Transition in Asia and Eastern and Central Europe: A Closed Door Two Open Windows?

TRANSITION IN ASIA AND EASTERN AND CENTRAL EUROPE: A CLOSED DOOR TWO OPEN WINDOWS?

NATHALIE H. FABRY
AND
SYLVAIN H. ZEGHNI

Foreword by
Bruce Kogut

NOVA SCIENCE PUBLISHERS, INC.
Huntington, NY

Senior Editors: Susan Boriotti and Donna Dennis
Coordinating Editor: Tatiana Shohov
Office Manager: Annette Hellinger
Graphics: Wanda Serrano
Book Production: Matthew Kozlowski, Jonathan Rose and Jennifer Vogt
Circulation: Cathy DeGregory, Ave Maria Gonzalez, Ron Hedges and Andre Tillman

Library of Congress Cataloging-in-Publication Data
Available Upon Request

ISBN 1-59033-020-X.

227 Main Street, Suite 100
Huntington, New York 11743
Tele. 631-424-6682 Fax 631-425-5933
E Mail: Novascience@earthlink.net

Printed in the United States of America

CONTENTS

FOREWORD

Bruce Kogut

Wharton School, University of Pennsylvania

The fall of the Berlin Wall in November of 1989 marked the ending of an era that consisted of the imposition of socialist planning on the previously capitalist economies in Central and Eastern Europe. This era lasted only 45 years, and yet left an institutional legacy that could not be eradicated quickly. Though sharing a common history, the former Soviet-dominated countries entered into transition with distinctive features, expectations, and above all, political realities.

Since the heady times of economics reform, the differences among countries have become even more transparent. Whereas a few countries, especially those sharing borders with western Europe, have returned to economic stability and at times growth, eastern Europe remains deeply troubled. Reforms are incomplete, the domestic politics are turbulent, and the future economic direction looks uncertain.

The economic evolution of communist countries in Asia is also highly uncertain, even if the political environment has the appearance of less turbulence. Both China and Vietnam are controlled by communist governments that are reluctant, to speak in euphemisms, to move to democracy. Nevertheless, both wish to pursue policies of economic growth, including the introduction of more market-oriented reforms.

In these complex interactions of politics and economics, foreign direct investment plays the role of a conduit of capital and expertise, of legitimization and of threat of foreign domination. It is not surprising that foreign companies are torn between the promise of unexplored markets and the hazards of unsettled environments. Governments too are caught between their desperate desire to find the resources to drive their economies, while they worry about selling assets at disadvantageous prices or losing sovereignty to foreign companies.

Governments made different choices in their attitude toward foreign direct investment. These choices were embedded within the larger policy decision whether to sell assets by auction or bids on the one hand, or by mass privatization on the other. In the first category, some countries, such as Hungary, saw foreign investment as a rapid way by which enterprises could be modernized and the economy integrated with the West.

Sales of state-owned enterprises were conducted by the placement of shares, and sometimes, control with foreign bidders. Occasionally, these sales were blocked by domestic opposition, either labor concerned about lay-offs or other business interests who did not want foreign competition or who wanted themselves to buy these assets.

In a few cases, sales of state assets were conducted by mass privatization. This method of sale created explosive situations afterwards, because capital markets were not sufficient to allow interested buyers to find sellers in an efficient way. Nor could foreign firms easily purchase these shares. In countries like Russia, insiders understood better the ways that control in such circumstances could be gained. Foreign firms were at a disadvantage and they looked therefore for joint venture partners or sought to participate as buyers of state-owned enterprises that were to be sold by auction or by bid.

In other words, mass privatization has not been successful in promoting foreign investment. In those countries that have chosen this policy, foreign firms have been limited to participating in the market for the purchase of those enterprises spared mass privatization itself. It is a conjecture (in which I believe) that mass privatization contaminated even the residual market for the sale of assets. By creating conditions that encouraged extra-legal ways to capture control over assets, mass privatization fomented the growth of powerful business groups who then had the political power to deter the sale of assets to foreign firms.

Leaving aside these speculations, it is clear that one of the most important sectors in transition economies is the banking sector. The legacy of the socialist system rendered the banks as powerful holders of debt in enterprises, as well as agents entangled in the complicated history of inter-firm payments. In almost all the transition economies in Europe, banking has posed unusual difficulty to governments. Even in relatively wealthy countries, such as the Czech Republic, banking has been the target of considerable domestic squabbling and has been slow to be opened to foreign investment. There is increasing convergence among many of the Central Europe countries, that foreign firms be allowed to invest and to dominate banking, because the alternative is the failure to develop the electronic payments systems, the capital depth, and efficiencies needed to support growth in the rest of the economy.

Despite more than a decade of experience, there remains still a remarkable controversy over the conclusions to be made from this transition experience. Surely, this history has made researchers and analysts more appreciative of the complexity of how economies work. It must be amusing for an older generation of economists to observe how these challenges have forced a return of interest to that branch of the social science once called "political economy". Since politics varies by country, the lesson of the enduring importance of political economy has also required an emphasis on studying transition in the comparative context of the variety of national experiences.

The chapters in this booked edited by Nathalie Fabry and Sylvain Zeghni embrace this comparative country methodology to understand foreign direct investment. The chapters are reasoned investigations into the relationship of direct investment to growth and transition. Behind these investigations lie the important play of politics and economics in understanding why countries with a similar past have yet varied wildly in their post-Soviet histories.

One might ask what is the general lesson to be learned from these national experiences. It would be a mistake to say that we know for sure that foreign direct investment is always desirable and a country should desire as much investment as it could attract. But it would also be reckless to give too much weight to the arguments against foreign direct investment, when we witness how poor are many of these countries and in desperate need they are of capital, technology, and better management. The subject of this book is vital to the future of these countries. The authors of these chapters are to be commended for the efforts to increase our understanding of the role that foreign investment has played, and may play, in the transition of Soviet economies to that which is still emerging.

INTRODUCTION

Nathalie H. Fabry
University of Marne-la-Vallée
Sylvain H. Zeghni
University of Marne-la-Vallée

Since the end of 1980s, in Central and Eastern European Countries (CEECs), Vietnam and China, a certain way to rule an economy based exclusively on a centrally-planed orientation has become obsolete. It is now "a closed door". Countries entered in transition[1]. Being a transition country is neither a destiny nor a fate. It should be a step toward industrialization and modernity. This process is historic and has no equivalent. Consequently, each country have to find itself its own direction and receipts according to its historical, political, human and cultural roots. From a single process - the transition - differentiated country profiles and transition path emerged. In this book we want to stress on "two open windows".

Firstly, a *geographical* perspective allows us to distinguish the Asian transition way and the European one's. In Asia, China and Vietnam aimed to create *market-oriented socialism.* In this system there is openness to international trade and inward foreign direct investment (FDI) but no major privatization and fundamental changes in political structure. The European way relies on privatization, democratic changes, openness and regional anchorage to European Union (for the majority of them). For a transition country, the problem is less to remain or not a communist country as Vietnam or China

[1] Transition started officially with the collapse of the Berlin wall in October 1989. The transition process is an irreversible movement towards reforms (political, social and economic) and more market oriented mechanisms. Seen in a strict economic perspective, transition process relies on three main areas of reforms, namely macroeconomic stabilization, real adjustment at the microeconomic level, and creation of institutional framework. See the special issue on Transition in *Thunderbird International Business Review*, vol. 41(1), January-February 1999 and *Transition Report* (annual issue) of the European Bank for Reconstruction and Development, London.

does. The problem is how may a transition country generate best conditions for sustained growth and prosperity. To achieve this purpose, these countries seem to rely on openness to foreign trade and investment.

Secondly, a comparison of *countries' ability to attract FDI* allows us to focus on the differentiated speed of the transition process. China since the post-Tienanmen openness (1992) has high GDP growth level and emerged as the most promising host country for foreign investors and export oriented industries. Vietnam, on the contrary, appears to be an unfilled promise: growth stagnation and falling inward-FDI. These Asian countries used the openness as a mean to overcome internal barriers to growth but not to converge to western-style democracies. China has deliberately chosen openness to install a twin transition process: a transition from centrally-planned economic system to a market-oriented one, and a transition from an agrarian society to a modern industrial society. The last dimension of the Chinese transition (i.e. the setting up of a modern industrial economic system) reveals deep-rooted problems that may potentially undermine the growth sustainability (State-owned enterprises corporate governance, financial institutions, education and skills, regional disparities). In Vietnam openness was a choice under constraints: the end of the anchorage to Soviet Union. This fundamental difference - openness deliberately chosen and actively managed (see China's WTO adhesion campaign) and not - may explain the relative failure of the Vietnamese reform framework.

CEECs become lately but progressively host countries for FDI. Among them, we may distinguish between countries that may access to the European Union enlargement process and countries that may not[2]. The collapse of Socialism in Eastern Europe has opened up the opportunity to transform centrally-planned economies into market economies. It also gives to the CEECs the opportunity to join - under convergence requirements - the European Union (EU). Thus, transition - in the early 1990s - and reorientation towards Western Europe - since the end of 1990s - have been the two decisive challenges for the CEECs since 1989. There is a considerable overlap between the reforms required during the transition process and the reforms required to join the EU. Consequently, the advanced transition countries will complete their transition path with the implementation of the *acquis communautaire*, the established institutional and regular framework of the EU. However, the CEECs have not yet the full capability to stand the market forces within the EU and to adopt all the obligations of EU membership as set out in the *acquis*. The CEECs still have to complete quite substantial reform tasks. Since the beginning of the transition, the anticipation of EU membership has helped the CEECs to progress sharply with their reforms. The prospect of uncertain or rather late EU accession due to delayed EU amendments by the present members[3] might jeopardize the zeal and the endeavors for reforms in the CEECs.

---

[2] Purpose of this non-integration may be different: insufficient economic reforms and unsafe growth basement (for example: Bulgaria) or political willingness to remain "independent" (example: Russia).

[3] See the recent Referendum in Irland (June 2001).

In other words, the transition process in Europe and in Asia is not unique and should be seen as a result of historic and institutional context. Consequently, facing a same range of problem, transition economies may give different responses that make their experience unique. But, transition economies have also various common characteristics such as risks, uncertainties, missing or inefficient markets (financial markets and institutions for example) and under performing markets.

In parallel, transition creates a window of opportunity for western firms. They can develop new market shares and benefit from low production costs and facilities. Thus, transition economies may rely on a FDI-led and exports-led industrialization and modernization to shift growth. But FDI may also accentuate structural problems in transitional host countries. For example, foreign firms may have to cope with local non-mature private sectors, institutions or markets. They also may have to fight against communist legacy that still provokes inertia and sticky behaviors.

More than a decade has passed, and it is possible to analyze and describe real advances in modernization but also to put forward existing and deep-rooted problems. As different contributors of the present book will show, the transition process has various components. Each component (political, institutional, social, and human) has its own timing. If the political and the institutional clock run relatively fast, the economic clock runs more slowly[4].

In chapter 1, N. Fabry focuses on the differentiated role that FDI could play in a transition economy, beyond the spillover analysis. By asking a specific question, *"In what measures can inward-FDI help a transition host country to operate an upgrading of its economy?"* the author shows that inward-FDI may have various direct and indirect effects on host countries at a macro and micro level. FDI's differentiated roles may be decomposed in *FDI-contributions* and *FDI-impacts*. The *FDI-contributions* make reference to the modernization and to the increased factor efficiency resulting from the reorientation of the production processes initiated by the foreign investors. Foreign firms are the main actors involved in these changes (introduction of modern facilities, and of modern methods and processes, which were proven successful elsewhere). The *FDI-impacts* put forward the host country's absorption capacities and the foreign investors' abilities to achieve the knowledge and best practice transfer within its affiliates. A causality test applied to CEECs, allows to conclude that none of these countries benefit from catching-up *vis-à-vis* industrial economies. FDI may help host countries to upgrade their economies but are not suited to replace industrial and technological changes for long-term growth.

In chapter 2, T. Mickiewicz, S. Radosevic and U. Varblane focus on the role of FDI as an agent of change in manufacturing. They examine the impact of FDI on employment structure as well as on job creation and job preservation. They also discuss the FDI's effects on productivity, wages and investment. Authors suggest that two major gains from FDI exist. Both are specific to post-communist economies. First, FDI may be instrumental in achieving short-term efficiency gains by improving allocation of resources, without necessity of large-scale investment. Second, in the longer run, the

[4] See Rupnick J. (1993), *L'autre Europe, crise du communisme*, Paris, Odile Jacob, Points.

important gain of FDI presence may consist of better access to financial resources, which facilitate investment and create basis for sustainable growth.

In chapter 3, using a specific firm-level data set, S. Zeghni shows that foreign investors in transition economies are characterized by low, rather than high, R&D intensity. He also finds that investors with higher R&D spending are more likely to engage in non-manufacturing projects than in local production. The empirical analysis links these results to weak protection of Intellectual Property Rights (IPRs). Such a weak protection deters FDI, especially investment in technology-intensive sectors that rely heavily on IPRs. Weak IPR protection also encourages investors to undertake non-manufacturing projects rather than local production. These results can be related to the greater scope for technology theft in the case of manufacturing FDI. The author shows that firms are much more concerned about IPR protection in a host country when they consider manufacturing FDI than when they plan investments in sales and distribution outlets. He also note that a larger market size increases the probability of foreign investment in manufacturing facilities, while the effects of transition progress and unit labor costs are not statistically significant. Finally, this chapter concludes that IPR protection affects the composition of FDI inflows. While studies of aggregate FDI flows have produced mostly inconclusive results, this firm-level analysis shows that FDI is sensitive to the strength of IPR protection. Furthermore, S. Zeghni adds to the transition literature by demonstrating empirically the positive impact of the transformation progress on the probability of a country being chosen as an FDI destination.

In chapter 4, M. Klimenko study industrial targeting policy to promote the development of selected industries (high growth potential) by the government of transition economies. The cases of success and failure of industrial targeting policy are numerous and well analyzed in the literature. M. Klimenko describes this policy as an optimal experimentation policy of an incompletely informed government. He attempts to model *"the characteristics of the process by which the governments select among several industries in which policy interventions are assumed to be justified on the grounds of welfare efficiency."* He proposes a normative issue of the long-run efficiency of such experimental policy activism in determining the country's pattern of specialization. He shows that even an optimal industrial targeting policy does not guarantee the country's long-run specialization according to its comparative advantage.

In chapter 5, M. Andreff and W. Andreff show that subcontracting is an intermediary form between trade and FDI. It is a frequent means of production relocation, technology transfer, improvement of managerial skills, product design adaptation to the world market. It is also a component of lean production and global outsourcing developed by transnational corporations in the framework of their new global strategies. Authors study international subcontracting through available macroeconomic and sectoral trade data registered under the customs classification of outward-processing trade (OPT) in the CEECs. They focus on the French OPT and show that France OPT in the CEECs has developed from 1993 to 1997 with a specific geographical orientation compared to EU-15 OPT. They show a substitution of French FDI to France OPT, during the same period in all the country subgroups of the CEECs. Finally, they find that in 1997, the sectoral patterns of French FDI and OPT in the CEECs are both different and complementary.

Transition countries need for banking system because the lack of credit is an extremely pressing problem. But in spite of western advisers, all attempts to establish immediately a banking system in the US or German-style have entirely failed over the past five years. As A. Tschoegl and K. Koford in chapter 6 mentioned it *"The appropriate models for transition economies are not the well-developed financial systems of today, but rather models drawn from periods of history when economies faced many of the same problems that currently face the Eastern Europeans. U.S. banking practices in the 19th century had some practices and institutions similar to those in Japan. European experience in the 19th century also provides evidence of varied institutions. Japan, both during the Meiji restoration and after World War II, developed new systems of credit that propelled the economy rapidly from a very low base in which almost no firms "deserved" credit by traditional standards."* Besides this historic perspective, the authors emphasize on the importance of economic groups in theory. Groups may be a *"natural and typical solution to a lack of accounting information and expertise"* and more generally to incomplete information. Moreover, groups may be the fundament for a new banking and financial system and a step toward a greater role for markets.

K. Iglicka, in chapter 7, focuses on the immigration into Poland, from both the East and the West, in the context of social and economic transformation. She emphasizes also the impact of this mobility on the labor markets. It appears that new and completely unexpected population phenomena occurred in Poland. Thus, Poland may serve as a model in the analysis of changes on labor markets from the perspective of immigrants' impact and role in this process. According to the author, the formation of a foreign labor force or immigrant enclave on the labor market is not a product of deliberate economic policy by the state or labor needs of the capitalist class, but depends on the initiative and resources of the immigrants themselves. The geography of migratory flows into Poland during the transition period reflects recent changes in the global division of labor. Highly skilled flows from the "West" and a small part of the flow from the "East" find an employment on the primary labor market. Immigrants have a regulated legal status and are used to supplement domestic labor force here. Decisive majority of the flows from the "East" finds an employment (legal or illegal) on the secondary labor market. Flows into the primary labor market are highly institutionalized whereas flows from the "East" reflect rather the dynamic process of migration that transforms temporary entries into settlement. In the future it is just immigrants from the "East" who would play an important role on both primary and secondary labor markets in Poland. Since the migratory potential lies on the "East" the process of globalization of migration will inevitable increase the flows from the "East" into Central European countries.

According to J. Jaussaud and J. Schnapper, transition countries seem to be a window of opportunity for Western Companies. As authors show, in chapter 8, the control of a plant abroad by a MNE is strategic. This question is particularly important in transition countries. The distribution of a joint venture's capital between partners and the expatriation policy of top executives constitute two essential instruments of control. On the basis of a sample of 394 Japanese multinationals' subsidiaries in China (218) and in Central and Eastern Europe (176), J. Jaussaud and J. Schnaaper compare the structure of the subsidiaries in these countries, and their expatriation policy. They found four major differences between plants in China and in the CEEC. First, the nature of the subsidiaries: in China a majority of plants have a production activity whereas in the CEEC they are generally limited to commercialization activities. Second the nature of the mode of entry: in China, most of the plants are joint ventures, whereas in the CEEC, most of them are wholly foreign owned subsidiary companies. Third, the nature of control: in China firms are directly held by the Japanese head offices, whereas in the CEEC they are frequently managed by the intermediary of another subsidiary company established in the European Union. Fourth, the expatriation policy is really different: the number of expatriated managers is clearly higher towards China than towards the CEEC.

The globalization of economic activity in general, and the growing role of multinational enterprises (MNEs) in particular, has directed attention toward the environmental consequences of these developments. Increasingly, MNEs activity in developing countries has become an issue for various normative initiatives at international level, in the OECD and in the WTO. However, there remains a pertinent need to gain a better understanding of the environmental implications of MNEs activity in developing countries. In chapter 9, N. Fabry and S. Zeghni examine the role of FDI in China with particular focus on its implications for the environment. An overview of policy and practices in environment protection is presented including a separate section devoted to the Chinese environmental regulatory framework regarding MNEs. The study shows that FDI generates both positive and negative effects on China's environment, but identifying the scale of such effect remains extremely difficult. As various FDI projects are located in the so-called pollution-intensive industries, the risk of environmental damage has increased. Authors argue that there seems to be greater environmental implications by FDI from the more developed countries in Asia than from developed countries. It is concluded that further examination at the firm level is highly desirable to provide a solid basis for the Government to formulate effective policy measures. Authors suggest that such case studies focus on the investigation of the cross border environmental management systems within the MNEs' integrated production networks, as well as on the identification of the actual level of technologies employed.

C. Pottier analyzes the most enigmatic Asian transition economy: Vietnam. Indeed, this country has potentially high growth perspectives but its performances are disappointing. Fundaments of this enigma have been studied elsewhere[5]. In chapter 10, the author emphasizes on the Vietnamese current economic difficulties. One fundamental feature of Vietnam's development strategy is its reliance on inward-FDI mainly in manufacturing and external trade. But the country has some difficulties to manage the transition process (internal reforms) and the rapid economic opening. The East Asian crisis (1997) provoked an important shock that revealed numerous blockages of the opening process. Lacking an open financial system, Vietnam was not directly affected but suffered the consequences of the crisis in terms of trade and inward-FDI. Investments have diminished rapidly since 1997 and consequently contributed to a net slowdown in growth. Two issues, therefore, emerged simultaneously: the adequacy of the opening

[5] See Fabry N. and Richet X. (1999), Investissements directs étrangers, attractivité et coopération industrielle au Viêt-nam, *Revue d'études comparatives Est-Ouest.*

process chosen by Vietnam (as revealed by the crisis), and the transition process itself. The aim of the author is firstly to illustrate the significant role of FDI in the Vietnamese economy. The analysis leads to an examination of the political options emerging in response to the strong slowdown in inward-FDI. Since the Vietnamese Communist Party already opted for a convergence towards market economy, the discussion is restricted to an examination of two questions. The first concerns the coherence and the rhythm of the transition process. The second concerns the way opening take place: how can Vietnam insert itself into the international division of labor resulting from the multinational corporations' networks? It is doubtful that in the near future growth will be rapid in Vietnam if the reduction in flows of FDI continues. In the short run, the government needs to improve the Vietnamese attractiveness.

Chapter 1

THE ROLE OF INWARD-FDI IN THE TRANSITION COUNTRIES OF EUROPE: AN ANALYTICAL FRAMEWORK

Nathalie H. Fabry
University of Marne-la-Vallée

1. INTRODUCTION

The transition process from the former centrally-planned economic system towards a market-led economy started in the late 1980's (Simai, 1999). Countries engaged in such a transition process need to replace, adapt and upgrade productive capabilities. They also need to acquire new skills and technology (Berg and al. 1996; Boycko and al. 1995) and more generally need to improve the factors' allocation and efficiency (Blanchard, 1996). These countries may achieve such a modernization and upgrading by importing foreign technologies and *western best practices* and by reaching some external help and financial support. In that context, studying the role of inward-Foreign direct investment (FDI) in transition countries appears to be an important quest.

In the present chapter we will focus on the differentiated role that FDI could play in a transition economy. The role of inward-FDI in the existing literature is often reduced or assimilated to spillover effects[1]. Recent studies of spillovers from FDI suggest that *"spillovers from FDI may occur from increased competition and labor turnover, or through demonstration, and may take place either in the foreign affiliate's own industry or among the affiliate's suppliers and customers in other industries"* (Blömstrom, Sjöholm, 1999, p.917). But even more studies stressed that spillovers do not lead to immediate economic results (Cohen and Levinthal, 1990; Verspagen and De Loo, 1999). Beyond the spillover analysis, we want to stress that inward-FDI may have various direct and indirect effects on host countries at a macro and micro level.

---

[1] For a survey on the contribution of FDI to host countries, see O'Donnell and Blumentritt, 1999.

Our question is the following: *"In what measures can inward-FDI help a transition host country to operate an upgrading of its economy?"* We will not put in perspective the ability of the host country to attract FDI. This point raises the *"attractivity analysis"* (Michalet, 1999) and the FDI *"determinants analysis"* (Dunning, 1993, 1995)[2]. We will however focus on the ability of the host country to take advantage of the presence of multinational firms.

FDI's differentiated roles may be decomposed on the one hand in *"FDI-contributions"* and on the other hand in *"FDI-impacts"*. The *"FDI-contributions"* make reference to the modernization and to the increased factor efficiency resulting from the reorientation of the production processes initiated by the foreign investors. Foreign firms are the main actors involved in these changes (introduction of modern facilities, and of modern methods and processes which were proven successful elsewhere). The *"FDI-impacts"* put forward the host country's absorption capacities and the foreign investors' abilities to achieve the knowledge and best practice transfer within its affiliates. The combination of these two elements allows us to appreciate the role of FDI and suggest an answer to our initial question. The existing literature does little to focus on the role of FDI in the host country under this analytical angle (Kalotay, 1999; O'Donnell and Blumentritt, 1999).

The chapter is organized as follows: Section 1 presents the specific transition context in which FDI occur, mainly in Europe (central and eastern countries, Baltic states, CIS). These countries deserve particular attention given their specificity. Unlike the developing countries and second generation Asian NIE's, the transition countries of Europe have at their disposal an educated labor force, but the qualifications do not always fit the western criteria of production (Dyker, 1997). Moreover, they don't always offer to the foreign investors optimal conditions of production and their attractiveness could appear weak in comparison to Asian or Latin American countries. Section 2 introduces the analytical framework and presents the role of inward-FDI in transition host countries. FDI bring first several elements of modernization and efficiency, and second, contribute to the transfer and to the diffusion of knowledge. These elements will permit us to analyze the role of FDI and their potential contribution to the transition economies' upgrading. The last section summarizes the main conclusions.

---

[2] Dunning (1993; 1995) in his « O.L.I. paradigm » tells us that FDI determinants rely on a combination of three categories: Firms *Ownership advantage*, host country *Localization advantage*, and internalization of *markets (Internalization advantage*). FDI determinants in transition economies are based on market and resources access (Lankes and Venables, 1996; Marinov and Marinova, 1999, Fabry and Zeghni, 2001), and on risks, uncertainties and hidden costs that foreign firms must manage in such markets (Estrin and Meyer, 1999; Firozzi, 1997; Sara and Newhouse, 1995).

2. Transition and Openness to FDI

2.1. FDI in Transition Economies of Europe: Some Data

The transition countries of Europe aren't among the countries that receive the more inward-FDI at the present time. Indeed, the group composed of Poland, Czech Republic, Romania, Hungary, Slovakia, and Russia receives fewer FDI than China or Latin American countries[3]. Even though the European countries of the former Communist block do not receive much FDI compared to the other zones (Latin America and Asia), several major features could be put in evidence:

- Inward-FDI constitute a transfer of long term saving and are therefore a steady financial support for host countries (Artus, 2000; Lipsey, 1999). As chart 1 suggests, FDI are a more stable source of capital entry for host countries than other forms of capital.

Chart 1:

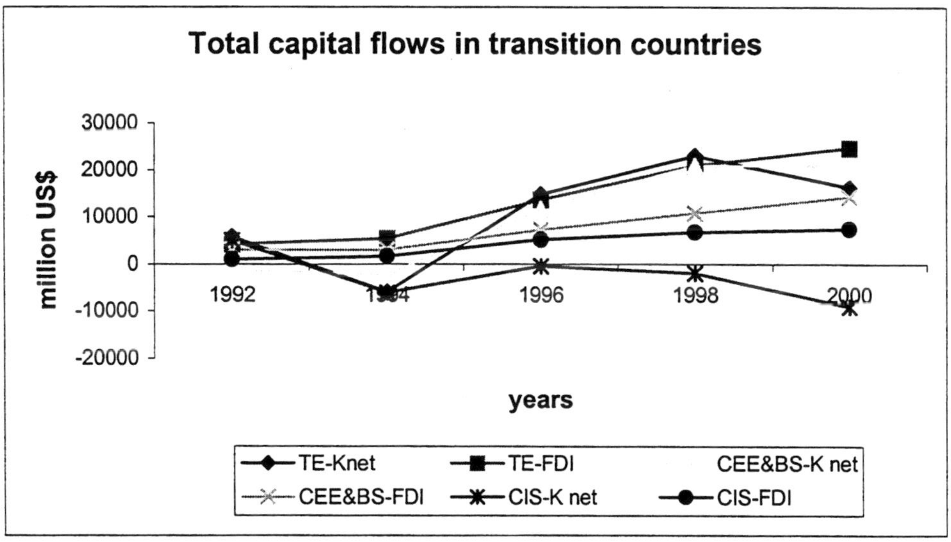

Notes: TE= all European transition economies, CEE&BS= central and eastern European countries and Baltic states, CIS= commonwealth of independent states, FDI= foreign direct investment, Knet= total capital inflows, net. **Sources**: EBRD (2000).

[3] In 1998, China received 2 634 millions USD of inward-FDI, ASEAN-3 (Indonesia, Philippines and Thailand) 334 million, Latin America 15 455 million, and Russia and central European countries 1 903 million. *Sources: JETRO (2000) « White paper on FDI ».*

- All republics and countries receive inward-FDI but to varying degrees. Host countries therefore are not homogeneous concerning inward-FDI reception (table 1). Except for political and economical endogenous risks linked to these kind of economies (Zeghni, 2001), and the small size of some countries or their weak industrial structures, the relative weakness of the inward-FDI results in the choice of State Owned Enterprises' privatization modalities (Bevan and Estrin, 2000). With the exception of Hungary, transition countries used to be reluctant to FDI. The reasons invoked are varied but all are relative to the willingness to give an advantage to national operators and in particular the *insiders* such as managers, employees or public actors (Labaronne, 1999, Sinn, Weichenrieder, 1997). Since 1999, CEEC have registered large FDI inflows. According to the *Transition Report* (EBRD, 2000) this may be explained by the progression in privatization and a possible access to the EU.

- Table 1 in terms of accumulated flows informs us of the relative developments of FDI in the European zone and especially their geographical spreading, first in the central and eastern countries (Hungary, Poland, Czech Republic and Slovakia), then in the CIS countries. Indeed, during the period 1991-95, FDI were concentrated at 61.9% on three Visegrad countries: Hungary (38,78%), Czech Republic (13,87%) and Poland (9,25%). From 1996, foreign investors did not invest strongly in Hungary (7,45% of accumulated-FDI during the period 96-99) but invested more in Poland (24,14%), in Romania (7,26%) or in the Russian Federation (11,18%).

Table 1: Inward-FDI Flows in European Transition Countries (1991-2000)

	1991	1992	1993	1994	1995	1996	1997	1998	1999	2000	Cumulated flows		
											1991-95	**1996-2000**	**1991-2000**
Central and eastern countries (CEE)													
Albania	8	20	45	65	89	97	42	45	51	92	**227**	**327**	**554**
	0.44%	*0.59%*	*0.89%*	*1.18%*	*0.67%*	*0.77%*	*0.24%*	*0.22%*	*0.23%*	*0.34%*	*0.78%*	*0.33%*	*0.43%*
Bulgaria	56	42	40	105	98	138	507	537	806	500	**341**	**2488**	**2829**
	3.08%	*1.25%*	*0.80%*	*1.91%*	*0.74%*	*1.09%*	*2.90%*	*2.58%*	*3.66%*	*1.85%*	*1.18%*	*2.49%*	*2.19%*
Croatia	Na	13	78	106	96	509	302	781	1350	450	**293**	**3392**	**3685**
		0.39%	*1.55%*	*1.93%*	*0.72%*	*4.03%*	*1.73%*	*3.75%*	*6.12%*	*1.67%*	*1.01%*	*3.39%*	*2.86%*
Czech Republic	Na	983	563	749	2526	1276	1275	2641	4912	6000	**4821**	**16104**	**20925**
		29.19%	*11.20%*	*13.63%*	*19.01%*	*10.10%*	*7.29%*	*12.67%*	*22.28%*	*22.20%*	*16.63%*	*16.10%*	*16.22%*
Hungary	1500	1471	2328	1097	4410	1987	1653	1453	1414	1650	**10806**	**8157**	**18963**
	82.60%	*43.68%*	*46.30%*	*19.96%*	*33.19%*	*15.73%*	*9.46%*	*6.97%*	*6.41%*	*6.11%*	*37.27%*	*8.16%*	*14.70%*
Macedonia	Na	0	0	24	13	12	18	175	30	100	**37**	**335**	**372**
		0.00%	*0.00%*	*0.44%*	*0.10%*	*0.10%*	*0.10%*	*0.84%*	*0.14%*	*0.37%*	*0.13%*	*0.33%*	*0.29%*
Poland	100	284	580	542	1134	2741	3041	4966	6642	10000	**2640**	**27390**	**30030**
	5.51%	*8.43%*	*11.54%*	*9.86%*	*8.54%*	*21.70%*	*17.40%*	*23.83%*	*30.13%*	*37.01%*	*9.10%*	*27.38%*	*23.28%*
Romania	37	73	87	341	417	415	1267	2079	949	500	**955**	**5210**	**6165**
	2.04%	*2.17%*	*1.73%*	*6.20%*	*3.14%*	*3.29%*	*7.25%*	*9.98%*	*4.30%*	*1.85%*	*3.29%*	*5.21%*	*4.78%*
Slovak Republic	82	100	107	236	194	199	84	374	701	1500	**719**	**2858**	**3577**
	4.52%	*2.97%*	*2.13%*	*4.29%*	*1.46%*	*1.58%*	*0.48%*	*1.79%*	*3.18%*	*5.55%*	*2.48%*	*2.86%*	*2.77%*
Slovenia	41	113	111	131	183	188	340	250	144	50	**579**	**972**	**1551**
	2.26%	*3.36%*	*2.21%*	*2.38%*	*1.38%*	*1.49%*	*1.94%*	*1.20%*	*0.65%*	*0.19%*	*2.00%*	*0.97%*	*1.20%*

	1991	1992	1993	1994	1995	1996	1997	1998	1999	2000	Cumulated Flows		
											1991-95	**1996-2000**	**1991-2000**
Commonwealth of Independent States (CIS)													
Armenia	Na	0	1	8	25	18	52	221	131	150	**34**	**572**	**606**
		0.00%	*0.02%*	*0.15%*	*0.19%*	*0.14%*	*0.30%*	*1.06%*	*0.59%*	*0.56%*	*0.12%*	*0.57%*	*0.47%*
Azerbaijan	Na	Na	0	22	282	661	1093	1024	510	274	**304**	**3562**	**3866**
			0.00%	*0.40%*	*2.12%*	*5.23%*	*6.25%*	*4.91%*	*2.31%*	*1.01%*	*1.05%*	*3.56%*	*3.00%*
Belarus	Na	Na	18	11	15	73	198	142	225	100	**44**	**738**	**782**
			0.36%	*0.20%*	*0.11%*	*0.58%*	*1.13%*	*0.68%*	*1.02%*	*0.37%*	*0.15%*	*0.74%*	*0.61%*
Georgia	Na	Na	0	8	6	54	236	221	96	109	**14**	**716**	**730**
				0.15%	*0.05%*	*0.43%*	*1.35%*	*1.06%*	*0.44%*	*0.40%*	*0.05%*	*0.72%*	*0.57%*
Kazakhstan	Na	Na	473	635	964	1137	1320	1143	1584	1500	**2072**	**6684**	**8756**
			9.41%	*11.55%*	*7.26%*	*9.00%*	*7.55%*	*5.49%*	*7.18%*	*5.55%*	*7.15%*	*6.68%*	*6.79%*
Kyrgyzstan	Na	Na	10	38.2	96	46.8	83	108.6	35.4	42	**144**	**316**	**460**
			0.20%	*0.69%*	*0.72%*	*0.37%*	*0.47%*	*0.52%*	*0.16%*	*0.16%*	*0.50%*	*0.32%*	*0.36%*
Moldova	Na	17	14	18	73	23	75	86	33	100	**122**	**317**	**439**
		0.50%	*0.28%*	*0.33%*	*0.55%*	*0.18%*	*0.43%*	*0.41%*	*0.15%*	*0.37%*	*0.42%*	*0.32%*	*0.34%*
Russian Federation	Na	Na	na	500	1663	1665	4036	1734	746	2000	**2163**	**10181**	**12344**
				9.10%	*12.52%*	*13.18%*	*23.09%*	*8.32%*	*3.38%*	*7.40%*	*7.46%*	*10.18%*	*9.57%*
Tajikistan	Na	Na	9	12	20	25	30	24	21	30	**41**	**130**	**171**
			0.18%	*0.22%*	*0.15%*	*0.20%*	*0.17%*	*0.12%*	*0.10%*	*0.11%*	*0.14%*	*0.13%*	*0.13%*
Turkmenistan	Na	Na	79	103	233	108	108	62	89	100	**415**	**467**	**882**
			1.57%	*1.87%*	*1.75%*	*0.86%*	*0.62%*	*0.30%*	*0.40%*	*0.37%*	*1.43%*	*0.47%*	*0.68%*
Ukraine	Na	200	200	151	257	526	581	747	489	750	**808**	**3093**	**3901**
		5.94%	*3.98%*	*2.75%*	*1.93%*	*4.16%*	*3.32%*	*3.58%*	*2.22%*	*2.78%*	*2.79%*	*3.09%*	*3.02%*
Uzbekistan	Na	9	48	73	-24	90	167	226	201	231	**106**	**915**	**1021**
		0.27%	*0.95%*	*1.33%*	*-0.18%*	*0.71%*	*0.96%*	*1.08%*	*0.91%*	*0.85%*	*0.37%*	*0.91%*	*0.79%*

	1991	1992	1993	1994	1995	1996	1997	1998	1999	2000	Cumulated flows		
											1991-95	**1996-2000**	**1991-2000**
Baltic States (BS)													
Estonia	Na	Na	156	212	199	111	130	575	222	250	**567**	**1288**	**1855**
			3.10%	*3.86%*	*1.50%*	*0.88%*	*0.74%*	*2.76%*	*1.01%*	*0.93%*	*1.96%*	*1.29%*	*1.44%*
Latvia	Na	43	51	279	245	379	515	303	331	300	**618**	**1828**	**2446**
		1.28%	*1.01%*	*5.08%*	*1.84%*	*3.00%*	*2.95%*	*1.45%*	*1.50%*	*1.11%*	*2.13%*	*1.83%*	*1.90%*
Lithuania	Na	Na	30	31	72	152	328	921	478	295	**133**	**2174**	**2307**
			0.60%	*0.56%*	*0.54%*	*1.20%*	*1.88%*	*4.42%*	*2.17%*	*1.09%*	*0.46%*	*2.17%*	*1.79%*
Total zone	**1816.00**	**3368**	**5028**	**5497**	**13286**	**12631**	**17481**	**20839**	**22046**	**27023**	**28995**	**100020**	**129015**
	100%	*100%*	*100%*	*100%*	*100%*	*100%*	*100%*	*100%*	*100%*	*100%*	*100%*	*100%*	*100%*

Sources: According to EBRD (1999 and 2000), Transition report. Data for 2000 are previsions

Notes: na. = not available. Data in brackets = weight (%) of the country in the total FDI in the region. Azerbaijan: data include portfolio investments and oil royalties paid to the government; Lithuania :data include reinvested earnings up to 1995 ; Slovenia: FDI definition changed in 1999. Before 1999, FDI includes foreign participation over 50%, 10% since 1999.

➢ Table 2 in terms of per capita FDI confirms the geographical spreading of inward-FDI in the Eastern European countries. In the period from 1996-99 (compared to 1991-1995), all the countries show a progression of the inward-FDI per capita ratio except Hungary, Albania and Turkmenistan. In Hungary, there is an effect of relative saturation of inward-FDI because the privatization process has been largely achieved. This situation does not compare in any way with those in Albania or Turkmenistan. In these two countries, foreign investors lack stability and economical perspectives (high risks). In the period from 1996-1999, fewer countries are under the 100$ per capita FDI ratio, but the leadership remains for the Visegrad countries and the Baltic countries, i.e. the candidate countries for the EU enlargement in the next decade.

Table 2: Inward-FDI per Capita

1991-1995 (A)		1996-1999 (B)		Variation (B)/(A) in %	
Georgia	2,59	Tajikistan	19,34	Hungary	-53,67
Belarus	4,22	Uzbekistan	29,54	Albania	-5,02
Uzbekistan	4,67	Ukraine	47,90	Turkmenistan	0,98
Armenia	5,86	Kyrgyzstan	51,04	Slovenia	10,78
Tajikistan	6,95	Russian Federation	51,12	Kyrgyzstan	52,11
Russian Federation	14,86	Belarus	58,85	Slovak Republic	79,05
Ukraine	15,53	Albania	70,94	Estonia	109,90
Macedonia	17,62	Moldova	87,91	Czech Republic	123,08
Moldova	28,37	Turkmenistan	93,13	Kazakhstan	133,01
Kyrgyzstan	33,56	Georgia	112,41	Latvia	166,44
Lithuania	35,85	Macedonia	117,50	Tajikistan	178,37
Bulgaria	38,69	Armenia	123,32	Ukraine	208,38
Romania	42,70	Bulgaria	204,58	Moldova	209,84
Azerbaijan	43,37	Romania	218,48	Russian Federation	243,93
Croatia	57,39	Slovak Republic	265,93	Romania	411,66
Poland	67,36	Kazakhstan	292,60	Bulgaria	428,76
Albania	74,69	Slovenia	313,50	Poland	521,47
Turkmenistan	92,22	Poland	418,60	Uzbekistan	532,64
Kazakhstan	125,58	Azerbaijan	466,93	Macedonia	566,89
Slovak Republic	148,52	Lithuania	486,76	Croatia	853,59
Latvia	197,20	Hungary	495,05	Azerbaijan	976,53
Slovenia	283,00	Latvia	525,42	Lithuania	1257,80
Czech Republic	378,64	Croatia	547,24	Belarus	1293,53
Estonia	383,11	Estonia	804,14	Armenia	2002,76
Hungary	1068,63	Czech Republic	844,66	Georgia	4235,71

Notes: Countries, per each period, are classified by increasing FDI per capita ratio. Class are as follow: 0-100 US$; 101-200US$; 201-500US$; over 501 US$.
Sources and notes as table 1

One notices a slight progression of FDI in the European zone and a relative geographical shift toward the "peripheral countries" or non CEEC. An element of explanation seems to reside in the fact that FDI is seen as a modernization vector. In economies characterized by missing capital, management skills, and internationalization experiences, FDI appear as a way to achieve and finance modernization of the production process and a successful insertion in the world economy[4].

2.2. The Specific Context of Transition

We present in this section an analytic framework in order to understand in what context inward-FDI take place. We will see that FDI are essentially the consequence of the economical openness of host countries but also of the capacity of the transition countries to stabilize their economic and political environment (Bevan and Estrin, 2000). Indeed, FDI accompany the reforms but do not precede them (or very rarely precede them). Foreign investors, in order to enter into business, need first a local demand, but also a stable environment and the existence of a private sector. The openness to FDI is not therefore a sufficient criterion to attract FDI. These FDI should find a law on FDI offering some guarantees to the investors in case of non-respect of the property rights. Investors should also find a reformed central and regional administration. It is necessary to add that foreign firms appreciate the existence of safe infrastructures and the presence of local industries which are able to procure them some subcontractors and some industrial partners[5].

We adopt a static comparative reasoning. Our starting point is a situation of pre-transition illustrated by the point A of figure 1. This point doesn't stay on the possibilities of production curve (PPC1) by reason of the numerous X-inefficiencies characterizing the former centrally-planned economies and of the given priority to the military industry and to extensive growth.

2.2.1. Transition Act 1: The Recession

The beginning of the transition causes a shock to the economy (switch from point A to point B). This B point represents an economical situation even less optimal relative to than the initial period. This situation is characterized not only by an output reduction but also by the apparition of unemployment and other dysfunctions such as inflation, budgetary and commercial deficit, increased risk, and uncertainty. In fact, this aggravation of general economic conditions may be explained by the downfall of the centrally-planned system. This downfall deprives the actors of their traditional references and marks without generating new rules in the short term. One observes a weakening of

---

4 Note that the Asian "miracle" and the high growth in Asia during the 80 and 90's is a good example for European countries. These Asian countries decided to finance their growth by promoting exports and inward-FDI.

5 For more details on FDI determinants in transition economies see Lankes and Venables (1996) and Bevan and Estrin (2000).

the principal mode of governance and of management (collapse of central planning, price liberalization) without the creation of new market mechanisms. Moreover, in a context of fierce international competition, the facilities and the qualifications reveal themselves very quickly as obsolete. In such a context, the only result is a reduction of the industrial output (Lankhuizen, 2000). This situation was characterized by Kornai (1994) of *"transformational recession"* and by Blanchard (1996) *"U-shaped response of output"*. From this stage, the challenge is to make the economy converge toward a more optimal situation.

Figure 1: Transition and the U-shaped Response of Output

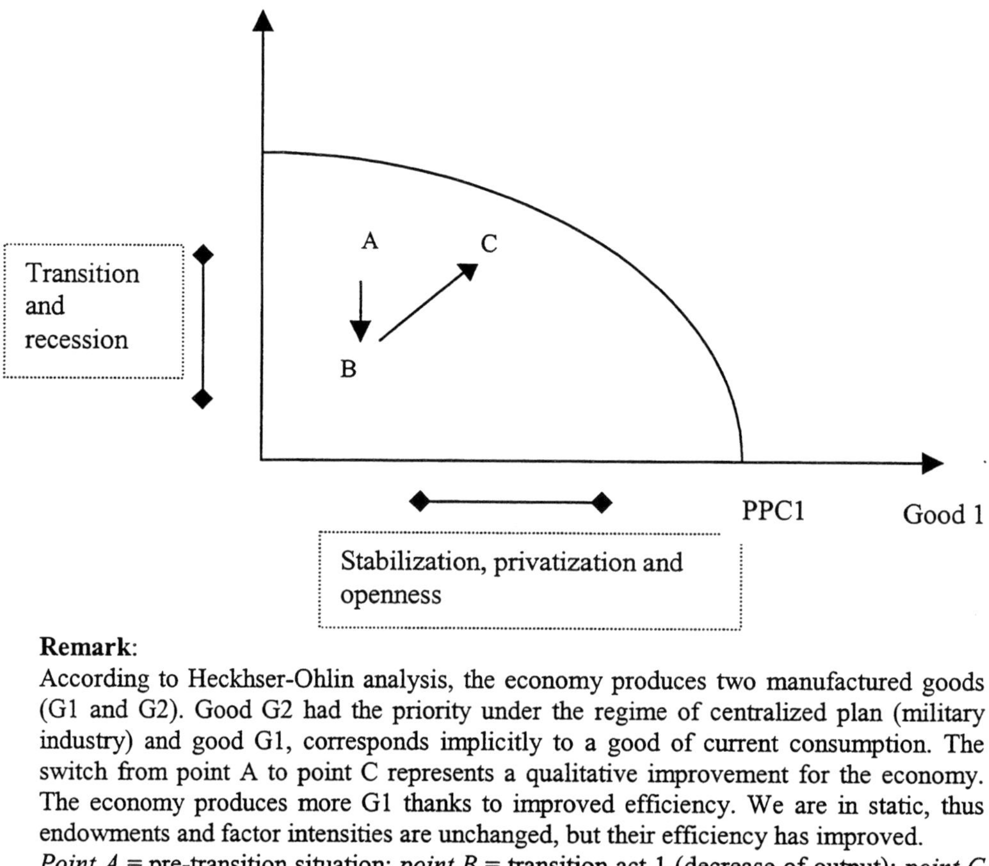

Remark:
According to Heckhser-Ohlin analysis, the economy produces two manufactured goods (G1 and G2). Good G2 had the priority under the regime of centralized plan (military industry) and good G1, corresponds implicitly to a good of current consumption. The switch from point A to point C represents a qualitative improvement for the economy. The economy produces more G1 thanks to improved efficiency. We are in static, thus endowments and factor intensities are unchanged, but their efficiency has improved.
Point A = pre-transition situation; *point B* = transition act 1 (decrease of output); *point C* = transition act 2 (stabilization, openness, privatization and modernization).
Sources: author's framework according to Blanchard (1996)

2.2.2. Transition Act 2: Macro Stabilization, Privatization and Openness to FDI

The objective of all transition economies is to grow. A macroeconomic stabilization and an institutional convergence towards market economy may reach this objective. According to our framework (figure 1), the economy should converge toward point C situated close to the border of the possibilities of production curve (PPC1). It is the reallocation and restructuring of the existing facilities, that is to say the development of the private sphere, the modernization of existing firms (state-owned enterprises (SOE)) and the stabilization of the macro level, which is going to help to reshape the activities. The state plays a major role in the transition by giving an impulsion to laws and legal framework, the institutions, the development of the infrastructures, the politics in favor of the private sector. In summary, the state needs to restructure itself (reduce the weight of the central administration in the activity) and to stabilize the macroeconomic level which will serve to support the economical activity.

Macro stabilization is obviously a necessity in order to allow a fast development of the activity. It deals with the monetary policy (essentially credit policy), the definition of an exchange rate policy, the struggle against inflation, the setting up of a fiscal policy, commercial openness, and the construction of legislation open to the development of private sector. The main problem is to create a coherent, transparent and efficient legal framework able to guarantee the respect of property rights, the protection of intellectual property and to define new labor rules. Macro stabilization acts also in fighting against corruption and administrative rigidities, in defining the procedures of bankruptcies, and in prices and wages liberalization (Johnson and al., 2000). The setting up of infrastructures and of robust institutions (in particular banking and financial institutions in order to drain off national savings toward the industry) are indispensable in order to pave the way to the market mechanisms.

The development of the private sector rests essentially on the SOE's privatization. In principle, this privatization could be open to the foreign investors under the shape of acquisition, of brownfield investments (calls for tender), of joint ventures or, rarer, of ex nihilo creation (Greenfield). In practice except for Hungary or Poland, privatization is specially reserved to the employees and/ or managers of the firm. It may also be devoted to public actors. All are insiders. If we take into account the former SOEs' characteristics (obsolescence of equipment and qualification), the weak financial capacities, the lack in management and cost analyze and/or risk management, the home enterprises do not have the human and financial means to acquire rapidly and efficiently the foreign practices and technology. Besides, privatization through insiders shows that these enterprises will be more concerned with protecting achievements than promoting modernization. Insiders fear that the search for performance may suppress jobs and urge workers to update their qualifications and working practices (Frydman and al., 1996; Aghion, Blanchard, and Burgess, 1994).

SOEs' privatization in the hands of insiders does not necessarily lead to a change of control system and governance. It leads even less to the adoption of performance and profitability objectives. Thus, the openness of the economies to inward-FDI is a means to improve the factors allowance and their efficiency. Numerous studies showed that firms involving foreigners have higher returns that those belonging to the insiders or those remained to the State (Labaronne, 1999). As Blanchard (1996 p. 106) specifies it, *"restructuring requires expertise and capital, and thus requires outside ownership ([n.a] FDI)."* In other words, FDI may push the host economy more quickly beyond point C presented in figure 1.

We are going to show that this FDI-contribution is relative, often diffuse, and that it doesn't have any automatic character.

3. The Role of Inward-FDI: an Analytical Framework

As presented in the introduction, our main question is the following: *"In what measures can inward-FDI help a transition host country to operate an upgrading of its economy?"* To answer this question, and to analyze the role of inward-FDI, two elements must be taken in consideration: the *"FDI-contributions"* and the *"FDI-impacts.* The *FDI-contributions* deals with the short term and the foreign investor's initiative. The *FDI-impacts* require a joined contribution of foreign investors and of the host country in the long term. Analyzing the role of inward-FDI in that manner may help us to understand the high importance of local conditions such as the host country's background, business institutions, and ability to develop absorptive capacities. Without such local conditions, the host country may not be able to benefit positively and extensively from inward-FDI. Our analytical framework will allow us to have a better understanding of FDI potential contribution to the upgrading of the transition economies.

3.1. The Twin Role of Inward-FDI in a Transition Economy

FDI may contribute to the improvement of the global factor's productivity and may influence positively the host country's growth. Such are the main teachings of recent economical literature[6]. Generally speaking, inward-FDI are thought of as a package of capital stocks, know-how, managerial skills, and technology. Their impact on the host country's growth is expected to be many-sided: industrial employment, labor qualification and job training, technology transfer, development of new activities such as services linked with FDI. The ultimate impact of FDI on the output growth in the recipient country depend on the spillover effects to domestic firms (Blomström, Kokko, 1998; Blomström, Kokko, Zejan, 2000). FDI lead to increasing returns in domestic productions, and increase in the value-added content of FDI-related productions. Local producers and subcontractors' products are more technology and know-how intensive. But the relationship between "inward-FDI and growth" is not so obvious and automatic (Fabry, Maximin, 2001).

Some blockages could appear and greatly attenuate the impact of inward-FDI on the host economies, especially concerning transition countries. Indeed, it seems insufficient to transpose western management rules in order to make a firm competitive and *a fortiori* in order to institute a climate of steady growth. For instance, unskilled human capital, unsafe infrastructures and legal system, weak absorption capacity of the transferred technology, and non-competitive financial institutions can indeed block the transmission phenomenon and reduce the impacts of FDI on growth (Lall 1998). It depends also on the human, political, institutional, and cultural base on which FDI are going to rest. In

6 See for instance: Balasubramanyam and al. (1996), Blomström, Kokko, Zejan (1994), Borensztein and al. (1998), Fabry, Maximin (2001), Haddad, Harrison (1993), Markusen and Venables (1997), De Melo (1999), O'Donnell and Blumentritt, 1999.

addition, the FDI effects are necessarily numerous and depend on the amount of achieved FDI as well as on their seniority in the country.

3.1.1. The FDI-Contributions: Transfers from Parent Firm to the Affiliates

The *FDI-contributions* concern *all the transfers* from the parent firm to the affiliates. These transfers are made of physical, financial and material flows (facilities, machines, equipment, and capital) but also of intangible assets like technology, expertise, know-how, methods, and organizational practices. Broadly seen, these transfers may be considered as a *knowledge transfer*. The transfers are made in order to modernize and adapt local factors to the foreign investor's criteria and managerial framework. Foreign firms want to introduce new equipment and machines, new methods and processes (production and distribution), new firm functions (marketing, accountancy, human resources) and new products. They have to transform former "socialist" production units into western-style business units. This implies a deep organizational learning for both host country and parent firm.

The expected results for the host country are modernization and its corollary, the increased efficiency of the factors. Indeed, the openness to FDI could be a means, in the short term, to improve the *allocative efficiency* and the *productive efficiency* of factors.

- Inward-FDI improve the *allocative efficiency* of factors while allowing the goods supply to approach the consumer's needs (or producer's). FDI introduce new services (bank, insurance, distribution), new products (consumer goods), and they contribute to reshape existing industries according to the international norms and criteria (food and beverage industries, pharmacy, automotive construction).

- Inward-FDI improve the *productive efficiency* of factors by developing a supply of goods and services at a better cost-quality level. Besides the capital paid for the acquisition of the local firms, the foreign investor imports a range of practices and abilities (accounting, cost-analyze, management rules, technology, equipment, processes, marketing). These numerous and varied contributions allows to upgrade the level of the products and processes to an international standard (ISO certification). This may open the way to the development and reorientation of the transition country's commercial exchanges (Lankhuizen, 2000). FDI can therefore contribute to the insertion of the host country in the world economy and facilitate its regional anchorage to the European Union. In addition, consumers will have a larger selection of products and will benefit from a better quality and lower prices.

Inward-FDI allows the host country to modernize and modify the production methods and to develop exports to western markets. These changes may occur rapidly. However they are indebted to the presence of foreign investors (importance of inward-FDI flows per capita, seniority of FDI in the country) and the performances remain dependent on the foreign firms.

3.1.2. The FDI-Impacts: Assimilation and Diffusion of the Transferred Knowledge

The *FDI-impacts*, of a more qualitative order, concern *assimilation* by local actors (within affiliates) of the transferred knowledge and finally its *diffusion* in the host country to the private sector (in the same industry or beyond). The question of the *assimilation* and *diffusion* of knowledge are important, particularly in a context still under the influence of practices and habits inherited from the former Soviet system. Indeed, if one considers that a firm represents a "social capital" registered in a specific spatial and temporal context (home country), one can question the transferability of this "social capital" in another environment (host country). One can also question the absorptive capacity of host country. As Audretsch (1999, p. 9) wrote: *"the marginal cost of transmitting knowledge, and especially tacit knowledge, rises with distance."*

- *Transferability* and *assimilation* concern above all the foreign affiliate level, whatever its legal form (IJV, greenfield, brownfield). The questions that arise are: *"How do foreign firms succeed in transferring their methods and managerial rules in the subsidiaries? How do foreign parents succeed in forming and qualifying local workers to new working practices? How do foreign parents succeed in motivating the workers and make them willing to assimilate new rules and habits?"* This puts the problem (rarely studied in the literature) of the link between the foreign firms, the knowledge transfer, and its assimilation within the affiliates by local workers (Fabry and Zeghni, 2000). In particular the transfer of best practices, which are responsive to the competitive advantage of the foreign firm, will be much more difficult to achieve. It is particularly true if the foreign enterprise competitive advantage' rests on tacit and complex knowledge (Maskell, Malmberg 1999, Simonin, 1999, Szulansky, 1999). Foreign firms entering transition economies must break old habits and develop a closer link between wage, qualification and productivity. In the absence of an efficient labor market, the foreign parent, to qualify local workers, needs to set up training programs. The training process can be divided into two complementary parts: on-the-job training (local demonstration and learning), and *off the job training* (formal schooling, seminars or visits from or/at the parent firm). The aim is to develop the learning capability of the local workers and to transfer western values of firms.
- The *diffusions* concern the host country and put the problem (now largely studied) of the spillovers generated on the local industrial structures (Blomström, Kokko, Zejan, 1994 and 2000; Blomström, Kokko, 1998). Foreign firms generate some vertical activities upstream and downstream (subcontractors, distribution). They can also generate new activities in services or industry. In any case, they incite local firms to modernize themselves and to actively upgrade their products to enrich the international standard. But spillovers point out the problem of the absorption capacity of the host country, that is to say its capacity to take advantage of the presence of foreign firms. This capacity reveals the transition country's potential as linked to its human capital endowment and its macro environment seen as a support to the development of a local entrepreneurship.

Figure 2 resumes FDI's twin role in host countries. The ultimate result should be that inward-FDI help the host country to upgrade its economy.

Figure 2: The Twin Role of FDI in Host Economy

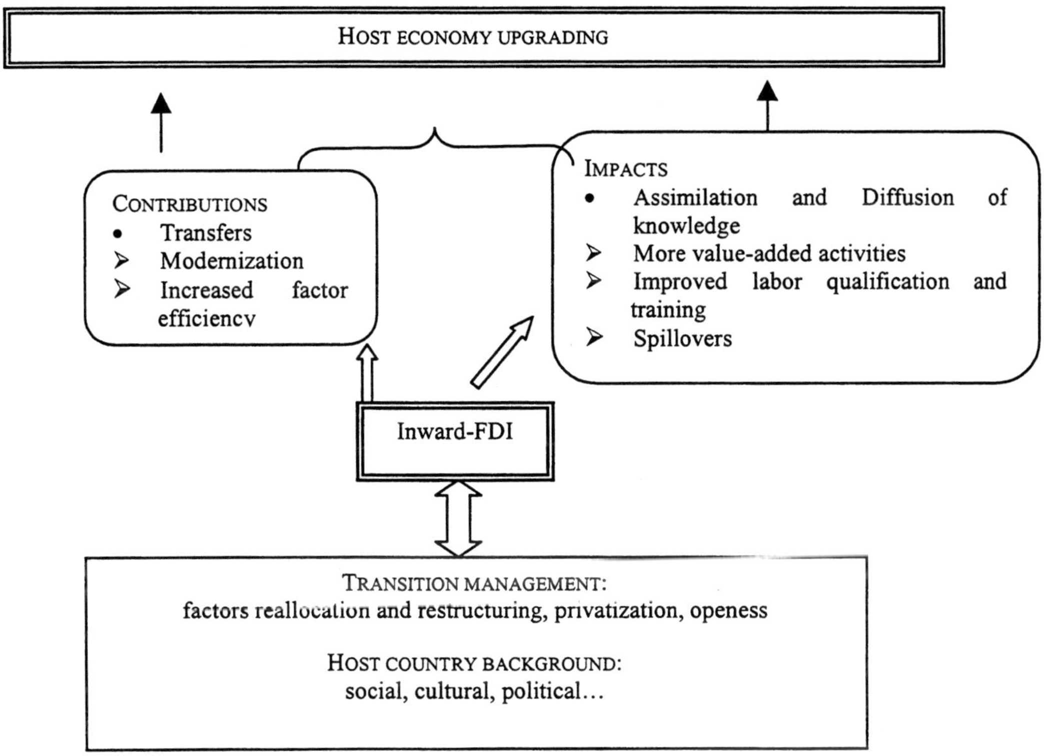

Legend:
- • Nature of the contributions and impacts
- ➢ Expected results

3.2. The Role of Inward-FDI in Host-Country's Upgrading

Beyond C point (figure 1), two representative cases of transition host countries' upgrading may be seen: the *exogenous-led upgrading* and the *endogenous-led upgrading.*

The *exogenous-led upgrading* is characterized by an important contribution of FDI to local output and exports. The local facilities are better used, the productive combinations are more efficient, and the productivity increases as well as the quality of the products. Besides, exports to western (European) markets are made easier. This situation is the consequence of an exogenous contribution of imported knowledge, techniques, capitals and methods. Schematically, it allows the host economy to pass C point and to shift toward point D on the production possibilities curve 1 (see figure 3).

The *endogenous-led upgrading* is characterized by an important contribution in terms of methods, facilities, capital and human capital. Two elements may accompany this upgrading. First, a modification of the organizational framework of the firms; second, a development of the local labor market (training, qualification, sectoral and geographical mobility). The presence of FDI goes beyond a simple modernization, efficiency of factors and growth of output. It rests on the actualization of transfers of expertise and tacit knowledge and of best practices of the foreign investor within the affiliates and through spillovers to local firms and markets. As a result, foreign production may become more intensive in added value creation as well as more diversified. As figure 4 suggests, this may allow the host country to shift from point C (or D) to point E on a second possibility of production curve (PPC2).

Figure 3: Exogenous-led Upgrading

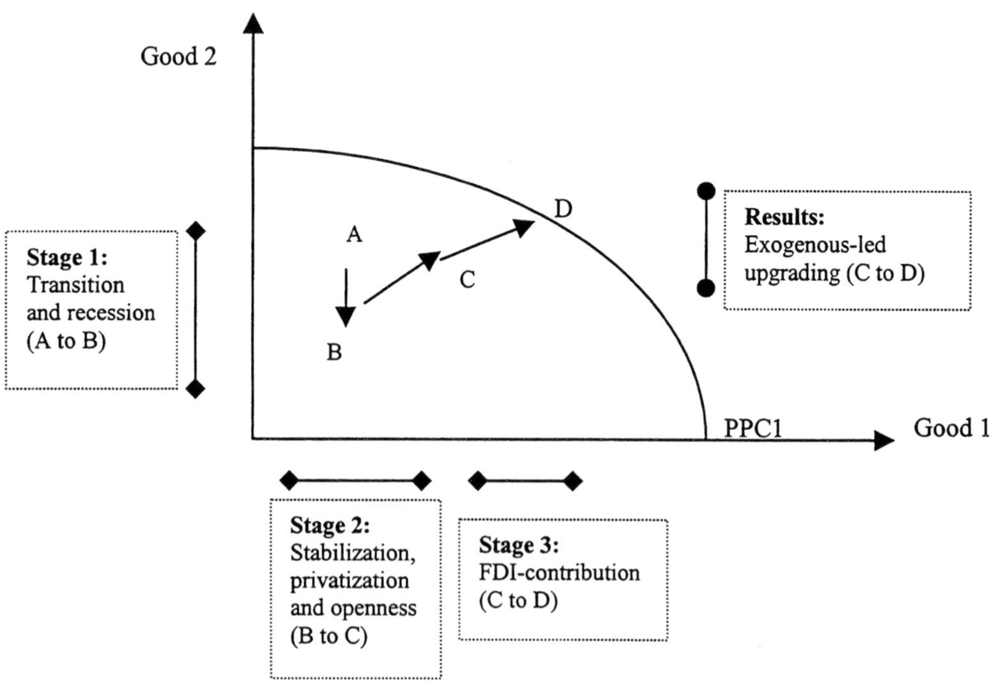

Figure 4: The Endogenous-led Upgrading

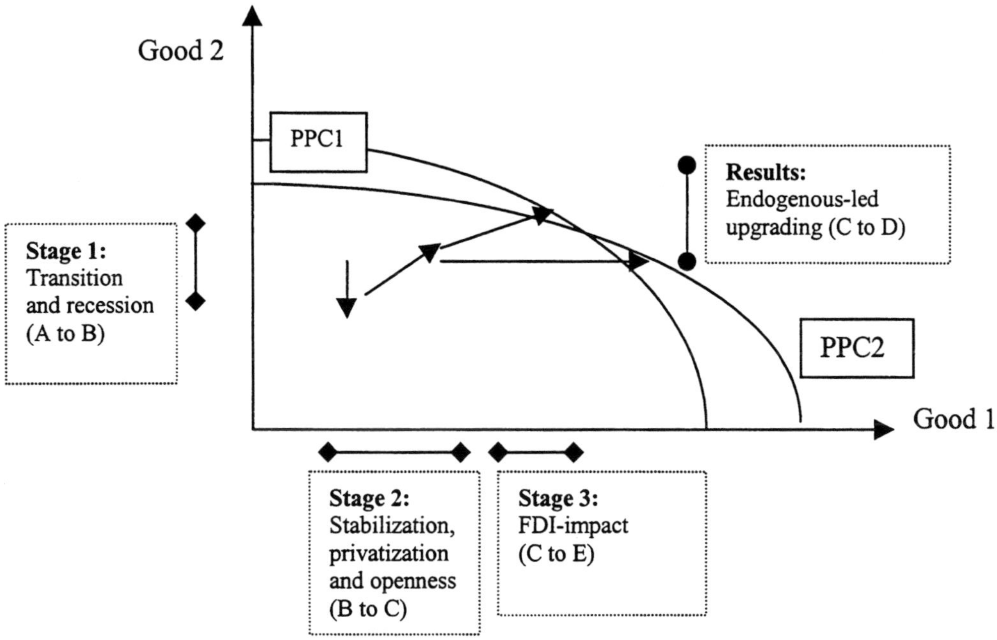

Table 3 presents a synthesis of the links between FDI-role and host economy upgrading. In the short run, FDI's role on local upgrading is strongly *exogenous* and may be resumed to the *FDI contributions*. In the longer run, FDI's role on local upgrading may become more *endogenous*. The capacity of the host country to take advantage of the presence of foreign firms determines the role of the inward-FDI into the economy and the reality of the transferred values and expertise.

Table 3: The Link between FDI-role and Host Country's Upgrading

	Exogenous-led Upgrading	**Endogenous-led Upgrading**
FDI Role	FDI contributions (short term)	Cumulative effect: FDI contributions and impacts (medium and long term)
Characteristics	*Exogenous contributions (transfers)*: improved and reoriented production processes, new equipment and machines, new products, capital import, new methods, New firm functions	*Assimilation of knowledge transferred* from parent firms to affiliates: technology, knowledge, know-how, best practices.... *Diffusion* of best practices and western management rules to local firms, spillovers.
Expected Results on Host Country	*Localized effects* within foreign subsidiaries (whatever the juridical form of the foreign affiliate): improved cost-quality linkage of products, improved factor efficiency, accelerator of firms modernization and restructuring	*Indirect effects* on host country: development of more complex and value-added activities within foreign subsidiaries *Direct effects* on host county: vertical linkages to local suppliers, subcontractors but also to other producers (diffusion of new methods and best practices in the host country - spillovers)
Next Step	Endogenous-led upgrading	Catching-up

3.3. A Simple Statistical Analysis of FDI's Role in Host-Countries

In a first step we made a Granger causality test to detect statistically a direction of causality for three variables: growth of output (GDP), exports (X) and inward-FDI (FDI). The aim of the simple statistical test is twofold. First, to know whether or not FDI contribute directly in boosting the growth of the recipient country; second, to learn about the relationship between FDI and exports. Exports should, in a first approach, approximate spillover effects and the nature of FDI activities more export oriented than local market-oriented.

From the 25 European transition countries, we selected from table 2 a sample of ten host countries. The selection criteria are as follows: (1) no country receiving FDI mainly in the oil sector (this excludes from the panel CIS members such as Azerbaijan, Kazakhstan, Kyrgyzstan, Uzbekistan...), (2) country with sufficient data over the 1991-2000 period. This second criterion excludes countries such as the Baltic States (Estonia and Lithuania) and CIS members (Belarus, Georgia). The Russian Federation, because of it emerging importance, is the only country that does not entirely fit this second criterion with missing data at the beginning of the period (1991 and 1992), and (3), countries with a cumulated FDI flow less than 0.4% in 1991-95 were excluded. Most of the CIS members and Macedonia, Croatia, Armenia are involved. Our selection is presented in the following table 4.

Table 4: Country Selection for the Causality Test

Countries	FDI per capita ratio		Evolution
	1991-1995	1996-2000	
Albania	74.7	70.9	Maintain in C1 with decrease (-5%)
Russian Federation	14.9	51.1	Maintain in C1 with increase (+244%)
Ukraine	15.5	47.9	Maintain in C1 with increase (+208%)
Bulgaria,	38.7	204.6	From C1 to C3
Romania,	42.7	218.5	From C1 to C3
Poland	67.4	418.6	From C1 to C3
Slovak republic,	148.5	265.9	From C2 to C3
Slovenia	283	313.5	Maintain in C3 with increase (+11%)
Czech republic,	378.6	844.7	From C3 to C4
Hungary,	1068.6	495.1	From C4 to C3 (decrease: -53,6%)

Notes: Class are as follow: C1 (0-100 US$); C2 (101-200US$); C3 (201-500US$); C4 (over 501 US$).
Sources: from table 2.

The main results of our causality test are gathered in the table 5.

Table 5: Granger Causality Tests (1991-2000)

	Null hypothesis	F-statistics	Probability	Results
	Inward-FDI and Host Country Growth (GDP)			
Albania	FDI does not Granger cause GDP	10.2236	0.04577	*Reject: FDI → GDP*
Russian Fed.	FDI does not Granger cause GDP	6.04915	0.09091	*Reject: FDI → GDP*
Hungary	GDP does not Granger cause FDI	4.16770	0.13615	*Reject: GDP → FDI*
Poland	GDP does not Granger cause FDI	37.1192	0.02623	*Reject: GDP → FDI*
Romania	GDP does not Granger cause FDI	3.52849	0.16292	*Reject: GDP → FDI*
	Inward-FDI and Host Country Exports (X)			
Bulgaria	X does not Granger cause FDI	49.8817	0.00499	*Reject: X → FDI*
Hungary	X does not Granger cause FDI	4.21941	0.13431	*Reject: X → FDI*
Poland	X does not Granger cause FDI	183.805	0.00541	*Reject: X → FDI*
Romania	X does not Granger cause FDI	9.94616	0.04744	*Reject: X → FDI*
Russian Fed.	X does not Granger cause FDI	42.1619	0.00742	*Reject: X → FDI*
	Exports (X) and Host Country Growth (GDP)			
Poland	X does not Granger cause GDP	7.79700	0.06481	*Reject: X → GDP*
Albania	GDP does not Granger cause X	4.97376	0.11153	*Reject: GDP → X*
Hungary	GDP does not Granger cause X	7.99652	0.06278	*Reject: GDP → X*
Ukraine	GDP does not Granger cause X	305.762	0.00326	*Reject: GDP → X*

Notes: Calculations are in logarithm. Time lag is (2) except for the Russian fed. (1). See annex 1 for more details.
Sources: EBRD reports (1999, 2000)

The relationship between FDI and GDP growth is not obvious and not automatic. We detected for Albania and the Russian federation a unidirectional causality from FDI to GDP. In Hungary, Poland and Romania, the causality works from GDP to FDI. For all other countries the causality is not strong (coefficient not significant) or bilateral (see annex 1). As FDI are supposed to boost host country exports, we expected a direction of causality from FDI to exports. The Granger test detected a direction of causality from exports to FDI in the five countries where the test coefficients are significant. Finally, in Albania, Hungary and Ukraine, "GDP causes exports" and in Poland, the statistical unidirectional causality goes from exports to GDP.

Table 6 summarized the results by causality direction and by country. One can observe that for three countries (Czech republic, Slovenia, and Slovak Republic) the Granger test never detects a direction of causality. On the contrary, tests always detect unidirectional causality for Hungary and Poland i.e. for most advanced transition host-countries. For the other countries of the sample, one (Bulgaria, Ukraine) or two (Albania, Romania, Russian Federation) directions of causality have been found. Causality tests are not sufficient to confirm the role of inward-FDI on host countries. But we may admit that the more significant the direction of causality for a country is, the more inward-FDI may play a significant role in the host country directly or indirectly via exports.

Table 6: Causality Direction for 10 Host Countries (1991-2000)

• FDI ⇨ GDP	Albania, Russian Federation		
• GDP ⇨ FDI	Hungary, Poland, Romania		
• FDI? GDP	Bulgaria, Czech republic, Slovenia, Slovak republic, Ukraine		
• FDI ⇨ X	None		
• X ⇨ FDI	Bulgaria, Hungary, Poland, Romania, Russian Federation		
• FDI? X	Albania, Czech republic, Slovenia, Slovak republic, Ukraine		
• GDP ⇨ X	Albania, Hungary, Ukraine		
• X ⇨ GDP	Poland		
• GDP? X	Bulgaria, Czech republic, Romania, Russian Federation, Slovenia, Slovak republic		
	Results by Countries		
Albania	FDI ⇨ GDP	GDP ⇨ X	
Bulgaria	X ⇨ FDI		
Czech republic	None		
Hungary	GDP ⇨ FDI	X ⇨ FDI	GDP ⇨ X
Poland	GDP ⇨ FDI	X ⇨ FDI	GDP ⇨ X
Romania	GDP ⇨ FDI	X ⇨ FDI	
Russian Federation	FDI ⇨ GDP	X ⇨ FDI	
Slovak republic	None		
Slovenia	None		
Ukraine	GDP ⇨ X		

Sources: annex 1

The correlation matrix may help us to gain a better understanding of the link between our three main variables: exports, FDI and GDP of the recipient country (table 7). In all countries of the selected panel the correlation coefficients of GDP-X relationship are higher than the coefficients of the FDI-GDP one. Exports seem to boost more deeply the host country's GDP than FDI. In Hungary FDI seem to be more local market oriented than elsewhere.

Table 7: Correlation Coefficient (1991-2000)

	FDI - GDP		FDI - X		GDP - X	
	Coef.	Rank	Coef.	Rank	Coef.	Rank
Albania	0.707	3	0.818	3	0.964	2
Bulgaria	0.644	5	0.395	8	0.650	9
Czech Rep.	0.654	4	0.741	5	0.938	3
Hungary	0.068	10	-0.0385	10	0.829	7
Poland	0.927	1	0,899	1	0.977	1
Romania	0.762	2	0.893	2	0.693	8
Russian Fed.	0.511	6	0.788	4	0.243	10
Slovak Rep.	0.484	7	0.646	6	0.916	5
Slovenia	0.334	9	0.613	7	0.833	6
Ukraine	0.467	8	0.364	9	0.932	4

Sources: annex 2

From these different statistical results we may put in perspective the following points:

- Most transition countries are still at stage 1 of FDI's role. They rely on an exogenous-led upgrading.

- Some countries like Hungary are at the crossroad and try to reach a more endogenous-led upgrading. As we show elsewhere (Fabry and Zeghni, 2000), even in Hungary some blockages of transfers and assimilation may be identified both at an affiliate level and at a nationwide level. More generally, to enter in an endogenous-led upgrading stage, host countries must develop skills and training of local workers and human capital.

- None of these countries benefit from catching-up *vis-à-vis* industrial economies. FDI, when accompanied by knowledge transfers, are not a gift for a host country. To benefit from FDI, a host country must develop absorptive capabilities of local human resources (Cohen and Levinthal, 1990; Keller, 1996). FDI helps countries to reach a more qualitative growth path. It is not a substitute to government policies (investment, R&D, education) to promote catching-up i.e. the reduction of the technology gap *vis-à-vis* advanced industrial countries.

4. Conclusion and Perspectives for Further Researches

The shift from an exogenous drive upgrading toward a more endogenous one is an important quest. It is also a difficult task. As we have seen it, some conditions must be reached such as:

- a relative high level of inward-FDI per capita in the host country and the seniority of these FDI;
- the ability of foreign firms to transfer *knowledge* (tacit and sticky) and to learn how to run an affiliate in transition countries;
- the absorptive capabilities of the host country and local firms (new habits and business rules);
- the importance of the local human capital (skills, training and qualification, entrepreneurship mood);
- a macro environment able to support the private sector (safe and reliable institutions and infrastructures) and to promote convergence towards markets.

Moreover, FDI may help host countries to upgrade their economies but are not suited to replace industrial and technological changes for long-term growth (Dycker, 1997; Dycker and Radosevic, 2000; EBRD, 2000). The endogenous-led upgrading characterizes the ability of the host country to take advantage of inward-FDI and to "attract" even more inward-FDI. Thus, an implicit question may be asked: *"does a transition country attract the inward-FDI that it deserves?"* In the end, one can ask if a transition country doesn't realize its potential more rapidly thanks to inward-FDI.

References

1. Aghion P., Blanchard O., and Burgess R. (1994). The behavior of state firms in Eastern Europe pre-privatization. *European Economic Review*. 38.
2. Artus P. (2000). *Comment corriger l'insuffisance de transfert d'épargne vers les pays émergents?* Document de Travail n°2000-40/EI. Caisse des Dépôts et consignations, juillet.
3. Audretsch D. (1999). *Knowledge spillovers and the role of small firms*. Communication at the international conference: "Knowledge spillovers and the Geography of innovation. A comparison of national systems of innovation. University of Jean Monnet - Saint-Etienne (France). July 1&2.
4. Balasubramanyam V., Salisu M., and Sapsford D. (1996). Foreign Direct Investment and Growth in EP and IS Countries. *The Economic Journal* (106), January.
5. Berg B., Kilvits K. and Tombak M. (1996). Technology Policy for Improving Competitiveness of Estonian Industries; *C 73 Series, ETLA - The research Institute of the Finnish Economy, Helsinki.*

6. Bevan A. and Estrin S. (2000), The determinants of FDI in transition economies, *William Davidson Institute, working papers n°342*, October.
7. Blanchard O. (1996). *The economics of post-communist transition.* Oxford: Clarendon Press
8. Blomstrom M., Kokko A., and Zejan M. (1994). Host Country Competition, Labor Skills, and Technology Transfer by Multinationals. *Weltwirtschaftliches Archiv*, Band 130, Heft 3.
9. Blomstrom M; Kokko A. (1998), Multinational corporations and spillovers, *Journal of Economic survey*, vol. 12, n°3.
10. Blomstrom M., Sjoholm F. (1999), Technology transfer and spillovers: does local participation with multinationals matter?, *European economic Review*, 43.
11. Blomstrom M., Kokko A., and Zejan M. (2000). *Foreign Direct Investment, firms and Host Country strategies*, Basingstoke, Mac Millan.
12. Borensztein E., de Gregorio J. and Lee J-W. (1998). How Does FDI Affect Economic Growth? *Journal of International Economics*, 45.
13. Boycko M., Schleifer A., and Vishny R. (1995). *Privatizing Russia.* Cambridge, MA: The MIT Press.
14. Cohen W. and Levinthal D. (1990). Absorptive capacity: a new perspective on learning and innovation. *Administrative Science Quarterly*. 35.
15. De Melo J. (1999). Foreign Direct investment-led growth: evidence from time series and panel data, *Oxford Economic Papers*, 51.
16. Dunning J. (1993). Multinational enterprises and the global economy, *Workingham, Addison-Wesley*
17. Dunning J. (1995). Reappraising the Eclectic Paradigm in a Age of Alliance Capitalism. *Journal of international Business Studies*, 3rd Quarter.
18. Dyker D. (ed.) (1997). *The Technology of Transition. Science and Technology Policies for Transition Countries*, Budapest: CIE.
19. Dycker D. and Radosevic S. (2000), Building the knowledge-based economy in countries in transition - from concept to policies, *SPRU Electronic Working Papers Series, paper n°36.*
20. EBRD - European Bank for Reconstruction and Development (1999), *Transition report: Ten years of transition*, London
21. EBRD - European Bank for Reconstruction and Development (2000), *Transition report: Employment, skills and transition*, London.
22. Estrin S., and Meyer K. (1999). Entry Mode Choice in Emerging Markets: Greenfield, Acquisition, Brownfield. *CIS-Middle Europe Center, London Business School, Discussion Papers Series, n°57*, February.
23. Fabry N. and Maximin B. (2001), FDI, Industrial Labour Transformation and Growth: The Case of South Korea, Malaysia and Thailand. In Andreosso-O'Callaghan B, Bassino J.P., Jaussaud J. editors. *The Changing Economic Environment in Asia,* Aldershot, McMillan (forthcoming).
24. Fabry N., and Zeghni S. (2000). *How to run an affiliate in transition economies? A foreign investor commitment perspective.* Communication at the 3rd EACES Paris Workshop, Impact of FDI and know-how Transfer on Restructuring, Spin off and

networking in Central and Eastern Europe and Asian Transition Economies, Marne-la-Vallée University (France), June 8&9.
25. Fabry N., and Zeghni S. (2000). International Joint venture in transition economies: a foreign investor commitment perspective. *GASI - Working Papers 2000-1. University of Marne-la-Vallée* (France).
26. Firozzi F. (1997). Multinationals FDI and Uncertainty: An Exposition, *Journal of Multinational Financial Management*, vol. 7(3).
27. Frydman R., Pistor K., and Rapaczynski A. (1996). Exit and voice after mass privatization: The case of Russia. *European Economic Review*. 40.
28. Haddad M. and Harrison A. (1993). Are There Positive Spillovers From Foreign Investment? *Journal of Development Economic*, vol. 42.
29. Johnson S., Kauffmann D., Mcmillan J., and Woodruff C. (2000). Why do firm hide? Bribes and unofficial activity after communism. *Journal of public Economics*. 76.
30. Kalotay K. (1999). *The other side of the location of international investment: the FDI absorptive capacity of host countries*. Communication at the 7th Conference les stratégies des FMN, localisation, impacts sur l'emploi, les exportations et la technologie. University of Paris 1 - Panthéon - Sorbonne. June 17&18.
31. Keller W. (1996). Absorptive Capacity: On the Creation and Acquisition of Technology in Development, *Journal of Development Economics* 49.
32. Kornai J. (1994). Transformational recession: a general phenomenon examined through the example of Hungary's development. *Discussion paper 1. Collegium Budapest.*
33. Labaronne D. (1999). *Les privatisations à l'est*, Paris, éditions Management.
34. Lall S. 1998. Changing Perceptions of FDI in Development, in Tharakan P.K. and Van Den Bulcke D. (editors), *International Trade, FDI and the Economic Environment*, London, McMillan.
35. Lankes H.P. and Venables A. (1996), FDI in economic transition: the changing pattern of investments. *Economics of Transition*. 4(2).
36. Lankhuizen M. (2000). Shifts in foreign trade, competitiveness and growth potential: from Baltics to "Bal-techs"? *Research Policy*. 29.
37. Lipsey R. (1999). The role of FDI in international capital flows. *NBER Working Papers* n°7094, December.
38. Marinov M. A., and Marinova S. T. (1999). Foreign investor strategy development in the Central and Eastern European context, *Thunderbird International Business Review*, vol. 40(1).
39. Markusen J. and Venables A. (1997). Foreign Direct Investment as a Catalyst for Industrial Development. *NBER Working Paper n°6241*.
40. Maskell P., and Malmberg A. (1999). Localized learning and industrial competitiveness, *Cambridge Journal of Economics*, vol.23 (2).
41. Michalet C-A. (1999), *La séduction des nations*, Paris, Economica.
42. O'Donnell S. and Blumentritt T. (1999). The contribution of foreign subsidiaries to host country national competitiveness. *Journal of International Management*, vol. 5.

43. Sara T. and Newhouse B. (1995). Transaction Costs and Foreign Direct Investment in Developing Countries, *International Advances in Economic Research*; vol. 1(4):
44. Simai M. (1999). When will the transition phase end?, *Thunderbird International Business Review,* vol.40(1):7-27
45. Simonin B. L. (1999). Ambiguity and the process of knowledge transfer in strategic alliance, *Strategic Management Journal*, vol. 20(7).
46. Sinn H. and Weichenrieder A. (1997). FDI, political resentment and the privatization process in Eastern Europe. *Economic Policy*, 24.
47. Szulanski G. (1999). The process of knowledge transfer: a diachronic analysis of stickiness, Working Paper 99-05, the Reginal H. Jones center for Management Policy, Strategy and organization, The Wharton School, Department of Management, Pennsylvania University, (*http://www-management.wharton.upenn.edu/jonesctr/papers/1999.htm*)
48. Verspagen B. and De Loo I. (1999). Technology spillovers between sectors and over time. *Technological forecasting and social change. 60.*
49. Zeghni S. (2001). Risk in Transition Economies: The Impact of Host Country Characteristics on FDI Inflows. In Fabry N. and Zeghni (editors) *Transition in Asia and Central and Eastern Europe: A closed door two open windows?*, New-York: Nova Science Publisher.

ANNEX 1: GRANGER CAUSALITY TESTS

	Null Hypothesis	F-statistics	Probability	Results
	Inward-FDI and host country growth			
Albania	GDP does not Granger cause FDI	0.50246	0.64832	Accept
	FDI does not Granger cause GDP	*10.2236*	*0.04577*	*Reject*
Bulgaria	GDP does not Granger cause FDI	0.52469	0.63767	Accept
	FDI does not Granger cause GDP	2.82304	0.20439	Accept
Czech rep.	GDP does not Granger cause FDI	1.06131	0.48513	Accept
	FDI does not Granger cause GDP	2.52203	0.28393	Accept
Hungary	*GDP does not Granger cause FDI*	*4.16770*	*0.13615*	*Reject*
	FDI does not Granger cause GDP	0.62964	0.59112	Accept
Poland	*GDP does not Granger cause FDI*	*37.1192*	*0.02623*	*Reject*
	FDI does not Granger cause GDP	2.42053	0.29235	Accept
Romania	*GDP does not Granger cause FDI*	*3.52849*	*0.16292*	*Reject*
	FDI does not Granger cause GDP	1.57005	0.34152	Accept
Russian Fed.	GDP does not Granger cause FDI	1.17542	0.35764	Accept
	FDI does not Granger cause GDP	*6.04915*	*0.09091*	*Reject*
Slovenia	GDP does not Granger cause FDI	0.15812	0.86043	Accept
	FDI does not Granger cause GDP	0.62722	0.59213	Accept
Slovak rep.	GDP does not Granger cause FDI	1.74528	0.31424	Accept
	FDI does not Granger cause GDP	0.49231	0.65328	Accept
Ukraine	GDP does not Granger cause FDI	0.97010	0.50759	Accept
	FDI does not Granger cause GDP	1.00145	0.49964	Accept
	Inward-FDI and Host Country Exports			
Albania	X does not Granger cause FDI	0.80747	0.52412	Accept
	FDI does not Granger cause X	1.62337	0.33281	Accept
Bulgaria	*X does not Granger cause FDI*	*49.8817*	*0.00499*	*Reject*
	FDI does not Granger cause X	0.33177	0.74102	Accept
Czech rep.	X does not Granger cause FDI	0.61102	0.62072	Accept
	FDI does not Granger cause X	0.44688	0.69114	Accept
Hungary	*X does not Granger cause FDI*	*4.21941*	*0.13431*	*Reject*
	FDI does not Granger cause X	0.58646	0.60957	Accept
Poland	*X does not Granger cause FDI*	*183.805*	*0.00541*	*Reject*
	FDI does not Granger cause X	1.22839	0.44875	Accept
Romania	*X does not Granger cause FDI*	*9.94616*	*0.04744*	*Reject*
	FDI does not Granger cause X	0.21270	0.81963	Accept
Russian Fed.	*X does not Granger cause FDI*	*42.1619*	*0.00742*	*Reject*
	FDI does not Granger cause X	7.81969	0068ü6	Accept

Inward-FDI and Host Country Exports (to be continued)				
Slovenia	X does not Granger cause FDI	0.28884	0.76785	Accept
	FDI does not Granger cause X	0.05256	0.94966	Accept
Slovak rep.	X does not Granger cause FDI	0.34215	0.74508	Accept
	FDI does not Granger cause X	0.13258	0.88294	Accept
Ukraine	X does not Granger cause FDI	0.68012	0.59520	Accept
	FDI does not Granger cause X	0.52800	0.65445	Accept
Host country Exports and Growth				
Albania	X does not Granger cause GDP	1.00249	0.46406	Accept
	GDP does not Granger cause X	*4.97376*	*0.11153*	*Reject*
Bulgaria	X does not Granger cause GDP	0.29316	0.76508	Accept
	GDP does not Granger cause X	0.29316	0.25554	Accept
Czech rep.	X does not Granger cause GDP	0.33707	0.73782	Accept
	GDP does not Granger cause X	3.55286	0.16174	Accept
Hungary	X does not Granger cause GDP	1.25274	0.40224	Accept
	GDP does not Granger cause X	*7.99652*	*0.06278*	*Reject*
Poland	*X does not Granger cause GDP*	*7.79700*	*0.06481*	*Reject*
	GDP does not Granger cause X	0.70200	0.56223	Accept
Romania	X does not Granger cause GDP	1.20579	0.41276	Accept
	GDP does not Granger cause X	0.56106	0.62087	Accept
Russian Fed	X does not Granger cause GDP	0.84924	0.39905	Accept
	GDP does not Granger cause X	0.18328	0.68638	Accept
Slovenia	X does not Granger cause GDP	0.65075	0.58244	Accept
	GDP does not Granger cause X	0.28184	0.77238	Accept
Slovak rep.	X does not Granger cause GDP	2.17681	0.31478	Accept
	GDP does not Granger cause X	2.80206	0.26302	Accept
Ukraine	X does not Granger cause GDP	35.9882	0.02704	Accept
	GDP does not Granger cause X	*305.762*	*0.00326*	*Reject*

Notes: Calculations are in logarithm. The time lag is (2) except for the Russian federation (1)

Sources: EBRD reports (1999; 2000)

ANNEX 2: CORRELATION COEFFICIENT (1991-2000)

Country		FDI	GDP	X
Albania	FDI	1		
	GDP	0.707	1	
	X	0.818	0.964	1
Bulgaria	FDI	1		
	GDP	0.644	1	
	X	0.395	0.650	1
Czech republic	FDI	1		
	GDP	0.654	1	
	X	0.741	0.938	1
Hungary	FDI	1		
	GDP	0.068	1	
	X	-0.0385	0.829	1
Poland	FDI	1		
	GDP	0,927	1	
	X	0,899	0,977	1
Romania	FDI	1		
	GDP	0.762	1	
	X	0.893	0.693	1
Russian Federation	FDI	1		
	GDP	0.511	1	
	X	0.788	0.243	1
Slovak Republic	FDI	1		
	GDP	0.484	1	
	X	0.646	0.916	1
Slovenia	FDI	1		
	GDP	0.334	1	
	X	0.613	0.833	1
Ukraine	FDI	1		
	GDP	0.467	1	
	X	0.364	0.932	1

Sources: EBRD reports (1999; 2000)

Chapter 2

FDI IN CENTRAL EUROPE: SHORT-RUN EFFECTS IN MANUFACTURING[1]

Tomasz Mickiewicz
University College London,
School of Slavonic and East European Studies
Slavo Radosevic
University College London,
School of Slavonic and East European Studies
Urmas Varblane
University of Tartu,
Faculty of Economics and Business Administration

1. INTRODUCTION

Central and Eastern European Countries (CEEC)[2] face difficult task of structural adjustment to both the initial post-communist transition shocks and to further disturbances linked to the process of EU accession. Foreign investors play important role in this process, bringing new technologies and capital and accelerating structural changes (Hunya 1998a, 1998b). This paper focus is on the role of FDI as an agent of change in manufacturing. We examine the impact of FDI on the structure of employment as well as

[1] This paper was prepared in the framework of the PHARE-ACE project R97-8112R, "Impact of Foreign Direct Investment on International Competitiveness of CEEC Manufacturing and EU Enlargement". In addition, the UK Economic and Social Science Research Council have funded part of the background work. We are grateful for comments on earlier version provided by the participants of the 6th EACES Conference, University of Barcelona, September 2000.

[2] Estonia is covered in our analysis, however, strictly speaking the country is located in northern, not central part of Europe (otherwise included in a separate category of Baltic States).

on job creation and job preservation. Next, we discuss effects on productivity, wages and investment. The data that form the basis of this paper are from *"Database on Foreign Investment Enterprises in Central European Manufacturing 1993 – 1998"*, prepared by the Vienna Institute for Comparative Economic Research (WIIW). It covers up to 23 branches of manufacturing industry in these countries by main economic indicators from balance sheets and income statements. Most data are presented separately according to the ownership of firms – for domestic and foreign owned sectors [3]. In co-operation with the Estonian Statistical Office comparable data on Estonia was added to the database, covering period from 1995 until 1998. Thus, our analysis refers to Poland, Czech Republic, Hungary, Slovenia and Estonia [4].

In the next section, we provide a brief general introduction into the issue. In the third section we present some stylized characteristics of FDI in transition economy. Employment structure is analyzed in section 4 and impact on employment level in section 5. Section 6 discusses potential effects of FIEs on productivity and wages, and in section 7, the focus is on investments. Finally, we provide conclusions.

2. Foreign Direct Investment

Multinational corporations (MNCs) play significant role in industrialized countries. However, its role is highly diversified. Amongst the OECD economies (1996), the share of foreign affiliates in employment is highest in Ireland (47%), France (25.8%) and Sweden (19.9%), and lowest in Japan (0.8%), Turkey (5.6%) and Germany (6.9%). It is striking that the comparable figure for new OECD members from Central Europe is already high: 42.8% for Hungary and 18.7% for the Czech Republic (OECD, 1999)[5]. Foreign companies have strong influence on manufacturing through types of jobs created regional distribution of new employment, dynamics of productivity and skill transfers. Direct effects are complemented by indirect or spillover effects. Indirect effects take place through movement of trained labor from foreign firms to other sectors as well as through the increase of employment in domestic subcontractors and learning processes therein. The integration of FDI into a local economy results often in a deep social change.

[3] All firms with some foreign share in their nominal or equity capital are counted as foreign investment enterprises (FIEs). Information about FIEs comes from national databases, which contain data of the income statements of firms. Even in the firms with minority foreign share, the foreign investor usually has a real control over the management. In that respect, FIEs do represent a population of firms that are usually defined as foreign direct investment (FDI). Nevertheless, we use the term FIEs whenever we explicitly refer to data on FIEs. For extensive methodological explanations see WIIW (1998).

[4] However, Czech data relate to firms with 100 employees and more, and Slovak to firms with 25 employees and more. That underestimates the share of domestic firms, as FIEs tend to be larger.

[5] WIIW database figures are lower, due to difference in definitions. We use OECD figure here to assure comparability with other OECD economies. However, figures on Poland - a third OECD member from CE - are not included in the OECD database.

Movement of labor and links with domestic subcontractors enable transmission of business culture, which includes corporate values, organizational structures and management practices (Mirza, 1998). All this may enhance both total factor productivity and labor productivity.

3. Characteristics of FDI and Progress in Reforms in Central Europe

With the opening of the CEEC economies, FDI has become an important mechanism of their integration into world economy, especially EU. Starting from the level of only 2.4bn USD in 1990 (1.5% of CEEC GDP), FDI in Central Europe has increased to 61.2 bn USD or 25 times (in 1998). Among CEEC, the relative importance of FDI is by far the highest in Hungary. High relative penetration of FDI in this economy could be partly explained by early inflows of FDI, which started immediately in 1990. Next early target country for foreign investors was Czech Republic. In mid-1990s, Poland took over the position of the main destination of FDI inflows among CEEC and has maintained it until now. Nevertheless, in terms of FDI stock per capita, Hungary remains still a clear outliner, the next two economies being Czech Republic and Estonia (Table 1).

Table 1: Data on FDI Stock in Transition Economies, 1989-1999.

Country	GDP 99/89 (%)	Cumulative FDI 99 (mln $)	Cumulative FDI per capita 99 ($)
Albania	95	454	137
Armenia	42	455	120
Azerbaijan	47	3592	448
Belarus	80	681	67
Bulgaria	67	2332	284
Croatia	78	3234	716
Czech Rep.	95	14924	1447
Estonia	77	1604	1115
FYR Macedonia	74	268	134
Georgia	34	622	116
Hungary	99	17770	1764
Kazakhstan	63	7356	494
Kyrgizstan	63	408	87
Latvia	60	2100	866
Lithuania	62	2012	545
Moldova	31	339	79
Poland	122	20047	518

Country	GDP 99/89 (%)	Cumulative FDI 99 (mln $)	Cumulative FDI per capita 99 ($)
Romania	76	5647	252
Russia	57	10344	71
Slovakia	100	2111	391
Slovenia	109	1400	701
Tajikistan	44	150	25
Turkmen	64	782	159
Ukraine	36	2751	55
Uzbekistan	94	790	32

Source: WIIW database (2000)

After ten years of post-communist transition, the differences among CEEC in terms of implementation of reforms and restructuring are significant. These differences are correlated with both the rate of growth of GDP and with the scale and nature of FDI that enter these economies. Generally, reforms create environment, which facilitate production, decrease costs and uncertainty and enables flexibility. Key stylized facts are (Lankes and Stern, 1998; Lankes and Venables, 1996; Meyer, 1998):

First, *market seeking* dominates among types of FDI entering the CEEC. Factor cost (efficiency seeking) considerations are secondary. Only jointly with attractive markets do lower factor costs attract inward FDI.

Second, economies which are characterized by most advanced reforms (as assessed, for instance, by EBRD transition indicators) are also characterized by higher share of (efficiency-seeking) *exporters* amongst FIE. Similarly, progress in reforms attracts more FIE, which are *local producers*, while FIE-*distributors* dominate in economies lagging in institutional transformation and recovery.

Third, *horizontal* type FDI projects are characteristic for less advanced CEEC economies. This may be linked to the fact that first mover advantages are highly relevant for distributors, i.e. in sales strategy rather than in production or acquisition of assets (local suppliers or exporters). Progress in transformation is associated with more *vertical* FDI (exporters) bringing them into EU and world production networks. In particular, export investment results in more "upstream" position of subsidiaries within the MNCs production chain, with almost half of the production sold within the corporation (Lankes and Stern, 1998).

Fourth, in advanced economies in transition, FDI is more *integrated into MNCs*, and more likely to be wholly owned. Countries further in transition have relatively more fully foreign owned projects.

Fifth, FDI enter into branches that have relatively stable and promising or *growing domestic markets* (Hunya 1997). They are not yet entering into collapsing branches with shrinking domestic markets.

Thus, FDI in less advanced CEEC is focused mainly on domestic markets and it is confined to the distribution parts of value-chain. This process is dominated by investment in trading, business support services and consumer goods operations targeting local markets.

High institutional instability and market uncertainty in the economies, which are less advanced in transition, are important but not insurmountable obstacles for this type of FDI. This explains the presence of FDI in those CEEC economies (for example, Ukraine) where high business risks would generally inhibit large-scale FDI inflows (Stern, 1997). Investors have opportunity to captivate local markets by being first. However, these advantages have to be balanced against economic risk and uncertainty. As a result of these opposing concerns, capitalization of FDI and their technology content are low, yet often include significant inflow of human capital in the form of transfer of managerial know-how, new organizational structures, management and marketing skills, access to distribution networks etc. However, in those circumstances, the overall impact of FDI is quite insignificant.

In more advanced transition economies, the basic conditions for FDI operations are improved. Here, foreign investors are setting up local suppliers to serve domestic market. Capitalization of investment projects increases and their time horizon expands, which increases the absolute numbers of foreign-controlled employment. Investments embody more technology than is the case of FDI focused on distribution. This requires diversified skill structure. In short, the economic effects are more substantial, both in terms of scale as well as structure.

In the parallel development, new subsidiaries are used as export platforms for labor intensive activities, which have been, delocalized from home countries. Again, the effects on CEES may be strong. Foreign investors start to shape employment according to the locational advantage of host economies. Inflows of Western technology, deepening co-operation with parent firms and better access to the distribution networks on the world market increase productivity in industry. These changes may induce reductions in employment in newly acquired firms but those may be often offset by increase in those enterprises, which are subcontractors of foreign firms.

In addition, portfolio of FDI expands through the emergence of strategic investments in utilities (telecommunications, energy) which are open to privatization in advanced reform economies. More generally, decreasing risks in advance reformers, growing domestic markets and cost differentials (in case of export oriented FDI), lead to expansion of FDI.

Given that the countries we want to analyze are advanced transition economies we would expect the structure of FDI to be an important factor in restructuring and change in manufacturing in the direction that would be more favorable for a long-term growth of CEES.

4. Foreign Direct Investment and the Structure of Employment

Similar to differences in the volume of FDI (Table 1), differences in the employment shares of FIEs in manufacturing among CEES economies are also significant. Already in 1993, more than 31% of employment in Hungary was in foreign owned firms. It increased to 44.9% in 1998. The share of foreign controlled manufacturing employment in other CEEC economies is growing as well, as it ranged from 13.1% to 26% in 1998 (Table 2).

Table 3 shows that the main targets for FDI are technology-intensive electrical machinery and car industry. In addition, foreign investors penetrate industries with relatively stable domestic markets, e.g. food, beverage and tobacco. Textiles, clothing and leather industries are less internationalized through FDI than other activities (except Estonia). Low penetration in coke and petroleum sector results from delay in privatization process (except Hungary)[6]. Same branches, which have typically low foreign penetration world-wide, have relatively higher foreign involvement in CEEC, for example, production of construction materials (see "other non-metallic minerals" in Table 3)[7]. With some delay, foreign presence is also growing in branches with great structural difficulties and oversized capacities, like steel industry.

In addition, there are some country specificities in foreign penetration across branches. For example, in Hungary, the coke and petroleum industry is practically taken over by foreign controlled firms (99.9% share of FDI in employment). Branches where the foreign presence is very high are office machinery (77.3%), chemicals (72.3%) and transportation equipment (79.1%). In the Czech Republic the major areas for FDI is again motor vehicles industry (55.9% share) and office machinery (56.3%). Similarly, in Poland, the presence of FIE in automotive sector is prominent as well (63.4%), but paper and paper products has the highest share of FIE (80.6%). The third key sector with FIE presence is radio and TV sets (45.7%). Exactly the same three sectors have the highest share in Slovenia, with 49% of FIE employment in automotive sector. In Estonia, both radio and office equipment and paper are again present in the first three sectors, however the country specific sector is textiles, with 55.8% of FIE employment, unlike other CEEC countries.

---

6 For detailed analysis on these problems see G.Hunya (1998b).

7 The growing construction activity in the region attracts acquisitions of cement and similar factories.

Table 2: The Shares of Foreign Firms in Total Employment of Manufacturing (%)

	1993	1998
Czech Republic	5.3	19.6
Estonia	9.5	20.8
Hungary	31.7	44.9
Poland	9.7	26.0
Slovenia	8.5	13.1

Source: WIIW Database on Foreign Investment Enterprises, Vienna (2000).

With higher level of FDI inflows, we would expect that the structure of FDI becomes more diversified. The data for Hungary shows that the high level of FDI is accompanied by high share (75%) of FIE in exports (Hunya, 1998b). Also, we find an increasing differentiation of FDI types among transition countries, as differences in FDI presence become larger across region. Data on branch structure of FDI may show some aspects of this diversification process.

Table 3: The Shares of Foreign Firms in Total Employment, Branches of Manufacturing, 1998 (%)

Visegrad-3:		Cz R	Hun	Pol	Slovenia			Estonia		
ISIC	Industries	% of FIE in 1998			ISIC	Industries	%FIE	ISIC	Industries	%FIE
15-16	Foodprod, bev, tobacco	19.9	41.0	27.3	15	Foodprod, beverage	8.2	15,16	Foodproducts, beverages	10.4
17	Textiles	14.3	38.3	11.1	16	Tobacco manufactures	*	17	Textiles	55.9
18	Wearing app, dressing	14.1	32.9	27.9	17	Textiles	9.2	18	Wearing apparel, dress.	14.2
19	Leather	6.6	47.8	14.7	18	Wearing apparel, dres	0.9	19	Leather	26.2
20	Wood	18.9	23.0	24.6	19	Leather	3.4	20	Wood	11.7
21	Paper and paper products	28.3	55.8	80.6	20	Wood	2.4	21	Paper and paper prod.	64.8
22	Publishing, printing	27.7	21.1	37.1	21	Paper& paper product	29.8	22	Publishing, printing	12.6
23	Coke and petroleum	0.0	99.9	1.0	22	Publishing, printing	7.2	23,24	Chemicals and coke	26.9
24	Chemicals	14.3	72.3	25.3	23	Coke and petroleum	0.0	25	Rubber and plastic	14.4
25	Rubber and plastic	29.0	41.0	41.7	24	Chemicals	14.3	26	Other non-met. minerals	38.1

	Visegrad-3:	Cz R	Hun	Pol		Slovenia			Estonia	
ISIC	Industries	% of FIE in 1998			ISIC	Industries	%FIE	ISIC	Industries	%FIE
26	Other non-met. Minerals	25.8	50.5	28.5	25	Rubber and plastic	20.2	27,28	Metals and products	14.3
27	Basic metals	4.5	36.6	7.1	26	Other non-met.miner	10.5	29	Machinery and eq. n.e.c.	8.2
28	Fabricated metals	14.8	30.8	15.8	27	Basic metals	15.6	30-33	Office, el., radio & med	50.1
29	Machinery and eq. n.e.c.	8.1	42.2	11.4	28	Fabricated metals	6.1	34,35	Motor veh., transp. eq.	20.2
30	Office machinery	56.3	77.3	27.0	29	Machin. and eq. n.e.c.	20.2	36,37	Furniture,others, recycl.	11.6
31	Electrical machinery	40.7	66.8	42.2	30	Office machinery	*			
32	Radio, TV set	38.2	46.4	45.7	31	Electrical machinery	17.1		*Standard deviation 1993*	*10.4*
33	Med., precision, opt. Ins	15.1	35.1	14.9	32	Radio, TV sets	29.9		*Standard deviation 1998*	*18.4*
34	Motor vehicles, trailers	55.9	79.1	63.4	33	Med,precision, opt inst	20.0			
35	Other transport equipm.	0.9	36.0	7.9	34	Motor vehicles, trailer	49.0			
36	Furniture, manuf. n.e.c.	15.9	25.7	44.9	35	Other transport equip	0.7			
37	Recycling	30.7	29.7	22.2	36	Furniture, man. n.e.c.	1.2			
	Standard Deviation 1993	*6.6*	*14.4*	*13.1*	*37*	Recycling	*			
	Standard Deviation 1998	*15.6*	*20.6*	*19.2*		Industr. with <3 FIEs	23.3			

Source: WIIW Database on Foreign Investment Enterprises, Vienna, (2000).

Below, we present correlation coefficients between four analyzed countries based on shares of FDI in employment in branches of manufacturing. However, it reveals no clear pattern of either similarity or dissimilarity. In 1998, the structure of FIE presence became quite similar in Czech Republic and Poland, however both countries differ in relation to Hungary.

Table 4A: The Correlation Coefficients for Shares of FDI in Employment in 1993

	PL93	CZ93	HU93
PL93	1.00	0.13	0.33
CZ93	0.13	1.00	0.23
HU93	0.33	0.23	1.00

Table 4B: The Correlation Coefficients for Shares of FDI in Employment in 1998

	PL98	CZ98	HU98
PL98	1.00	0.67	0.10
CZ98	0.67	1.00	0.28
HU98	0.10	0.28	1.00

Standard deviations in branch structure of FIE employment (Table 3 above), show that there is increasing dispersion in FIE penetration. Both in 1993 and 1998, dispersion is higher in economies with higher share of FDI, starting with Hungary, next Poland and Czech Republic[8].

In order to analyze the structural impact of FDI on employment, we calculated changes in employment in different branches of manufacturing industry for 1993-1998 and separated contribution of FDI to net balances. In order to compare directly change in FIE sector with the aggregate changes, we express both changes as a rate of change measured against initial *aggregate* (total) employment (Table 5 below).

Table 5: Changes in Employment, Branches of Manufacturing, 1993-1998 (%)

ISIC-code	Industries	Poland		Czech R		Hungary	
		dT/T	dFIE/T	dT/T	DFIE/T	dT/T	dFIE/T
15-16	Foodproducts, beverages, tobacco	-12.8	13.8	-4.9	5.5	-9.5	0.5
17	Textiles	-37.8	3.2	-32.2	9.3	-1.0	9.1
18	Wearing apparel, dressing	-21.4	5.6	-13.5	10.4	25.3	11.7
19	Tanning and dressing of leather	-43.6	4.6	-50.5	0.7	-7.1	20.3
20	Wood	1.6	15.1	-39.4	8.5	7.7	7.2
21	Paper and paper products	-9.4	9.6	-16.8	17.9	-4.3	0.6
22	Publishing, printing	2.8	24.4	1.5	24.5	-2.1	-3.1

[8] Data for Slovenia excludes sectors with small number of FIE, therefore standard deviation cannot be calculated.

ISIC-code	Industries	Poland		Czech R		Hungary	
23	Coke and petroleum	-14.4	0.7	-70.0	0.0	-28.3	66.2
24	Chemicals	-9.0	18.0	-2.0	8.1	-8.7	22.4
25	Rubber and plastic	11.4	37.2	25.2	23.7	40.0	24.4
26	Other non-metallic minerals	-10.4	17.8	-20.3	8.8	7.9	14.1
27	Basic metals	-3.3	2.0	-21.4	2.6	5.5	27.3
28	Fabricated metals	16.0	11.5	-18.5	7.2	8.5	9.1
29	Machinery and equipment n.e.c.	-22.1	5.1	-32.8	3.4	3.0	19.1
30	Office machinery	-7.5	14.1	-59.7	22.7	56.9	66.6
31	Electrical machinery and app.	7.6	32.8	17.2	43.0	75.4	51.1
32	Radio, TV set	-32.1	10.0	12.9	42.4	38.4	36.1
33	Medical, precision, opt. instruments	-6.5	9.9	-28.9	1.2	2.4	4.3
34	Motor vehicles, trailers	1.5	43.5	-3.4	26.1	28.8	65.7
35	Other transport equipment	-23.8	4.0	-32.7	-1.3	39.7	2.1
36	Furniture, manufacturing n.e.c.	3.7	24.8	-28.3	10.5	0.0	4.8
37	Recycling	25.7	14.1	-31.0	21.2	348.0	106.3
D	Total manufacturing	-12.3	13.1	-19.8	9.8	7.4	16.5

Note: dT/T - change in aggregate employment (93-98) divided by aggregate employment (98); dFIE/T -change in FIE employment (93-98) divided by aggregate employment (98)
Source: Calculations based on the WIIW Database (2000).

We want to analyze the extent to which the change in the foreign investment enterprises sector differs from general trend. However, we will not analyze changes in employment behavior of domestic vs. foreign firms, as we would face serious problems in their interpretation. If we were to focus on distinction between domestic vs. foreign, we would be measuring the aggregate effect of both the changes in ownership of enterprises and changes in their employment behavior. This is especially risky given very short time period for which data is available.

Table 5 shows several interesting features. First, unlike the initial period of transition (see: Mickiewicz and Bell, 2000), the employment generation in Hungary is already on the agenda. With 7.4% more jobs in 1998 as compared with 1993, the Hungarian manufacturing stands apart from the two other economies, where the dominant mode of adjustment is still passive adjustment through lay-offs. Second, despite big relative differences between countries and sectors, foreign controlled firms have capacity to either create or preserve employment. In all three economies, FIE operate either as buffer to further erosion of employment or significantly contribute to employment creation.

To analyze the structural dimension in more detail, we classified all branches of manufacturing industry into four groups depending on their characteristics of employment dynamics:[9]

- First group consists of branches of industry where employment, both total and in FIEs, is decreasing (Type 1). This may suggest that *rationalization in the sector is taking place to a great extent through layoffs in both domestic and foreign controlled firms.*

- Second group includes branches, where total employment is declining, but employment in FIEs is increasing (i.e. the FIEs sector is not strong enough to balance a decline of the domestic enterprises) (Type II). These are *sectors undergoing heavy restructuring* process after privatization, however they have clear *potential for future growth*, as indicated by the interest from foreign investors. Growth in FIEs' employment may result from new job creation but also from take-overs of the existing domestic firms.

- Third group would include those sectors where the overall employment is increasing but where FIEs experience decline in employment (Type III). In this group, FIEs firms would decrease employment, in spite overall growth. This is *a sector, where competitive advantages of FIEs are either small or there are important structural differences between the domestic and FIC sector and the logic of growth of FIEs is different from domestically controlled firms.* However, empirically this category is irrelevant, as there is no such a sector in our data set.

- Fourth group consists of branches where, both overall and FIE, employment is increasing (Type IV). These are sectors, which have *passed initial restructuring* and have *good prospects for development.*

The results are presented in Table 6, where all branches of manufacturing industries of Poland, Czech Republic and Hungary are classified according to the four types of employment patterns.

[9] This classification was first introduced in Mickiewicz et al. (2000).

Table 6: Classification of Branches of Manufacturing Industries by the Type of Employment Change

ISIC-code	Industries	Czech Rep	Hungary	Poland	II in all three	IV in all three
			A. Low Technology			
15+16	Foodproducts, beverages, tobacco	II	II	II	1	
17	Textiles	II	II	II	1	
18	Wearing apparel, dressing	II	IV	II		
19	Tanning and dressing of leather	II	II	II	1	
			B. Resource and Scale Intensive			
20	Wood	II	IV	IV		
21	Paper and paper products	II	II	II	1	
22	Publishing, printing	IV	I	IV		
23	Coke and petroleum		II	II		
24	Chemicals	II	II	II	1	
25	Rubber and plastic	IV	IV	IV		1
26	Other non-metallic minerals	II	IV	II		
27	Basic metals	II	IV	II		
28	Fabricated metals	II	IV	IV		
			C. Medium and High Technology			
29	Machinery and equipment n.e.c.	II	IV	II		
30	Office machinery	II	IV	II		
31	Electrical machinery and app.	IV	IV	IV		1
32	Radio, TV set	IV	IV	II		
33	Medical, precision, opt. Instruments	II	IV	II		
34	Motor vehicles, trailers	II	IV	IV		
35	Other transport equipment	I	IV	II		
36	Furniture, manufacturing n.e.c.	II	IV	IV		
37	Recycling	II	IV	IV		
D	Total manufacturing	II	IV	II		

Source: Calculations based the WIIW Database; classification into groups A-C, after Landesmann (2000).

Table 6 shows marked differences between countries in types of employment changes. In most of Hungarian branches the growth of the overall employment is accompanied by growth of employment in FIEs' sector. In 16 out of 23 branches, FIEs have complemented the general trend of growth in employment (type IV). In Poland, in 8 out of 23 branches there was increase in both the overall and FIEs' sector employment. However, in most branches, employment in FIEs increased while the overall employment went down (Type II, 15 branches). In Czech Republic, reduction of employment still dominates, as only 4 branches were in Type IV.

These differences may suggest more advanced stage of restructuring in Hungary, after the first phase of general reduction in excessive initial employment levels (see: Mickiewicz and Bell 2000). This conclusion is additionally supported by the fact that for Hungary, Type IV branches are concentrated in high technology group of manufacturing. Virtually all the branches in this group are Type IV. In contrast, Type 4 branches are evenly spread between high technology group and resource/scale intensive group for both Poland and the Czech Republic. Nowhere is Type IV present in low technology branches, except just one case out of twelve – it is clear, that those are not growing branches for all the three Visegrad countries. This general trend may support the Landesmann (2000) findings that the comparative advantage in Central Europe is shifting from low-tech to medium/high tech branches (also, comp. Radosevic and Hotopp, 1999).

In addition to those general trends, we can get some additional insights from analysis on the branch level. If we define as a common trend the same change that occurs in three countries we can discern several common patterns (see last two columns of Table 6):

First, in electrical machinery and apparatuses in all three countries, both the overall employment and employment in foreign controlled sector, has risen (Type IV). Similar pattern is present in rubber and plastics. This suggests that in those sectors, the downsizing phase of restructuring is over and it may indicate a mutual favorable interaction of demand and technological factors.

One should not overlook five additional sectors, which are Type IV in both Hungary and Poland, and Type II in Czech Republic. Those are: motor vehicles, machinery and equipment, fabricated metals, recycling and wood. The situation in the Czech Republic may be temporary, and the sectors may have also clear potential in employment creation for the future.

Textile, leather, food products, paper and chemicals are all sectors, which are attractive to foreign investors, but increase in foreign controlled employment cannot counter balance the overall decrease in employment. We speculate that those are the sectors, which are still in downsizing phase of restructuring, while the foreign presence indicate potential for future growth (Type II).

Significantly higher frequency of Type II and Type I (in other transport equipment) in Czech R. confirms the general impression about delayed micro restructuring in the economy, where foreign investors substitute for domestic structural weaknesses (see Table 5 and 6). Contrary to this, Hungary is the case of the mature stage of FDI and active restructuring.

The most interesting difference between Hungary and the two other economies is employment generation in "machinery and equipment n.e.c". In Czech R. and Poland this branch is in crisis with foreign investors succeeding to preserve some employment. Overall, this branch is the biggest loser of employment in both Poland and Czech Republic. In Hungary, contrary to this bleak picture, this branch is generating new employment, both aggregate and in the FIE sector.

5. Foreign Direct Investment and the Level of Employment

Despite potentially positive long-run effects of FDI on skill profile of employment in host countries the relationship between FDI and level of employment is far from being understood. This relationship is influenced by a plethora of different macro and micro factors, which makes their assessment in a comprehensive manner difficult. A review of employment effects of FDI by OECD (1995) points out that there is *"no general conclusion (...) regarding neither the sign of employment effects nor their magnitude. The broad range of results is a reflection of both the complexities of the analysis and methodological shortcomings, combined with the generally poor data availability in most countries" (p. 140)*. Similarly, the UN report (UN 1999) concludes that *"The balance (...) is likely to vary among host countries and industries. Effects may also vary over time. A short-term loss of employment may be more than offset by longer-term gains if FDI raises the competitiveness, efficiency and export-orientation of domestic firms (...)." (p. 261)*

To complicate the task even further, the post-communist economies bear some unique characteristics. Under "real socialism", excessive employment or "labour hoarding" was an endemic part of the economy of shortage (Kornai, 1986). Factor markets were as much affected by shortages as final product markets and the rational response of the enterprises was to hoard. It was the volume of production, not profit, which was maximized. With "soft budget", this maximization was not subject to financial but to real constraints (ibid.).

At the outset of economic transition it was obvious that it will be impossible to maintain levels of employment from socialist period. Hence, the slowdown of employment reduction and protection of employment has become one of the main objectives of economic (or rather: social) policy. The ambiguity of the FDI role results from the fact that by imposing more efficient corporate governance, it can facilitate restructuring process, leading to employment reductions and on the other hand, it may create new employment alongside expanded output, due to access to new export markets in particular.

Taking into account constraints imposed by data availability, we are able to check some short-run effects of FIE presence on aggregate levels of employment, using sectoral data for 1997-8, for Poland, Czech Rep., Hungary, Estonia and Slovenia. We estimated the following equation:[10]

---

[10] For details on methodology and recent results, based on firms survey, see: Christev and FitzRoy, (2000).

(1) $\Delta[ln(employment)]_{ij} = \Delta[ln(sales)]_{ij} + \Delta[ln(wages)]_{ij} + FIE_{ij} + (country\ dummy)_j + \varepsilon$

Here, *i* corresponds to manufacturing sector, *j* to country and *FIE* to the percentage share of FIE in equity of sector *i*. Both sales and wages were transformed into constant prices, by using CPI 1998 index for all countries [11], to eliminate artificial effects caused by different rates of inflation. The results of two alternative specifications are given below.

Table 7A: Estimated Employment Equation (Dependent Variable: Dlnempl)

Variables	Coefficients	Std. Error	Standardized Coefficients	t	Sig.	95% Confidence Interval for B		Collinearity Statistics	
			Beta			Lower Bound	Upper Bound	Tolerance	VIF
(Constant)	-8.756E-03	.036		-.247	.806	-.079	.062		
DLNSALES	.510	.063	.648	8.140	.000	.386	.634	.751	1.332
DLNWAGES	-.529	.161	-.274	-3.294	.001	-.848	-.210	.687	1.456
SLOVENIA	1.451E-02	.036	.039	.402	.688	-.057	.086	.497	2.012
HUNGARY	4.485E-02	.042	.126	1.061	.291	-.039	.129	.339	2.953
CZECHREP	-7.763E-02	.036	-.218	-2.157	.034	-.149	-.006	.467	2.141
POLAND	-7.962E-03	.036	-.022	-.223	.824	-.079	.063	.476	2.099
FIEEQU98	-2.097E-04	.000	-.046	-.475	.636	-.001	.001	.506	1.978

Number of observations: 105; R square: 0.54; F statistics: 16.1.

Table 7B: Estimated Employment Equation (Dependent Variable: Dlnempl)

Variables	Coefficients	Std. Error	Standardized Coefficients	t	Sig.	95% Confidence Interval for B		Collinearity Statistics	
			Beta			Lower Bound	Upper Bound	Tolerance	VIF
(Constant)	-1.017E-02	.023		-.452	.652	-.055	.034		
DLNSALES	.515	.060	.654	8.633	.000	.396	.633	.817	1.223
DLNWAGES	-.496	.140	-.257	-3.536	.001	-.774	-.218	.888	1.126
CZECHREP	-8.554E-02	.026	-.240	-3.273	.001	-.137	-.034	.873	1.146

Number of observations: 105; R square: 0.53; F statistics: 37.4.

Both equations are not entirely satisfactory, especially given that the intercept term is insignificant. However few indicative results are clear. It seems that the manufacturing sector is a coherent unit of analysis for employment dynamics. Moreover, the above results are consistent with literature, indicating negative impact of wage dynamics and

[11] Taken from EBRD (1999).

positive impact of production dynamics on employment (both significant and robust to specification). Country dummies are insignificant, except the Czech Republic, indicating that both labour market setting and the basic logic of employment creation is similar in most countries. In particular, it is interesting to notice that the dummy for Poland is insignificant, provided that the privatisation clauses protecting employment were imposed on foreign investors more frequently than elsewhere. Apparently, the impact of this is not visible. Significant result for the Czech Republic dummy may be explained by different macroeconomic environment after the currency crisis and its impact on responsiveness of employment in relation to production.

From the point of view of this study, the most important result however is that presence of FIE in a given sector has no systematic impact on overall employment dynamics. This is consistent with existing literature (see discussion at the beginning of this section).

6. Foreign Direct Investment, Wages and Productivity

Post communist economies of Central Eastern Europe have been characterized by distorted structures of both wages and employment. We discussed employment in the previous section. As far as wages are concerned, traditionally, skilled employees were relatively underpaid (see: Mickiewicz and Bell, 2000). As a consequence - at least initially – it was relatively easy for foreign companies to offer incentives to attract skilled workers from existing domestic businesses. Thus, the short-run external effects on existing domestic businesses could be negative. Moreover, in the short term, there may not be much need for training as foreign firms may rely on existing stock of highly qualified employees. Only in the long term, new training and practice in the foreign firms may bring additional increase in skills. Ultimately, that in turn may lead to positive spillovers into domestic sector, resulting from both the flows of trained employees and learning through co-operative links.

To make discussion more focused, let us introduce simple notation, where: W – wage of qualified labor, VMP - value of marginal product of qualified labor and subscripts d and f relate to activities of domestic and foreign sectors correspondingly. Initial wage distortions in a sector d correspond to the situation, where highly qualified workers in the domestic sector are underpaid, that is:

(2) $W_d < VMP_d$

With liberalisation, foreign firms initiate some new activities (or take over some old). The important point here is that while those would not necessary be higher value added in comparison with the domestic sector, the foreign sector can still take advantage of the initial distortions in wage structures. Thus, in some cases, we may well expect:

(3) $VMP_f < VMP_d$

And taking into account (2), it is feasible that:[12]

(4) $W_d < W_f < VMP_f < VMP_d$

The practical meaning of equation (4) is that due to the initial wage distortions, we may have some negative short-run external effects of foreign investment resulting from restructuring of employment. Because of the opportunity of arbitrage, the foreign sector may hire employees below their skills and that may lead to some loss in value added [13]. Simultaneously, the domestic sector may not be able to respond by increasing wages, either because of financial constraints, due to imperfections in the financial markets, or because of the egalitarian wage schemes, which are persistent due to insiders' control. This reasoning may be one of the possible explanations of the Knell (2000) result, which shows that FDI does not generate convergence in productivity of domestic firms in short/medium term. Thus, the productivity increase in FDI sector may come at cost of the domestic sector in transition economies. Yet, the overall (aggregate) productivity in a given sector may rise, just because of the negative effects on the domestic companies. Because of the potential disruptive effect on the domestic sector, some domestic firms are forced to exit, which would also lead to increase in average productivity. Thus, the aggregate positive effect comes from the change in the skill composition of employment (unskilled workers in the domestic sector becoming unemployed).

The argument above lead to two empirical hypotheses:

- The presencc of FDI in a given sector may have short-run effect on average sector productivity, before any effects of investments.
- The presence of FDI in a given sector of the economy may have no short-run spill-over effects on accelerating wage growth above current productivity levels (this is corollary to the previous hypothesis, given in addition that domestic firms are not able to respond to wage competition from the foreign sector.

The data does not contradict the above hypotheses. Estimations of both wage and productivity equations are presented below.

Wage equation is estimated as [14]:

(5) $\Delta[ln(wages)]_{ij} = \Delta[ln(sales/employment)]_{ij} + FIE_{ij} + (country\ dummy)_j + \varepsilon$

---

[12] In particular, in case of FIE focused on domestic markets (market-seeking as contrasted with efficiency-seeking).

[13] Example may be useful. Foreign pharmaceutical companies hire highly qualified medical doctors to work as sale representatives, much below their skills. Initial wage distortions make it is feasible. No formal evidence can be given here, but authors are familiar with other examples of employees being hired below their skill levels in foreign firms.

[14] Again, for methodology and recent estimations of wage equations based on firms surveys, see: Grosfeld and Nivet, (1999); Christev and FitzRoy, (2000).

As illustrated by Table 8, presence of foreign firms in a given sector has no impact on wages. Even if they are paying higher wages than the domestic sector (see equation 4), the effect is probably counter-balanced by deterioration of the relative position of domestic firms, which may be loosing skilled employees and are unable to match the wage offer, due to financial constraints.

It is interesting to notice that country effects for both Hungary and Poland are robust to specification. Both economies seem to be characterized by higher pressure on wages than the other three economies (Czech Republic, Slovenia, Estonia). One may speculate on possible differences in labor market institutions and wage setting mechanisms (see: Mickiewicz and Bell, 2000, chapter 5).

Table 8A: Estimated Wage Equations (Dependent Variable: Dlnwages)

Variables	Coefficients	Std. Error	Standardized Coefficients	t	Sig.	95% Confidence Interval for B		Collinearity Statistics	
			Beta			Lower Bound	Upper Bound	Tolerance	VIF
(Constant)	8.471E-02	.019		4.355	.000	.046	.123		
DLNPROD	.159	.045	.300	3.556	.001	.070	.248	.892	1.121
SLOVENIA	-6.543E-03	.022	-.034	-.303	.762	-.049	.036	.498	2.007
HUNGARY	8.327E-02	.024	.450	3.471	.001	.036	.131	.377	2.651
CZECHREP	-1.699E-03	.021	-.009	-.081	.935	-.043	.040	.498	2.006
POLAND	4.605E-02	.021	.249	2.216	.029	.005	.087	.502	1.991
FIEEQU98	-4.067E-06	.000	-.002	-.015	.988	-.001	.001	.510	1.959

Number of observations: 105; R square: 0.38; F statistics: 9.9.

Table 8B: Estimated Wage Equations (Dependent Variable: Dlnwages)

Variables	Coefficients	Std. Error	Standardized Coefficients	t	Sig.	95% Confidence Interval for B		Collinearity Statistics	
			Beta			Lower Bound	Upper Bound	Tolerance	VIF
(Constant)	8.133E-02	.009		8.641	.000	.063	.100		
DLNPROD	.162	.043	.304	3.762	.000	.076	.247	.943	1.061
HUNGARY	8.585E-02	.016	.464	5.531	.000	.055	.117	.875	1.142
POLAND	4.887E-02	.015	.264	3.194	.002	.019	.079	.901	1.110

Number of observations: 105; R square: 0.38; F statistics: 20.4.

Productivity equation takes into account effects of both employment reductions and investment (current and previous period). Thus, it distinguishes between three different restructuring strategies - downsizing, investment-led, and one based on improved efficiency resulting from FIE presence (hypothesis *I* above):

(6) $\Delta[ln(valueadded/employment)]_{ij} = \Delta[ln(employment)]_{j} + ln(investment)_{ijt} + ln(investment)_{ijt-1} + FIE_{ij} + (country\ dummy)_j + \varepsilon$

As data for Estonia are not available, the number of observations is smaller than in the previous cases. Investment variables [15] have expected signs, but are not statistically significant. The most robust variable is clearly change in employment. The percentage of foreign companies in a given sector has expected sign, i.e. is associated with faster growth in productivity. Thus, foreign direct investment may be interpreted as a source of productivity growth, which is alternative to employment reductions (downsizing). When (insignificant) country variables are eliminated from equation, the variable for foreign presence becomes highly significant. Thus, the tentative conclusion is that the presence of the foreign firms have some positive short-run effects on productivity.

Table 9A: Estimated Productivity Equations (Dependent Variable: Dlnvaem)

Variables	Coefficients	Std. Error	Standardized Coefficients	t	Sig.	95% Confidence Interval for B		Collinearity Statistics	
			Beta			Lower Bound	Upper Bound	Tolerance	VIF
(Constant)	5.421E-02	.045		1.204	.232	-.035	.144		
DLNEMP	-.324	.081	-.412	-3.979	.000	.486	-.162	.778	1.286
LNINVA97	1.358E-02	.024	.062	.557	.579	-.035	.062	.667	1.500
LNINVA98	1.743E-02	.013	.131	1.294	.199	-.009	.044	.812	1.231
SLOVENIA	-4.808E-02	.034	-.166	-1.399	.166	-.116	.020	.592	1.689
HUNGARY	6.094E-02	.046	.217	1.311	.193	-.032	.153	.304	3.285
POLAND	-2.838E-02	.033	-.101	-.850	.398	-.095	.038	.589	1.697
FIEEQU98	5.629E-04	.001	.152	1.095	.277	.000	.002	.431	2.320

Number of observations: 90; R square: 0.32; F statistics: 5.4

Table 9B: Estimated Productivity Equations (Dependent Variable: Dlnvaem)

Variables	Coefficients	Std. Error	Standardized Coefficients	t	Sig.	95% Confidence Interval for B		Collinearity Statistics	
			Beta			Lower Bound	Upper Bound	Tolerance	VIF
(Constant)	-2.625E-02	.021		-1.265	.209	-.067	.015		
DLNEMP	-.352	.076	-.447	-4.653	.000	-.502	-.201	.930	1.075
FIEEQU98	1.401E-03	.000	.379	3.947	.000	.001	.002	.930	1.075

Number of observations: 90; R square: 0.25; F statistics: 14.8.

15 (Net) investment variables were linearly transformed to eliminate negative figures, before logarithms were taken.

7. INVESTMENT

Already, when discussing wages, we pointed out that post-communist domestic manufacturing sectors face financial constraints. As a consequence, firms have to rely on internal sources of finance. Investment is related not to the long term net present value of the firm, but rather to its current cash flow[16]. Here, the role of foreign firms is to provide alternative source of finance. This leads to the following specification of investment equation:[17]

(7) $ln(investment)_{ij} = ln(net\ profit)_{ij} + FIE_{ij} + (country\ dummy)_j + \varepsilon$

The results are presented in Table 10, below[18]:

Table 10.A: Estimated Investment Equations (Dependent Variable: Lnin98)

	Coefficients	Std. Error	Standardized Coefficients	t	Sig.	95% Confidence Interval for B		Collinearity Statistics	
			Beta			Lower Bound	Upper Bound	Tolerance	VIF
(Constant)	-75.514	23.572		-3.204	.002	-122.389	-28.639		
LNPR98	6.975	1.982	.351	3.519	.001	3.033	10.917	.680	1.470
SLOVENIA	.911	.443	.206	2.056	.043	.030	1.793	.672	1.489
HUNGARY	.510	.620	.119	.823	.413	-.722	1.742	.323	3.093
POLAND	-1.099	.440	-.257	-2.496	.015	-1.975	-.223	.640	1.563
FIEEQU98	8.157E-03	.007	.145	1.214	.228	-.005	.022	.476	2.102

Number of observations: 90; R square: 0.43; F statistics: 12.5.

[16] On further discussion on this point and earlier empirical results on the link between cash flow and investment, see: Mickiewicz, (1996).

[17] Profit is a crude approximation for cash flow, but we have no better here.

[18] Again, profit variable was were linearly transformed to eliminate negative figures, before logarithms were taken.

Table 10.B: Estimated Investment Equations (Dependent Variable: Lnin98)

	Coefficients	Std. Error	Standardized Coefficients	t	Sig.	95% Confidence Interval for B		Collinearity Statistics	
			Beta			Lower Bound	Upper Bound	Tolerance	VIF
(Constant)	-83.039	21.685		-3.829	.000	-126.154	-39.923		
LNPR98	7.610	1.822	.383	4.176	.000	3.987	11.233	.802	1.247
SLOVENIA	.792	.418	.180	1.895	.062	-.039	1.624	.752	1.331
POLAND	-1.264	.391	-.295	-3.233	.002	-2.042	-.487	.808	1.237
FIEEQU98	1.148E-02	.005	.204	2.142	.035	.001	.022	.745	1.342

Number of observations: 90; R square: 0.43; F statistics: 15.8.

Country dummies, Hungary in particular, are strongly correlated with FIE shares in equity. Nevertheless, dummy for Hungary is least significant and when eliminated, the equation shows expected effect of FIE presence on investment. Current cash flow (here, as approximated by profits) and presence of foreign firms seem to be alternative factors enhancing investment levels in manufacturing industries.

8. Discussion and Conclusions

First, among CEEC economies, Hungary is a country which has already the structure of employment most similar to the most developed European "North" (see Jackman and Pauna, 1997; Mickiewicz and Bell, 2000). This structural similarity suggests that Hungary is the best prepared to create positive direct and indirect effects of FDI, including focus on high-tech branches of manufacturing.

Differences in privatisation methods significantly affected FDI inflows. Also, the political commitment and quality of state governance do play a role. Many transition countries (Czech Republic in particular) used *vouchers* (*privatisation securities*) as the fastest method for implementing the privatization reform. It proved to be relatively quick method, but made participation of foreign investors difficult. Hungary is the country, which have chosen the direct sales method as the major mode, giving equal access to all bidders, including foreign investors. Enterprises were sold to the local or foreign buyers, most often provided that they guarantee certain amount of investments and jobs during next years. Many analysts initially perceived this piecemeal approach to privatisation as time consuming and not very promising. However, the data indicates that Hungarian privatisation path resulted in efficient restructuring.

Our estimations suggest that there are significant differences between CEEC economies in sectoral patters of employment, wages and investment. Poland is characterised by lower investment and higher wage pressure. First may be explained by more pronounced potential for efficiency gains from mere allocation of resources.

However, high wage pressure may cause problems in the future. Wage pressure is also high in Hungary, which in the future may reduce/eliminate positive impact of restructuring.

Third, as a more general result, both short run productivity growth and investment seem to be affected by the presence of foreign companies, which coincides with the conclusions presented by Landesmann (2000). Thus, this paper suggest that there are two major gains from FDI, which are specific to post-communist economies:

A. FIE may be instrumental in achieving short-term efficiency gains by improving allocation of resources, without necessity of large-scale investment.
B. In the longer run, the important gain of FIE presence may consist of better access to financial resources, which facilitate investment and create basis for sustainable growth.

REFERENCES

1. Christev A. and FitzRoy F. (2000) Employment and Wage Adjustment: Insider and Outsider Control in a Polish Privatisation Panel Study, *Discussion Paper*, No. 0003, CRIEFF, University of St. Andrews.
2. EBRD (1997-1999), *Transition Report 1997-1999*, London, European Bank for Reconstruction and Development.
3. Grosfeld I. and Nivet J.F. (1999), Insiders power and wage setting in transition: Evidence from a panel of large Polish firms, 1988-1994, *European Economic Review*, Vol. 43, p. 1137-1147.
4. Hunya G. (1997), Large privatisation, restructuring and foreign direct investment, in Zecchini S. (ed.), *Lessons from the Economic Transition. Central and Eastern Europe in the 1990s*, Dordrecht, Kluwer, p. 275-300.
5. Hunya G.(1998a), *Relationship between FDI, Privatisation and Structural Change in CEECs*, paper prepared for the Conference on Privatisation, Corporate Governance and the Emergence of Markets in Central-Eastern Europe, FIT, Berlin, May 22-23, mimeo.
6. Hunya G. (1998b), Integration of CEEC manufacturing into the European corporate structures by direct investments, *MOST-MOCT*, No 1.
7. Hunya G. and Stankovsky J. (1999), *Foreign Direct Investment in Central and East European Countries and the Former Soviet Union*, WIIW-WIFO Database, Vienna.
8. Jackman R. and Pauna C. (1997), Labour Market Policy and the Reallocation of Labour across Sectors, in Zecchini S. (ed.), *Lessons from the Economic Transition. Central and Eastern Europe in the 1990s*, Dordrecht, Kluwer, p. 373-392.
9. Knell M. (2000), FIEs and productivity convergence in central Europe, in: Hunya G. (ed.), *Integration through Foreign Direct Investment*, Cheltenham, Edward Elgar.
10. Kornai J.(1986), *Contradictions and Dilemmas*, Cambridge MA, MIT Press.

11. Landesmann M. (2000), Structural Change in the Transition Economies, 1989 to 1999", wiiw *working Paper*, No. 269.
12. Lankes H.P. and Stern N. (1998), Capital flows to eastern Europe and the former Soviet Union, *EBRD Working Paper*, No. 27.
13. Lankes H.P. and Venables A.J. (1996), Foreign direct investment in economic transition: the changing pattern of investments, *Economics of Transition,* vol. 4(2).
14. Meyer K. (1998), *Direct Investment in Economies in Transition*, Cheltenham, Edward Elgar.
15. Mickiewicz, T. (1996), The State Sector during Economic Transformation: Employment, Wages and Investment, *Communist Economies and Economic Transformation*, Vol. 8 (3), p. 393-410.
16. Mickiewicz, T. and Bell J. (2000), *Unemployment in Transition. Restructuring and Labour Markets in Central Europe*, Amsterdam, Harwood Academic Publishers.
17. Mickiewicz, T., Radosevic S. and Varblane U. (2000), FDI: From Job Destruction to Job Creation. Evidence from Transition Economies, 1993-1996, in Weresa M. (ed.), *Foreign Direct Investment in Poland*, London, UCL.
18. Mirza H. (1998), Transitional Corporations as agents for the transition of business culture to host countries, in: *Privatization, Enterprise Development and Economic Reform. Experiences of Developing and transitional Economies*, Cook, Kirkpatrick R.C. and Nixson F. (eds.), Cheltenham, Edward Elgar.
19. OECD (1995), *Foreign Direct Investment, Trade and Employment*, OECD, Paris.
20. OECD (1999), *Measuring Globalisation: The Role of Multinationals in OECD Economies*, OECD, Paris.
21. Radosevic. S. and Hotopp U. (1999), The product structure of Central and Eastern European trade: the emerging patterns of change and learning, *MOST - MOCT*, 2.
22. Stern R. (1997), Foreign Direct Investment, Exports, and East West Integration: Theory and Practice, in: Cooper R. and Gacs, J. (eds.), *Trade Growth in Transition Economies. Export Impediments for Central and Eastern Europe*, Cheltenham, Edward Elgar.
23. UN (1999), *World Investment Report. Foreign Direct Investment and the Challenge of Development,* United Nations, New York and Geneva.
24. WIIW (1998; 2000), *Database on Foreign Investment Enterprises in Central European Manufacturing. Austria, the Czech Republic, Hungary, Slovenia, 1993-96*, Vienna, The Vienna Institute for International Economic Studies.

Chapter 3

RISK IN TRANSITION ECONOMIES: THE IMPACT OF HOST COUNTRY CHARACTERISTICS ON FDI DETERMINANTS

Sylvain H. Zeghni
University of Marne-la-Vallée

1. INTRODUCTION

After the collapse of communism, the Central and Eastern Europe Countries (CEECs) and the Commonwealth of Independent States (CIS) began their transformation to a market economy in the hope of achieving economic growth and higher living standards. As De Castro & Uhlenbruck (1997) or Simai (1999) have shown it, transition process is linked to the historic and institutional context of each country and of its initial level of development.

These transition economies are characterized by numerous uncertainty and risks linked to market failures like property rights, legal code, intellectual property protection (Ferrantino, 1993; Zloch-Christy, 1995 a, b; Firozzi, 1997; Sharp & Barz 1997; Zecchini 1997; Estrin & Meyer, 1999); institutional, administrative and political uncertainty; missing markets (labor and financial markets) (Zloch-Christy, 1995 a, b; Meyer, 1998); habits and practices inherited from the old centrally planned economy as bureaucracy, corruption, weak corporate governance.

Upgrading production technologies is one of the crucial challenges facing the transition countries[1]. Policy-makers in the region perceive foreign direct investment (FDI) as a means of obtaining capital and new technology (Dunning & Rojec, 1993;

[1] The technological gap between transition economies and developed countries is quite substantial. For example, in 1985 engineering exports from CEECs earned less than thirty per cent of the average unit value received by all exporters of similar products, and technology of the exported goods was often twenty years behind (World Bank, 1996, p. 3)

EBRD 1994; Fabry, 2001). Attracting FDI has become a main objective of government's policy throughout CEECs and the CIS. Transition economies hope that FDI will contribute to upgrade their production technologies. Since multinational enterprise (MNEs) generally transfer their most recent technologies to their affiliates, while only older ones are sold or licensed outside the firm, FDI may be the only way for many countries to gain access to the latest and especially to certain key technologies. Additionally, FDI inflows can produce indirect benefits through the turnover of workers trained by MNEs and the technical assistance that MNEs provide to local suppliers. Governments tend to perceive FDI in technology-intensive sectors as the most beneficial to their countries. This belief is reflected in the greater bargaining power of MNEs with higher R&D spending in negotiations with local authorities. Leaving aside the question of whether such beliefs are justified and whether there exist technology spillover from FDI[2], this study investigates whether transition economies indeed receive the kind of FDI they are hoping for.

The highly skilled labor force and engineering traditions combined with low labor costs in the region are perceived as magnets that should attract FDI into technology-intensive sectors (Zloch-Christy, 1995a; Fabry, Zeghni, 2001). The proportion of scientists and engineers engaged in R&D activities is larger in CEECs and the CIS than in Latin America and many East Asian countries. The extent of R&D activities in the CEECs, measured in terms of US patents, is equal to or greater than in Southern Europe. R&D spending in the region, as a percentage of GNP is also high when compared to Southern European Countries (Radosevic, 1996)[3]. Thus, the belief of transition economies to receive technology-intensive FDI has some justification.

Overall, the achievements of transition economies in terms of attracting FDI have been mixed[4]. Apart from the success stories of Hungary and the Czech Republic, FDI inflows have been quite modest (Fabry, 2001) and the magnitude of investment flows was very small in the first years of transition. The situation improved in 1995 when the inflows almost doubled relative to the previous year. Nevertheless, transition economies have received little FDI by international standards.

The connection between technological capabilities of a firm and its decision to undertake FDI is highlighted in Dunning's (1988) *"OLI paradigm"*, which explains activities of multinational corporations in terms of ownership (O), localization (L) and internalization advantages (I). When selling its products abroad, a firm is at least initially disadvantaged relative to local producers. Thus, in order to compete effectively with

---

[2] While Blomstrom & Wolff (1994) find evidence of technology spillover from FDI in Mexico, Haddad & Harrisson (1993) do not observe such effects in Morocco. Using data from Uruguay, Kokko, Tansini & Zejan (1996) show that spillovers take place in plant with moderate gaps *vis-à-vis* foreign firm, but not when the gap is large.

[3] In the Soviet innovation system, however, a large share of R&D funds was committed to the military and space exploration without many technological spillovers to other industries. In contrast to Japan or Western Europe, enterprise R&D accounted for only a small fraction of total R&D outlays in the Soviet Union (Knell, 1996).

[4] See for example UNCTAD 1997 ; World Bank 1996 ; Radosevic & Dyker 1997 ; Druzic, 1997.

indigenous firms, a foreign producer must possess some ownership advantages. They can take the form of a superior production technology or improved organizational and marketing systems, innovatory capacity, trademarks, reputation, or other assets. Ownership advantages assure a firm's ability to enter the host country's market, but do not explain why the foreign presence should be established through production rather than exports. This issue is, in turn, addressed by localization advantages that arise due to differences in factor quality, costs and endowments, international transport and communication costs, overcoming trade restrictions, and host government policy. The last advantage, internalization, explains why a foreign firm prefers to retain full control over the production process instead of licensing its intangible assets to local firms. This decision is generally attributed to high transaction costs involved in regulating and enforcing licensing contracts.

Weak Intellectual Property Right (IPR) protection increases the probability of imitation, which erodes a firm's ownership advantages and decreases localization advantages of a host country. At the same time, a weak IPR system increases the benefits of internalization, since it is associated with a larger risk of the licensee's breaching the contract and acting in direct competition with the seller. An inadequate IPR regime, therefore, deters FDI and encourages exporting. A strong IPR system may also have a negative impact on FDI by making licensing a viable alternative to direct investment. Thus, the overall relationship between the level of IPR protection and FDI is ambiguous.

The empirical studies of FDI show that *"multinationals tend to be important in industries and firms with four characteristics: high levels of R&D relative to sales; a large share of professional and technical workers in their workforce; products that are new and/or technically complex; and high levels of product differentiation and advertising. These characteristics appear in many studies, and I have never seen any of them contradicted in any study"*(Markusen, 1995, p. 172).

Lipsey, Blomström and Kravis (1990) find that high levels of R&D relative to sales are also typical of MNEs investing in less developed countries (LDCs). Their examination of U.S. companies indicates that firms undertaking investments in LDCs are more R&D-intensive than investors in developed countries. This is the case in manufacturing as a whole as well as in every industry. It is particularly true for Asian developing countries. The econometric analysis performed by Yu (1990) on a sample of U.S. MNEs confirms the positive relationship between R&D intensity and the probability of a firm investing in LDCs. Furthermore, Dunning (1988) points out that within manufacturing industry, the pattern of involvement by MNEs in LDCs as a whole is broadly comparable to that in developed countries. In both groups, MNEs are most frequently present in sectors characterized either by above average technological intensity or product differentiation. FDI activities are also found to be positively associated with a firm's size (see e.g., Grubaugh, 1987; Meyer, 1995) and a firm's previous exporting and investment experience (Braunerjelm and Svensson, 1996).

On the host country side, the results of empirical studies indicate that FDI is positively related to national income, population size and national income per capita (Dunning, 1992; Braunerjelm and Svensson, 1996). The first two variables reflect market size and scale effects while the third controls for the purchasing power of local consumers. The investigations of the relationship between real wage costs and FDI produce mixed conclusions.

The results of empirical studies exploring the impact of IPR protection on FDI are mostly inconclusive. Ferrantino (1993) doesn't finds statistically significant relationship between the extent of U.S. affiliate sales in a foreign country and that country's membership in an international patent or copyright convention. Similarly, Maskus and Konan (1994), who employ the Rapp and Rozek (1990) index of IPR protection, do not obtain statistically significant results.

Thanks to a unique firm-level data compiled from a worldwide survey of companies conducted by the EBRD in 1995 covering 25 transition economies, we are able to examine the nature of FDI in the region in greater depth than earlier research which concentrated mostly on aggregate inflows and case studies. We extend Rodricks (1991) investment model and use it in the investigation of factors affecting FDI inflows. This model predicts that a firm's decision to undertake FDI is positively correlated with the host country's size, progress in reform and trade barriers, and negatively related to entry cost, regional tensions and lack of intellectual property right protection (IPRP).

The plan of this chapter is as follows: in the next section we describe and modify the Rodrick's model. Then, we discuss first our hypothesis about the link between the country characteristics and the FDI inflows, second we investigate our hypothesis about the composition of FDI and the country characteristic and last we describe our data. The final section presents our results.

2. MODEL'S CHARACTERISTICS

As we have seen in the introduction, the experiences of transition economies in terms of FDI have been very diverse, ranging from impressive inflows into Hungary, the Czech Republic and Poland, to hardly any FDI in several former Soviet Republics. Thus, an examination of characteristics of transition economies can provide us with valuable insights about factors influencing FDI inflows. In this section we extend Rodrick's (1991) model of investment and use it as a framework in the investigation of host country characteristics affecting FDI inflows.

2.1. Basic Model

In a context of the opening of a new country or region to foreign goods a firm have the choice to export or to produce in this country. While engaging in FDI has the potential for yielding higher profits because of proximity to customers, savings on transportation costs, tariffs, labor cost differentials, etc., it also involves higher risk. We assume that a firm's profit from exporting is equal to E each period, while that from FDI amounts to R. When undertaking production in a foreign country, a firm has to incur a fixed cost. There are two components of the fixed cost: a country specific cost (η) that is the same for all firms (as for instance, registration fees and procedures) and a firm specific cost (ε) that can be thought of as the cost of organizing foreign production (lowered by the existence of prior sales in the region and previous multinational experience). Since we assume that a firm has production facilities in the home country, there is no transport costs in the case of exporting.

Further, we assume that an investor decides how to supply the market at the beginning of the first period and immediately executes the plan. Events adversely affecting profits from FDI can only take place in the second period. With probability (π), the returns to FDI drop to zero in the second period and the firm is forced to exit incurring a cost (s). This sudden drop in returns may be attributable to expropriation, unexpected changes in tax code or other regulations, bureaucratic delays, corruption, crime, violation of intellectual property rights or regional tensions and political instability. A firm will choose FDI over exporting if:

$$R-\eta-\varepsilon+\pi\left(\frac{0-s}{1+r}\right)+(1-\pi)\left(\frac{R}{1+r}\right)>E+\frac{E}{1+r} \qquad (1)$$

$$\Rightarrow (R-E)\left(\frac{2+r}{1+r}\right)-\pi\left(\frac{s+R}{1+r}\right)-\eta>\varepsilon$$

There exists a cut-off value of (ε*) such that a firm will undertake FDI only if its fixed cost is below the cut-off, that is, if ε < ε*, where

$$\varepsilon^*=(R-E)\left(\frac{2+r}{1+r}\right)-\pi\left(\frac{s+R}{1+r}\right)-\eta \qquad (2)$$

We assume that R is sufficiently greater than E to make ε* positive, since otherwise FDI would never take place. The model implies that the difference between the returns to FDI and exporting must be greater in countries with a positive probability of profits from FDI dropping to zero than in host economies where this threat does not exist. Thus π can be viewed as equivalent to a tax on direct investment.

2.2. Our Modifications

We assume that a foreign firm enjoys a temporary monopoly power (first mover) in the host country and faces an inverse demand function (p = a-bx), where p denotes price, x quantity (x_E or x_R depending on whether a firm exports or undertakes FDI), and a is a parameter related to host country size. We assume that a>0 and b>0. An exporting firms profit is equal to $E=\left[\frac{p}{(1+\tau)}-w(1+t)\right]x_E$ each period, where w is the home country wage rate, (τ) is a proportional tariff, and (t) denotes transportation cost[5]. Thus, the firm will export $x_E = [a - w(1+t)(1+\tau)]/2b$ units and receive each period a profit equal to $E = \frac{[a - w(1+t)(1+\tau)]^2}{4b(1+\tau)}$.

A firm that undertakes FDI receives each period ($R = (p-w^*)x_R$), where w^* is the host country wage rate[6]. Thus, it produces $x_R = (a-w^*)/2b$ units and its profit equals $R = (a-w^*)^2/4b$. We assume that both FDI and exporting are profitable undertakings, thus $x_E>0$ and $x_R>0$. This implies that $a>w(1+t)(1+\tau)$ and $a>w^*$[7]. Again, a firm will choose FDI if $\varepsilon>\varepsilon^*$, where ε^* can now be written as:

$$\varepsilon^* = \frac{2+r}{4b(1+r)}\left\{(a-w^*)^2 - \frac{[a - w(1+t)(1+\tau)]^2}{(1+\tau)}\right\} - \frac{\pi}{4b(1+r)}\left[4bs + (a-w^*)^2\right] - \eta \qquad (3)$$

We can normalize w to one and rewrite the above expression in terms of the relative wage ratio $W= w^*/w=w^*/1=w^*$ to get:

$$\varepsilon^* = \frac{2+r}{4b(1+r)}\left\{(a-W)^2 - \frac{[a - (1+t)(1+\tau)]^2}{(1+\tau)}\right\} - \frac{\pi}{4b(1+r)}\left[4bs + (a-W)^2\right] - \eta \qquad (4)$$

We assume there are many firms that differ only by their fixed cost (ε) and that all firms with the cost below the cut-off undertake FDI. Thus the lower "cut-off" cost is, the larger is the total investment in a host country. We also find that:

$$\frac{\partial \varepsilon^*}{\partial \pi} = -\left[\frac{4bs + (a-W)^2}{4b(1+r)}\right] < 0 \qquad (5)$$

$$\frac{\partial \varepsilon^*}{\partial W} = -\left[\frac{(a-W)}{2b(1+r)}(r+2-\pi)\right] < 0 \qquad (6)$$

since $\pi<1 \Rightarrow r+2-\pi>0$

$$\frac{\partial \varepsilon^*}{\partial t} = \frac{(2+r)[a-(1+t)(1+\tau)]}{2b(1+r)} > 0 \qquad (7)$$

$$\frac{\partial \varepsilon^*}{\partial \tau} = \frac{(2+r)}{4b(1+r)(1+\tau)^2}[a-(1+t)(1+\tau)][a+(1+t)(1+\tau)] > 0 \qquad (8)$$

[5] In these countries this hypothesis is very realistic because of the poor infrastructure during the period we have studied.

[6] Note that we do not include fixed costs here, since they are incurred only once.

[7] These assumptions will be used to sign some of the derivatives presented below.

$$\frac{\partial \varepsilon^*}{\partial a} = \frac{[2+r-\pi](a-W)(1+\tau)-[a-(1+t)(1+\tau)](2+r)}{2b(1+r)(1+\tau)} \quad (9)$$

$$\frac{\partial \varepsilon^*}{\partial a} > 0 \text{ if } \frac{[a\tau+(1+\tau)(1+t-W)](2+r)}{(a-W)(1+\tau)} > \pi \quad (10)$$

$$\frac{\partial \varepsilon^*}{\partial \pi} = -1 < 0 \quad (11)$$

Thus, the cut-off cost (and the number of foreign investors) decreases as the risk associated with undertaking FDI (π) goes up, as the country specific entry cost (η) increases, and as host country wages go up relative to the home wage rate (W). In the contrary, the number of investors rises with increasing tariff (τ) and transportation costs (t). It also increases with host country size (a) if the probability of returns to FDI dropping to zero is not very large, that is if the condition (10) above is true. The intuition for this finding is the following. An increase in the market size of a host country makes FDI more profitable relative to exporting because of tariffs, savings on transportation and possibly labors costs. However, as the market size expands larger the expected loss incurred in the case of FDI relative to exporting outweighs the increase in the expected loss. Therefore, undertaking local production becomes more profitable and a large number of investors choose this option. Note that the left-hand side of the inequality (10) is always positive if wages in the host country are lower than those in the home country, which is certainly true in the case of transition economies.

3. The Test

We present our empirical proposals, and our data and methodology. Our propositions are divided in two parts. The first examine the relationship between firm's decision to choose a country as a FDI country and the host country characteristics. The second explore the relationship between host country characteristics and the function of investment project.

3.1. Our Proposals

3.1.1. Impact of Host Country Characteristics on FDI Inflows

We test the above model's predictions by examining the relationship between a firm's decision to choose a country as an FDI destination and the host country's market size (corresponding to (a) in the model); risks associated with engaging in FDI which include lack of reform progress, weak intellectual property rights protection and regional tensions (π); an index of registration procedures (a proxy for the country specific entry cost (η)), and dummies for membership and applicant status in WTO[8] (reflecting the impact of trade barriers, (τ)).

Previous empirical studies have found the host country's market size to be an important determinant of FDI inflows[9]. Since many transition economies have experienced significant declines in real incomes, GDP may not be an appropriate measure of their potential market size. Therefore, in the estimation we employ three variables: population size (reflecting market potential), GDP per capita (measuring actual purchasing power of local consumers) and GDP growth rate (taking into account changes in the market size).

Uncertainty about the returns to FDI can arise from the risk of expropriation as well as from new legislation adversely affecting repatriation of profits and tax rates, bureaucratic delays etc. The perceived riskiness of CEECs and the CIS has often been cited as a factor discouraging foreign capital inflows (Zloch-Christy 1995b; Estrin & *al.* 1997; Hunya, 1997). Lankes and Venables (1996) find a negative association between EBRD indicators and country risk as perceived by the interviewed firms, with the rank correlation coefficient equal to -0.89. Thus, in the empirical analysis we employ the average of the EBRD indicator as a proxy for risks associated for countries affected by regional tensions.

Weak intellectual property rights protection (IPRP) can also be a source of uncertainty about the returns to FDI. This is mostly the case in R&D intensive industries and for firms possessing innovative technologies. The lack or inadequacy of IPRP in transition economies is reflected by the fact that many of them have been placed on the US Special 301-watch list. It's possible that the fear of intellectual property rights infringement has discouraged foreign companies from undertaking FDI in the region[10]. To investigate this issue empirically, we construct an index capturing the strength of intellectual property right legislation and its enforcement in the CEECs and the CIS during the period studied (see annex II).

To capture the size of entry costs we include an index reflecting the complexity of the registration procedures. Entry costs might have played a significant role in an investor's decision since, at least in the initial period of the transformation, the registration procedures in the CEECs and the CIS were not very straightforward and varied across the

[8] We choose this criterion because during the period studied, much of these countries have not pre-adhered to the European Union.

[9] See for example Dunning (1992), Caves (1996), Braunerjelm & Svensson (1996) or Hallward-Driemeier (1996).

[10] Several western law firms active in CEECs and the FSU confirmed that their clients, who were potential or actual foreign investors, expressed concerns about weak IPRP in the region. It is also likely that firms planning to invest in countries with low IPRP find it more difficult to obtain funds, since banks take the intellectual property rights regime into account when estimating potential returns to investment (see Maskus, 2000).

region[11]. Since detailed data on tariffs and other trade barriers are not available for most of the transition economies, we employ dummy variables for membership and applicant status in WTO.

Our model also suggests including relative wages in the regression analysis. Since the productivity of labor force in CEECs and the CIS is lower than in developed countries, using unit labor costs would be more appropriate. Unit labor costs are, however, available only for a few countries and they are strongly correlated with the GDP per capita (the correlation is equal to 0.90). Therefore, we do not use them in estimation[12].

Foreign investment can also be attracted by the presence of natural resources. Since we are primarily interested in exploring the impact of government's policy on the magnitude and nature of FDI inflows, we exclude firm in the oil, gas and coal sector from the estimations. Even if such firms were only engaged in the distribution of imported products at the time the survey, these activities may have been undertaken as a prelude to exploitation of the host country's natural resource endowment.

To control for unobserved firm characteristics, we use dummy variables for all firms. The Hausman test confirms that including firm fixed effects is more appropriate than employing a random effect model. The dependent variable takes on the value of one if firm i has invested in country c, and zero otherwise. Thus the model is estimated in the following form:

$$Y_{ic}^{*} = d_i + X_c\beta + u_{ic}$$

$$Y_{ic} = 1 \text{ if } Y_{ic}^{*} > 0$$

$$Y_{ic} = 0 \text{ otherwise}$$

where d_i represent firm dummies and X_c is a vector of host country characteristics: population size, GDP per capita, GDP growth, transition progress, IPRP, entry costs, number of telephone lines per hundred inhabitants and dummies for regional tensions, WTO membership and WTO applicant status. Firms without any projects in the region drop out of the estimation because of dummy variables. Thus, the regression is estimated on the subsample of investors only, and it is not necessary to employ weights.

3.1.2. Composition of FDI and Host Country Characteristics

We explore here the relationship between host country characteristic and the function of investment projects. We also investigate the nature of inflows FDI into high and low

[11] For instance, one EBRD-supported FDI project in the region required seventy signatures of officials to clear applicable licensing and regulatory hurdles (Lankes & Stern, 1997, annex I, p. 2).

[12] Note that the OECD survey (1994) show that only 9.3% of investors view low labor costs as the prime reason for the attractiveness of the region, as compared to 80% who point to the actual and potential market size. Low labor cost in transition economies is perceived by many investors as short-term benefits.

technology sectors. First, we focus on the investor's choice of local production versus non-manufacturing FDI by estimating the following model:

$$Y_{ic}^{*} = X_i\delta + X_c\beta + u_{ic}$$

$$Y_{ic} = 1 \text{ if } Y_{ic}^{*} > 0$$

$$Y_{ic} = 0 \text{ otherwise}$$

where Y_{ic} takes the value of one if firm i have existing or planned manufacturing investment in country c and zero if firm has decided to engage in non-manufacturing project (i.e., distribution or a representative office). X_i denotes firm specific variables: firm size, advertising intensity, R&D intensity and production diversification, while X_c is a vector of host country characteristics: GDP, transition progress, IPRP and unit labor cost. Since the sample consists of investors only, there is no need for using weights. We correct, however, for the possibility that the errors are correlated across observations for the same firm. We also employ industry dummies and exclude firms in the oil, gas and coal sector.

In the case of host country characteristics, we expect to observe a positive marginal effect of GDP, since a larger market size encourages local production due to economies of scale and greater savings on transportation cost[13]. According to Mansfield (1994), foreign investors undertaking production in a host country are more concerned about IPRP than those engaging in distribution only. Therefore, we anticipate that a stronger IPRP regime encourages local manufacturing and thus that the marginal effect of the IPRP index will be negative. Higher unit labor costs are likely to have a negative effect on the probability of manufacturing FDI. Deeper reforms may be perceived by foreign firms as less easily reversible. Thus, greater progress in transition may encourage investors to engage in manufacturing projects, which have a longer payoff period.

3.2. Data and Methodology

Thanks to a unique firm-level data set, we are able to examine the nature of FDI in the region in greater depth than earlier research, which concentrated mostly on aggregate inflows and case studies. The data set, compiled a worldwide survey of companies conducted by the EBRD in 1995, covers twenty-five transition economies. It contains information on both firm and host country characteristics as well as on types of investment project.

While the aggregate figures show the amount and distribution of FDI across the region, they can provide only limited insights about the nature of investment flows. In

[13] Of course, if the production is primarily destined for exports, the size of the local market becomes less important.

January 1995, a brief questionnaire was sent out to all companies (about 9.500) listed in the Worldscope database[14]. Responses were obtained from 1405 firms that answered questions regarding undertaken and planned investment in CEECs and the CIS. Additionally, information on function of the project (manufacturing, distribution, and representative office) was collected. 117 of the survey respondents were chosen for in-depth interviews whose results discussed in Lankes and Venables (1996).

The data set does not include any information on the time when each investment was undertaken (date of entry). Since the magnitude of FDI inflows was marginal before 1989, the information collected pertains mostly to the period 1990-1994[15]. Thus, the data set is well suited for making inferences about the nature of FDI inflows and host county policy that influenced them during the first six years of transition. The data obtained from the survey were supplemented with firm specific information from Worldscope. The response rate in the survey was close to fifteen percent.

3.3. The Results

We can distinguish two level for our results: (1) our results about the nature of FDI inflows; (2) our results about the impact of host country characteristics on FDI inflows.

3.3.1. Nature of FDI Inflows: Our Results

We begin our examination of firms investing in transition economies with a brief look at the distribution of investors across industries. In addition to the sectoral breakdown of investing firms, table 1 presents the average value of firm R&D outlays relative to sales in each sector, first of all firms listed in Worldscope and then for investors in the sample.

Both high and low technology sectors seem to attract FDI[16]. In the majority of high technology sectors, however, investing firms are less R&D intensive than the average firm in their industry. In electronics (the second most R&D intensive sector), the R&D outlays of an average investor (relative to sales) are equal to about 61% of the corresponding figure for the whole sector. In the most research oriented industry, drugs, cosmetics and health care products, the R&D intensity of an average investor reach only 38% of the industry mean. The situation is similar in the case of machinery and equipment or electrical products. The exceptions include chemical and automotive

[14] Worldscope is a commercial database that provides detailed financial statements, business descriptions and historical pricing information on thousand of public companies located in more than fifty countries.

[15] CEECs and the FSU were virtually closed to FDI before 1989, see Meyer (1995), Hunya (1997).

[16] In this subsequent exercises, we use the term « high technology sectors » to refer to industries with average R&D spending exceeding in value one percent of sales. These industry averages were calculated for the population of firms in Worldscope. Half of the sectors qualify as high technology under this definition.

sectors. The mean R&D outlays of investors amount to 3.07% of sales, as compared to 4.53% for the population of firms. Thus, average investors tend to be less R&D intensive.

Table 1. Sectoral Distribution of Investors in the Sample

	R&D/Sales*100 (all firms in worldscope)	R&D/Sales*100 (all firms in the sample)	Number of firms with FDI in the region (in the sample)	% of all firms with FDI in the region (in the sample)
Miscellaneous	4.11	2.49	54	14.17
Financial			49	12.86
Construction	0.58	2.06	32	8.40
Machinery & Equipment	2.95	2.72	27	7.09
Oil, gas & coal	0.73	1.20	26	6.82
Electronics	11.23	6.90	23	6.04
Chemicals	2.98	3.86	21	5.51
Metal & metal prod.	0.99	1.43	20	5.25
Food & beverage	0.62	0.80	19	4.99
Diversified	1.72	0.89	16	4.20
Utilities	0.75	0.91	13	3.41
Electrical	2.38	1.67	11	2.89
Retailers	0.02	0.00	11	2.89
Drugs, cosmetics & health care product	20.38	7.75	10	2.62
Paper	0.70	0.54	10	2.62
Automotive	2.31	3.81	9	2.36
Transportation	0.00	0.00	9	2.36
Recreation	0.92		7	1.84
Textiles & apparel	0.61	0.36	5	1.31
Printing & publishing	0.12	1.07	4	1.05
Aerospace	6.03	7.54	3	0.79
Tobacco	0.18		2	0.52
TOTAL	**4.53**	**3.07**	**3.81**	**100**

Detailed descriptions of variables are presented in appendix 1. All variables pertain to 1993 with the exception of multinational experience, which refer to 1989 to avoid endogeneity problems[17]. We also include industry dummies to control for industry

[17] The share of foreign assets in a firm's total assets would obviously be affected by its investment in transition economies. Since, however, CEECs and the FSU were virtually closed to foreign

specific effects that makes FDI more prevalent in some sectors as well as source country dummies.

Because of different response rates of investors and non-investors, estimating an ordinary probit would lead to inconsistent results; fortunately this problem can be corrected by applying weights. We assume that the response rate for all investors was equal to the rate at which firms with FDI in CEECs answered the survey (15%). Furthermore, we assume that all non-investors had the same probability of responding, equal to 12%. We estimated this figure from the overall and the investor response rate. For each group, the inverse of their response is used as a weight. The results, presented in terms of marginal effects evaluated at the weighted sample means, can be found in table 2. For dummy increases from 0 to 1.

Table 2. Characteristics of Investors. Probit Model

	FDI in the region	FDI in the region	FDI in the region
Firm size (billion USD)	0.0027*** (0.0009)	0.0022** (0.0010)	0.0024*** (0.0 010)
R&D intensity	-0.0048 (0.0031)	-0.0774** (0.0039)	-0.0073** (0.0039)
Advertising intensity	0.0027*** (0.0010)	0.0036*** (0.0013)	0.0033*** (0.0012)
Regional experience	0.1647*** (0.0378)	0.2230*** (0.0786)	0.1995*** (0.0777)
Multinational experience		<0.0001 (0.0006)	<0.0001 (0.0006)
Sales per employee			<0.0001 (0.0001)
Number of obscrvations	305	134	133
χ^2	81.10	50.61	56.17
d.f.	25	22	23
Prob>χ^2	0.00	0.00	0.00
Pseudo R^2	0.23	0.28	0.30
Log Likelihood	-80.38	-32.48	-31.65
Obs. P	0.11	0.11	0.11
Pred. P	0.06	0.05	0.05

Results reported in terms of marginal effects. <0.0001 denotes coefficients with absolute value smaller than 0.0001. *** significant at 1% level, ** at 5% level, * at 10% level. Dummies for industry groups and sources countries have been included

investment until late 1989, including the 1989 share of foreign assets does not pose such problems. The 1988 value might be even more appropriate but we refrained from using it since it would increase the number of missing observations.

As anticipated, we find that a firm's size is positively related to the probability of investing in CEECs and the CIS. Large firms are likely to be better endowed with tangible and intangible assets necessary for investment. They may be more interested in finding new markets since they are more likely to outgrow their domestic market. In transition economies, larger firms also tend to have greater bargaining power in negotiations with local authorities. Consistent with earlier studies, we observe that higher advertising efforts increase the probability of investing. Multinational experience and labor intensity, on the other hand, do not appear to have a statistically impact on the investment decision. Thus, we confirm Meyer's (1995) finding that firms with more labor-intensive production are not more inclined to engage in FDI in the region.

Furthermore, the results show that firms with previous sales experience in the region are more likely to invest than inexperienced counterparts. One should keep in mind, however, that the experience gained by exporting to pre-transition CEECs and the Soviet Union differed from that acquired in the Western world. Since the potential to learn about consumer tastes in centrally planned economies was very limited, foreign firms benefited mostly from making personal contacts with local officials and managers and learning about socioeconomic peculiarities of the region[18].

Unlike studies of FDI in other parts of the world, we find that R&D intensity is a significant negative predictor of investment in transition economies. The higher R&D outlays relative to sales are, the lower is the probability of a firm to undertake FDI in the region. Thus, our findings contradict the widespread view that the skilled and inexpensive labor force would attract technology-intensive FDI into transition economies[19]. Our results are consistent with Dunning's analytical framework of ownership advantages since it is technological superiority relative to local producers that enables a foreign firm to compete successfully. Given the technological gap between transition economies and developed countries, it is quite likely that even firms with R&D spending below their industry average can be successful in the region. Our results, however, are surprising in the light of the finding of Lipsey and al. (1990), Yu (1990) and Dunning (1988) that high level potential of R&D relative to sales are typical of firms investing in less developed

---

18 For the importance of experience in transition economies as a source of personal contacts see King (1997) and Bakos (1995), for the role of previous trading relationship in the context of Japanese FDI see Michalet (1999) and OECD (1994), for the evidence from case studies see Estrin and al. (1997).

19 When the measure of multinational experience is includes in the model, the number of observations drops due to missing values. It is conceivable that the R&D intensity becomes statistically significant only because of the decreased number of observations rather than because of the new model specification. This is, however, not the case. In the original model (presented in column 1), R&D intensity is significant at the 12% level of confidence. When we decrease the number of observations to 134 and use the same model specification, the R&D variable appears to be significant at the 10% level. After the measure of multinational experience is included, R&D achieve the 5% significance level. Note that this regression includes the oil, gas and coal sector (which has been removed from other model in this study) because our goal is to draw conclusions about all investors in the region. Excluding this sector from the sample, however, does not affect the signs or significance levels of marginal effects.

countries. We continue the investigation by examining characteristics of investors choosing different project functions. We estimate a multinomial logit with the project type as the dependent variable. The project types includes manufacturing (possibly accompanied by distribution); distribution (but no manufacturing); and representative office only[20]. The Hausman test could not reject the assumption of the independence of irrelevant alternatives, thus confirming that it is appropriate to use the multinomial logit. The results are presented in terms of marginal effects evaluated at sample means as we see in table 3 and 4.

Table 3 Choosing Project Function. Multinomial Logit Model

	Manufacturing	**Distribution (but no manufacturing)**	**Representative office only**
Firm size (billion USD)	0.0014 (0.0014)0	.0003 (0.0015)	-0.0017 (0.0018)
Advertising intensity	**-0.0076***** **(0.0019)**	-0.0015 (0.0019)	**0.0091***** **(0.0016)**
R&D intensity	**-0.0426***** **(0.0066)**	**0.0162***** **(0.0054)**	**0.0264***** **(0.0048)**
Number of observations	514		
χ^2	78.49		
d.f.	6		
Prob > χ^2	0.00		
Log Likelihood	-515		
Obs. P	0.37	0.34	0.29
Pred. P	0.35	0.37	0.28

Results are reported in terms of marginal effects. *** significant at 1% level, ** significant at 5% level, * significant at 10% level. Significant figures are bold. Oil, coal and gas sector has been excluded

[20] The survey did not include extraction activities as a possible answer to the question about the function of an investment project. We suspect that firms engaged in excavation of natural resources referred to their activities as manufacturing for the purposes of the survey. Since we are specifically interested in the characteristics of investors undertaking local production, we excluded the oil, gas and coal sector to avoid taking into account excavation projects. However, when this sector is included in the regression, the sign patterns and significance levels remain the same, and the magnitudes of the marginal effects are barely affected. The only exception is the firm size, which is positively related to the probability of manufacturing FDI with the effect being significant at the 10% level.

Table 4 Choosing Project Function. Multinomial Logit Model

	Manufacturing	Distribution (but no manufacturing)	Representative office only
Firm size (billion USD)	0.0017 (0.0014)	<0.0001 (0.0016)	-0.0017 (0.0018)
Advertising intensity	**-0.0084***** **(0.0020)**	-0.0009 (0.0019)	**0.0092***** **(0.0017)**
R&D intensity	**-0.0418***** **(0.0065)**	**0.0158***** **(0.0054)**	**0.026***** **(0.0048)**
Product diversification	-0.0619 (0.0108)	0.0144 (0.0102)	0.0024 (0.0099)
Number of observations	514		
χ^2	81.61		
d.f.	8		
Prob > χ^2	0.00		
Log Likelihood	-513.17		
Obs. P	0.37	0.34	0.29
Pred. P	0.35	0.37	0.28

Results are reported in terms of marginal effects. *** significant at 1% level, ** significant at 5% level, * significant at 10% level. <0.0001 denotes marginal effects with absolute value smaller than 0.0001. Significant figures are bold. Oil, coal and gas sector has been excluded

These findings indicate that an increase of one standard deviation in R&D outlays relative to sales decreases the probabilities of a distributional project and a representative office by 6 and 10 percent, respectively. Similarly, an increase in advertising intensity discourages local production and encourages representative offices. Thus firms with characteristics typical of MNEs (i.e. large spending on advertising and R&D relative to sales) are most likely to have only a representative office. As Meyer (1995) suggest, it may be more difficult for firms with a less diversified product portfolio to alter their product profile in response to the changing competitiveness in term of labor costs. Although we obtain a negative marginal effect of product diversification in the case of manufacturing investment, it is not statistically significant. Similarly, the marginal effects of firm size do not appear to be statically significant.

Governments tend to view manufacturing in technology-intensive sectors as the most desirable form of FDI. We find evidence that transition economies fail to attract this kind of investment. There are several possible explanations for these findings. First, foreign firms may try to take advantage of low labor cost in the region and undertake production of low technology, labor-intensive goods for exports. This explanation, however, does not seem very plausible. Surveys of foreign investors in CEECs and the CIS indicate that labor costs are of only secondary importance (Lankes and Venables, 1996). In table 2, we show that labor intensity of the production process does not affect a firm's decision to invest in the region and thus confirm Meyer's (1995) result that foreign firms in transition economies are mostly not motivated by labor costs.

A second hypothesis is that weak protection of intellectual property right deters investors with more sophisticated technologies from engaging in local production. Investors may fear that locating production facilities in a country with a weak IPR regime may increase the probability of technology theft. Our results are consistent with the findings of Mansfield (1994) who surveyed US manufacturing firms about the importance of IPR protection for their investment decision. He found that in the case of investment in sales and distribution outlets, only about 20% of respondents were concerned with IPR protection. In the case of investment in rudimentary production and assembly facilities, 30% of respondent viewed IPR protection as important. This percentage increased to 50-60% for investment in manufacturing components and complete products and to 80% in the case of R&D facilities.

Finally, technology-intensive sectors may exhibit greater economies of scale since they require a higher initial investment. Thus, manufacturing in these sectors may be deterred by insufficient local demand, which may be a result of the drop in real income experienced by all economies in the region in the initial phase of transformation. Foreign firms in such sectors may, however, be willing to set up a distribution network or a representative office to support their export presence on the market. We will investigate these hypotheses in the next paragraph.

3.3.2. Impact of Host Country on FDI Inflows

Table 5 presents the estimation results from several variants of the model. We find that all three variables measuring market size have a significant and positive impact on the probability of a country being chosen as an investment destination. An increase in the GDP per capita of one standard deviation above the mean is associated with 15.1% increase in the probability that the country received FDI. It is conceivable that GDP per capita represents not only the purchasing power of the population but also the quality of infrastructure in a host country. To examine this issue, we include in the estimation the number of telephone lines per hundred inhabitants and find that its marginal effects is positive and significant. This modification, however, does not affect the magnitude of the marginal effect or the significance level of GDP per capita and produces only slight changes in the marginal effects of other variables. In general, FDI inflows can affect the growth rate of a host country's GDP. One of the advantages of this study is that it is not the case here. CEECs and the CIS had been virtually closed to FDI until the end of 1989 and the aggregate FDI inflows remained very small throughout the period covered by the data set.

Table 5 Probit Estimates of the Model

	All FDI	All FDI	All FDI	All FDI	All FDI
Populations (millions)	0.001*** (0.0001)	0.001*** (0.0001)	0.001*** (0.0001)	0.001*** (0.0001)	0.001*** (0.0001)
GDP per capita (thousand $)	0.033*** (0.0045)	0.033*** (0.0045)	0.029*** (0.0050)	0.029*** (0.0047)	0.028*** (0.0050)
GDP Growth	0.003*** (0.0005)	0.003*** (0.0005)	0.002*** (0.0006)	0.003*** (0.0006)	0.002*** (0.0008)
Transition Progress	0.024*** (0.0056)	0.018*** (0.0060)	0.025*** (0.0055)	0.008 (0.0056)	0.011* (0.0065)
IPR protection Index	-0.022*** (0.0054)	-0.020*** (0.0052)	-0.018*** (0.0051)	-0.017*** (0.0047)	-0.016*** (0.0048)
Regional tensions			-0.029** (0.0085)	-0.014 (0.0127)	-0.018 (0.0123)
Entry cost index			0.006** (0.0028)		0.003 (0.0035)
WTO member				0.040*** (0.0152)	0.042*** (0.0158)
WTO applicant				0.044*** (0.0132)	0.039*** (0.0143)
Telephone lines (per 1000 inhabitants)		0.001*** (0.0005)			
Number of obs.	6246	6246	6246	6246	6246
χ^2	2273	2280	2282	2295	2296
d.f.	351	352	353	354	355
Prob > χ^2	0.00	0.00	0.00	0.00	0.00
Pseudo R^2	0.44	0.44	0.44	0.44	0.44
Log Likelihood	-1457	-1453	-1452	-1446	-1445
Obs. P	0.15	0.15	0.15	0.15	0.15
Pred. P	0.04	0.03	0.03	0.03	0.03

Results are reported in terms of marginal effects. *** significant at 1% level, ** significant at 5% level, * significant at 10% level. Firm dummies have been included in all regressions but are not reported. Oil, coal and gas sector has been excluded

As expected, we find the marginal effect of transition progress to be positive and statistically significant. Thus, we empirically confirm the widespread belief that countries more advanced in transformation are more attractive FDI destinations. We also find that the regional tensions decrease the probability of foreign investment. Furthermore, the results show inadequate IPR protection discourages foreign investors. This effect is statistically significant at the 1% level. Changes in IPR protection from the Romanian level to that of Poland increases the probability of FDI by more that, 11%. Protection of intellectual property rights has been a neglected issue in the earlier literature on transition economies[21].

As anticipated, more liberal entry procedures attract foreign investors. Contrary to the model's predictions, we find that lower trade barriers (to the extent that membership or application for membership in WTO reflects them) encourage FDI. The impact of both dummy variables is statistically significant. This situation may arise from the fact that foreign investors tend to import equipment as well as many of their inputs, at least in the initial period. It is also possible that the access to the WTO Dispute Settlement has a positive impact on firm's decision to undertake FDI.

Next, we re-estimate the model taking into account foreign investment in manufacturing facilities only. The results, presented in table 6 are similar in terms of the sign patterns and the significance level to those in table 5. One of the exceptions in the number of telephone lines, which does not appear to be statistically significant.

Table 6 Probit Estimates of the Model

	Manufacturing FDI	Manufacturing FDI	Manufacturing FDI	Manufacturing FDI	Manufacturing FDI
Populations (millions)	0.001*** (0.0001)	0.001*** (0.0001)	0.001*** (0.0001)	0.001*** (0.0001)	0.001*** (0.0001)
GDP per capita (thousand $)	0.020*** (0.0045)	0.020*** (0.0046)	0.016*** (0.0045)	0.016*** (0.0047)	0.012*** (0.0048)
GDP Growth	0.002*** (0.0006)	0.002*** (0.0006)	0.001*** (0.0006)	0.002*** (0.0007)	0.001 (0.0009)
Transition Progress	0.019*** (0.0060)	0.015*** (0.0069)	0.019*** (0.0060)	0.007 (0.0058)	0.013* (0.0069)
IPR protection Index	-0.019*** (0.0060)	-0.018*** (0.0059)	-0.014*** (0.0055)	-0.013*** (0.0051)	-0.012*** (0.0051)
Regional tensions			-0.030* (0.0070)	-0.023 (0.0096)	-0.029* (0.0080)
Entry cost index			0.005* (0.0030)		0.006* (0.0037)

[21] Stronger IPR protection in Hungary, the Czech Republic and Poland could conceivably be a result of the pressure exercised on these countries by the US government, since american companies accounted for a large portion of FDI inflows in each of these economies. While some pressure was exercised in the case of Poland which was placed on the Priority Watch List in 1992 and 1993 and on the Watch List in 1994 and 1995, neither Hungary nor the Czech Republic or former Czechoslovakia found themselves on either of the lists in the same period.

	Manufacturing FDI	Manufacturing FDI	Manufacturing FDI	Manufacturing FDI	Manufacturing FDI
WTO member				0.031** (0.0162)	0.036** (0.0177)
WTO applicant				0.027** (0.0131)	0.016 (0.0129)
Telephone lines (per 1000 inhabitants)		0.001 (0.0005)			
Number of obs.	4014	4014	4014	4014	4014
χ^2	1059	1060	1067	1071	1074
d.f.	227	228	229	230	231
Prob > χ^2	0.00	0.00	0.00	0.00	0.00
Pseudo R^2	0.38	0.38	0.38	0.38	0.38
Log Likelihood	-879	-878	-875	-873	-872
Obs. P	0.11	0.11	0.11	0.11	0.11
Pred. P	0.03	0.03	0.03	0.02	0.02

Results are reported in terms of marginal effects. *** significant at 1% level, ** significant at 5% level, * significant at 10% level. Firm dummies have been included in all regressions but are not reported. Oil, coal and gas sector has been excluded

We also experimented with replacing our measure of IPR (see appendix 2) protection with an update version of the patent rights index by Ginarte and Park (1997). This index is highly correlated with our IPR measure (.74) and produces results very similar to those found in table 5 trough 8. Since it is available for only nine transition economies, we chose to present result based our measure.

Additionally, we estimated models in which our IPR index was replaced with a dummy variable for countries with the weakest IPR regimes (corresponding to the index vale of 3). The results produced by these models were consistent with the findings presented here.

3.3.3. Composition of FDI and Host Country Characteristics

The results, presented in table 7 confirm our earlier findings that less R&D and less advertising-intensive as well as less diversified firms are more likely to engage in local production. As anticipated, market size has a positive marginal effect on the probability of an investor to undertake local production rather that non-manufacturing FDI. We also find that weak IPR protection has a large negative effect on the probability of engaging in manufacturing FDI and that the effect is statistically significant. A decrease in IPR protection from the level of Poland to that of Romania lowers the probability of FDI focusing on local production by 21.5%. This result may be due to the greater scope for technology theft in the case of manufacturing projects. The effects of reform progress and unit labor cost are not statistically significant. The latter result is consistent with the evidence, that foreign investors are not motivated by low labor costs in the region.

Governments tend to favor FDI in technology intensive sectors. To examine what host country characteristics encourage this type of FDI, we re-estimate the model interacting host country variables with dummies for high and low technology industries. We estimate the model for all FDI and for manufacturing projects only, defining as high technology sectors where the average R&D expenditure exceeds 1% of sales. We hypothesize that weak IPR protection has a larger deterring effect in the case of technology-intensive sectors. Since undertaking local production in such sectors may also require a greater initial investment (presumably because the cost of equipment is higher), thus creating economies of scale, we anticipate that market size have a greater positive effect on technology-intensive FDI.

Table 7 Manufacturing vs. Non-Manufacturing Projects. Probit Model

	Manuf./Non Manuf	Manuf./Non manuf.	Manuf./Non manuf.
Firm size (billion $)	0.0008 (0.0019)	0.0014 (0.0018)	0.0013 (0.0018)
R&D intensity	-0.0375*** (0.0103)	-0.0370*** (0.0097)	-0.0344*** (0.0079)
Advertising intensity	-0.0101** (0.0046)	-0.0132*** (0.0046)	-0.0139*** (0.0046)
Product diversification	-0.0365* (0.0202)	-0.0364* (0.01096)	-0.0391** (0.0192)
GDP (billion $)	0.0017*** (0.0005)	0.0020*** (0.0006)	0.0017*** (0.0005)
Transition progress	-0.0307 (0.0622)	-0.0672 (0.0807)	0.0317 (0.0634)
IPR protection index	-0.0809* (0.0460)	-0.1236* (0.0660)	
Unit labor cost		0.0013 (0.0031)	0.0004 (0.0022)
No. Of obs.	429	357	387
χ^2	65.76	70.76	89.88
d.f.	20	20	20
Prob > χ^2	0.00	0.00	0.00
Pseudo R^2	0.18	0.19	0.19
Log likelihood	-234	-195	-209
Obs. P	0.38	0.40	0.38
Pred. P	0.35	0.36	0.35

Results are reported in terms of marginal effects. ***significant at 1% level, **significant at 5% level, * significant at 10% level. Oil, coal and gas sector has been excluded. Industry dummies have been included in all regressions but are not reported. Standard errors have been corrected to take into account possible correlation between errors from the observations for the same firm.

Results presented in the first two columns of the table 8 indicate that both high low technology industries are discouraged by weak IPR protection. The marginal effects are very similar in size, and the difference in the magnitude of the probit coefficients, from which these marginal effects have been derived, is not statistically significant. One should keep in mind, however, that intellectual property rights do not play an equally important role in all technology-intensive industries. For instance, Mansflield (1995) mentions that IPR protection may be less crucial in sectors such as automobile production, in which firms frequently cannot make use of a competitor's technology without much complex and expensive input. Thus, we re-estimate the model classifying as high technology only four R&D-intensive sectors which, as surveys indicate, tend to rely heavily on IPRs. They include drugs, cosmetics and health care products; chemicals; machinery and equipment; electrical equipment[22]. When all FDI is are taken into account (see column 3 in table 8), the deterring impact of inadequate IPR protection is almost twice as large for the IPR sensitive industries than for the other sectors. The marginal effects are significant at the 1% level and the difference between the underlying probit coefficients is significant at the 1% level as well. However, when we estimate the model for manufacturing FDI alone, weak IPR protection has a larger impact on the 4 high technology sectors, but the differences between the underlying coefficients is not statistically significant.

As Lall (1997, p. 244) point out, strong protection of intellectual property not only decreases the threat of IPR infringement but also plays a significant role: "*...the signaling value of the intellectual property regime has become extremely important in recent years. In general, countries that seek to attract technology-intensive foreign investment also offer strong protection to those investments*". It is likely that potential investors perceive the adequacy of the IPR regime as an indication of the government's attitude toward FDI, which would explain why all kinds of FDI, and not only those in technology-intensive sectors, are deterred by a weak IPR regime.

[22] See Mansfield (1995) and Baldwin (1996)

Table 8 High and Low Technology Sectors. Probit Model

	All Hi Tech sectors		IPR Sensitive Hi Tech sectors	
	All FDI	**Manuf. FDI**	**All FDI**	**Manuf. FDI**
Hi tech sectors * GDP (billion $)	0.0009*** (0.0000)	0.0007*** (0.0000)	0.0009*** (0.0000)	0.0007*** (0.0000)
Other sectors * GDP (billion $)	0.0008*** (0.0001)	0.0007*** (0.0001)	0.0008*** (0.0000)	0.0007*** (0.0000)
Hi tech sectors * transition progress	0.0448*** (0.0065)	*0.0195**** *(0.0069)*	0.0263** (0.0111)	0.0157 (0.0101)
Other sectors *transition progress	0.0444*** (0.0090)	*0.0501**** *(0.0099)*	0.0487*** (0.0059)	0.0371*** (0.0069)
Hi tech sectors * IPR protection index	-0.0564*** (0.0064)	-0.0414*** (0.0069)	-0.0843*** (0.0057)	-0.0467*** 0.0102)
Other sectors * IPR protection index	-0.0573*** (00086)	-0.0331*** (0.0088)	-0.0498*** (0.0057)	-0.0367*** (0.0066)
No. of obs.	6246	4014	6246	4014
χ^2	2178	1039	2184	1034
d.f.	352	228	352	228
Prob > χ^2	0.00	0.00	0.00	0.00
Pseudo R^2	0.42	0.37	0.42	0.37
Log likelihood	-1504	-889	-1501	-892
Obs. P	0.15	0.11	0.15	0.11
Pred. P	0.04	0.03	0.04	0.03

Results are reported in terms of marginal effects. *** significant at 1% level, ** significant at % level; * significant at 10% level. Bold figures indicate that the difference between the underlying coefficient is statistically significant at 1% level, bold italics mark a difference significant at 5% level. Oil, coal and gas sector has been excluded. Firm dummies have been excluded in all regressions but are not reported.

As anticipated, we find some indication that a host country's GDP has a larger impact on technology-intensive industries than on low technology sectors. This difference appears to be significant at the 10% level in the first column of table 8. The progress in reforms, on the other hand, encourages FDI inflows into both sectors with the marginal effect being larger for low technology industries. The difference in magnitudes is statistically significant only in the second column of table 8.

To sum up, our results provide evidence that stronger IPR protection and a larger market size encourage investors to undertake local production rather than to engage in distribution or open a representative office. Weak IPR protection discourages FDI in both high and low technology sectors, with this effect being significantly stronger for 4 R&D-intensive sectors in which intellectual property rights play a particularly prominent role.

4. Conclusion

Governments all over the world compete fiercely to attract FDI. This is also true of policy makers in CEECs and the CIS who hope that FDI can contribute to upgrade production technologies in their countries. Even leaving our skepticism about the scope of FDI for technology transfer, we provide evidence that the reality does not fit the expectations of the host countries policy makers in the region. The examination of investor's characteristics shows those FDI inflows in transition economies concentrate in low technology activities. We find in our sample that firms characterized by low R&D intensity are more likely to invest in the region that firms with relatively large R&D spending. We also observe that higher R&D outlays increase the probability that an investor will engage in distribution rather that in local production.

Furthermore, our analysis shows that while larger population size, per capita income and GDP growth rate encourage foreign investment slow progress in reform and regional tensions act as deterrent to FDI. We construct an index of IPR protection and find that a weak IPR regime has a negative impact on foreign investment inflows. It not only deters FDI in general but it also discourages foreign investors from undertaking local production and encourages them to engage in non-manufacturing projects. The negative effect of inadequate IPR protection is particularly strong in four technology-intensive sectors: drugs, cosmetics and health care products; chemicals; machinery and equipment; electrical equipment. As we have shown, firms in these sectors tend to view IPRs as more important than their counterparts in other industries.

Since CEECs and the CIS were virtually closed to FDI before 1989, their "sudden opening" to foreign investment can be compared to a natural experiment. This characteristic of our dataset presents us with a unique opportunity to estimate the effect of IPR protection and other country characteristics on FDI in absence of investment history. It is possible that in earlier studies, the lack of controls for past policy variables and investment history has obscured the impact of IPR protection on FDI. Our results, therefore, suggest than more research is needed to improve our understanding of the implication of IPR regimes for the magnitude and composition of FDI inflows. Shedding more light on this issue could potentially encourage many developing countries to re-evaluate their policy on IPR protection.

References

1. Baldwin J., (1996), The use of intellectual property rights by Canadian manufacturing firms: Findings from the innovation survey, mimeo. *Statistics Canada*.
2. Bakos G., (1995), Magyar Suzuki: Case study of Japanese investment, in: Zloch-Christy I., ed., *Privatization and Foreign Investments in Eastern Europe*, London: Praeger, pp. 197-214.

3. Blomström M. and Wolff E., (1994), Multinational corporations and productivity convergence in Mexico, in: Baumol W., Nelson R. and Wolff E., eds., *Convergence of Productivity. Cross-National Studies and Historical Evidence,* Oxford: Oxford University Press.
4. Braunerhjelm P. and Svensson R., (1996), Host country characteristics and agglomeration in: foreign direct investment, *Applied Economics* 28, pp. 833-840.
5. Caves R. E, (1996), *Multinational enterprise and economic analysis*, Second Edition Cambridge: Cambridge University Press
6. De Castro J. O., and Uhlenbruck K. (1997) Comparing privatization characteristics in former communist, developing and developed countries, in Ullmann H. A., and Lewis A. (Eds). *Privatization and entrepreneurship. The managerial challenge in Central and Eastern Europe*, Binghamton: The Haworth Press.
7. Druzic I. (1997), Regional dispersion of foreign direct investment in Eastern Europe, in Shamar S. ed., *Restructuring Eastern Europe. The microeconomics of the transition process.* Cheltenham: Edward Elgar Publisher, pp. 97-110.
8. Dunning J. H., (1988), *Multinationals, Technology and Competitiveness*, London: Unwin Hyman
9. Dunning J. H. (1992), *Multinational enterprise and the global economy.* Wokingham: Addison-Wesley Publishing Company
10. Dunning J. H. and Rojec M., (1993), *Foreign Privatization in Central & Eastern Europe* (CEEPN, Ljubljana, Slovenia).
11. EBRD. *Transition Report*. (EBRD, London). Various years.
12. ECE. 1995. *Economic Bulletin for Europe*. Vol. 47. Geneva.
13. Estrin S., Hughes K. and Todd S., (1997), *Foreign direct investment in Central and Eastern Europe: Multinationals in transition London and Washington*: Pinter / Royal Institute for International Affairs
14. Estrin S., and Meyer K. (1999). Entry Mode Choice in Emerging Markets: Greenfield, Acquisition, Brownfield. *CIS-Middle Europe Center, London Business School, Discussion Papers Series, n°57*, February.
15. Fabry N., and Zeghni S. (2001) The Japanese Foreign Direct Investment in China: the Case of Dalian and Shanghai, *Global Business and Finance Review,* may.
16. Fabry N. (2001), The role of FDI in transition economies, in Fabry N. & Zeghni S. eds., *Transition in Asia and Central and Eastern Europe: A closed door two open windows?*, New-York: Nova Science Publisher
17. Ferrantino M. J. (1993), The effect of intellectual property rights on international trade and investment, *Weltwirtschaftliches Archiv*, 129 pp. 300-331
18. Firozzi F. (1997), Multinationals FDI and Uncertainty: An Exposition, *Journal of Multinational Financial Management*, vol. 7(3): 115-125.
19. Frydman R., Gray C. and Rapazynski A. (Eds.) (1996) *Corporate Governance in Central Europe and Russia*, vol. 1, London and Budapest: Central European University Press.
20. Ginarte J. C. and Park W. G., (1997), « Determinants of patent rights: A cross-national study », *Research Policy* 26, pp. 283-301.

21. Grubaugh S. G., (1987), Determinants of direct foreign investment, *Review of Economics and Statistics* 69, pp.149-152.
22. Haddad M. and Harrison A., (1993), Are there positive spillovers from direct foreign investment? Evidence from Morocco, *Journal of Development Economics* 42, pp.51-74.
23. Hallward-Driemeier M., (1996), *understanding foreign direct investment by firms: Market pull, cost push and knowledge accumulation*, mimeo, MIT.
24. Havlik P., (1996), Exchange rates, competitiveness and labour costs in Central and Eastern Europe, *WIIW Research Report* No. 231 (WIIW, Vienna).
25. Hunya G., (1997), Large privatisation, restructuring and foreign direct investment, in: Zecchini S. ed., *Lessons from the economic transition. Central and Eastern Europe in the 1990s*. Dordrecht, Boston and London: Kluwer Academic Publishers, pp. 275-300.
26. International Intellectual Property Alliance. *Special 301 Recommendations*. Various years.
27. International Telecommunication Union & OECD, (1994), *Telecommunication Indicators for Economies in Transition*, Paris: OCDE
28. Jermakowicz W. and Drazek C., (1993), Joint venture laws in Eastern Europe: A comparative assessment in: Artisien P., Rojec M. and Svetlicic M. eds., *Foreign Investment in Central and Eastern Europe,* New-York: *St. Martin's Press*, pp. 149-68.
29. King L. P., (1997), *Strategic restructuring: Making capitalism in post-communist Eastern Europe*. Paper prepared for the conference Organization Change in Transition Economies at The William Davidson Institute, Ann Arbor, September 26-28.
30. Knell M., (1996), Structural adjustments and growth: Is eastern europe catching up?, in: Knell M., ed., *Economics of Transition. Structural Adjustments and Growth Prospects in Eastern Europe,* Cheltenham: *Edward Elgar*, pp. 1-24.
31. Kokko A., Tansini R. and Zejan M. C., (1996), Local technological capability and productivity spillovers from FDI in the Uruguayan manufacturing sector, *Journal of Development Studies*, 32, pp. 602-11.
32. Lall S., (1997), Investment, technology and international competitiveness, in: Dunning J. H. & Hamdani K. A., eds., *The New Globalism and Developing Countries New York*: United Nations University Press, pp. 232-59.
33. Lankes H.-P. and Stern N., (1997), Capital flows to Eastern Europe and the former Soviet Union, *EBRD Working Paper* No. 27.
34. Lankes H.-P. and Venables A. J., (1996), Foreign direct investment in economic transition: The changing pattern of investments, *Economics of Transition* 4, pp. 331-347.
35. Lipsey R. E., Blomstrom M. and Kravis I. B., (1990), R&D by multinational firms and host country exports, in: Evenson R. E. and Ranis G., eds., *Science and Technology. Lessons for Development Policy,* San Francisco: Westview Press, pp. 271-300.

36. Mansfield E., (1994), Intellectual property protection, foreign direct investment and technology transfer, *IFC Discussion Paper* No. 19.
37. Markusen J. R., (1995), The boundaries of multinational enterprises and the theory of international trade, *Journal of Economic Perspectives* 9, pp. 169-189.
38. Maskus K and Konan D., (1994), Trade related intellectual property rights: Issues and exploratory results, in Deardoff A. and Stern R. (eds), *Analytical and negotiating issues in the global trading system*, Ann-Arbor: University of Michigan Press, p. 401-446
39. Maskus K. E. (2000), Intellectual property and foreign direct investment, *Working Paper n°0022, CIES, University of Adelaide* (Australia)
40. Meyer K., (1995), Direct foreign investment in Eastern Europe. The role of labor costs, *Comparative Economic Studies* 37, pp. 69-88.
41. Meyer K., (1998), *Direct Investment in Economies in Transition* Cheltenham: Edward Elgar
42. Michalet C.-A., (1999*), La séduction des Nations ou comment attirer les investissements*, Paris: Economica
43. OECD, (1994), *Assessing Investment Opportunities in Economies in Transition.* Paris: OCDE
44. Radosevic S., (1996), Prospects of building science and technology capabilities in Central and Eastern Europe, in: Knell M. ed., *Economics of Transition. Structural Adjustments and Growth Prospects in Eastern Europe*. Cheltenham: Edward Elgar, pp. 185-209.
45. Radosevic S. and Dyker D., (1997), Technological integration and global marginalization of Central and East European economies: The role of FDI and alliances, in: Sharma S. ed., *Restructuring Eastern Europe. The Microeconomics of the Transition Process*, Cheltenham: Edward Elgar, pp.111-127.
46. Rapp R. T. and Rozek R. P. (1990), Benefits and costs of intellectual property protection in developing countries, *Journal of World Trade* 24, p. 75-102
47. Rodrik D., (1991), Policy uncertainty and private investment in developing countries, *Journal of Development Economics* 36, pp. 229-242.
48. Sharp M. and Barz M., (1997), Multinational companies and the transfer and diffusion of new technological capabilities in Central and Eastern Europe and the former Soviet Union, in Dyker D. A. ed*., The Technology of Transition. Science and Technology Policies for Transition Countries*. Budapest: Central European University Press, pp. 95-125.
49. Simai M. (1999), When will the transition phase end?, *Thunderbird International Business Review,* vol.40(1):7-27
50. UNCTAD, (1997), *World Investment Report* 1997: Transnational Corporations, Market Structure and Competition Policy. United Nations.
51. World Bank, (1996), *World Development Report* 1996. From Plan to Market New York: Oxford University Press.
52. Yu, C.-M. J., (1990), The experience effect and foreign direct investment, *Weltwirtschaftliches Archiv* 126, pp. 561-79.

53. Zecchini S. (1997) ed., *Lessons from the transition: Central and Eastern Europe in the 1990s*, Dordrecht: Kluwer Academic Publisher
54. Zloch-Christy I., (1995a), Introduction: Foreign investment and the transition in post-communist Europe, in: Zloch-Christy I. ed., *Privatization and Foreign Investments in Eastern Europe*. London: Praeger, pp. 1-10.
55. Zloch-Christy I., (1995b), Economic transformation, external imbalances, and political risk in post-communist Eastern Europe, in: Zloch-Christy I. ed., *Privatization and Foreign Investments in Eastern Europe*. London: Praeger, pp. 215-238.

APPENDIX I. VARIABLES EMPLOYED IN THE EMPIRICAL ANALYSIS

Drawing on the theoretical and empirical literatures, the following firm and host country characteristics are examined in the study:

Firm size	➢ measured by the firm's sales in US dollars
R&D intensity	➢ measured by R&D outlays as a percentage of net sales
Advertising intensity	➢ proxied by selling, general & administrative expenses as a percentage of net sales (note that this is a standard proxy in the literature and has been used by, for instance, Grubaugh, 1987
Product diversification	➢ the number of four-digit SIC codes describing a firm's activities
General multinational experience	➢ proxied by the share of foreign assets in a firm's total assets
Regional experience	➢ denoted by a dummy variable indicating whether a company had a trading relationship with the region before 1990
Capital intensity of production	➢ proxied by sales per employee in US dollars
Dummies for high and low R&D and advertising sectors	➢ for the former the cut-off value was one percent of net sales, while for the latter it was equal to twenty percent of net sales
The host country's market size	➢ measured by population size
Purchasing power	➢ measured by GDP per capita
Change in market size	➢ measured by GDP growth rate
Transition progress	➢ represented by the average of EBRD transition indicator (transition indicator rate the progress of a country's reforms in the following areas: price liberalization and competition, trade and exchange system, large-scale privatization, small-scale privatization, enterprise restructuring, and banking reform. See EBRD (1994, p. 11).
IPR index	➢ constructed by the author based on the information from Special 301 Recommendations prepared by the International Intellectual Property Alliance (note that lower index values imply stronger IPR protection)
Entry costs	➢ index of required registration procedures derived by Jermakowicz and Drazek (1993, Table 9.4, pp. 158-9); the first half of 1991; see description below; note that lower values indicate more complicated registration procedures

A dummy variable equal to one if a country has been affected by regional tensions and zero otherwise	➢ such tensions have been present in Armenia, Azerbaijan, Croatia, Georgia, FYR Macedonia and Tajikistan, according to World Bank, 1996, p. ix
Unit labor costs relative to the Austrian level	➢ source: Havlik, 1996
Number of main telephone lines per 100 inhabitants	➢ Source: International Telecommunication Union and OECD, 1994
WTO membership and applicant dummies	➢ as of 1995 according to EBRD, 1997

All information on firm characteristics other than that from the survey was obtained from the *Worldscope* database and pertains to fiscal year 1993 (from 4/93 to 3/94). Multinational experience, which refers to 1989 to avoid endogeneity, is the only exception[23]. 30 Host country data refer to 1993 and are taken from the *EBRD Transition Report* (EBRD, 1997) unless otherwise noted. The transition indicator pertain to 1994, since it is the earliest year for which they are available. Note that even though the data set contains 1,405 firms, not all information is available for all firms. Therefore, the number of firms used in the econometric analysis is much smaller, and the number of observations varies among regressions.[24]

Index of Registration Procedures Mandatory for Foreign Investors	
Points	Description
1	Multi-stage process requiring consent of more than one government institution
2	All J-V registrations require consent of a government institution
3	Only majority foreign owned firms require government permit
4	Free registration

Source: Jermakowicz and Drazek (1993, Table 9.3 and 9.4, pp. 156-9).

[23] It is possible that other variables (e.g. advertising intensity) are also subject to the endogeneity problem. To explore this possibility we estimated our models with all of firm specific variables referring to 1989 and the results were not significantly different. Since, there are fewer missing values for 1993, we decided to present the results pertaining to that year.

[24] Note that the proportion of investors in the sample is equal to 27%. When we take into account only firms for which all data are available, the proportion of investors equals 29%.

APPENDIX II.
IPR INDEX

We construct an index capturing the strength of IPR legislation and its enforcement in CEECs and the CIS. Although, the data cover the period until January 1995, we use the end of that year as a reference point in the rating to take into account the anticipation of the changes. The table below presents the rating criteria. A higher value of the index corresponds to weaker IPR protection.

Index of Intellectual Property Protection	
Points	Description
1	Close to adequate IPR legislation present by the end of 1995 ; some enforcement efforts undertaken
2	Close to adequate IPR legislation present by the end of 1995 ; no enforcement efforts undertaken
3	No reform of IPR legislation undertaken by the end of 1995

Source: constructed by the author based on IIPA Special 301 recommendations (various years)

Chapter 4

EXPERIMENTATION IN EXPORT PROMOTION POLICIES IN TRANSITION AND DEVELOPING ECONOMIES*

Mikhail M. Klimenko
University of California at San Diego

1. INTRODUCTION

Many governments in industrializing and transition economies have implemented industrial targeting policies to promote the development of selected industries which were believed to have high growth potential. The cases of success and failure of these policies are well documented and have been thoroughly analyzed by many authors (see, for example, Westphal (1982), Krueger (1985), Wade (1990), Rodrik (1995, 1996), Lall (1996)). Two major types of market failure were cited as justification for these government interventions in the market mechanism. One type of market failure leads to allocative distortions in the markets for existing goods and the other type inhibits the introduction of new goods and activities in the economy. Imperfect competition or information asymmetries are among the major causes of the former type of market failure. Causes of the latter type of market failures are rooted either in coordination problems[1] or non-appropriability of external benefits from innovation and investments

*I would like to thank Edward Lazear, John McMillan, Barry Naughton, James Rauch, John Roberts, Robert Wilson, Phillipp Afêche, Michael Herron, T.L. Lai and participants at seminars at the Stanford University Graduate School of Business, at the Graduate School of International Relations and Pacific Studies at the University of California at San Diego, and at Stockholm Institute of Transition Economics and East European Economies for helpful discussions. I am especially grateful to Paul Krugman for his constant encouragement and help.

[1] A simultaneous entry of firms in several complementary industries may be a precondition of high rates of economic growth. In vertically integrated industries, the possibility of differing

into new activities leading to a less than socially desirable rate of entry of new firms (see Bardhan (1971), Young (1991), Hoff (1997)).

The literature on industrial targeting policies has been focused on the timing and type of government interventions as well as on the specifics of the market structure, which can justify such policies from the welfare efficiency standpoint. An interesting characteristic of many papers is that while they elaborate in great detail on finely-tuned subsidies or tariffs, they also typically contain a caveat that governments are unlikely to be competent enough to adopt and correctly implement such policies. While we do not subscribe entirely to this view, we agree that the targeting policies which theory prescribes to the governments are very complex and the governments have only limited capacity to implement such policies. Given their limited targeting capacity, the governments often have to choose how to allocate their policy effort between different industries which require intervention. Thus, while justification and design of a specific policy intervention are important, this paper attempts to model another ingredient of industrial targeting policy, i.e., the characteristics of the process by which the governments select among several industries in which policy interventions are assumed to be justified on the grounds of welfare efficiency.

After describing a government's industrial targeting program as an optimal experimentation policy of an incompletely informed government, we address the normative issue of the long-run efficiency of such experimental policy activism in determining the country's pattern of specialization. In particular, we show that even an optimally designed industrial targeting policy does not guarantee the country's long-run specialization according to its comparative advantage. In fact, if the long-run specialization according to comparative advantage is taken as criteria, then, despite concomitant coordination problems, private experimentation by firms may be superior to centralized experimentation by a government implementing an industrial targeting policy[2]. This suggests that overcoming market coordination failures should not be used as an unconditional justification for targeted promotion of industries selected by the government.

1.1. Stylized Facts from the Experience of East European, Latin American and Asian Countries with Industrial Targeting Policies

Some Eastern European transition economies and some less developed countries of Latin America and Asia tried to identify technologies in which they were most

degrees of coordination in the entry of upstream and downstream firms creates multiple equilibria. Targeting the "right" sectors can help to overcome "underdevelopment traps", i.e., bad equilibria characterized by the lack of entry of new firms producing essential intermediate inputs and complementary producer services. Potential coordination problem inherent in the economic development were analyzed, for example, by Murphy et. al. (1989), Matsuyama (1997) and Rodrik (1996).

[2] Matsuyama (1997) makes a similar point.

competitive by targeting different industries with their export promotion policies. The Korean government selectively promoted infant industries by means of investment subsidies and licensing of capital and technology inflows. According to Westphal (1982), the Korean government's promotion policies were characterized by highly flexible decision-making about which industries to promote and how to do so. Priorities at all levels were revised through continual monitoring of targeted industries. On several occasions, the government put aside its initial plans for promoting particular industries (e.g., heavy engineering and chemical industries) when additional information indicated that they would not achieve international competitiveness within a reasonable length of time.

In contrast to Korea, industrial targeting policies in Eastern European and Latin American countries were more ad hoc and were based on trial-and-error methods rather than a systematic search for the best alternative. For example, the governments of Mexico and Brazil in the 1970s and of Poland, Hungary and the Czech Republic in the early 1990s encouraged foreign direct investments in the vertically related segments of their auto manufacturing industries. A typical western car maker responded to this policy with a proposal to set up low-skilled labor-intensive kit assembly plants. The car makers intent was to initially produce for the relatively small local markets and to expand later into the markets of industrialized countries. In most cases, the car makers asked for tariff protection in return for their investments.

However, the carmakers' strategies often suffered due to local constraints. For instance, inventory controls, optimal scheduling and just in time supply parts delivery are extremely important factors in modern car assembly technology. Since these countries had no networks of maintenance and production parts suppliers, most parts sought by car manufacturers had to be shipped from abroad. At the same time the local infrastructure was extremely weak. This resulted in very slow and unreliable deliveries, which led to poor scheduling and underutilization of costly equipment. To overcome irregularity in the supply of parts assembly plants had to accumulate large inventories of parts, which resulted in very high overhead costs. Thus the productivity of both labor and capital were decreased and substantial work-in-process inventory generated interest charges that were higher than necessary. Consequently, Western automakers were unable to achieve high productivity in the labor-intensive downstream assembly operations. A few years after opening their assembly plants, multinational auto companies in Mexico and Brazil changed their strategies. A similar phenomenon can be observed these days in the strategies of carmakers in Hungary, Poland and the Czech Republic.

As part of the strategy shift, final assembly plants were complemented and sometimes substituted with a new generation of capital- and skilled-labor-intensive upstream technologies, which were less dependent on the infrastructure. Some companies ventured to build sophisticated stamping, body shop and engine production facilities, which were, at the time, considered, unsuited to the countries' low-skilled labor. Surprisingly, the match between these technologies and the labor in Latin America, and later in the countries of Eastern Europe, proved to be much better than expected. The most notable examples in Mexico are Ford's automotive engine plant in Chihuahua, built in 1983, which exports 90% of its output to the U.S., and Nissan's engine plant serving the company's U.S. car assemblers. In Eastern Europe, General Motors and Opel successfully operate an engine plant in Szentgotthard (Hungary), and Volkswagen is developing an engine facility near its Skoda plant in the Czech Republic.

In Eastern Europe, the promotion of foreign direct investment in automobile manufacturing industry was undertaken against the background of the policy of pursuing closer economic integration with the European Union. As a part of the Association Agreements with the EU, in 1994 Eastern European governments began to dismantle tariffs, which were initially granted to foreign car manufacturers that made direct investments. However, with relatively small demand in Eastern European markets, Western car makers found it impossible to increase sales to realize cost advantages through economies of scale and become profitable without tariff protection. On the other hand, Western car markets had very inelastic demand. Car sales there could only be increased if prices were reduced even further below the prices of cars assembled in the developed countries. But such price reductions were hardly possible because assembly plants in the region were much less productive than their Western European counterparts.

One way car manufacturers could reduce costs was to manufacture auto parts locally rather than to import them from West. In Eastern Europe, like in Mexico, the need to bring parts from abroad coupled with poor local infrastructure, inhibited the use of just-in-time inventory control methods and resulted in high overhead costs. This meant that auto plants in the region operated at a disadvantage compared to U.S. and Western European plants. The development of a local network of maintenance and production parts suppliers could have improved productivity. At the same time the skilled labor required for upstream auto manufacturing (e.g., the production of car engines) was abundant in the countries of Eastern Europe. While initially there were very few proposals from Western firms to develop projects in this segment of the auto industry, such proposals are now numerous. Many firms, which had already built assembly plants, are now offering to develop skilled-labor-intensive parts production.

In summary, the examples of Western car manufacturers in Latin America and in Eastern Europe point to the following *stylized fact*: In the course of their import substitution policies, governments promoted foreign investments into an auto assembly industry because it was believed that their countries' comparative advantage was in the production of low-skilled labor-intensive goods and in industries where the technology is static and simple to learn. Later it became clear that due to the specifics of car assembly operations, the advantages of low-cost labor could not compensate for the lack of good local infrastructure. While neither the governments nor Western multinationals expected that investments in capital-intensive upstream technologies would be successful, problems with the local infrastructure forced the multinationals to test these technologies in conjunction with the local labor. It turned out that upstream production of some supply parts, in particular car engines, was much more efficient than downstream assembly.

This new information changed the perceptions of governmental policy makers and auto firms' managers about what automotive production process can be most competitive in lesser developed countries. Now, the export flow of sophisticated components from developing and transition economies to industrialized countries is almost as large as the flow of assembled cars in the reverse direction. Thus, by *experimenting* with the promotion of foreign direct investments in different segments of the auto industry, Mexican, Brazilian and Eastern European governments *learned* that their nations were more competitive in manufacturing capital-intensive upstream products rather than in labor-intensive downstream assembly.

Motivated by these stylized facts this paper studies the effects of learning through experimentation in international trade policies. After analyzing characteristics of the industrial targeting policy of an optimally experimenting government, we consider the long-run pattern of specialization to which the country will converge as a result of such policy.

1.2. An Overview of Related Literature

The issue of optimal experimentation is not new in economics. There is extensive literature on optimal Bayesian learning in uncertain economic environments when an individual agent's action not only provides immediate reward, but also delivers information leading to the reduction of uncertainty. This information may be valuable for selecting future actions. For example, a monopolist faced with an uncertain demand curve may decide to produce so as to maximize expected current profits based on his current beliefs or to vary his output from period to period deliberately so as to accumulate information about the location of the demand curve. Rothschild (1974), McLennan (1984) and Aghion et al. (1991) study problems of this type.

The present work is closely related to models of optimal sequential investment decisions under uncertainty about the future payoffs. Weitzman (1979), Roberts and Weitzman (1981), Bernanke (1983), Dixit and Pindyck (1994) examine projects with sequential outlays using models that stress the trade-off between the costs of waiting for the arrival of new information and taking uninformed actions immediately.

Another strand of literature closely related to this work is based on rational expectations models. Blume and Easley (1984), Anderson and Sonnenschein (1982), Jordan (1985), Easley and Kiefer (1988), Banks and Sundaram (1992) explore conditions under which economies generate enough information to assure that optimally-acting agents eventually learn the true distributions of the stochastic shocks in the economy. This issue motivated the current study of the long-run results of government experimentation with targeting different industries. The main result of Section 6 of this paper is that for any set of targeted industries, we can determine whether a country will specialize in this set in the limit with positive or zero probability. Eventual specialization in a given industry occurs because the government always favors in its policy the same technology which was initially selected for the promotion. On the other hand, there will be technologies which survive the selection policy in the long run only with zero probability. With probability one the government will target these technologies only in finitely many periods and will never learn the true competitiveness of its country in these technologies because the government's posterior beliefs will be updated only a finite number of times.

The analysis in this paper draws on several themes in the literature on international trade. The problem of the government's experimentation with export promotion policies and infant industry protection is related to the literature analyzing export-oriented development strategies in Asia, Latin America and Easten Europe [Westphal (1982), Kuo (1983), Krueger (1985), Rodrik, (1995, 1996)].

Analyses of industrial targeting in earlier papers on 'strategic trade policy' were motivated by the recognition of the fact that government intervention can be welfare-enhancing when markets are characterized by imperfect competition, information asymmetries or leaning-by-doing. Papers by Brander and Spencer (1985), Spencer and Brander (1983), Krugman (1984) and Dixit and Grossman (1986) incorporate imperfect competition. Grossman and Horn (1988) and Bagwell and Staiger (1989) employ models of *adverse selection* to explore the possibility that infant-industry protection or export subsidies may be welfare-improving in the markets for experience goods, the quality of which can be learned only after the purchase. The issue of optimal design of trade policy in the absence of perfect information was also studied by Dinopoulos et al. (1995) who employed techniques from the literature on contracting under asymmetric information to examine the optimal industrial targeting when domestic firms have private knowledge of their learning economies. Hoff (1997) presented a two-period model that rationalized policy intervention as a means of overcoming informational barriers to entry.

Rodrik (1996) analyzes the potential coordination problem inherent in the economic development of middle-income countries that are well endowed with skilled labor but lack physical capital. Interdependence of investment and entry decisions in the upstream and downstream segments of vertically linked high technology industries imply that such countries may follow either a favorable high-tech high-income growth path or an unfavorable low-tech and low-income route. This interdependence creates a coordination problem, which the government may help to overcome by implementing policies stimulating private investments into specialized upstream producer services. Such policies will facilitate the transition of the economy from the bad equilibrium to the good one. The framework presented in this paper takes Rodrik's justification of the government's intervention into the private-sector investment decision as a starting point and analyzes the long-run implications of the process by which the government selects specific industries for promotion.

The problem faced by a government trying to allocate its limited targeting capacity to the industries with uncertain characteristics is directly related to a class of statistical problems studied under the general heading of multi-armed bandit (MAB) problems. The techniques developed to solve the MAB problems are the main methodology used in this paper to analyze how a government learns which industries are the best candidates for promotion.[3]

[3] The classical MAB framework considers a Bernoulli reward processes, or 'arms', with different unknown success probabilities. The arms are 'pulled' one at a time and the objective is to achieve a high overall success rate by selecting at each stage the next arm to be pulled on the basis of current information about the different probabilities for success. An optimal selection rule for the case of a two-armed bandit was discussed by Bellman (1956), however as recently

1.3. Organization of the Chapter

The chapter is organized as follows. Section 2 describes the government's decision problem, introducing the objective function, the specific sources of uncertainty, and the timing of decisions and realizations. Next, Section 3 gives an overview of the theoretical tools available to solve the multi-armed bandit problem and shows how they can be applied to the problem at hand. Section 4 discusses the properties of the dynamic allocation indices (Gittins indices) in the context of the present model and considers their economic implications for the government's targeting policy based on promoting the industries with the highest current index. This section shows how the main characteristics of an industry affect its Gittins index and thereby the chances of being selected for promotion by the government's optimal policy. Section 5 is concerned with the characterization of the targeting policy for a problem in which the government can promote more than one industry at each decision time. The concepts of asymptotic and turnpike optimality are introduced in this section to show that while the policy based on the Gittins index is no longer optimal, it is very close to the optimal policy in terms of its value and in terms of the actions it prescribes. In Section 6 the paper turns to the limit time behavior of the sequence of decisions on the promotion of a set of industries and characterizes the long-run pattern of specialization of a country. Section 7 concludes with a description of some open questions.

2. THE FRAMEWORK[4]

In order to explain the theoretical framework of this paper it is helpful to consider two countries, East and West. West has a set N of competitive industries ($i = 1,..., N$) with increasing marginal cost technologies. The technologies are employed by risk-neutral firms, which have total costs of producing output x defined by $TC_i^W = F_i + w^W \gamma_i^W x^2$ (although we may assume some other form of increasing marginal costs). γ_i^W is a non-negative productivity parameter denoting the quality of the match of technology i with

as the 1970s the derivation of such rule had been regarded as a challenge difficult to the point of hopelessness. The problem had essentially been solved by Gittins (see Gittins and Jones (1974) and Gittins (1989)) who showed that optimal strategies may be obtained by solving a family of stopping problems that associates with each arm an index. This index is known as the *dynamic allocation index,* or the *Gittins index.* Since then several authors considered the problem, in particular by Whittle (1980) and Berry and Fristedt (1985). Whittle (1981) extended the result of Gittins to the case of an 'arm-acquiring bandit,' i.e., when new arms arrive according to a stochastic process with known distribution of arrivals. Banks and Sundaram (1992) considered the case of a denumerable-armed (i.e., countably infinite-armed) bandit. Karatzas (1984) and Mandelbaum (1987) offered continuous-time formulations of the MAB problem.

[4] Readers interested in the proofs of the results that are omitted in the body of the paper can find them in the Appendix of Klimenko (1998).

labor in West[5]. The fixed cost F_i consists of capital and variable cost $w^W \gamma_i^W x^2$ consists of the wages w^W paid to hired labor. In competitive industries profits are equal to zero and therefore prices equal average costs. Because firms maximize profits, the industry price is also equal to marginal cost. Thus, by setting the average cost AC_i^W equal to the marginal cost MC_i^W,

$$\frac{F_i + w^W \gamma_i^W x^2}{x} = 2w^W \gamma_i^W x, \tag{2.1}$$

we can determine the equilibrium price $p_i^W = 2\left(F_i w^W \gamma_i^W\right)^{\frac{1}{2}}$ and output $x_i^W = \left(\frac{F_i}{w^W \gamma_i^W}\right)^{\frac{1}{2}}$ in industry i in West. We further assume that there exists a small country, East, where the wages are lower than in West: $w^W > w^E$. However, there is uncertainty as to how well technology i will match with the skills of local labor in East. This uncertainty is captured by the cost/productivity parameter $\tilde{\gamma}_i^E$, which can be either low (high productivity) with some unknown probability $\tilde{p}_i$ or high (low productivity) with probability $(1-\tilde{p}_i)$. The probability $\tilde{p}_i$ measures the quality of the match between technology i and local labor in East. The productivity parameter enters the total cost equation for a firm in industry i in East the same way as for a firm in a similar industry in West:

$$\widetilde{TC}_i^E = F_i + w^E \tilde{\gamma}_i^E x^2. \tag{2.2}$$

We assume that transportation costs are negligible, and that the market for good i is very small in East. Therefore it only makes sense to produce in East in order to sell in West. Since West is much larger than East, the terms of trade between the two countries are determined by the supply and demand conditions in West. If a firm in industry i decides to produce in East, it will have to sell its product at the price prevailing in West. Therefore, given the price in West, the output and the expected profit of a risk-neutral firm i producing in East can be determined from expected profit maximization equation:

[5] The framework of this paper is very similar to that of Jovanovic (1979), which describes a worker whose productivity depends on the unknown quality of the match between a worker's skills and a job's technology. The worker's compensation in each period is equal to her expected productivity. She updates the beliefs about the true match parameter and future wages at the current job after observing the output generated using the job's technology. The Jovanovic's interpretation of the turnover inspired this paper's treatment of the problem of a country's government trying to find an industry which has the best productivity match with the local economic environment and thereby ensure the country's specialization in the production of goods in which it has a comparative advantage.

$$\max_{x_i^E} E\left(\tilde{\Pi}_i^E\right) = \max_{x_i^E} E\left[2\left(F_i w^W \gamma_i^W\right)^{\frac{1}{2}} x_i^E - F_i - w^E \tilde{\gamma}_i^E x_i^{E2}\right]$$
$$= \max_{x_i^E}\left[2\left(F_i w^W \gamma_i^W\right)^{\frac{1}{2}} x_i^E - F_i - w^E \bar{\gamma}_i^E x_i^{E2}\right] \qquad (2.3)$$

where $\bar{\gamma}_i^E = E(\tilde{\gamma}_i^E) = E\left(\tilde{p}_i \gamma_i^{E\,low} + (1-\tilde{p}_i)\gamma_i^{E\,high}\right)$.

Thus, we assume that firms entering East make production plans based on their expectations of the quality of the match between their technologies and the Eastern labor. The planned output of a firm i in East is:

$$x_i^E = \frac{\left(F_i w^W \gamma_i^W\right)^{\frac{1}{2}}}{w^E \bar{\gamma}_i^E}. \qquad (2.4)$$

A firm with technology i makes an investment in East and operates its technology for one period to produce the targeted output defined in (2.4). At the end of the period, the firm observes its total cost and learns the realization of random variable $\tilde{\gamma}_i^E$. This information becomes public and the beliefs about $\tilde{p}_i$ are updated according to Bayes rule. The profit and the expected profit are given by

$$\tilde{\Pi}_i^E = F_i\left[\frac{w^W \gamma_i^W}{w^E \bar{\gamma}_i^E}\left(2 - \frac{\tilde{\gamma}_i^E}{\bar{\gamma}_i^E}\right) - 1\right] \text{ and, } E\left(\tilde{\Pi}_i^E\right) = F_i\left[\frac{w^W \gamma_i^W}{w^E \bar{\gamma}_i^E} - 1\right]. \qquad (2.5)$$

Suppose that n_i firms possessing technology i have applied to the Eastern government for a license to establish production facilities in East.[6] A firm with technology i would prefer to open a facility in East only if this allows it to make a non-negative profit from selling in West; otherwise, it would rather open a new facility in West where it would earn zero profit. We assume that the numbers n_i are small relative to the total number of firms in the industry i in West so that even if all n_i open facilities in East, this would not affect the Western competitive price.

6 The origin of these firms is irrelevant to the purpose of our model. These can be branches of Western firms, joint East-West ventures or Eastern firms which acquired Western technology. In the sequel we will focus on the case of Western firms relocating their production to the East by opening branch plants. With some modifications in assumptions the results of our model can be extended to new firms of local or joint (i.e., East-West) origin.

If $w^E \bar{\gamma}_i^E < w^W \gamma_i^W$, i.e., the expected marginal costs of producing in East are lower than the marginal costs of producing in West, then a firm from industry i has a positive expected profit from producing in East. The Eastern government can tax almost all of this profit by imposing a license fee or an investment tax. If production in East is characterized by expected loss, then in order to attract firms to East, the local government must offer subsidies equal to the expected loss.[7]

Following Brander and Spencer (1987), we assume that wages in East are fixed above the market clearing level. Therefore, some workers who would like to work at the going wage are unemployed. An aggregate labor market with a disequilibrium fixed wage might reasonably approximate, for our purposes, the complex structure that leads to unemployment in transition and developing economies. In the presence of unemployment, the welfare which East receives from the relocation of a firm i from West to East is a sum of the collected tax (or subsidy) and wages which are paid by the firm i to the newly employed local workers:

$$\tilde{W}_i^E = E\left(\tilde{\Pi}_i^E\right) + w^E \tilde{\gamma}_i^E \frac{F_i w^W \gamma_i^W}{\left(w^E \bar{\gamma}_i^E\right)^2} = F_i\left[\tilde{k}_i - 1\right], \tag{2.6}$$

where the dichotomous random variable $\tilde{k}_i$ can have two realizations:

$$k_i^{high} = \frac{w^W \gamma_i^W}{w^E \bar{\gamma}_i^E}\left(1 + \frac{\gamma_i^{E\,high}}{\bar{\gamma}_i^E}\right) \text{ and } k_i^{low} = \frac{w^W \gamma_i^W}{w^E \bar{\gamma}_i^E}\left(1 + \frac{\gamma_i^{E\,low}}{\bar{\gamma}_i^E}\right). \tag{2.7}$$

The Eastern government and potential entrants in industry i are assumed to have common beliefs about the unknown probability $\tilde{p}_i$ of a good match between technology i and Eastern labor. The match characteristic $\tilde{\gamma}_i^E$ as well as its function $\tilde{k}_i$ are Bernoulli random variables with unknown parameter $\tilde{p}_i$.

Given the prior expectation of the probability of the good match $\bar{p}_i$, the expected value $Ek_i(\tilde{p}_i) = k_i(\bar{p}_i) = \bar{p}_i k_i^{low} + (1 - \bar{p}_i)k_i^{high} = 2\frac{w^W \gamma_i^W}{w^E \bar{\gamma}_i^E}$ can be interpreted as a

[7] To avoid the time inconsistency problem of the 'obsolescing bargain' (see Brander and Spencer (1987)) in which the relative bargaining power of the government and the firm change systematically over the life of an agreement, we assume that the Eastern government can credibly precommit itself to the announced level of investment tax or subsidy. Therefore, the Eastern government in our model does not exploit the change in the relative bargaining position arising after a firm has incurred the sunk costs.

measure of comparative advantage of East in industry *i*.[8] Hence, a welfare-maximizing, risk-neutral government has the immediate expected reward function:

$$\overline{W}_i(\overline{p}_i) = F_i\left[k_i(\overline{p}_i) - 1\right] = F_i\left[2\frac{w^W \gamma_i^W}{w^E \overline{\gamma}_i^E} - 1\right]. \qquad (2.8)$$

Finally, the following assumption is made about the nature of the process of targeting the new industries for promotion. The Eastern government has the capacity to license at most K new firms from K different industries at a time. This can be explained by a two tier structure of the selection process. Each tier is endowed with a limited amount of a critical resource required for the evaluation of industries and making a decision on which of them to develop in East by attracting a firm with the appropriate technology. The lower tier consists of N agencies responsible for the expert evaluation of each of the N technologies. These agencies act as parallel servers for N independent queues. At every moment of time each agency has enough capacity to evaluate at most one potential entrant in the corresponding industry. After N firms from N distinct industries have been selected at the lower tier, the next decision is adopted at the single interindustry agency of the higher tier. This agency has the capacity to evaluate and select at most K firms (K N) from N passed up from the lower tier. For example, the higher tier agency may be a finance ministry which determines on the basis of technological evaluations of the lower tier agencies the size of the tax or the subsidy for the potential entrants from N industries.

The Eastern government, using its two-tier decision structure, will try to allocate its targeting capacity[9] to those technologies which would allow it to maximize the total expected welfare from the entry of selected firms. If the capacity K of the Eastern government allows it to register firms from more than one industry at a time, then we would define the set of industries targeted at time t as the *set of leading sectors* S_t. Given the described decision making process, S_t includes firms from K different industries, one firm from each industry.

[8] This measure of comparative advantage reflects not only the competitiveness of East in industry i but also incorporates the welfare gains through the wages paid by a firm i to the workers in the East. The true measure of competitiveness of country East in industry i is the ratio of the average cost of producing the good i in the East to the expected average cost of producing the same good in West.

[9] The terms targeting, licensing, sanctioning and registration capacity will be used interchangeably. Each of them reflects East's limited ability per unit of time to accommodate the entry of firms with new technologies.

3. Sequential Selection of Industries and the Multi-Armed Bandit

This sections characterizes the optimal pattern of attracting the industries to East by the government that wants to maximize its total expected welfare from all investments made by Western firms beginning to produce in East.

The Eastern government's task of maximizing the discounted flow of welfare rewards while looking for industries which have the best match with local labor can be formulated as a 'multi-armed bandit' (MAB) problem. In statistical decision theory the MAB framework describes a type of Markov decision problem that deals with the issue of finding the optimal strategy for a gambler who plays against a gambling machine with N independent arms[10] and can pull K arms at each time. K is referred to as the capacity of the gambler. The reward which the gambler receives for pulling an arm is a random variable which is a function of a stochastically evolving state.[11]

The state variable in the context of industrial targeting is the posterior distribution of the probability of a good match for a firm with technology i. In the Bernoulli case with the dichotomous match characteristic which is assumed in this paper[12] the state variable for industry i at time t is summarized by the number s of realizations of the good match which have taken place in the first t-1 trials.[13]

In this paper the prior beliefs about the probability of high reward $\widetilde{p}_i$ (i.e., the quality of technology i) are represented by the beta probability density function with the parameters (r,n):

---

[10] Historically the first application of the MAB models was in clinical trials where the problem was usually described in terms of sequentially assigning patients to one of N independent treatments.

[11] The discrete-time version of the MAB problem in which the gambler can pull only one arm at a time (K = 1) has received considerable attention beginning with the seminal work of Gittins and Jones (1974) and Whittle (1980). They prove that if the state of the arms evolve in a Markovian fashion, it is possible to associate each arm with a function of its state, now called the Gittins index, such that the gambler can optimize the total discounted reward by sequentially engaging the arms with the maximal current Gittins index. These ideas are extended by Varaiya et. al. (1985) and Mandelbaum (1986) who have relaxed the assumption about the Markovian structure of reward by allowing arbitrary reward processes. Mandelbaum (1986) also provides a very elegant formulation of the problem as one of controlling a process with multidimensional time parameter. Karatzas (1984), Epplet (1986) and Mandelbaum (1987) also offer continuous-time formulations of the problem and prove that the Gittins index strategy of pulling the arm with maximal current index is optimal in continuous time as well as in discrete time. The main significance of the Gittins index result is that it allows to decompose the N-dimensional control problem into N one-dimensional problems.

[12] In another set-up the task may be to identify the true mean of a normal random variable. The decision maker is uncertain about the *mean* and perceives it as a *random variable* having a continuous distribution with unknown mean and known variance.

[13] This is because the number of successes in a given number of trials is a *sufficient statistic* for the Bernoulli reward process.

$$f(p_i) = \frac{1}{B(r,n)} p_i^{r-1}(1-p_i)^{n-r-1}$$

where $B(r,n) = \int_0^1 t^{r-1}(1-t)^{n-r-1}dt$. Therefore, after any sequence of n' trials (n' new entries of firms with technology i in East) with r' successes (r' realizations of good match), the posterior beliefs will be the beta distribution with parameters $(r+r', n+n')$. The mean and the variance of any beta distribution with parameters (r,n) is $\overline{p} = \frac{r}{n}$ and $v = \frac{\frac{r}{n}(1-\frac{r}{n})}{n+1}$, respectively.[14]

Using these properties of the beta p.d.f. one can simplify the notation by identifying the state $x_j(t)$ of the random reward process with the mean of the posterior beta probability distribution represented as the ratio of the number of successes to the total number of trials. Therefore, the state variable after n' new entries of firms with technology i in East is defined by

$$x_i(t) = \frac{r+r'}{n+n'}.$$

If the number of potential Western investors with technology j into the Eastern economy were unlimited, then, assuming that the prior distribution of p is uniform, the process $\{x_j(t), t \geq 1\}$ is a Markov chain on the state space $X_j = \{r/n, r = 1, 2, \ldots; n = 2, 3, \ldots\}$. When the number of firms with technology j wishing to invest in East is limited by n_j, the state variable evolves according to a finite state Markov chain with an absorbing state corresponding to entry of all Western firms which wanted to operate in East with technology j.[15]

The indicator control variable $\Delta u_i(t)$ is equal to one if the government allocates its targeting capacity to industry i by sanctioning an entry of a firm with technology i at time t. $\Delta u_i(t)$ is zero if no Western firm is given a license to enter industry i in East at time t.

The process of industrial targeting is formalized by an allocation strategy which is an N-valued stochastic process denoted by $u(t)=\{u_1(t), u_2(t), \ldots, t \geq 0\}$. Its i-th coordinate denotes the cumulative number of new Western firms licensed in industry i in East by the end the first t 'clock time' intervals of implementing this strategy, $u_i(t) = \sum_{s=1}^{t} \Delta u_i(s)$.

---

[14] Assuming that prior distribution of p is uniform $U[0,1]$, this is equivalent to the beta distribution with the parameters (1,2) and the mean 1/2. After a successful trial the mean of the posterior beliefs becomes 2/3, etc.

[15] The absorbing state for industry j can be thought of as a state in which the Eastern government receives a deterministic welfare reward equal to zero at every period after all the firms in this industry have already entered the East.

The random vector $u(t)$ can be viewed as an 'investment time' parameter that satisfies the following properties:

$$t = \sum_{i=1}^{N} u_i(t); \tag{3.1a}$$

$$\{u(t) \leq s\} \in F(s),\ s \in S \tag{3.1b}$$

where S is a set equipped with the partial order $r = (r_1,...r_N) \leq s = (s_1,...s_N)$ iff $r_i \leq s_i$, $i = 1,...N$; and $F(s)$, is a sigma algebra representing information about the quality of the match between Eastern labor and technologies $i = 1,...,N$ after the entry of $s = (s_1,...s_N)$ foreign firms equipped with these technologies.

After $u_i(t) = u$ investments the beliefs about the quality of technology i evolve into the state $x_i(u)$ and conditional on these beliefs allowing one more entry into industry i gives the government the expected reward $\overline{W}_i(x_i(u))$ defined by (3.5). After observing the realization of this reward consisting of the tax and wages paid to Eastern workers the government updates its beliefs about the unknown probability of the good match, and the state becomes $x_i(u+1)$. The accumulated rewards are discounted by a factor β.

The stochastic reward process associated with licensing entry of foreign firms in industry i is defined as

$$\widetilde{W}_i(x_i) := \left\{\widetilde{W}_i(x_i(u)), F_i(u-1)\right\}_{u=1}^{\infty} \tag{3.2}$$

For a state of the posterior beliefs $x_i(u)$, the reward $\widetilde{W}_i(x_i(u))$, is a $F_i(u-1)$-measurable random variable reflecting the fact that the government's knowledge about technology i is determined by the number of foreign firms u which entered industry i in East.[16]

Thus, the government having the capacity to target up to K industries at each time solves the following problem:

---

[16] $F_i(u_i(-1))$ is the sigma algebra generated by the prior distribution of the probability of the good match between the technology i and the Eastern labor. Furthermore, we assume that information is never forgotten by the policy makers which is formally defined by $F_i(u-1) \subseteq F_i(u)$ and $F_i(\infty) := \sigma\left(\bigcup_{u=1}^{\infty} F_i(u)\right)$ $\forall\ i = 1,...,N, \forall u = 0,1,2,...$. Since the productivities of different technologies in the East are independent, so are the σ-algebras $F_i(\infty)$.

$$\max_{\{\Delta u(t)\}_{t=1}^{\infty}} E\sum_{i=1}^{N}\sum_{t=0}^{\infty}\beta^t\widetilde{W}_i(x_i(u_i(t)))\Delta u_i(t)$$

$$\begin{aligned}&\text{s.t. almost surely} \sum_{i=1}^{N}\Delta u_i(t)\leq K,\\ &\qquad \Delta u_i(t)\in\{0,1\},\\ &\qquad \Delta u_i(t)\text{ is } \sigma\left(\bigcup_{i=1}^{N}F_i(u_i(t-1))\right)\text{- measurable}\\ &\qquad i=1,\ldots,N \text{ and } t=0,1,\ldots\end{aligned} \tag{3.3}$$

The last constraint in (3.3) is the clock time information constraint: an assignment of K available licenses to different industries at time t must be based on information available from the actions taken by time t-1.

The sequence of vectors $\{\Delta u(t)\}_{t=0}^{\infty}$ represents the choice of industries which are targeted as time progresses by sanctioning entry of foreign firms with respective technologies so as to maximize the expected total discounted welfare. In choosing between a firm with a technology in which East is believed to have a comparative advantage (i.e., the one which has high r/n) and a firm from an industry in which it has little experience (and so a poor estimate of a true probability of the good match), the government experiences a conflict. From the point of view of immediate expected yield, it would be better to sanction an investment by the first firm. However, if long term performance is important (i.e., the discount factor is not too small), it may be preferable to test the second industry which has a chance of having a higher productivity than the first. Therefore, from the long-term point of view, the acquisition of additional information may be worth more than the immediate yield, i.e., experimentation may be justified.

In the context of our model, the limit of the sequence of partial sums $E\sum_{i=1}^{N}\sum_{t=0}^{\infty}\beta^t\widetilde{W}_i(x_i(u_i(t)))\Delta u_i(t)$ denotes the expected stream of investment tax revenues received by the Eastern government and wages paid out to Eastern workers employed at the new plants[17]. The Gittins indices $M_i(x_i(u))$, also known as the dynamic allocation indices (DAI), for the reward sequences $\widetilde{W}_i(x_i(u))$ represent the guaranteed rewards which make the options of continuing the targeting of industry i and of stopping the promotion of that industry (with the retirement reward $M_i(x_i(u))$) equally attractive. The following formulation of the Gittins index is due to Mandelbaum (1986) who showed that, under certain conditions, the essential supremum in (3.4) is attained by a positive F_i-measurable 'investment' stopping time,

[17] To ensure the existence of the sequence's limit, we assume that expected total discounted reward from targeting any of the industries is finite: $E\sum_{u=1}^{\infty}\beta^u\left|\widetilde{W}_i(x_i(u))\right|<\infty$ for all i.

$$M_i(x_i) = ess\sup_{\tau>0} \frac{E\left\{\sum_{u=0}^{\tau-1} \beta^u \tilde{W}_i(x_i(u)) \middle| x_i(0)=x_i\right\}}{E\left\{\sum_{u=0}^{\tau-1} \beta^u \middle| x_i(0)=x_i\right\}}. \tag{3.4}$$

Since *ess sup* is attained it is replaced by *max* in the rest of this paper. When the government is constrained to target only one industry at a time (K=1), the Gittins index strategy prescribing to target the industry with the greatest current index is optimal for the problem (3.3). Formally, the optimal strategy is define by

$$u(t+1)=u(t)+e_i \text{ if } M_i(x_i(u_i(t))) = \max_{1\leq j\leq N}\{M_j(x_j(u_j(t)))\} \tag{3.5}$$

where e_i is the i-th unit vector.

The index for any uncertain technology i is equal to the expected immediate reward with an upward adjustment reflecting the possibility of resolving uncertainty about the future rewards by selecting this technology. Thus, the learning component of the index is defined to be the difference between the index itself and expected immediate reward. For two technologies with the same expected immediate rewards, the learning component should be larger for the technology in which the reward rate is more uncertain and therefore the value of new information is greater. This is analogues to increasing values of stock options when underlying stock variability increases.

4. The Optimal Selection of Technologies

In this section we analyze the optimal targeting strategy of the Eastern government when its targeting capacity is limited to one industry at a time (K=1). The government's experimentation with different technologies in search of the industries in which its country has the greatest comparative advantage is different from the gambler's task in the classical MAB problem in one important respect. While the gambler is always assumed to pull at least one arm, the Eastern government has an option not to promote any of the technologies available in West if it believes that East would not have sufficient comparative advantage in any of them. More formally, the government in our problem can opt to terminate the process altogether and then receive a guaranteed zero reward every unit of time after termination. To take this into account, we adapt the MAB problem to the purpose of our analysis by allowing the government to set the control variable $\Delta u_i(t) = 0$ for all N reward processes rather than to only $N-1$ processes, like it is done in conventional MAB problems.

If one assumes that all foreign investors want to invest in East in only one industry i, the government's problem is to find the optimal stopping time for a Markov chain which describes the evolution of the state variable $\{x_i(t),\ t\geq 1\}$. The initial state of the Markov chain $x_i(0) = r/n$ corresponds to beta (r, n) prior distribution of the probability of a good match between local labor and the foreign technology, $\tilde{p}_i$. As time progresses the state variable is determined by the parameters of the posterior beta distribution. If the new entry occurs when the state of beliefs is *r/n*, then it brings to East the expected reward $\overline{W}_i(r/n)$. At anytime the government can stop the Western firms' entry forever by setting $\Delta u_i(t) = 0$ and then collect deterministic zero reward at each period after stopping.[18] Thus, the government's problem is to find the stopping time τ that maximizes

$$E\left\{\sum_{t=0}^{\tau-1} \beta^t \tilde{W}_i(x_i(t)) + \sum_{t=\tau}^{\infty} \beta^t \cdot 0 \middle| x_i(0) = x_i \right\} \tag{4.1}$$

Proposition 1: *The optimal time for the government to stop investments in industry i is determined by*

$$\tau^* = \min\{t \geq 0 : M_i(x_i(t)) \leq 0\} \tag{4.2}$$

where $M_i(x_i(t))$ is the Gittins index for industry i as defined by 4.7.

Proposition 1 has an important implication for the case when there are Western firms willing to invest in more than one industry in East. Given the assumption that the government can apply controls $\Delta u_i(t) = 0$ to all industries at the same time and continue receiving deterministic zero reward each period thereafter, the government will stop entry by new firms in all industries if the Gittins index for each of them is non-positive. In this case, non-action is preferred to the experimentation

The government's right to license new foreign firms has option-like qualities. Every registration of a new firm in industry *i* in East can be viewed by the government as exercising a call option. The striking price here is zero because we assume that the licensing per se has a very small cost to the government and therefore any new firm which is expected to bring positive welfare to East is "in the money". The difference from a typical call option is that the price of the "underlying stock" (i.e., the welfare reward from licensing one more firm with technology *i*) is revealed in our case at every decision time not exogenously by the market, but rather endogenously from the actions of the government testing the unknown technology. To arrive at the moment of decision about registering the *k*-th firm in industry *i*, the government has to accumulate all positive or negative welfare rewards associated with registering the $k-1$ preceding firms.

The optimal policy for the Eastern government is at each stage to license a firm in the industry which has the highest index $M_i(x_i)$ greater than zero. If $M_i(x_i)$ is equal to zero for all *i*, then there are no technologies in the set *N* which are worth developing in East given

[18] Simple logic shows that it is never optimal to interrupt the investment process for a few periods and then resume it again.

both the priors about the comparative advantage of East in these industries and possible learning through experimentation with firms in these industries.[19]

Table 1 summarizes a numerical example of the index-based targeting policy of the Eastern government that can select every period one of the three industries A, B, C for targeted promotion[20]. The government is assumed to have uniform (i.e., beta (1,2)) priors on the probability of a good match for all technologies. The number of Western firms willing to start producing in East is n for all industries, i.e., $n_i = n$, $i = 1, 2, ..., N$. By setting $k_i^{high} - k_i^{low} = 1$ for any i, the variance of comparative advantage is normalized to be the same for all technologies, i.e., $Var(k_i(\tilde{p}_i)) = \frac{1}{12}(k_i^{high} - k_i^{low})^2 = \frac{1}{12}$, $i = 1, 2, ..., N$. Note that under such normalization the difference in variability of welfare reward among technologies is entirely determined by the sunk costs F_i.

Table 1: An Example of Calculation of the Gittins Indices

Industries i	F_i *\$ million*	$k_i(1/2)$	$\overline{W}_i(1/2)$ *\$ million*	$M_i(1/2)$		
				n_i=2	n_i=3	n_i=4
A	10	1.1	1	5.82	6.36	6.73
B	50	0.98	-1	5.09	8.89	9.21
C	100	0.95	-5	0	5.77	10.63

In Table 1, the index $M_i(1/2)$ is increasing in n_i, i.e., the number of Western firms wishing to obtain a license to invest in East. The increase of the index in n_i is similar to the increase in the value of the regular call option with the time to maturity: the government can try more firms with a given technology and wait until more information accumulates about the true level of comparative advantage of East in the corresponding industry.

When the number of firms available for experimentation is sufficiently large ($n_i' \geq 4$), higher sunk costs, F_i, lead to a higher index regardless of whether the immediate reward is positive or negative. This shows that the larger the size of the government's 'bet', the more valuable the information gained by additional experimenting. As one can see from

---

[19] If $M_i(r'/n') = 0$ for all i, then choosing control $\Delta u_i(t)$=1 for all i is equivalent to applying control $\Delta u_i(t)$=0 to any of the existing processes and at the same time setting control $\Delta u_i(t)$ to some hypothetical process $\tilde{W}_j(x_j(t))$ which always yields reward zero with certainty. But this is simply equivalent to stopping the whole "multi-armed" process.

[20] Beale (1979), Chen and Katehakis (1986), Varaiya et. al. (1985) and Yoshida (1993) have described algorithms to compute the indices for reward processes evolving according to the finite state Markov chains. We followed an algorithm described by Beale (1979) to calculate the indices for three technologies in the example summarized in Table 1.

the immediate rewards and the indices for projects B and C, the value of the additional information gained through learning can sometimes outweigh a large immediate expected loss.

Under the assumption that $k_i^{high} - k_i^{low} = 1$, the variance of welfare reward is given by

$$Var\left(\tilde{W}_i(r/n)\right) = F_i^2 \frac{(1 - r/n)r/n}{n+1}, \; i = 1, 2, ..., N. \tag{4.3}$$

This suggests that both an increase in F_i and an increase in the uncertainty about the quality of the match between the foreign technology and local labor as measured by the variance of the beta (r, n) random variable, $\frac{(1-r/n)r/n}{n+1}$, lead to an increase in the variance of welfare reward and thereby an increase in the value of experimentation. Therefore, $M_i(r/n)$ should be increasing in the variance of reward very much like the value of the call option is increasing the variance of the underlying stock. The following proposition summarizes the properties of the index which play an important role in the sequel.

Proposition 2: *The dynamic allocation index $M_i(r/n)$ in the government's decision problem is a non-negative function continuously increasing in F_i and increasing in the variance of the match quality parameter p_i. For industry i with n_i potential Western entrants, the index $M_i(r/n)$ is increasing in n_i.*

Figure 1 provides the graphic illustration of the analytical advantage that can be gained by using the Gittins dynamic allocation index (DAI) in this model. It is assumed again that initial beliefs about the probability of a good match between labor and technology are the same in all industries, with priors on the probability of a good match given by the p.d.f. beta (1,2). The measure of variation in comparative advantage, $k_i^{high} - k_i^{low}$ equals unity[21], and the number of firms willing to invest in East, n_i, is sufficiently large and assumed to be the same for all industries. Thus, industries differ only in terms of the required sunk costs, F_i, and the expected comparative advantage coefficient under the uniform priors, $\bar{k}_i(1/2)$. A finite or countably infinite number of industries is assumed to be uniformly spread within the area N on Figure 1 which also shows a number of iso-welfare and iso-DAI curves.

[21] Since any realization of the coefficient of comparative advantage is non-negative (i.e., k_i^{high}, $k_i^{low} \geq 0$), the assumption that $k_i^{high} - k_i^{low} = 1$ imposes a constraint that $\bar{k}_i(1/2) \geq 1/2$. A technology i with $\bar{k}_i(1/2) = 1/2$ must have $k_i^{high} = 1$ which means that even under the most optimistic posterior beliefs beta (r,n), the welfare from registering a firm with such technology is not positive. Hence, when $\bar{k}_i(1/2) = 1/2$ we have $M_i(r/n) = 0$ for any posterior beliefs beta (r,n).

Figure 1: Iso-Welfare and Iso-DAI Curves for the State Beta (1,2).

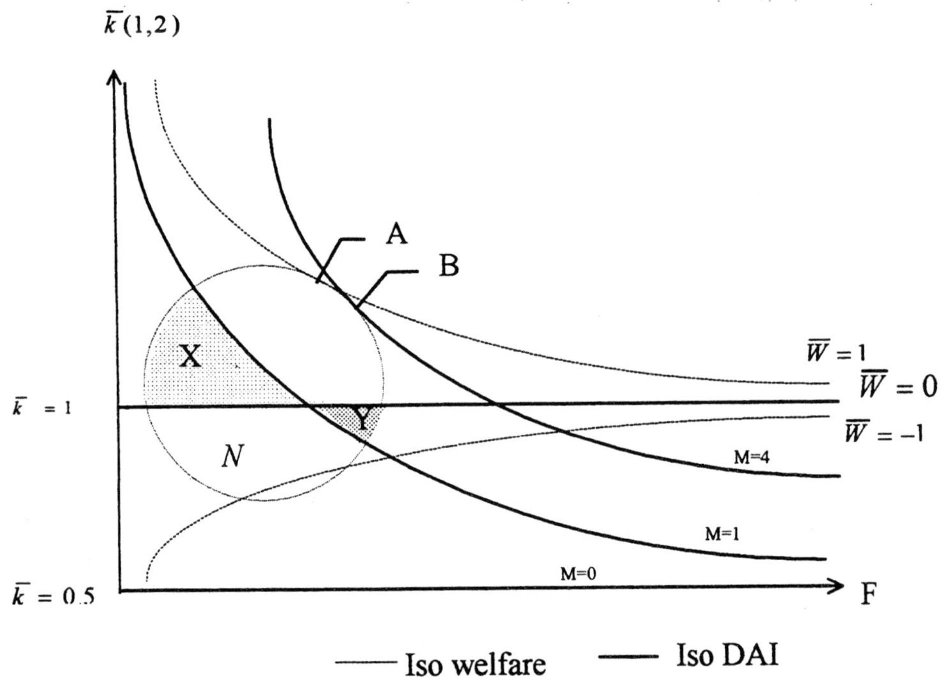

As shown in Figure 1, the Eastern government would prefer industry A to industry B according to the myopic criterion of maximizing immediate expected reward but not according to the index policy criterion. One can clearly see that, depending on the shape of the "cloud" of industries *N*, there are industries which yield negative expected welfare (industries in the area Y) and in which East does not have any comparative advantage. However, these industries might get priority under the government's targeting policy over the industries in the area X which yield positive immediate welfare. One can also infer from Figure 1 that according to the index criterion and contrary to the myopic criterion, large sunk costs *F* always make an industry more attractive to develop because they have a larger variance of reward and, therefore, a larger Gittins index.

As the number of potential entrants n_i in the industry *i* increases (for example with the size of the industry in West) the scope for experimentation also increases, and this leads to a higher dynamic allocation index. As n_i goes to one, the Gittins index converges to the immediate reward. Based on this one can hypothesize that a large industry which tends to have a larger number of potential entrants in East is likely to be on the top of the industrial policy priority list of the Eastern government even when prior information indicates that East does not have a comparative advantage in that industry.

For example, in the automobile industry the efficiency scale of upstream components manufacturing is larger than the efficiency scale of downstream assembly operations. Therefore the downstream segment of automobile manufacturing is dispersed among many assembly plants while the upstream components segment is represented by relatively few independent production units each of which produces a substantial portion of the segment's output. This may be one of the reasons why in less developed and transitional economies the risk averse Western firms initially were more willing to set up kit automobile assembly plants rather than build component plants.

Since there were many offers by Western firms to build relatively small assembly plants, the governments of the host countries had a lot of room to experiment with how well this segment of the auto industry was suited to their economies. This may explain why Eastern European governments welcomed the automobile assembly firms by creating very favorable entry conditions for them even though there were many other alternative products which Eastern Europe is believed to be able to produce more cheaply, if equipped with corresponding Western technologies. One of these alternatives is the car engine industry which is not as crowded as the automobile assembly and has a much smaller number of firms willing to establish production facilities in Eastern Europe. Thus, even though the prior beliefs were such that the countries of Eastern Europe should have chosen to specialize in engines rather than assembly if they wanted to maximize their immediate welfare gains, the long-run learning considerations led to the initial specialization in automobile assembly which brought lower immediate payoff.

5. THE TARGETING OF MULTIPLE INDUSTRIES

In this section we briefly consider the implications of relaxing the constraint on the number industries which the government can simultaneously target for promotion. Unfortunately, the optimal strategy for a version of the targeting problem in which the policy maker can at each time select up to $K > 1$ industries cannot be described in terms of the Gittins indices. It is known that for the multi-armed bandit problem, the policy of selecting the arms with the K largest indices may be suboptimal.

This version of the MAB problem belongs to the class of *NP*-complete problems which are characterized by the extreme computational complexity of finding an optimal strategy and usually solved by enumerative methods such as the branch-and-bound method. However, a computationally simple heuristic whose performance is arbitrarily close to optimal often exists even in those cases in which the problem of finding an optimal solution has been proved *NP*-hard. For example, Whittle (1988) conjectured and Weber and Weiss (1990) proved that in most cases the index policy provides a very good heuristic for the solution of multi-armed bandit problems in which a gambler can pull more than one arm at a time.

When the discount factor approaches one the Gittins index priority policy for the MAB problem with $K > 1$ provides a heuristic which in the long run is almost optimal both in terms of the value of this policy and in terms of the actions it prescribes. The first of these two results was proved by Ishikida and Varaiya (1994) who addressed the issue of asymptotic optimality of the Gittins index priority policy for $K > 1$. In our previous work[22] we proved the validity of the second result by showing that in the long run the fraction of decision times during which the prescription of the index policy contravenes the prescriptions of the optimal policy is zero[23]. Therefore, by following the Gittins index heuristic over a long time horizon the policy maker will be using optimal actions most of the time.

In the context of optimal industrial targeting, asymptotic optimality and turnpike optimality of the Gittins index heuristic suggest that the government, which has the targeting capacity $K > 1$, can solve satisfactorily a problem for which the optimal solution is intractable. The need for consideration of near optimality (ε-optimality) rather than "full" optimality in optimal learning problems was demonstrated by Easley and Kiefer (1989). We follow their example (although in a different context) and assume in modeling the government's industrial targeting policy that the decision maker uses an almost optimal and simple index strategy rather than the computationally complex optimal strategy.

6. The Long-Run Industrial Structure and Stochastic Survival of Technologies

This section develops a characterization of the set of industries in which the Eastern government will specialize in the long-run if its policy of selecting firms from different industries at every decision time t is governed by the index policy as defined above. To do this we analyze the stochastic properties of the process of selection of firms by the government. Similar issue was studied by Banks and Sundaram (1992). They analyzed the multi-armed bandit framework in which the arms can be of a finite number of types and the gambler has the capacity to pull only a single arm at a time. The techniques used here closely parallel that approach.

Suppose that at each time t there is a priority ordering of the available technologies $I(t) = (1_t, 2_t, \ldots, N_t)$ which ranks the them by the size of their indices $M_{1_t}(x_{1_t}(t)) \geq M_{2_t}(x_{2_t}(t)) \geq \ldots \geq M_{N_t}(x_{N_t}(t))$.

Then the *set of leading sectors* (i.e., the set of industries targeted at time t by registering new firms in these industries) is formally defined by $S_t = \{j_t : j_t \leq K\}$.

Now we relax the assumption that firms with specific technologies can only come in limited numbers from West. Instead we assume that after all n_i Western firms from

---

[22] See Klimenko (1998).

[23] The derivation of this result was inspired by Weiss' work (1992, 1994) on optimal scheduling of stochastic jobs on parallel servers. Borrowing from his terminology the present paper refers to this result as the *turnpike optimality* of the Gittins index heuristic for the MAB problem. The exact result which Weiss (1992) refers to as turnpike optimality is that the Gittins index heuristic takes optimal action most of the time as the number of arms becomes infinite.

industry i have established production in East, East "learns" to generate copies of technology i internally, i.e., firms with the same technology can emerge in unlimited numbers in East. However, we retain the assumption that Eastern demand for products manufactured in industry i is very small. Therefore, all new firms in that industry in East produce in order to sell in the larger Western market where the competitive price is not driven down by the emergence of new suppliers because the demand is growing at the same rate as the supply. Therefore, the prices, the expected profits or losses of new firms, and the expected welfare of the Eastern government are the same as in Section 2[24].

The initial set of leading sectors S_0 consists of industries with the K highest indices given the prior beliefs

$$\bar{p}_i^0 = \frac{r_i}{n_i},\ i = 1, 2, ..., N. \text{ Let } m^* = \sup_{j \in N \setminus S_0} M_j(\bar{p}_j^0) \cdot \tag{6.1}$$

Define $\bar{p}_i^\tau$ to be the posterior probability of the good match between the technology i and Eastern labor at time τ. Then the set of leading sectors will remain unchanged by time t (i.e., $S_0 = S_1 = ... = S_t$) if the beliefs about the quality of match updated after every new entry, $\bar{p}_i^\tau$, satisfy the inequality $M_i(\bar{p}_i^\tau) \geq m^*, i \in S_0$ for $\tau = 1, 2, ..., t$. To analyze which industries remain in the set S_t in the long-run, i.e., as time t goes to infinity, we will try to characterize the probability distribution of the number of periods during which the above inequality remains valid.

To eliminate the trivial cases, we assume that the set N contains only "competitive" technologies, implying that for each technology i in N, the random quality parameter of match includes in its support such an outcome which allows i to "overtake" by some time τ other technologies and be included in the set of leading sectors S_τ under some vector of posterior probabilities of the good match $\bar{p}^\tau = (\bar{p}_1^\tau, ..., \bar{p}_N^\tau)$. Therefore, under this condition even those technologies which were not included in S_t under one vector of beliefs still have a chance of eventually getting into this set if the technologies which are currently in S_t perform in an unsatisfactory way and the beliefs about their quality deteriorate. Formally, this condition is determined by:

$$\bigcap_{i \in N} \left[E\left(\tilde{W}_i \middle| \bar{p}_i = 0\right)\ E\left(\tilde{W}_i \middle| \bar{p}_i = 1\right) \right] \neq \varnothing \tag{6.2}$$

---

[24] It is also assumed that the set N of available technologies is such that it makes sense for the government to experiment with any of them; that is we rule out the situation when the support of a random productivity parameter can yield negative (positive) expected welfare even under the most optimistic (pessimistic) beliefs about the quality of match with the local labor. More formally, we rule out the technologies for which $E\left(\tilde{W}_i \middle| \bar{p}_i = 1\right) < 0$ $\left(E\left(\tilde{W}_i \middle| \bar{p}_i = 0\right) > 0\right)$, where $\bar{p}_i$ is the expected probability of a good match.

The support of the random variable $\widetilde{\gamma}_i$ is denoted by $\Gamma_i = \left\{\gamma_i^{low},\ \gamma_i^{high}\right\}$, $i \in S_o$. The two outcomes in the support correspond to the realizations of the productivity parameter $\widetilde{\gamma}_i$ under the good and bad match between local labor and technology i.

The sequences of realizations of high and low productivity after t consecutive entries of new firms in industry i are the elements of the t-fold Cartesian product of Γ_i denoted by $\Gamma_i^t = \times_{\tau=1}^{t} \Gamma_i$. Then for each technology $i \in S_o$ and each true probability p_i of high realization of productivity, the probability of observing a specific sequence $\gamma_i^t = (\gamma_{i1},...,\gamma_{it}) \in \Gamma_i^t$ of γ_i^{low} and γ_i^{high} is defined by $Prob\left(\widetilde{\gamma}_{ik} = \gamma_{ik}, k \le t \middle| p_i\right) = p_i^s (1-p_i)^{t-s}$, where $s = \sum_{k=1}^{t} \mathbf{1}_{\{\widetilde{\gamma}_{ik} = \gamma_{ik}^{low}\}}$ is the number of high productivity realizations after t entries of firms in the industry i. Then the industry i will still remain in the initial set of leading sectors S_o for at least t periods if the sequence of beliefs $\left\{\overline{p}_i^{\tau}\right\}_{\tau=1}^{t}$, derived according to the Bayes rule from a sequence of realizations of productivity $\gamma_{i1},...,\gamma_{it}$ and from the prior belief $\overline{p}_i^0 = \frac{r_i}{n_i}$, satisfies the inequalities $M_i(\overline{p}_i^{\tau}) \ge m^*$, $\tau = 1, 2, ..., t$.

Denote by $\mathcal{D}_i^t$ the set of all t-element vectors of realizations of productivity after registering t consecutive firms in industry i, such that after these realizations the industry i still remains in the initial set of leading sectors S_o. Clearly, $\mathcal{D}_i^t \subset \Gamma_i^t$. Then the probability that industry i will still be in the set S_o by time t given that the true probability of high productivity (good match) is p_i is defined by

$$Q_{p_i}(t) = \int_{\mathcal{D}_i^t} P\left(\gamma_i^t \middle| p_i\right) d\gamma_i^t . \tag{6.3}$$

Therefore the probability that the set S_o consisting of K industries characterized by the vector of the true probabilities of high reward $p=(p_1,..., p_K)$ will remain unchanged by time t is given by

$$Q_{\mathbf{p}}^{S_0}(t) = \prod_{i \in S_0} Q_{p_i}(t) \tag{6.4}$$

Define $U_{p_i} = \lim_{t \to \infty} Q_{p_i}(t)$ to be the probability that technology i will remain in the initial set of leading sectors of East in the *long-run* given that the true probability of the good match between this technology and the local labor is p_i. Similarly, the probability that the country East will specialize in the long-run in the same set of industries in which it specializes at time t = 0 is given by $U_p^{S_0} = \lim_{t \to \infty} Q_p^{S_0}(t)$. Both limits exist because $Q_{p_i}(t)$ and $Q_p^{S_0}(t)$ are non-increasing in t and bounded.

We would like to determine under what conditions the country East will eventually specialize in the same set of industries as the one it targeted at the beginning of its learning process by licensing the entry of firms with the corresponding technologies. The main result of this section is formulated in the following proposition.

Proposition 3: *For each industry $i \in S_o$ there exists a certain probability p_i* such that*

1) *if $p_i < p_i$* then* $U_{\mathbf{p}}^{S_0} = 0$; *if $p_i < p_i$*, $\forall i \in S_o$ then* $U_{\mathbf{p}}^{S_0} = 0$;

2) *if $p_i \geq p_i$*then* $U_{p_i} > 0$; *if $p_i \geq p_i$*, for all $i \in S_o$ then* $U_{\mathbf{p}}^{S_0} > 0$

The above proposition makes it possible to determine how good the technology has to be in reality so that given that the government had sufficiently good priors about its productivity, once it is selected for promotion, it performs well enough to stand a chance to continue to be promoted in the long-run. The latter would lead with positive probability to East's eventual specialization in the given technology.

According to Proposition 3 for each industry i in the initial set of leading sectors S_o which East promotes given the initial beliefs $\bar{p}^0 = (\bar{p}_1^0, ..., \bar{p}_N^0)$ about the quality of match between available technologies and the local labor, we can find a certain probability p_i* such that if the true probability of the good match is below p_i*, then East will not specialize in i in the long-run almost surely and will eventually abandon i in favor of some other technology which currently is not in the set of leading sectors.

Conversely, if the true probabilities of the good match between local labor and technologies exceed a certain level p_i* for all $i \in S_o$, then with some positive probability, the set of industries which the government began to promote initially will survive in the long-run and East will eventually specialize in the industries from that set.

Note that Proposition 3 can also be stated in terms of the true coefficient of comparative advantage $k_i(p_i)$ because it is an increasing function of p_i. Interestingly, there can be a situation in which a country with probability one does not specialize in the long run in an industry in which it has very high true comparative advantage $k_i(p_i)$. While some technologies may be superior than the others in terms of the country's true comparative advantage, they may be not good enough (i.e., $k_i(p_i) < k_i(p_i^*)$) to remain in the set of leading sectors forever even if they were targeted at some time. When this happens the long run specialization in these truly best technologies occurs with probability zero and at the same time with some positive probability East eventually specializes in the 'wrong' technologies which are not the best among available technologies but exceed the critical bounds $k_i(p_i^*)$ and can perform well enough not to induce the government to look for better technologies.

This result suggests that government experimentation in the form of industrial targeting policy may not be the best means of overcoming coordination problems in economic development if the long-run efficiency of such experimentation is taken into account. Even optimally designed industrial targeting policies justified by the logic of coordination failures in the market may lead in the long run to the country's specialization in the industries in which it doesn't have comparative advantage.

7. CONCLUSION

The existing literature on industrial targeting develops sophisticated policies which governments should adopt in response to the specific market failures in industries. The problem is that very often market failures characterize multiple industries and the governments have limited capacity to develop appropriate policy response for each industry and rank the industries in terms of prospective welfare gains from policy intervention. Therefore, this paper addresses the issue of allocating a government's limited targeting capacity among several industries deserving policy intervention.

The proposed model puts the issue of optimal learning while conducting a trade policy within the framework of the specific type of sequential decision problem, namely the multi-armed bandit problem. Within this framework, the optimal policy of a government which wants to learn in what industries its country has the greatest comparative advantage and at the same time maximize the flow of welfare resulting from targeting different industries for promotion is based on the Gittins dynamic allocation index. The paper discusses how characteristics of the policy based on selecting the industries with the highest Gittins indices depend on economic properties of the technologies defining those industries.

This paper also addresses the issue of a country's long-run pattern of specialization emerging from the index promotion policy. Although this analysis has been rather abstract, its lessons are likely to be of practical interest in important concrete settings. The following result may be relevant to the policy makers not only in Eastern European transition economies but also in developed industrialized economies trying to acquire new technologies. It was shown that even the optimal targeting policy may fail to lead to the country's long-run specialization according to its comparative advantage. This possibility of the long-run specialization in the "wrong" set of industries reduces the value of industrial targeting policy as a form of government intervention designed to selectively overcome coordination failures.

Although decentralized private experimentation by firms may be costlier in the short run because of possible market imperfections, in the long run it may lead to more efficient specialization outcome for the country as a whole.

Among the issues that the paper leaves open is the design of an optimal learning policy when the pool of new technologies is not static but rather varies as a result of technical change. For example, it can be assumed that new industries/technologies arrive according to some stochastic process (e.g. Poisson). Then we can model the government's problem in the context of the so-called 'arms-acquiring bandit' which also has a solution based on the Gittins index.

An interesting extension of the model considered in this chapter would be a framework incorporating a cost of changing a country's specialization to alternative technologies. Such modification would make the multi-armed bandit framework more applicable to the analysis of trade policy. It is not clear whether the Gittins index policy would continue to be optimal in this setting.

REFERENCES

1. Aghion, P., Bolton, P., Harris, C. and Jullien, B. (1991), Optimal Learning by Experimentation, *Review of Economic Studies,* 58, p. 621-654.
2. Anderson, R. And Sonnenschein, H. (1982), On the Existence of Rational Expectations Equilibrium, *Journal of Economic Theory,* 26, p. 261-278.
3. Bagwell, K. and Staiger, R. (1989), The Role of Export Subsidies When Product Quality is Unknown, *Journal of International Economics,* 27, p. 69-89.
4. Banks, J. and Sundaram R. (1992), Denumerable-Armed Bandits, *Econometrica,* 60, p. 1071-1096.
5. Banks, J. and Sundaram R. (1994), Switching costs and the Gittins index, *Econometrica,* 62, p. 687-694.
6. Bardhan, P.K., (1971), On Optimum Subsidy to a Learning Industry: An Aspect of the Theory of Infant-Industry Protection, *International Economic Review,* 12, p. 54-70.
7. Beale, E. M. L. (1979), Discussant of J. C. Gittins, *Journal of Royal Statistical Society*, Ser. B, 41, p. 171-172.
8. Bellman, R. E. (1956), A Problem in the Sequential Design of Experiments, *Sankhya,* 16, p. 221-229.
9. Bernanke, B. (1983), Irreversibility, Uncertainty, and Cyclical Investment, *Quarterly Journal of Economics,* 98, p. 85-106.
10. Berry, D. and Fristedt, B. (1985), *Bandit Problems: Sequential Allocation of Experiments*, London, Chapman and Hall.
11. Blume, L. and Easley, D. (1984), Rational Expectations Equilibrium: An Alternative Approach, *Journal of Economic Theory,* 34, p. 116-129.
12. Brander, J. and Spencer, B. (1985), Export Subsidies and International Market Share and Rivalry, *Journal of International Economics,* 18, p. 83-100.
13. Brander, J. and Spencer, B. (1987), Foreign Direct Investment with Unemployment and Endogenous Taxes and Tariffs, *Journal of International Economics,* 22, p. 257-279.
14. Chen, Y. R. and Katehakis, M. N. (1986), Linear Programming for Finite State Multi-Armed Bandit Problems, *Mathematics of Operations Research,* 11, p. 180-183.
15. Dinopoulos, E., Lewis, T. and Sappington, D. (1995), Optimal Industrial Targeting with Unknown Learning-by-Doing, *Journal of International Economics,* 38, p. 275-295.
16. Dixit, A. and Grossman, G. (1986), Targeted Export Promotion with Several Oligopolistic Industries, *Journal of International Economics,* 21, p. 233-249.
17. Dixit, A. and Pindyck, R. (1994), *Investment Under Uncertainty,* Princeton, Princeton University Press.

18. Easley, D. and Kiefer, N. M. (1988), Controlling a Stochastic Process with Unknown Parameters, *Econometrica*, 56, p. 1045-1064.
19. Epplet, W. (1986), Continuous-Time Allocation Indices and Their Discrete-Time Approximations, *Advances in Applied Probability,* 18, p. 724-746.
20. Gittins, J. C. (1989), *Multi-Armed Bandit Allocation Indices*, Wiley, Chichester.
21. Gittins, J. C. and Jones, D. (1974), A Dynamic Allocation Index for the Sequential Allocation of Experiments, in J. Gani et al. (eds.), *Progress in Statistics*, Amsterdam, North Holland, p. 241-266.
22. Grossman, G., and Horn, H. (1988), Infant-Industry Protection Reconsidered: The Case of Informational Barriers to Entry, *Quarterly Journal of Economics,* 103, p. 767-787.
23. Hoff, K. (1997), Bayesian Learning in an Infant Industry Model, *Journal of International Economics,* 43, p. 409-436.
24. Ishikida, T. and Varaiya, P. (1994), Multi-Armed Bandit Problem Revisited, *Journal of Optimization Theory and Applications,* 83, p. 113-154.
25. Jordan, J.S. (1985), Learning Rational Expectations: The Finite State Case, *Journal of Economic Theory,* 36, p. 257-276.
26. Jovanovic, B. (1979), Job-Search and the Theory of Turnover, *Journal of Political Economy,* 87, p. 972-990.
27. Karatzas, I. (1984), Gittins Indices in the Dynamic Allocation Problem for Diffusion Processes, *Annals of Probability,* 12, p. 173-192.
28. Klimenko, M. (1998) Optimal Learning and Experimentation in Export Promotion Policies, *IR/PS, UC San Diego, Research Report No. 99-02.*
29. Krueger, A. (1985), The Experience and Lessons of Asia's Super Exporters, in V. Corbo et al. (Eds.) *Export-Oriented Development Strategies: The Success of Five Newly Industrializing Countries*, Westview Press, Boulder, CO
30. Krugman, P. (1984), Import Protection as Export Promotion: International Competition in the Presence of Oligopoly and Economics of Scale, in Kierzkowski, Henryk, ed. *Monopolistic Competition and International Trade*. Oxford University Press, New York, p. 180-193.
31. Kuo, S. (1983), *The Taiwan Economy in Transition*, Westview Press, Boulder, CO.
32. Lall, S. (1996), *Learning from Asian Tigers*, Macmillan, London.
33. Mandelbaum, A. (1986), Discrete Multi-Armed Bandits and Multi-parameter Processes, *Probability Theory and Related Fields,* 71, p. 129-147.
34. Mandelbaum, A. (1987), Continuous Multi-Armed Bandits and Multiparameter Processes, *Annals of Probability,* 15, p. 1527-1556.
35. Matsuyama, K. (1997), Economic Development as Coordination Problems, in Aoki et. al., (eds.) *The Role of Government in East Asian Economic Development: Comparative Institutional Analysis*. Oxford University Press, New York, p. 134-162.
36. Mclennan, A. (1984), Price Dispersion and Incomplete Learning in the Long Run, *Journal of Economic Dynamics and Control,* 7, p. 331-347.
37. Murphy, K., Shleifer, A., Vishny, R. (1989), Income Distribution, Market Size, and Industrialization, *Quarterly Journal of Economics*, 104, p. 537-564.

38. Roberts, K. and Weitzman, M. (1981), Funding Criteria for Research, Development, and Exploration Projects, *Econometrica,* 49, p. 1261-1288.
39. Rodrik, D. (1995), Getting interventions right: How South Korea and Taiwan grew rich, *Economic Policy,* 20, p. 53-107.
40. Rodrik, D. (1996), Coordination Failures and Government Policy: A Model with Applications to East Asia and Eastern Europe, *Journal of International Economics,* 40, p. 1-22.
41. Rothschild, M. (1974), A Two-Armed Bandit Theory of Market-Pricing, *Journal of Economic Theory,* 9, p. 185-202.
42. Spencer, B. and Brander, J. (1983), International R & D Rivalry and Industrial Strategy, *Review of Economic Studies,* 50, p. 707-722.
43. Varaiya, P., Walrand, J. and Buyukkoc, C. (1985), Extensions of the Multiarmed Bandit Problem: The Discounted Case, *IEEE Transactions on Automatic Control,* AC-30, 426-439.
44. Wade, R. (1990), *Governing the Market,* Princeton University Press, Princeton.
45. Weber, R. R., and Weiss, G. (1990), On an Index Policy for Restless Bandits, *Journal of Applied Probability,* 27, p. 637-648.
46. Weiss, G. (1992), Turnpike Optimality of Smith's Rule in Parallel Machines Stochastic Scheduling, *Mathematics of Operations Research,* 17, p. 255-270.
47. Weiss, G. (1994), On Almost Optimal Priority Rules for Preemptive Scheduling of Stochastic Jobs on Parallel Machines, *Advances in Applied Probability,* 27, p. 821-839.
48. Weitzman, M. (1979), Optimal Search for the Best Alternative, *Econometrica,* 47, p. 641-654.
49. Westphal, L. (1982), Fostering Technological Mastery by Means of Selective Infant-Industry Protection, in M. Syrquin and Teitel S. (Eds.) *Trade, Stability, Technology and Equity in Latin America,* Academic Press, New York.
50. Whittle, P. (1980), Multi-Armed Bandits and the Gittins Index, *Journal of Royal Statistical Society*, Ser. B, 42, p. 143-149.
51. Whittle, P. (1981), Arm-acquiring Bandits, *The Annals of Probability,* 9, p. 284-292.
52. Whittle, P. (1988), Restless Bandits: Activity Allocation in a Changing World, in J. Gani, ed., A Celebration of Applied Probability, *Journal of Applied Probability,* 25 A, p. 287-298.
53. Yoshida, Y. (1993), Optimal Stopping Problems for Multiarmed Bandit Processes with Arms' Independence, *Computers and Mathematics with Applications*, 26, p. 47-60.
54. Young, A., (1991), Learning-by-doing and the Dynamic Effects of International Trade, *Quarterly Journal of Economics,* 106, p. 369-405.

Chapter 5

OUTWARD-PROCESSING TRADE AND FOREIGN DIRECT INVESTMENT FROM FRANCE INTO EAST EUROPEAN COUNTRIES

Madeleine Andreff
University of Marne-la-Vallée
Wladimir Andreff
University of Paris 1 – Panthéon - Sorbonne

1. INTRODUCTION

The break-up of the former communist regime, the first years of transition towards a market economy in Eastern Europe and the self-dissolution of the former CMEA (Council of Mutual Economic Assistance) have triggered a move towards the integration of Eastern European countries (EECs) into the world economy through the privileged channels of economic relationships with, and aid from, the European Union (Andreff and Andreff, 1995). Such an integration process is based on a significant reorientation of EEC foreign trade, from the former CMEA partners to the West, and on an increasing inflow of foreign direct investment from Western (European) home countries into the new transitional economies. French trade and foreign direct investment (FDI) have obviously been affected by this overall reorientation, quite unexpectedly, and outward-processing trade linking relocated production by French main contractors to EEC subcontractors has become a significant mode of entry in post-communist economies.

There are several modes of entry for a Western (French) firm in any host country, and in particular in post-communist transitional economies. One is trade, another one is FDI. In between, one finds the so-called "new forms of investment" (Oman 1984), in the OECD parlance, *i.e.* joint ventures, minority-controlled affiliates, co-production, international subcontracting, technical assistance, licensing, franchising, management agreements and turnkey plants. The higher transaction costs on a foreign market, the more "internalized" mode of entry; like a wholly or majority-owned affiliate; the lower transaction costs, the more externalized mode of entry like trade, then turnkey plants. International subcontracting fits with not too high and not too low transaction costs, when industrial enterprises shift a part of or all their manufacturing process to a foreign country, as a component of an either horizontally or vertically linked production system. It requires a segmentation and a relocation abroad of a sequence of - or all - the firm's production process, and unavoidably triggers international trade flows (a cross border trade of inputs and semi-finished products). Thus, it actually appears to be an intermediary form between trade and FDI. Subcontrating is a frequent means of production relocation, technology transfer, improvement of managerial skills, product design adaptation to the world market, just like FDI, while it saves on capital expenditures, equity involvement and corporate governance costs - like trade. Finally, it is a component of lean production and global outsourcing developed by transnational corporations in the framework of their new global strategies (Andreff, 1996). In order to implement these strategies, transnational firms pay special attention to building an efficient network of suppliers at a lower degree of vertical integration, which means a bundle of autonomous enterprises strongly interrelated through subcontracting and outward processing trade (Halpern 1994). From the European Union's point of view, "*a subcontracting relationship exists whenever a business (subcontractor) acts for the account of another (main contractor) undertaking in the process of working and making a specific product to plans and technical specifications supplied by the main contractor, who has final economic responsibility*" (quoted from UNECE 1995 - p. 110, note 263).

We focus, in this chapter, on international subcontracting looked at through available macroeconomic and sectoral trade data registered under the customs classification of outward-processing trade (OPT) which more precisely refers to fashioning subcontracting. The latter means that exports of semi-finished products flow from the main contractor's country (here France) and, after some fashioning, imports of more elaborated intermediary products - or even final products - flow back from the subcontractor's to the main contractor's country. OPT is thus considered sometimes as a sub-category of countertrade, a transaction where exports and imports are linked (Neale and Sercu, 1993). EECs are understood *lato sensu* as to encompass 27 countries, even though some of them are not geographically located in Central Europe, while all of them have once been members of either CMEA or the Federal Republic of Yugoslavia:

1. CEFTA countries: the Czech Republic, Hungary, Poland, Slovakia and Slovenia[1],
2. the Balkan countries: Albania, Bosnia-Herzegovina, Bulgaria, Croatia, Macedonia, Romania and Yugoslavia (Serbia-Montenegro),
3. the Baltic states: Estonia, Latvia, Lithuania, members of the Baltic Free Trade Area,

[1] In the period covered by our study (1993-1997), Bulgaria and Romania were not yet a CEFTA member (CEFTA: Central European Free Trade Area).

4. CIS countries: Armenia, Azerbaijan, Belarus, Georgia, Kazakhstan, Kyrgyzstan, Moldova, Russia, Tajikistan, Turkmenistan, Ukraine and Uzbekistan, members of the Commonwealth of Independent States.

Our first task is to assess the development of France OPT with the various EEC subgroups in terms of evolution, relative share in overall trade, major products (sectors) concerned, and comparative specialization (Section 2 below). Note that France OPT has been largely a one-way avenue so far, *i.e.* companies in the EECs have been processing intermediate inputs, semi-finished or final products for French enterprises and not the reverse. This is quite logical if one refers to the determinants of international subcontracting and OPT.

The determinants of fashioning subcontracting abroad with OPT are various. It is crystal clear that the bilateral flow of OPT export and reimportation would have no (or less) interest for an EU main contractor if it should be taxed twice at the border. Therefore, the first determinant of OPT is that some countries, free trade areas or customs unions apply a specific customs regime to OPT; such a customs regime has been introduced in the European Community (EC) in 1986. It allows temporary export of EC (then EU) products to be transformed, mended, fashioned or integrated into a more elaborated product on an assembly line and, afterwards, to be reimported with an overall or partial exemption from customs duties and with a partial avoidance of quantitative quotas, if any. The objective of the OPT customs regime is to avoid taxation of EU commodities that are contained in imports achieved by an EU member country. Only the value added abroad is submitted to taxation; this *fiscal* OPT regime is open to any manufactured product. Therefore, the OPT advantage, compared to regular trade with customs duties, is its duty-free or slightly taxed character. As a privileged trade treatment, OPT helps improving the trade gain of the main contractor. In order to benefit from the specific OPT customs regime, the subcontractor and the main contractor must be legally independent entities, otherwise the international flows of semi-finished products will be considered as intra-company trade. This *definitely differentiates OPT from FDI.*

A second customs regulation relates to *economic* OPT. It refers exclusively to clothing and textiles, and essentially allows for preferential tariff quotas on reimports of goods processed abroad (UNECE, 1995). In order to qualify for the special provisions of economic OPT an EU producer must satisfy a number of conditions which include, *inter alia*, that the goods sent abroad for processing should originate in the EU and the value of outward processing should not exceed 50% of the EU producer's output.

Another determinant of outward processing is widely considered in the economic literature to be a lower production cost - in particular a lower unit labor cost - in the subcontractor's country. A low transport cost between the two countries involved, and the capacity it offers to avoid tariff barriers, namely when the main contractor's country has erected some protection measures against sensitive imports from the subcontractor's low-wage country (Graziani, 1998), are also supposed to trigger OPT. All the three factors might have been relevant in international relationships between France and the EECs. Transport costs are not very high due to geographical proximity between France and the EECs, and are on a decreasing trend with technological improvement in international transport. Unit labor costs were lower in the EECs than in France by a wide margin at the dawn of the transition process, due to low real wages in the East, even lowered in hard currencies by the initial devaluation of new post-socialist currencies. However, with the economic recovery in the second half of the nineties, the labor cost gap with France has slightly narrowed after labor productivity and real wage have increased in most EECs (Andreff, 1999a), and this may well be a determinant for French firms to switch from OPT to a more domestic demand-oriented FDI in the coming years. This would mean that the labor cost comparative advantage which favored OPT with the EECs would be superseded by a market demand comparative advantage, fueled by higher incomes (wages) and purchasing power, attractive to foreign investors. This assumption remains to be tested (see Section 3).

It is often argued (UNECE, 1995) that OPT with the EECs is a way, for an EU (French) stagnating sector, to cope with strong competition from foreign (namely Asian) suppliers. The argument is obviously relevant for the textile and clothing industry - which concentrates the great bulk of EU (France) OPT with the EECs - as well as for the footwear industry where Community producers have lost market shares both abroad and at home; it pertains less to machine building and electrical equipment industries, for instance. Nevertheless, in any case, OPT with the EECs is a lever to improve the competitiveness of EU producers, on the basis of low labor costs, and once these costs start to grow, OPT enables EU producers having yet a foot in the door to swiftly switch to FDI. On the other hand, participating to subcontracting and OPT with an EU main contractor is likely to upgrade the industrial competitiveness of East European subcontractors and improve the quality of their products.

Some other prerequisites must be met to determine OPT (Andreff and Boudier-Bensebaa, 2001). The host (subcontractor's) country must offer industrial partners with existing production capacities that can fit with the technical and economic norms of the main contractor. This means that a EEC is likely to attract OPT if it exhibits a competitive advantage of its producers over those located in other EECs and developing countries. The host country must also have reached an institutional and political stability - in other words an acceptable level of country-risk[2] - a satisfying business climate, and must secure private property rights. Unlimited imports of intermediate products and unrestricted exports of processed goods have to be guaranteed. It results from these prerequisites that the EECs have an uneven access to OPT.

Being intermediary forms of trade in goods and trade in factors of production (Schmidt and Naujoks, 1994), and thus intermediary means between direct trade and FDI, international subcontracting and OPT are often regarded as a temporary or transitional phenomenon (Lankes and Venables, 1996) which must be substituted in the long run by either direct trade or FDI, depending on the worsening or improving investment climate

[2] An acceptable country-risk for OPT may sometimes be unbearable for FDI since OPT does not result in either capital investment or ownership of a production facility abroad. The subcontractor remains with his/her property rights and has to cope with his/her (host) country risk, investment climate, labor market situation (for instance, firing excess manpower which should have been done by the foreign investor in case of FDI), and so on.

and risks in the host country (Andreff, 2000). In the short run, OPT is more flexible than FDI insofar as it requires no capital investment, and this makes it more easily adaptable to a risky economic environment such as the one of the EECs in the early years of transition. Now, another question addressed to, in our chapter, is to know whether an emerging substitution of FDI to OPT is yet at work in the relationships between France and the EECs (Section 3). Such a substitution might bring with it, in the future, an increasing share of FDI and a shrinking OPT between France and both the EECs areas. By the same token, OPT might cease to be "*more important than either direct trade or FDI as a source of interdependence between EU and the EECs*" as it was phrased in the case of clothing (Corado 1994, p.16). In the background of this substitution process, it remains to see whether French FDI and OPT in the EECs develop in a similar or contrasted range of manufacturing industries (Section 4).

We do not analyze here whether the EU-EEC interdependence through OPT is promising or not, whether its possible substitution by FDI will increase or decrease the adjustment cost of EECs' laggard industries and, in a nutshell, we neglect all the microeconomic dimensions which should take place in a more comprehensive analysis of OPT and FDI relationships. We do not focus either on the historical dimension of East-West OPT in Europe. In the former planned economies, OPT was nearly the only possibility of creating direct links with convertible currency markets outside the vertically organized and state controlled foreign trade (Hamar, 1998) but, since custom-based foreign trade statistics was only introduced in the 1990's in the EECs, data for the earlier years are not comparable. FDI was forbidden or when it was allowed, since the 1970's in some CMEA countries, it was limited to a very few number of foreign affiliates. Thus, as a specific category of countertrade, some OPT has developed before 1990 between Eastern Europe and EC members, first of all Germany. For instance, according to an OECD survey (Zaleski and Wienert, 1980), subcontracting with OPT was yet representing 7.4% of the overall number of identified East-West technological transfer and industrial cooperation operations in 1978 (the other forms of transfer were licensing, turnkey projects, co-production and joint ventures). German OPT with CMEA countries was witnessed as soon as 1971 and in 1988 its share was 57% of all the German OPT with the world (Boudier-Bensebaa and Brezinski, 2000). France OPT with CMEA countries was markedly lagging behind at the time. In 1988, France had a lower share than the EC average (10.9%) for OPT reimportation in her overall import from the EECs (CGP 1999).

2. Evolution and Specialization of French Outward-Processing Trade with East European Countries: An Empirical Assessment[3]

2.1. An Evolving Geographical Orientation

France OPT export with our 27 sampled EECs has reached 214 million Ecus in 1993 and 300 million Ecus on the reimportation side. The ratio (percentage) of OPT export to overall France-EEC export was 4.7%. The relative importance is quite similar for France OPT reimportation from the EECs with a 6.4% ratio (Table 1). In 1997, OPT export had grown up to 352 million Ecus to the EECs, and OPT reimporation from the EECS was up with 514 million Ecus. The average annual growth of France-EEC OPT reimportation, from 1993 to 1997, has been 14.4% while France-EEC OPT export has grown slightly slower (13.2% per year). French export for further processing in the EECs have become increasingly significant. In 1998, OPT reimportation from the EECs has stagnated at 514 million Ecus, and OPT export has *fallen* down to 243 million Ecus (-31%), probably the first sign of the vanishing comparative advantage of OPT foreseen for 1998-1999 since the specific customs regulation has come to an end in 1998 for OPT between the EU and CEFTA countries, and in Bulgaria in 1999..

France OPT basically has not grown faster than overall trade, between 1993 and 1997, except for OPT reimportation from the EECs whose share in overall import is slightly higher in 1997 than in 1993; the share of France OPT export to the EECs has declined during the same period of time. Last not least, OPT with France *creates trade surplus* for the EECs (a surplus of 86 million Ecus in 1993, 162 million Ecus in 1997 and 171 million Ecus in 1998), an impact which must be appreciated by countries suffering from an overall trade deficit (except Russia).

Table 1 – French Outward Processing Trade with East European Countries: percentage of overall trade and evolution, 1993-1997

1993	Export	Import
Outward processing trade *	214339	299506
OPT in % of overall trade	4.7	6.4
1997	**Export**	**Import**
Outward processing trade *	352195	513618
OPT in % of overall trade	3.5	6.6
Annual growth in 1993-1997	13.2	14.4

* In thousand Ecus. **Source:** Annex 1

[3] Data have been collected from Eurostat and the Chelem data bank by Marie-José Desaigues (ROSES)

Now, let us briefly compare our results on France OPT with the EECs to European Union OPT with the same geographical area [4]. In 1993, OPT export to the EECs amounted to 7.8% of overall export of the EU-12, and the percentage was 10.5% for reimportation. Thus, *French enterprises were much less involved in OPT with the EECs than average European* (in particular German) *firms*. The same conclusion applies to 1997 when EU-12 OPT export reached 6.1% of EU-12 overall export and 8.9% on the reimportation side [5]. But both French and EU OPT shares in overall trade with the EECs are on a *decreasing trend* in 1997 compared to 1993.

A more detailed view is provided in Annexes 1 and 2. *Balkan countries have the highest share of OPT export and reimportation in overall trade with France*, compared to CEFTA, CIS and the Baltic states. This is mainly due to the very high ratios observed for Romania (and to some extent Bulgaria). Romanian OPT reimportation to France is in the range of one quarter of overall import from Romania (26% in 1993, 23% in 1997). Among CEFTA countries, Hungary had a ratio which compared to Romania for reimportation in 1993 (23%), but it dropped down to 11% in 1997, explaining the drop of CEFTA OPT reimportation to France from 10% in 1993 to roughly 8% in 1997. Note that OPT reimportation in overall import is not significant from the Baltic states and is still low - though growing- from CIS countries. As to OPT export from France, Romania and Hungary come first for the ratio to overall export, ahead of Poland, while Balkans are ahead of CEFTA, CIS and the Baltic states. *Some ratios are decreasing from 1993 to 1997*, except for Balkan OPT export and reimportation, and Baltic and CIS reimportation. CEFTA front runners in OPT with France have been successfully challenged by the Balkan countries, first of all Romania, and to a lesser extent by the newcomers from the CIS. This latter might well be the next area of France OPT expansion after 1999, when the window of opportunity would be closed in the ten associated Central Eastern European Countries (CEECs which gathers CEFTA countries, Baltic states and Bulgaria). Such a move of OPT, among the EECs, from CEFTA to the Balkan countries has already been witnessed from 1992 to 1995: *"OPT has also been moving from the CEECs with higher wages (especially Hungary and Slovenia) to the Balkan countries"* (Lemoine, 1998 - p. 159). What reveals new, with our more recent data for France OPT, is a possible second switch toward CIS which is also expected from other EU main contractors' countries (UNECE, 1995).

The distribution of France OPT with the various subgroups of EECs is provided in Annex 2. From 1993 to 1997, the market share of CEFTA decreases in both OPT export and reimportation between the overall EECs and France whereas the Balkans' share sharply increases as well as the CIS share (the Baltic states' share also increases but remains very small). In 1997, CEFTA roughly accounts for one half (52%) of France OPT export to the EECs, the Balkans for one third (36%), the CIS for one tenth (11%)

---

[4] relying, for the latter, on the data elaborated on in Andreff and Boudier-Bensebaa (2001); all the comparisons with EU-15 OPT with the EECs are based on this reference

[5] The same results are obtained if one takes into consideration the EU-15 instead of the EU-12. In 1995, EU-15 OPT export accounted for 7.2% of EU-15 overall export (5.6% in 1997) and EU-15 OPT reimportation amounted to 9.3% of EU-15 overall import (8.4% in 1997).

and the Baltic states for less than 1%. As regards reimportation, CEFTA is a bit over two fifths (43%) of all France OPT reimportation from the EECs, the Balkans are nearly one third (31%), the CIS reaches one quarter (26%) and the Baltic states are under 1%. In 1998, CEFTA has gained ground in France OPT export (64%) while the Balkans (29%) and the CIS (7%) have lost ground. The distribution between the three areas remains practically unchanged in France OPT reimportation in 1998, compared to 1997. In EU-15 OPT export to the EECs in 1997, CEFTA attracts a 61% share, the Balkan countries 26%, the CIS 7% and the Baltic states 6%; in the EU-15 OPT reimportation, in 1997, the respective shares are: 58% for CEFTA, 29% for the Balkans, 9% for the CIS and 5% for the Baltic states. Thus, *France OPT is less oriented toward CEFTA and the Baltic states* (privileged areas of German main contractors) and *more Balkan- and CIS-oriented* than the EU-15 OPT.

France-EEC OPT *is geographically concentrated on four major partner countries* (MPC): the Czech Republic, Hungary, Poland and Romania [6] attract together 66% of France OPT export in 1993, and 71% in 1997, while their share in France OPT reimportation is 65% in 1993 and 57% in 1997. In this respect, French business concentrates its OPT in roughly the same proportion in the same EECs as European business does. In 1997, the four MPCs were concentrating 68% of EU-15 OPT export and 66% of EU-15 OPT reimportation with all the EECs, whereas the share of these four countries is only 49% of overall EU-15 export to, and 46% of overall EU-15 import from all the EECs.

2.2. Sectoral (Product) Concentration

Turning now to the sectoral (product) distribution of France OPT with the EECs, we have calculated the Herfindal-Hirschman concentration index by product (Table 2) given by:

$$HHI = 100\sqrt{\sum_k MS_k^2}$$

where MS_k stands for the market share of the product *k* in the overall OPT market (export or import). OPT is rather concentrated, in particular for reimportation. Between 1993 and 1997, the product concentration of France reimportation from the EECs slightly weakens, while concentration grows for France OPT export.

Sectoral (product) concentration is also crystal clear when assessed on the basis of two-digit product groups (Annex 3). The first ten product items weigh 80% in France OPT export to the EECs in 1993; the first ten reimported items concentrate a more

[6] Russia is only the seventh partner in the French main contractors' export (after Bulgaria and Ukraine) in 1997; on the other hand, Russia is the second partner in France outward processing reimportation, but the latter's share in overall import from Russia is small and very much concentrated on one product (28 in the classification).

important share of OPT reimportation, roughly 97%. OPT export are even more concentrated on the first ten products (85%) in 1997 and the first ten OPT reimportation products remain with a 97% share of the total. *The degree of concentration is higher in France OPT than in EU-15 OPT with the EECs* in 1997 which is only 75% on the export side and 91% on the reimportation side for the first ten products.

Table 2 – Product Concentration Index of France Outward

Processing trade with the EECs, 1993-1997		
Year	**Export**	**Import**
1993	28.89	54.94
1997	33.25	51.75

Authors' calculation of the Herfindal-Hirschman index from Eurostat.

In terms of product structure, in 1993, textile products accounted for 47% of France OPT export to the EECs, and clothing reached 25%. OPT reimportation of textile products was practically nil from the EECs while clothing was making the great bulk of reimportation (70%). France OPT actually *was achieving a vertical division of labor in the textile-clothing industry with the relocation of the more labor intensive downstream parts of the production process* (clothing) in lower labor cost areas such as the EECs in 1993. Wool, cotton and synthetic fibers were the major items exported by French main contractors. Hosiery, other clothing, apparels, togs, rags and footwear were the major items reimported from EEC subcontractors. The picture has not basically changed in 1997, but the share of textiles has declined to 38% in France OPT export to the EECs while the share of clothing has also decreased to 64% in France OPT reimportation from the EECs. The reimportation of textiles remains practically nil. Cotton and synthetic fibres are still major OPT exports in all areas in 1997, while wool remains important in the EEC export structure. Hosiery, other clothing, apparels, togs, rags and footwear remain significant items in the reimportation. *The 1993 division of labor is still lasting in 1997, but the whole textile-clothing industry is loosing some ground in favor of other product subgroups* in France OPT with the EECs. Exactly the same scheme is observed in EU-15 OPT trade with the EECs in the textile-clothing industry.

After the textile-clothing industry, two other product subgroups have a non-negligible participation in France OPT with the EECs. One is electrical equipment: 2% in OPT export to the EECs and 3% in OPT reimportation from the EECs in 1993. The share of *electrical equipment in France OPT trade with the EECs has much increased* up to 1997 and has gained ground over the textile-clothing share. In 1997, its share in OPT export to the EECs is 17%, and it is of 8% in OPT reimportation from the EECs. Another product subgroup is worth being mentioned: machine building weighs 2% in France OPT export to the EECs in 1993, and less than 1% in OPT reimportation from the EECs. Its share *also increases from 1993 to 1997* when it reaches 3% of OPT export to the EECs, and 1% in OPT reimportation from the EECs. Electrical equipment and machine building producers seem to be, in some way, the followers of textile-clothing main contractors in

France OPT with Eastern Europe. This means that *electrical equipment and machine building industries would probably supersede the textile-clothing industry in OPT relocation of production* to the EECs after the total liberalization of the latter's industrial foreign trade with France (and EU-15).

Some specific products must be briefly alluded to. The French leather-saddlery industry has also proceeded to the same downstream division of labor as the textile-clothing industry has done in the EECs, exporting leather (2% of OPT export to the EECs in 1997) and reimporting leather products (less than 1% of OPT reimportation from the EECs). Chemical products are relatively important in OPT with the EECs, in particular in France reimportation from the CIS, but this latter is concentrated on one country, Russia, and one product, the item 28 in the standard product classification which refers to precious metals, radioactive elements and isotopes. This OPT flow relates to the treatment of fissile materials for the French nuclear industry in Russian nuclear plants, which has been initiated long ago in the former Soviet-French co-operation.

A comparison of the product structure between France and EU-15 OPT with the EECs in 1997 reveals no surprise. The major items exported by EU-15 to the EECs in this framework are connected to the textile-clothing industry (wool, cotton, synthetic fibres, and then clothing) and the most significant reimportation is the one of clothing (hosiery, other clothes, apparels, togs, rags and footwear). Electrical equipment is of a comparable importance in France and EU-15 OPT export and reimportation while machine building is twice more important in EU-15 than in France OPT with the EECs. A last point is to be made, derived from the already noticed (CGP 1999) product concentration on textile-clothing and electrical equipment: *the product distribution of EU (and France) OPT is quite specific compared with the product distribution of their overall trade, with the EECs*. In overall trade, EU imports from the EECs are concentrated first on clothing, but then on motor cars, steel, machine building, chemical products and then on electrical equipment and furniture (Andreff, 1998, Lemoine and Freudenberg, 1999). The first EU exports to the EECs are machine building, then motor cars, chemical products, textiles, and then electrical equipment and food. It clearly appears that subcontracting resorts to a vertical division of labor which is quite specific and relies on an international specialization which is different from the one of EU (France) overall trade with the EECs.

2.3. EEC Specialization in Outward Processing Trade with France

The determinants of international specialization are similar in the trade of intermediary products and in the trade of final goods, as soon as the production process is internationally segmented (Fontagné *and al.*, 1995). OPT is a subset of both trade in intermediary products (main contractor's country exports and thus subcontractor's country imports) and trade in final goods (reimportation by the main contractor's country and thus exports of the subcontractor's country). Therefore, we can use the current analyses of international specialization in either intermediary products or final goods, in the case of OPT. Products that are exported by France to be processed in the EECs are intermediary products (or semi-finished products or spare parts) while they are reimported in the form of final goods (and semi-finished products and spare parts). The consequence is that *OPT exports and OPT imports usually do not belong exactly to the same position in the standard product classification*. Thus, EECs' OPT imports are achieved for products in the production of which they have a comparative disadvantage, and their OPT export (after processing) consists in final goods (or spare parts) in the production of which they have a comparative advantage. But, due to the specificity of OPT, it is even more relevant to assess the relative position of different East European countries and subgroups, as regards their specialization, than their obvious comparative advantages and disadvantages towards France. We first use the Balassa index of revealed comparative advantage:

$$t_{jk} = \frac{X_{jk}/X_{j.}}{X_{.k}/X_{..}} \quad \text{and} \quad u_{jk} = \frac{M_{jk}/M_{j.}}{M_{.k}/M_{..}}$$

in which X_{jk} stands for OPT exports of the product k from the EEC (j) to France; $X_{.k}$ stands for OPT exports of the product k from all extra-EU countries to France; $X_{j.}$ stands for overall OPT exports from the EEC (j) to France; and $X_{..}$ stands for overall OPT exports from all extra-EU countries to France (the same definitions apply for M = imports). But we have interpreted the Balassa index in a specific way in order to adapt it to the OPT case. One EEC (j) is considered to have a "subcontracting or OPT comparative advantage" in the product k if the ratio of the relative export structure is higher than 1 and if the ratio of the relative import structure is higher than 1. The higher ratio of an EEC, the higher its rank in the hierarchy of France OPT partners.

In EEC OPT exports of clothing products to France, the Balkans (mainly due to Romania) have the most important comparative advantage, followed by CEFTA (mainly duc to Hungary and Poland) in 1997 (Annex 4.1). This comparative advantage is more significant in OPT clothing exports to France than to EU-15. A comparative advantage in textiles appears for CEFTA, primarily due to Poland and the Czech Republic. On the other hand, in electrical equipment and machine building, we observe no comparative advantage or even a slight disadvantage, except for electrical equipment exported from the Czech Republic in 1997. This specialization structure on the EEC OPT export side in fact lasts since 1993.

In EEC OPT imports from France, their major comparative advantage is in textiles in 1997, first for the CIS countries and then CEFTA and the Balkans (Annex 4.2). In OPT imports of clothing, the most significant comparative advantage is for the Balkan countries (primarily due to Romania), followed by CEFTA (mainly due to Poland) and the CIS countries. On the other hand, in electrical equipment and machine building there is a strong comparative disadvantage. The same specialization structure and country hierarchy prevailed in 1993. As a matter of fact, the comparative advantage is more marked in EEC OPT imports from France, for most products, than from EU-15.

The specialization index based on the *contribution to the trade balance* gets rid off the impact of macroeconomic factors on a country competitiveness and sticks to the structural dimensions of international specialization. This index compares, for each product, the real trade balance between two countries to a "normal" trade balance, which is proportional to the share of each product in the overall trade between these two countries. This index here is weighted by the value of overall trade between each EEC and France in order to take into account the difference between the commercial sizes of these countries:

$$f_{jk} = \left[(X_{jk} - M_{jk}) - \frac{X_{jk} + M_{jk}}{\sum_k (X_{jk} + M_{jk})} * \sum_k (X_{jk} - M_{jk}) \right] * \frac{100}{\sum_k (X_{jk} + M_{jk})}$$

When the index is higher than zero, it means a comparative advantage in the product k for the country j, *i.e.* for an EEC, and an index lower than zero means a comparative disadvantage. The index is exclusively calculated here for OPT with France.

The index is, as expected, lower than zero for textile products and higher than zero for clothing in 1993 and 1997 (Annex 5). The negative contribution of textiles to the trade balance weakens from 1993 to 1997 in France OPT with all the sampled areas. The most negative contribution in textiles is the one of CEFTA (primarily due to Hungary and Poland), then come the CIS and the Balkans in 1997. The most positive contribution in clothing is the one of CEFTA (mainly Hungary and Poland), and then come the Balkan countries in 1997. The contribution of machine building to the trade balance is small but rather negative. In 1993, the contribution of electrical equipment was small and positive for CEFTA and the four MPCs, and it turned out into a negative contribution for CEFTA (primarily due to Hungary) in 1997. For all other areas electrical equipment always had a small and negative contribution.

3. Outward-Processing Trade in the Face of Growing Foreign Direct Investment: A Transitional Phenomenon

The entry of FDI in the EECs has markedly accelerated between 1993 and 1997 (Table 3) from both the overall world and France. The world FDI inflow in the EECS is concentrated (60%) on CEFTA countries in 1993 but partly moves eastwards to the CIS (45%) and southwards to the Balkans (10%) in 1997. As a result, the world inward FDI stock in the EECs is less concentrated on CEFTA countries in 1997 (56%) than in 1993 (77%). The French FDI inflow in the EECS is even more concentrated on CEFTA countries (97%) in 1993 - with the Czech Republic as the first host country and then Hungary, Poland and Slovakia -, and practically non existent in the Baltic states and the CIS. In 1997, the concentration of French FDI flow on CEFTA countries has slightly diminished (67%) and has left some room for FDI flow to the Balkans (22%) and the CIS

(11%): the main countries attracting French FDI in Eastern Europe are first Poland, and then Romania, the Czech Republic, Hungary and Russia. In terms of inward stock into the EECs, French FDI in 1997 remains more concentrated than world FDI first on CEFTA countries (the Czech Republic, then Hungary, Poland, Slovenia and Slovakia), second on the Balkans (Romania, then Yugoslavia, Croatia and Bulgaria), while it is less geared towards the CIS (Russia, then Ukraine and Kazakhstan) and the Baltic states (only in Latvia).

Table 3 – Inflow and Inward Stock of Foreign Direct Investment

In the EECs from the world and from France, 1993-1997								
	FDI inflow				**FDI inward stock**			
*From the world * to :*	1993	%	1997	%	1993	%	1997	%
• **EECs**	**8301**	**100**	**22409**	**100**	**15001**	**100**	**81288**	**100**
• CEFTA	4988	60.1	8792	39.2	11605	77.4	45500	56.0
• Balkans	307	3.7	2303	10.3	910	6.1	6471	8.0
• Baltic states	237	2.8	1143	5.1	303	2.0	3461	4.2
• CIS	2769	33.4	10171	45.4	2183	14.5	25856	31.8
*From France ** to :*	1993	%	1997	%	1993	%	1997	%
• **EECs**	**1678**	**100**	**6668**	**100**	**3441**	**100**	**17198**	**100**
• CEFTA	1622	96.7	4451	66.8	3129	90.9	13138	76.4
• Balkans	56	3.3	1488	22.3	96	2.8	2392	13.9
• Baltic states	0	0	0	0	0	0	23	0.1
• CIS	0	0	729	10.9	216	6.3	1645	9.6

* In million dollars, Source: UNCTAD (1999); ** In million francs, **Source**: Banque de France

The question to be addressed now is to assess whether this geographical distribution is accompanied with a substitution (or a crowding out) of OPT by FDI. We focus on this issue only in the case of France OPT and FDI, though it pertains to the renewal of a more general debate in the economic literature today (Altzinger, 1999, Brenton and di Mauro, 1998) about the substitutability or complementarity between FDI and trade, initiated by Mundell (1957) who advocated the substitutability thesis (for the complementarity thesis, see Fontagné and Pajot, 1998). It has been shown, for instance, that the growth of EEC exports coincides with a strong presence of FDI in some sectors, the automotive industry being the best example (Lemoine and Freudenberg, 1999), a fact which supports the complementarity hypothesis. It is also expected, at least for CEFTA countries, that both trade and FDI will be similar in the future to what they have been in the last few years (Sass, 1999), expressing a low profile support to complementarity. A more precise analysis should include the determinants of FDI. If FDI is market seeking, one must expect FDI and exports to be potential substitutes; they must be complementary if efficiency-seeking transnational corporations relocate their production in low (unit labor) cost host countries. Some recent econometric exercises (Alessandrini and Bosco, 1998) have not been able to demonstrate that globally complementarity is prevailing over substitutability for FDI and trade with the EECs. Complementarity is significant in some sectors such as chemicals and electrical equipment. Substitutability prevails in food, milk and derivatives, metals, rubber and plastics. Evidence is mixed in machine building, textiles and clothing. These results highlight the non linearity of the relationship between trade and FDI which is usually assumed outside the context of Eastern Europe (Markusen and Venables, 1995). But outward processing trade is not direct trade.

Now we look at the possible substitution effect between France OPT and FDI, from 1993 to 1997. We have calculated an aggregated market value of inward flows in the EECs, summing up OPT exports and FDI inflows from France (Annex 6). In 1993, the share of OPT (46%) was yet lower than the one of FDI (54%). In 1997, the share of OPT has diminished (26%) to the benefit of FDI. Let us *distinguish a simple substitution effect from a crowding out effect*. If a smaller increase of an OPT export from France to one EEC subgroup (like CEFTA, CIS, Balkans) responds to a bigger increase of FDI from France to the same subgroup, then elasticity of OPT to FDI is lower than 1. Thus, in an overall increasing market for OPT and FDI, the share of FDI grows faster than the share of OPT, and the former partly substitutes to the latter. We call this a substitution effect. On the other hand, if a decrease in OPT export from France to one EEC subgroup responds to an increase in FDI from France to the same subgroup, then elasticity is negative (lower than zero). Here OPT is partly crowded out by FDI.

At first sight, from 1993 to 1997, FDI is gaining ground over OPT, exhibiting *a substitution effect* insofar as OPT is still growing, but slower than FDI does (Annex 6). The relative share of OPT basically declines in the CIS, from 100% to 27%, in the Balkans, from 86% to 36%, then in the four MPCs, from 33% to 21%. Table 4 suggests that there is *no crowding out* of OPT by FDI in any EEC subgroup (no negative elasticity). Except CIS countries which have not welcomed any significant French FDI in 1993, the strongest substitution of FDI to OPT is witnessed for the four major OPT partners of France: from 1993 to 1997, each increase of, say, one Ecu of French FDI is accompanied with a 0.31 Ecu increase of OPT. Then comes the CEFTA countries: a 0.27 Ecu increase in OPT for each Ecu increase of FDI, and then come the Balkan countries (0.06 Ecu in OPT increase for each Ecu of FDI increase). Anyway, weaker or stronger, a *substitutability relationship* is exhibited between OPT and FDI.

Table 4 - Substitution Elasticities of France

OPT to FDI in the EECs from 1993 to 1997	
All East European countries	0.22
CEFTA countries	0.27
of which the four major partners (MPCs)	0.31
Balkan countries	0.06
CIS countries	infinite

Authors' calculation from Eurostat and Banque de France

How can we explain the observed tendency of French FDI to substitute to OPT in the EECs? A first simple factor is that the duty-free advantage of OPT was on the brink of disappearing in 1997, and it was rather sensible for French main contractors to give up OPT. This explains why the pace of OPT has slowed down, not why FDI has accelerated, except if some French firms have taken over their former EEC subcontractors, or have invested in some local processing enterprises in the host country. We lack microeconomic evidence here to support this view. The quality of the processed goods has probably increased in the EECs throughout the industrial co-operation with French firms, in particular when the local subcontractor has restructured and sharply adjusted to the main contractor's requirements. Again, microeconomic evidence is needed to confirm such an assumption, but we know that the quality of various EEC exports has increased in particular in machine building and textile-clothing by mid-nineties, compared with late eighties (Landesmann and Burgstaller, 1997). In the same vein, resulting from years of subcontracting work with French firms, a possibly increased competitiveness of EEC subcontractors have made them more autonomous from (or even competing with) their main contractors, so that the latter then have preferred to turn to FDI.

We would test more precisely two assumptions. As to the first one, OPT is a strategy of producers looking for lower unit labor costs abroad. On the other hand, some econometric studies (Andreff and Andreff, 1997; Andreff, 1999b; Meyer 1998) have successfully tested the hypothesis that a large part of FDI in the EECs has been determined by market demand so far, and thus has been achieved by Western firms conducting a market-seeking strategy. Under this assumption OPT and FDI are expected to be complementary as long as unit labor costs are low in the EECs, OPT being undertaken in a cost-minimizing strategy and FDI being much more kept for market-seeking strategies. But, since the unit labor cost increases in the EECs, OPT becomes less attractive than a demand-oriented FDI, the latter being fueled by income (wage) increases, and this *may pave the way for a partial substitution of FDI to OPT*. The second assumption starts from the idea that FDI requires a better investment climate and country-risk than OPT and, then, the substitution of FDI to OPT *reflects a better, safer and more stable economic and political environment* in most EECs in 1997 than at the dawn of the transition, basically due to economic recovery, structural and institutional change, and soft changeover of political power between parties. To make the test feasible, we would reduce this factor to the eight EBRD qualitative indicators of progress in the transition process that encompass: large-scale privatization; small-scale privatization; governance and enterprise restructuring; price liberalization; trade and foreign exchange system; competition policy; banking reform and interest rate liberalization; and securities markets and non-bank financial institutions. A second test relies on the country-risk evaluation of the EECs.

In 1993, the labor cost per hour was 1.34 DM in Romania, 1.68 DM in Bulgaria, 2.70 DM in Slovakia, 3.01 DM in the Czech Republic, 3.45 DM in Poland, 4.54 DM in Hungary as against 42.67 DM in West Germany (Schroeder, 1995). According to another estimation, the gross wage per month per employee was, in 1993, 30.3 Ecus in Ukraine, 53.0 Ecus in Russia, 87.9 Ecus in Romania, 99.7 Ecus in Bulgaria, 127.3 Ecus in Croatia, 149.5 Ecus in Slovakia, 170.5 Ecus in the Czech Republic, 184.2 Ecus in Poland, 252.8 Ecus in Hungary, 570.2 Ecus in Slovenia, as compared to 1900.8 Ecus in Austria (Havlik, 1998) and 1730.2 Ecus in France. Once their low level of productivity is taken into account, the EECs are still left with a considerable advantage in unit labor costs (Nagarajan, 1994). The unit labor cost, including indirect costs, in CEFTA and the Balkan countries was between one tenth and two fifths of the Austrian level in 1993: 7.8% in Ukraine, 9.3% in Russia, 17.2% in Bulgaria, 17.6% in Slovakia, 18.5% in the Czech Republic, 20.4% in Romania, 26.6% in Croatia, 29.9% in Poland, 31.9% in Hungary and 40.8% in Slovenia, according to Havlik's calculation. Gross wages have increased after the mid-nineties, the productivity as well, but, on average, less than real wages (Andreff, 1999a) so that the unit labor cost is on a growing trend in the EECs. This trend is evidenced in Table 5, except for Hungary, in 1993-1998.

Table 5 - Annual Change in D-Mark Unit Labor Cost in Some EECs, 1993-1998 (in %)

Country	1994	1995	1996	1997	1998	1993-1998
Bulgaria	(-32.1)	5.4	(-21.0)	44.1	36.6	11.3
Croatia	33.6	25.9	2.0	0.4	(-1.2)	70.2
Czech Republic	11.3	1.5	10.0	0.9	4.3	30.8
Estonia	61.7	35.2	19.2	(-5.1)	24.0	206.6
Hungary	(-3.6)	(-19.1)	(-3.4)	0.6	(-4.7)	(-27.8)
Latvia	85.7	2.8	(-0.9)	18.4	2.6	129.8
Lithuania	85.2	23.3	30.4	32.8	11.9	342.3
Poland	(-6.2)	2.9	9.0	3.0	3.2	11.9
Romania	(-1.4)	(-4.2)	0.4	(-7.3)	40.2	23.3
Russia	79.8	(-4.9)	54.6	16.9	n.a.	n.a.
Slovakia	0.7	5.5	14.0	12.9	(-5.0)	30.0
Slovenia	(-2.1)	3.7	(-1.6)	4.8	2.8	7.6

Source: EBRD (1999).

Coming to the test of our assumptions, we have unfortunately to work on small country samples, not only because the EECs are twenty-seven, but also due to missing data for some countries as regards, for instance, the unit labor cost, or for those EECs in which FDI or OPT is non existent in some years. With a small number of observations (smaller than thirty), it is not much significant to undertake sophisticated analyses based on linear regression. We have thus calculated rank correlation between FDI and OPT on the one hand, and various aforementioned economic variables or indicators on the other hand. Such a methodology is recommended in order to test the dependence or independence between two variables on the basis of small samples, because this method does not depend on the underlying distribution of variables (namely it does not depend on the assumption of a Gaussian distribution).

The Spearman rank correlation is calculated as follows: $r_S = 1 - \frac{6\sum_i d_i^2}{n(n^2-1)}$

where d_i stands for the difference between the two rankings of a country, according to two variables, and n is the sample size. Looking at the Spearman table, we can conclude at a concordance (a positive coefficient close to 1) or a discordance (a negative coefficient close to -1) or no relation (a coefficient close to zero) between the ranks for the two variables. If the coefficient of rank correlation is not significant, then the two variables are independent.

The first test consists in verifying whether French FDI is attracted by the market size of the EECs. Taking GDP as a proxy for the market size of each country, we have calculated the rank correlation between French FDI inflows and GDP of host countries for eighteen EECs whose data is available in 1997. We observe (Table 6) a concordance between the two variables, which are significantly correlated, a result that supports the idea of a primarily *market-seeking strategy followed by French firms investing in the EECS.*

Table 6 – Rank Correlation between FDI, OPT and Other Variables and Indicators

Variable 1	Variable 2*	Rank correlation Coefficient	CEECs number	Level of significance	Test
French FDI 1997	GDP 1997	0.5996	18	1%	significant
French FDI 1994	Variation of ULC in 1993	0.4048	8	35%	non significant
French OPT 1994	Variation of ULC in 1993	(-0.4818)	11	15%	non significant
French FDI 1997	Variation of ULC in 1996	(-0.5182)	11	10%	non significant
French OPT 1997	Variation of ULC in 1996	(-0.4000)	11	20%	non significant
French FDI 1997	Average EBRD indicator 1996	0.4971	16	5%	significant
French OPT 1997	Average EBRD indicator 1996	0.1649	19	50%	non significant
French FDI 1994	Country-risk rank in 1993	(-0.3818)	10	17%	non significant
French OPT 1994	Country-risk rank in 1993	(-0.5607)	15	3.5%	significant
French FDI 1997	Country-risk rank in 1996	(-0.6882)	16	0.5%	significant
French OPT 1997	Country-risk rank in 1996	(-0.5158)	19	2%	significant

* variation of ULC: variation of D-Mark unit labour cost as given in Table 6 - average EBRD indicator: average note obtained by a country with the 8 EBRD indicators - country-risk ranking published in Euromoney

We have calculated the rank correlation between French FDI (then OPT) of one year and the variation of the unit labor cost in the previous year, in view of assessing whether FDI (OPT) does react or not to a change in labor cost. The test is achieved at the beginning and at the end of our observation period. The correlation coefficient is negative, as expected, meaning that a lower unit labor cost should be in concordance with a higher FDI or OPT (with the exception of FDI in 1994, but this is probably due to the small number of observations). However, the test is not significant, at the usual 5% threshold, for either the relation between FDI and the unit labor cost or the relation between the latter and OPT. *Labor cost is not a major determinant of French FDI in the CEECs* which confirms a result found for all FDI in the region (Andreff and Andreff, 1997; Meyer, 1998). What is more surprising, given the importance of labor cost in the literature on production relocation and OPT, is the absence of a significant relation between OPT and the unit labor cost, at least in the French case. Coming back to our first assumption, the first part of it is acceptable: this is a market-oriented FDI that substitutes to OPT between France and the EECs. But the second part is not: this substitution is not much triggered by the increase of a labor cost in the EECs that has often been supposed to be influential on OPT.

Then, we turn to our second assumption. The rank correlation between French FDI in the EECs in 1997 and the average of the eight EBRD indicators of institutional improvement in 1996 is significant, at the 5% threshold, and exhibits a positive sign. This means that *the more a EEC has developed its market-oriented institutions in the previous year, the more it will attract a French FDI inflow in the current year*. On the other hand, even if the relation between OPT and the average EBRD indicator shows the expected positive sign, the rank correlation coefficient is weak and the test is not significant at all. Thus, it seems that (French) FDI requires more institutional preconditions to be attracted into the host countries (EECs) than OPT to be developed with the same partners. Once the market-friendly institutional framework has been upgraded in a number of EECs, FDI tends to substitute to OPT, in particular in those EECs more advanced in institutional reforms (roughly speaking, the CEFTA countries). Such a factor is also likely to explain that CEFTA countries, due to more comprehensive institutional reforms, have attracted more FDI than Balkan countries, whereas the latter are now challenging the former as regards OPT expansion. Finally, the absence of a significant relation between OPT and market-friendly institutions is also meaningful in retrospect, if we refer to the pre-transition period when OPT was yet linking West European (French) firms to East European subcontractors while the institutional framework was not incentive to (or was forbidding) FDI.

Our last calculated rank correlation is between French FDI (OPT) and the ranking of the EECs as to their evaluated country-risk one year before. In 1994, the correlation between OPT and the country-risk is significant and has the expected negative sign, meaning that *the higher country-risk, the lower OPT*. There is no significant relation between French FDI and country-risk which is quite understandable because French firms has only achieved investments in a small sub-sample of ten EECs (out of twenty-seven) and are absent, as direct investors, from most EECs in 1994. The picture has changed in 1997. The country-risk, on average, has improved (lowered) in most EECs and this factor has heavily contributed to attract French FDI in the region (sixteen countries out of twenty-seven). The *correlation between FDI and country-risk has become even more significant than the one linking OPT and country-risk* in 1997; this result fits with the evidence of FDI substituting to OPT in an upgraded economic and political environment in a number of EECs.

4. The Sectoral Pattern of French Direct Investment into the Central Eastern European Countries

The knowledge of the FDI sectoral distribution in the EECs is rather scarce and blurred. The great bulk of what is known has recently been gathered by UNCTAD (1999) for the ten CEECs, four CIS countries (Belarus, Moldova, Russia, and Ukraine) and two Balkan countries (Bosnia-Herzegovina, Croatia) in 1997. From this overall picture a first trend emerges: the inward FDI stock is more concentrated on the tertiary sector than on the secondary sector in Bosnia, Estonia, Hungary, Latvia, Lithuania, Moldova, Russia, Slovakia and Slovenia. It is more invested in manufacturing than in services industries in Bulgaria, Croatia and Romania; the distribution is fairly balanced between the two sectors in the Czech Republic, Poland and Ukraine, while FDI is more involved in the primary sector in Belarus (whose share is also significant in Russia). Manufacturing FDI is mostly present in the food industry, chemicals, metal products, electrical machinery and equipment, and to some extent in the automotive industry (basically in four CEECs). FDI in services is concentrated in trade and finance-banking-insurance whereas it is non negligible in transport-telecommunications, real estate, construction, and electricity and water distribution (basically in Hungary, Moldova and Slovenia for the latter service industry). Let us consider these features as a sort of world average sectoral pattern of FDI flowing into the EECs.

Compared with the above-described average, the sectoral structure of French FDI flow to the EECs, in 1997, appears rather specific. FDI inflow from France is present in only 16 EECs: seven CEECs (Bulgaria, the Czech Republic, Hungary, Poland, Romania, Slovakia, and Slovenia), seven CIS countries (Armenia, Azerbaijan, Georgia, Kazakhstan, Russia, Turkmenistan, and Ukraine) and two Balkan countries (Albania, Croatia). In seven of them, French FDI inflow is fully concentrated (100%) on the tertiary sector in 1997, which is the case of Armenia, Azerbaijan, Bulgaria, Georgia, Kazakhstan, Slovenia and Ukraine, where it is basically attracted in trade and finance, and then in real estate. In other EECs, these three latter services industries gather a prominent share of French FDI inflow as well. The value of French FDI inflow is actually significant in the manufacturing industry in only six countries: the Czech Republic, Hungary, Poland, Romania, Russia and Slovakia (48% of overall FDI, though it makes a small amount in million francs in this country). For the first five of them, the FDI sectoral distribution is exhibited in Table 7: except in Romania, *French FDI in the services industry is bigger than in the manufacturing industry*, showing a pattern roughly similar to the one of the overall French FDI in the world, though less geared towards manufactured products.

Table 7 - Sectoral Pattern of French FDI in five East European Countries, 1997 (in %)

Sector	French FDI flow to:					
	Czech Rep.	Hungary	Poland	Romania	Russia	The world
Agriculture, fishing	0	0.9	0	0	0	0.02
Mining, quarrying, petroleum	0	0	0	0	0	0.1
Manufacturing products	31.7	6.5	31.9	92.3	12.3	42.7
Electricity, gas. water	0.3	61.8	0	0	0	0.8
Building industry, civil engineer.	0.3	1.5	1.1	0.7	30.0	0.8
Services, of which :	67.6	29.3	67.0	7.0	57.7	55.5
Trade	3.0	15.5	17.4	0.4	24.9	10.0
Finance, banking, insurance	45.5	6.5	10.4	4.1	6.4	15.1
Real estate, rental activities	18.5	6.9	27.9	2.0	26.0	26.9

Source: Banque de France.

A more detailed view of the French FDI distribution by industry, in the manufacturing sector of the five countries, is provided in Annex 7. Within the manufacturing industry, in 1997, French FDI in the world is first concentrated in electrical machinery and equipment, and in chemicals; then come the food industry, the automotive industry, the oil industry and machine building. All other industries (including textile and clothing) have a share roughly lower than 2% of the overall French manufacturing investment abroad. We do not find exactly the same pattern for French FDI in the four EECs (the data for Romania gives a few information). While FDI is significant in chemicals in all countries, it is absent in electrical machinery and equipment. French FDI in the food industry is ahead in the Czech Republic and Poland and still well involved in Hungary, but it is non existent in Russia. Machine building is much attractive to French FDI in Russia and over the (world) average in the Czech Republic and Poland. A Hungarian specificity is to attract the great bulk of French manufacturing investment in the non-ferrous metallurgy (in fact the aluminum industry) whereas the Czech one is to concentrate an over average share of French FDI in textile-clothing, the automotive industry and the ferrous and non ferrous metallurgy.

Now it is of interest to compare the distribution of French FDI by industry with the industrial pattern of French OPT in the five EECs. Considering the OPT pattern, the concentration is on textile-clothing as against chemicals and the food industry in the case of FDI, with the exception of Russia where OPT is more concentrated than FDI in chemicals. The second most important industry for French-EEC OPT is electrical machinery and equipment while there is no French FDI at all in this industry in 1997. On the other hand, the share of machine building is higher in FDI than OPT for Hungary, Poland and Russia, whereas it is lower for the Czech Republic. In Hungary and the Czech Republic, the small share of metallurgy in French OPT cannot compare with the significant share of French FDI in this manufacturing industry. Such a contrasted distribution pattern suggests an industrial complementarity between French FDI and OPT in the EECs, an assumption which must be submitted to further testing once more detailed data will be available. Thus, we reach the following conclusion: *while French FDI is substituting to French OPT with the EECs as the time is going on, what remains in 1997 is a rather complementary industrial structure between FDI and OPT* the French firms are involved in. This finding is quite consistent with our previous empirical analysis showing that the determinants of French FDI are different from the determinants of French OPT, and that the latter are vanishing while the former are strengthening. Since the sectoral patterns of FDI and OPT are different and complementary, this means that the substitution of the former to the latter over the years must also be interpreted as a *sectoral shift of the French stakes* in the EEC manufacturing industry, primarily from textile-clothing and electrical equipment to chemicals and the food industry.

5. Conclusion

Our main findings are that France OPT in the EECs has developed from 1993 to 1997 with a specific geographical orientation compared to EU-15 OPT with the EECs, and a product concentration on the textile-clothing industry. We have found a substitution of French FDI to France OPT, from 1993 to 1997, in all the country subgroups of the EECs. In 1997, the sectoral patterns of French FDI and OPT in the EECs are quite different and complementary, meaning that the substitution of FDI to OPT is going alongside with a sectoral shift of the French penetration in the EEC manufacturing industry.

References

1. Alessandrini S. and M.G. Bosco (1998), Trade and Foreign Direct Investment: Are they complementary or substitute? An econometric analysis on three CEE countries, *CEPS Conference*, Brussels, 24-25 April.
2. Altzinger W. (1999), Is FDI Becoming a Substitute for Exports? Empirical Evidence of Austria's Integration with Eastern Europe, *Emergo*, 6 (1), p. 86-98.
3. Andreff M. (1998), La spécialisation du commerce entre l'Union européenne et les pays d'Europe centrale et orientale: quelle évolution?, *Revue d'Etudes comparatives Est-Ouest*, 29 (4), p. 161-189.
4. Andreff M. and W. Andreff (1995), Economic Disintegration in Eastern Europe: Towards a New Integration?, in B. Dallago, G. Pegoretti, eds., *Integration and Disintegration in European Economies*, Aldershot: Dartmouth.
5. Andreff M., W. Andreff (1997), L'investissement direct étranger en Russie et dans les pays de la Communauté des Etats Indépendants: emploi et attractivité, in J. de Melo, P. and P. Guillaumont, eds., *Commerce Nord-Sud, migration et délocalisation. Conséquences sur les salaires et l'emploi*, Paris: Economica.

6. Andreff M., W. Andreff, and F. Boudier-Bensebaa (2001), Sous-traitance internationale de façonnage et trafic de perfectionnement passif entre les pays de l'Union européenne et de l'Europe de l'Est, *Revue d'Etudes comparatives Est-Ouest*, n° 2.
7. Andreff W. (1996), *Les multinationales globales*, Paris: La Découverte.
8. Andreff W. (1999a), Nominal and Real Convergence - At What Speed?, in J. van Brabant, ed., *Remaking Europe. The European Union and the Transition Economies*, Lanham: Rowman & Littlefield.
9. Andreff W. (1999b), The Global Strategy of Multinational Corporations and their Assessment of Eastern European and C.I.S. Countries, in V. Tikhomirov, ed., *Anatomy of the 1998 Russian Crisis*, Contemporary Europe Research Centre, The University of Melbourne.
10. Andreff W. (2000), Foreign direct investment in Central and Eastern Europe, Keynote speech, 3rd EACES workshop in Paris: *Impact of foreign direct investment and know how transfer on restructuring, spin off and networking in Central and Eastern Europe and Asian transitional economies*, University Marne la Vallée, 8-9 June (EACES: European Association for Comparative Economic Studies).
11. Boudier-Bensebaa F., and H. Brezinski (2000), *Outward-Processing Trade Between Germany and the Central Eastern European Countries*, VIth ICCEES World Congress, Tampere, 29 July - 3 August.
12. Brenton P., and F. di Mauro (1998), The Potential Magnitude and Impact of FDI Flows to CEECs, Centre for European Policy Studies, *Working document, n° 116*, February.
13. CGP (1999), *L'élargissement de l'Union européenne à l'est de l'Europe: des gains à escompter à l'Est et à l'Ouest*, Commissariat Général du Plan, Paris: La Documentation Française.
14. Corado C. (1994), Trade with Central and Eastern Europe: Impacts on members of the EC, *CEPR Discussion paper series*, n° 1004, August.
15. EBRD (1999), *Transition report 1999*, European Bank for Reconstruction and Development, London.
16. Fontagné L., M. Freudenberg, and D. Unal-Kesenci (1995), Régionalisation et échanges de biens intermédiaires, *Document de travail du CEPII*, n° 95, 11 décembre.
17. Fontagné L., and M. Pajot (1998), Investissement direct à l'étranger et commerce international. Le cas français, *Revue Economique*, 49 (3), p. 593-606.
18. Graziani G. (1998), Globalization of production in the textile and clothing industries: The case of Italian foreign direct investment and outward processing trade in Eastern Europe, in J. Zysman, and A. Schwartz, eds., *Enlarging Europe: The Industrial Foundations of a New Political Reality*, A BRIE/Kreisky Forum Project, IAS, Berkeley: University of California.
19. Halpern L. (1994), Comparative Advantage and Likely Trade Pattern of the CEECs, *CEPR Discussion paper*, n° 1003, September.
20. Hamar J. (1998), How to integrate into the global markets: Recent experiences with OPT and MNCs in Hungary (an update), in *Integrating the Enterprise Sphere of*

Central-European Countries in Transition into European Corporate Structures, Phare-Ace n° 95P-2003.R.

21. Havlik P. (1998), Labour Cost Competitiveness of Central and Eastern Europe, *MOCT-MOST*, 8 (2), p. 13-33.
22. Landesmann M., and I. Burgstaller (1997), Vertical Product Differentiation in EU Markets: The relative position of East European producers, *WIIW Research Report*, n° 234a.
23. Lankes H.P., and A.J. Venables (1996), Foreign direct investment in economic transition: The changing pattern of investments, *Economics of Transition*, 4 (2), p. 331-347.
24. Lemoine F. (1998), Integrating Central and Eastern Europe in the regional trade and production network, in J. Zysman, and A. Schwartz, eds., *Enlarging Europe: The Industrial Foundations of a New Political Reality*, A BRIE/Kreisky Forum Project, IAS, Berkeley: University of California.
25. Lemoine F., and M. Freudenberg (1999), Les pays d'Europe centrale et orientale dans la division du travail en Europe, *Economie internationale*, 80, p. 3-35.
26. Markusen J., and A.J. Venables (1995), Multinational Firms and the New Trade Theory, *NBER Working paper, n° 5036.*
27. Meyer K. (1998), *Direct Investment in Economies in Transition*, Cheltenham: Edward Elgar.
28. Mundell R. A. (1957), International Trade and Factor Mobility, *American Economic Review*, 47 (3), p. 321-335.
29. Nagarajan N. (1994), EU-CEEC trade in textiles and clothing: market access and future prospects, *European Economy, n° 6,* European Commission, Luxembourg.
30. Neale C.W., and P. Sercu (1993), Countertrade in International and Domestic Markets, *International Trade Journal*, 7 (3), p. 271-294.
31. Oman C. (1984), *New Forms of International Investment in Developing Countries*, Paris, OECD.
32. Sass M. (1999), Trade and Foreign Investment: The Case of Hungary and the EU, *Emergo*, 6 (1), p. 49-64.
33. Schmidt K.D., and P. Naujoks (1994), Outward processing in Central and East European transition countries: Issues and results from German statistics, *Kiel working papers, n° 631, Institut für Weltwirschaft, Kiel.*
34. Schroeder C. (1995), Arbeitkosten in Südostasien und in den Reformstaaten Mittel und Osteuropas, *IW Trends*, n° 1, p. 29-41 (IW Köln).
35. UNCTAD (1999), *World Investment Report. Foreign Direct Investment and the Challenge of Development*, United Nations, New York & Geneva.
36. UNECE (1995), Outward-processing trade between the European Union and the associated countries of Eastern Europe: The case of textiles and clothing, *Economic Bulletin for Europe*, Economic Commission for Europe, United Nations, Geneva.
37. Zaleski E., and H. Wienert (1980), *Transfert de techniques entre l'Est et l'Ouest*, OCDE, Paris.

ANNEX 1: FRANCE OUTWARD PROCESSING TRADE WITH THE EECs:

Values and percentage in overall trade, 1993 and 1997

	Poland	Czech Rep.	Hungary	Romania	CEFTA	Baltic st.	Balkans	CIS	**EECs**
Export 1993									
OPT *	43214	11398	41198	45600	123169	608	53429	37133	214339
OPT/OT % **	5.66%	2.75%	10.87%	11.55%	5.95%	0.58%	7.21%	2.31%	4.74%
Import 1993									
OPT *	56728	13387	67139	57684	166913	739	67509	64345	299506
OPT/OT % **	9.72%	5.58%	23.39%	26.02%	10.31%	0.71%	13.51%	2.63%	6.41%
Export 1997									
OPT *	64500	21986	75564	88640	182359	1090	128578	40168	352195
OPT/OT % **	3.12%	2.06%	9.20%	16.35%	3.53%	0.41%	12.25%	1.11%	3.48%
Import 1997									
OPT *	88365	24399	77669	100501	219138	2858	157353	134269	513618
OPT/OT % **	8.58%	4.38%	11.48%	23.93%	7.70%	1.52%	22.44%	3.36%	6.64%

* Outward processing trade, in thousand Ecus - ** Ratio of OPT to overall trade in percentage - **Source**: Eurostat

ANNEX 2: DISTRIBUTION OF FRANCE OUTWARD PROCESSING TRADE BY COUNTRY AND GEOGRAPHICAL AREA 1993 AND 1997

	Poland	Czech Rep.	Hungary	Romania	CEFTA	Baltic st.	Balkans	CIS	**EECs**
Export 1993	20.16%	5.32%	19.22%	21.27%	57.46%	0.28%	24.93%	17.32%	100.00%
Import 1993	18.94%	4.47%	22.42%	19.26%	55.73%	0.25%	22.54%	21.48%	100.00%
Export 1997	18.35%	6.25%	21.50%	25.22%	51.88%	0.31%	36.38%	11.43%	100.00%
Import 1997	17.20%	4.75%	15.12%	19.57%	42.67%	0.56%	30.64%	26.14%	100.00%

Source: Eurostat

ANNEX 3: DISTRIBUTION OF FRANCE-EEC OUTWARD PROCESSING TRADE BY PRODUCT, 1993 AND 1997

Export 1993						Import 1993					
CEFTA			EECs			CEFTA			EECs		
Product code	%	cumul. %	Product code	%	cumul. %	Product code	%	cumul. %	Product code	%	cumul. %
51	15.55	15.55	61	15.26	15.26	62	59.73	59.73	62	48.68	48.68
55	14.33	29.88	55	14.26	29.52	61	15.22	74.95	61	20.72	69.40
62	7.80	37.68	51	10.90	40.42	64	12.95	87.89	28	11.71	81.11
41	7.31	44.99	62	8.90	49.31	85	5.46	93.35	64	8.24	89.34
54	6.92	51.91	28	7.81	57.12	42	1.37	94.72	85	3.12	92.46
52	6.39	58.30	52	5.70	62.82	63	1.35	96.07	87	1.16	93.62
60	6.39	64.69	54	5.64	68.46	73	0.65	96.72	33	1.09	94.71
61	5.80	70.49	41	4.48	72.94	53	0.47	97.18	42	0.80	95.50
64	5.40	75.88	60	4.17	77.11	84	0.42	97.61	63	0.76	96.26
59	4.68	80.57	64	3.20	80.30	95	0.32	97.93	94	0.51	96.77
Textile	58.63		Textile	46.93		Textile	0.79		Textile	0.51	
Clothing	14.39		Clothing	24.65		Clothing	76.29		Clothing	70.16	
Mach. B*	0.95		Mach. B*	1.88		Mach. B*	0.42		Mach. B*	0.38	
Elect.**	3.63		Elect.**	2.24		Elect.**	5.46		Elect.**	3.12	

Export 1997						Import 1997					
CEFTA			EECs			CEFTA			EECs		
Product code	%	cumul. %	Product code	%	cumul. %	Product code	%	cumul. %	Product code	%	cumul. %
85	30.28	30.28	61	19.00	19.00	62	52.35	52.35	62	42.92	42.92
55	13.84	44.11	85	17.13	36.13	85	18.62	70.97	61	20.17	63.09
61	9.24	53.35	55	14.06	50.19	61	15.84	86.82	28	18.57	81.66
51	8.82	62.17	62	10.67	60.86	84	3.01	89.83	85	8.34	90.00
52	4.71	66.88	51	7.88	68.75	63	2.63	92.45	64	3.19	93.19
58	4.65	71.53	52	5.16	73.91	64	1.44	93.89	84	1.42	94.60
62	4.41	75.94	58	3.39	77.30	87	1.22	95.12	63	1.17	95.77
84	3.77	79.71	28	3.14	80.44	73	0.83	95.95	87	0.74	96.52
54	2.68	82.38	84	2.58	83.02	42	0.82	96.76	42	0.46	96.98
60	2.65	85.03	41	2.29	85.31	53	0.81	97.58	55	0.42	97.39
Textile	41.90		Textile	37.93		Textile	1.16		Textile	0.97	
Clothing	14.37		Clothing	30.11		Clothing	70.82		Clothing	64.25	
Mach. B*	3.77		Mach. B*	2.58		Mach. B*	3.01		Mach. B*	1.42	
Elect. **	30.28		Elect. **	17.13		Elect. **	18.62		Elect.**	8.34	

Mach. B* = Machine Building - Elect.** = Electrical Equipment - **Source**: Eurostat.

ANNEX 4.1: REVEALED COMPARATIVE ADVANTAGES OF THE EECs IN OUTWARD PROCESSING EXPORT TO FRANCE

Annex 4.1a: Export to France in 1997

Product	Poland	Czech Rep.	Hungary	Romania	CEFTA	Baltic st.	Balkans	CIS
28	0.00	0.00	0.00	0.00	0.00	0.00	0.00	14.98
41	0.00	0.00	0.00	0.00	0.37	0.00	3.42	0.00
Textile	**5.46**	**2.77**	**0.34**	**0.09**	**2.70**	**189.87**	**0.14**	**0.03**
of which 50	0.00	0.00	4.19	0.00	1.86	0.00	0.00	0.00
51	0.05	0.16	1.55	0.32	0.68	665.77	0.56	0.00
52	0.28	23.76	0.00	0.55	3.08	0.00	0.63	0.11
54	2.76	0.00	4.39	0.00	4.00	0.00	0.00	0.00
55	1.73	0.08	0.68	0.08	1.06	635.74	0.19	0.07
58	0.07	0.00	0.00	0.00	0.03	0.00	0.00	0.00
60	0.74	11.47	0.22	0.08	1.74	0.00	0.05	0.00
Clothing	**3.18**	**0.83**	**3.24**	**4.02**	**2.96**	**0.75**	**3.65**	**1.15**
of which 61	2.51	1.28	2.77	8.37	2.46	0.00	6.70	0.12
62	3.35	0.57	3.51	2.49	3.09	1.04	2.60	1.58
64	0.02	0.02	0.25	0.15	0.73	0.00	4.24	0.00
Mec.Eqt (84)	**0.08**	**0.61**	**0.05**	**0.01**	**0.13**	**0.00**	**0.01**	**0.01**
Elect.Eqt(85)	**0.94**	**2.35**	**1.02**	**0.07**	**1.02**	**0.00**	**0.07**	**0.00**
90	0.06	0.00	0.02	0.00	0.03	0.12	0.02	0.02

Annex 4.1b: Export to France in 1993

Product	Poland	Czech Rep.	Hungary	Romania	CEFTA	Baltic st.	Balkans	CIS
28	0.00	0.00	0.00	0.00	0.00	0.00	0.00	19.22
41	0.26	6.51	2.27	0.00	1.52	0.00	0.00	0.11
Textile	**3.34**	**4.15**	**0.51**	**0.39**	**1.74**	**12.56**	**0.44**	**0.10**
of which 50	0.00	0.00	0.00	0.00	0.00	0.00	0.00	0.00
51	4.17	83.48	1.09	1.98	8.55	0.00	1.69	0.25
52	0.83	0.00	0.26	0.00	0.46	0.00	2.88	0.09
54	0.84	0.00	0.39	0.00	0.44	0.00	0.00	0.00
55	3.16	27.04	3.07	2.88	4.48	26.96	2.46	0.98
58	0.04	0.00	0.05	0.00	0.03	0.00	0.00	0.01
60	0.26	0.00	0.99	0.00	0.52	0.00	0.00	0.15
Clothing	**2.70**	**1.45**	**3.04**	**3.20**	**2.70**	**3.20**	**3.04**	**1.33**
of which 61	3.05	1.34	1.64	7.71	2.20	0.55	7.06	0.82
62	2.57	1.48	3.56	1.78	2.87	4.06	1.78	1.53
64	4.11	13.96	1.63	0.21	5.02	0.00	1.76	0.00
Mach.B* (84)	**0.03**	**0.02**	**0.01**	**0.02**	**0.02**	**0.01**	**0.01**	**0.02**
Elect. (85)**	**0.29**	**0.49**	**0.31**	**0.00**	**0.27**	**0.19**	**0.00**	**0.01**
90	0.02	0.28	0.03	0.00	0.05	0.00	0.08	0.06

Source: Eurostat

ANNEX 4.2: REVEALED COMPARATIVE ADVANTAGES OF THE EECS IN OUTWARD PROCESSING IMPORT FROM FRANCE

Annex 4.2a: Import from France in 1997

Product		Poland	Czech Rep.	Hungary	Romania	CEFTA	Baltic st.	Balkans	CIS
28		0.00	0.00	0.00	0.00	0.00	0.00	0.00	62.69
41		0.45	1.28	0.02	0.00	1.76	0.00	4.22	0.01
Textile		**4.81**	**0.48**	**4.26**	**1.97**	**4.23**	**8.96**	**2.72**	**5.43**
of which	50	0.12	0.00	0.26	0.05	0.18	0.00	0.04	0.00
	51	7.09	0.41	7.30	3.69	6.95	34.92	4.10	8.84
	52	2.69	0.42	1.14	1.21	2.37	2.86	2.54	3.80
	54	6.01	0.21	9.33	2.75	7.00	17.51	3.19	5.03
	55	8.16	1.03	4.86	3.39	5.72	2.32	4.47	10.63
	58	1.01	0.46	7.95	0.88	3.99	18.19	1.78	1.18
	60	3.50	0.00	3.26	0.97	3.39	5.29	0.97	2.92
Clothing		**4.41**	**1.92**	**1.26**	**13.01**	**2.64**	**0.00**	**10.74**	**2.13**
of which	61	4.82	2.04	1.26	13.67	2.87	0.00	12.08	0.03
	62	3.29	1.17	1.26	12.30	2.05	0.00	9.00	5.34
	64	0.00	0.11	0.83	0.00	0.36	0.00	4.70	0.00
Mach.B*	**(84)**	**0.24**	**1.59**	**0.10**	**0.05**	**0.34**	**0.00**	**0.05**	**0.35**
Elect.**	**(85)**	**0.42**	**1.17**	**0.94**	**0.12**	**0.68**	**0.00**	**0.09**	**0.01**
90		0.02	0.11	0.32	0.00	0.15	0.39	0.00	0.10

Source: Eurostat

Annex 4.2b: Import from France in 1993

Product		Poland	Czech Rep.	Hungary	Romania	CEFTA	Baltic st.	Balkans	CIS
28		0.00	0.00	0.00	0.00	0.00	0.00	0.00	33.90
41		5.62	3.56	1.24	0.20	4.90	0.00	0.74	0.00
Textile		**3.61**	**2.82**	**4.69**	**1.49**	**3.82**	**5.51**	**1.72**	**2.42**
of which	50	0.04	0.01	0.17	0.00	0.29	0.00	0.01	0.01
	51	6.32	2.83	9.40	2.26	7.04	5.22	2.06	2.08
	52	2.02	3.07	1.19	0.32	1.74	0.00	0.70	2.17
	54	8.04	1.06	5.21	2.08	5.69	40.60	3.08	2.80
	55	3.85	2.23	8.34	3.97	4.73	1.03	4.12	5.54
	58	1.22	0.36	1.80	0.19	1.54	1.11	1.14	0.89
	60	2.49	4.63	5.24	0.29	3.96	8.15	0.28	1.24
Clothing		**3.45**	**1.37**	**2.69**	**13.39**	**2.77**	**0.73**	**12.08**	**0.81**
of which	61	3.81	0.35	0.26	18.66	2.09	0.00	17.09	0.18
	62	2.55	2.32	5.67	7.63	3.40	0.86	6.58	1.60
	64	7.43	30.22	2.62	0.75	10.48	0.00	0.76	0.00
Mach.B*	**(84)**	**0.02**	**0.32**	**0.02**	**0.19**	**0.06**	**0.12**	**0.18**	**0.26**
Elect.**	**(85)**	**0.16**	**0.22**	**0.11**	**0.00**	**0.12**	**0.00**	**0.01**	**0.01**
90		0.03	0.45	0.00	0.04	0.06	0.00	0.32	0.00

Source: Eurostat

Annex 5: Contribution of Outward Processing Trade to the Foreign Trade Balance of the EECS (in Percentage)

Annex 5a: In 1997

Product		Poland	Czech Rep.	Hungary	Romania	CEFTA	Baltic st.	Balkans	CIS
28		0.00	0.00	0.00	0.00	0.00	0.00	0.00	15.43
41		-0.21	-0.59	-0.01	0.00	-0.81	0.00	-1.94	0.00
Textile		**-22.11**	**-1.80**	**-21.03**	**-9.69**	**-20.20**	**-2.87**	**-13.30**	**-19.04**
of which	50	-0.08	0.00	-0.17	-0.03	-0.12	0.00	-0.02	0.00
	51	-4.39	-0.26	-4.61	-2.33	-4.37	-11.07	-2.57	-3.98
	52	-2.61	-0.04	-1.14	-1.19	-2.29	-2.27	-2.49	-2.68
	54	-1.12	-0.04	-1.78	-0.52	-1.32	-2.68	-0.60	-0.68
	55	-9.54	-1.24	-5.84	-4.07	-6.81	23.71	-5.34	-9.11
	58	-0.57	-0.27	-4.63	-0.51	-2.30	-8.47	-1.03	-0.49
	60	-1.32	0.20	-1.27	-0.37	-1.28	-1.65	-0.37	-0.81
Clothing		**25.36**	**4.64**	**35.29**	**12.69**	**27.99**	**7.20**	**14.27**	**5.64**
of which	61	0.31	0.83	6.87	4.88	3.28	0.00	2.06	0.25
	62	24.23	3.53	28.39	7.81	23.77	7.05	12.21	5.39
	64	0.02	0.00	0.07	0.14	0.64	0.00	3.18	0.00
Mach.B*	**(84)**	**-0.37**	**-1.88**	**0.04**	**-0.17**	**-0.38**	**0.00**	**-0.17**	**-1.27**
Elect.**	**(85)**	**-0.72**	**-4.52**	**-11.63**	**-2.01**	**-5.78**	**0.00**	**-1.28**	**-0.13**
90		0.06	-0.12	-0.34	0.00	-0.13	-0.23	0.03	-0.06

Source: Eurostat

Annex 5b: In 1993

Product		Poland	Czech Rep.	Hungary	Romania	CEFTA	Baltic st.	Balkans	CIS
28		0.00	0.00	0.00	0.00	0.00	0.00	0.00	4.37
41		-4.11	-2.59	-0.85	-0.15	-3.56	0.00	-0.55	0.00
Textile		**-26.43**	**-20.57**	**-33.82**	**-11.17**	**-28.26**	**-39.06**	**-12.93**	**-17.17**
of which	50	-0.03	0.00	-0.14	0.00	-0.24	0.00	-0.01	-0.01
	51	-6.82	-2.59	-9.77	-2.45	-7.55	-5.70	-2.23	-2.13
	52	-3.64	-5.62	-2.05	-0.59	-3.12	0.00	-1.25	-3.71
	54	-4.79	-0.64	-2.98	-1.25	-3.38	-24.44	-1.85	-1.58
	55	-5.68	-2.96	-11.87	-5.90	-6.93	-1.15	-6.12	-7.77
	58	-0.53	-0.16	-0.75	-0.08	-0.67	-0.49	-0.50	-0.37
	60	-1.97	-3.71	-3.97	-0.23	-3.11	-6.52	-0.22	-0.92
Clothing		**28.64**	**16.84**	**33.89**	**10.29**	**30.25**	**42.83**	**11.40**	**15.45**
of which	61	5.18	4.14	5.01	0.76	4.60	1.88	0.69	2.39
	62	23.43	12.69	28.86	9.62	25.37	40.91	10.79	13.07
	64	3.32	10.15	1.35	0.08	3.69	0.00	2.04	0.00
Mach.B*	**(84)**	**0.11**	**-2.09**	**0.01**	**-1.24**	**-0.26**	**-0.83**	**-1.20**	**-1.58**
Elect.**	**(85)**	**0.40**	**1.43**	**1.34**	**0.00**	**0.89**	**1.94**	**-0.12**	**0.09**
90		-0.02	-0.41	0.04	-0.07	-0.04	0.00	-0.47	0.08

Source: Eurostat

Annex 6: French Foreign Direct Investment and Outward Processing Export in the EECs in 1993 and 1997

		MPCs	CEFTA	Baltic st.	Balkans	CIS	EECs
				1993			
		MPCs	**CEFTA**	**Baltic st.**	**Balkans**	**CIS**	**EECs**
OPT	value	141410	123169	608	53429	37133	214339
	%	37.15%	33.45%	100.00%	86.33%	100.00%	45.82%
FDI	value	239279	245019	0	8459	0	253479
	%	62.85%	66.55%	0.00%	13.67%	0.00%	54.18%
Distribution FDI		94.40%	96.66%	0.00%	3.34%	0.00%	100.00%
Total =	FDI+OPT	380689	368188	608	61888	37133	467818
				1997			
		MPCs	**CEFTA**	**Baltic st.**	**Balkans**	**CIS**	**EECs**
OPT	value	250690	182359	1090	128578	40168	352195
	%	22.88%	21.28%	100.00%	36.31%	26.66%	25.85%
FDI	value	844993	674509	0	225493	110473	1010476
	%	77.12%	78.72%	0.00%	63.69%	73.34%	74.15%
Distribution FDI		83.62%	66.75%	0.00%	22.32%	10.93%	100.00%
Total =	FDI+OPT	1095683	856868	1090	354071	150641	1362671

MPCs = Major Partners Countries: Poland, the Czech Republic, Hungary and Romania
Source: Banque de France for FDI (Francs converted into Ecus at 1993 and 1997 average exchange rates), Eurostat for OPT

ANNEX 7: SECTORAL DISTRIBUTION OF FRENCH FOREIGN DIRECT INVESTMENT AND OUTWARD PROCESSING TRADE IN THE MANUFACTURING INDUSTRY OF FIVE EAST EUROPEAN COUNTRIES (1997, IN %)

Sector	French FDI flow to					
	The World	**Czech Rep**	**Hungary**	**Poland**	**Romania**	**Russia**
Food industry	6.2	47.8	14.1	47.4	0.0	0.0
Textile clothing	1.3	10.7	0.0	0.3	0.0	0.0
Wood, printing, edition	2.2	0.3	1.6	5.1	0.0	0.0
Refined petroleum prod.	3.4	0.0	0.0	0.0	0.0	0.0
Chemicals	25.9	8.1	26.6	24.0	1.0	19.6
Rubber, plastics	0.4	0.3	0.0	0.4	0.0	0.0
Ferrous and non ferrous met.	1.4	13.2	56.3	0.0	0.7	0.0
Machine building	3.1	7.3	1.6	9.4	0.0	25.0
Electrical Machin and equipt	36.9	0.0	0.0	0.0	0.0	0.0
Motor cars	5.2	12.4	0.0	1.0	0.0	0.0
Other transport equipment	1.4	0.0	0.0	0.0	0.0	0.0
Non specified manufact.prod.	12.6	0.0	0.0	12.3	98.3	55.4
Total	100.0	100.0	100.0	100.0	100.0	100.0

Sector	French OPT export to				
	Czech Rep	**Hungary**	**Poland**	**Romania**	**Russia**
Food industry					
Textile clothing	49.1	15.3	71.7	90.3	20.0
Wood, printing, edition					
Refined petroleum prod.					
Chemicals	0.0	0.0	0.0	0.0	73.8
Rubber, plastics					
Ferrous and non ferrous met.	0.4	4.8	0.1	0.1	0.1
Machine building	1.1	17.5	2.6	0.6	4.4
Electrical machine and equipt	42.6	52.2	18.7	5.3	0.6
Motor cars	0.0	0.4	0.0	0.0	0.0
Other transport equipment	0.0	0.1	0.4	0.0	0.0
Non specified manufact.prod.					
Total	100.0	100.0	100.0	100.0	100.0

Source: Banque de France for FDI and Eurostat for OPT

Chapter 6

DEVELOPING CREDIT MARKETS IN EASTERN EUROPE: LESSONS FROM BANKING HISTORY[1]

Kenneth J. Koford
University of Delaware
Adrian E. Tschoegl
Wharton School, University of Pennsylvania

1. BACKGROUND AND MAJOR HYPOTHESES

After the collapse of communism, Eastern European firms' need for credit immediately became apparent. Both private and state firms were short of investment capital and even working capital. The lack of liquidity forced many firms to curtail their operations. Firms also failed to pay their bills due to a shortage of working capital, leading to a cascade of payment failures. Much of the collapse of output in Eastern Europe has been due to the lack of credit (Commander and Coricelli 1995), and the shortage of credit has slowed the growth of new private firms.

Western advisers, led by the IMF and World Bank, argued that these problems showed the need to establish immediately a U.S. or German-style banking system that would be these nations' main conduit for credit. (There have also been efforts to create securities markets, which we discuss below). Most countries have tried to do this, helped by a large amount of international assistance. However, the efforts have almost entirely failed over the past five years, leaving policy-makers puzzled and concerned that their advice on restructuring Eastern European banking has been unsuccessful. They wonder why established banks fail to lend to new private firms, and why private firms have become closely tied to some of the new private banks. The World Bank, in particular, has

---

[1] K. Koford presented an earlier, and substantially different, version at the Conference on Emerging Financial Markets: Implications for Economic Development, American University, May 1996.

engaged in considerable self-evaluation and even self-criticism along these lines (for example, in sponsoring the two volumes on credit co-edited by Masahiko Aoki).

Economic theorists have become over-committed to the current U.S./U.K. model of a financial system because of its familiarity and its emphasis on arms-length market relations. Certainly, for large, sophisticated markets with good financial data on the borrowers, an arms-length, data-based financial system is highly appropriate. However, this market-based system may not be appropriate or even possible elsewhere.

First, U.S.-style arms-length banking requires accounting data on firms' assets and income that is reasonably accurate. Second, German-style close ties between banks and borrowers requires experienced and skillful bankers who understand and can control a firm's operations and management without adequate accounting information. Neither of these requirements is satisfied in Eastern Europe and neither is likely to be satisfied for many years. Yet the lack of credit remains an extremely pressing problem.

The appropriate models for transition economies are not the well-developed financial systems of today, but rather models drawn from periods of history when economies faced many of the same problems that currently face the Eastern Europeans. U.S. banking practices in the 19th century had some practices and institutions similar to those in Japan. European experience in the 19th century also provides evidence of varied institutions (Cameron 1972; Cameron et al. 1967). Japan, both during the Meiji restoration and after World War II, developed new systems of credit that propelled the economy rapidly from a very low base in which almost no firms "deserved" credit by traditional standards.

We will argue below that history demonstrates the important role that economic groups can play in the development of credit systems. Hence, the credit systems of the transition economies should encourage rather than impede the formation of economic groups. In such groups, a closely-knit group of business owners also own and control a bank. Within a group, the bank bases its lending on close association between borrower and lender. Rather than being an aberration or pathology, such groups are the natural and typical solution to a lack of accounting information and expertise.

We think that examining these historical patterns in countries that have had considerable economic success can provide two benefits. The first benefit is in providing models to improve lending policies in Eastern Europe. There may be a broader policy implication for less developed countries (LDCs) as well as most LDCs are following Japan in having close ties between banks and firms (Amsden 1989; McKinnon 1993).

The second benefit is in helping us develop a more complete economic theory of credit, an important problem in incomplete information. By reexamining an important form of institution, the group, we may expand the range of institutions that economic theorists accept. In particular, institutions involving personal knowledge and personal contact are much more important in the real world than in economic theory (Hayek 1948; Sowell 1980). Emphasizing the importance of institutions involving personal knowledge may help revitalize economic theory.

2. THEORETICAL MODEL AND LITERATURE REVIEW

While all financial systems perform the same basic functions, depending on their structure some may perform specific functions better or worse than others. How effectively a financial system performs depends, in part, on the fit or lack of it between the financial system and the economy that it serves, as each evolves over time. A well-designed financial system is not only appropriate now, but can evolve as the economy changes to be appropriate in the future.

Effective financial systems allocate capital to the "best" (or highest return for risk) projects, thereby maximizing value added for a given capital cost. Thus they identify and provide capital for those firms and entrepreneurs with good projects but insufficient resources. Furthermore, effective financial systems equalize and may lower the cost of capital and thus increase potential output. Financial systems lower the cost of capital by borrowing (allocating time-deferral) from the most patient, by allocating risk to the least risk averse, and by transforming risk and liquidity through credit contracts and risk pooling. These are not trivial tasks and it is clear that finance matters to development (de Gregorio and Guidotti 1995; King and Levine 1993).

The structure of a financial system consists of the channels through which funds flow and the form these flows take. The flow of funds from those individuals and institutions with funds to invest and lend to those firms and individuals with projects requiring funding can occur directly through securities markets and indirectly through intermediaries. The form may be debt (bank or bond) or equity.

The overall model is of a single huge "pool" of credit allocated according to price, following supply and demand principles. Credit varies by risk class, and risk too is priced in these markets. When funds flow directly via securities markets, financial firms act as brokers, market-makers or traders for marketable securities. The financial firms facilitate the operating of the market (borrowers and lenders finding each other) but do not replace the market. These financial firms are not in fact intermediaries.

Alternatively, funds may flow through intermediaries that act as principals, holding or issuing non-marketable securities; the intermediary may hold or issue marketable securities as well, but it is the substitution of an entity to issue or buy securities that markets cannot issue or buy that constitutes intermediation. Financial intermediaries must obtain other people's investment funds, often by issuing demand deposits or insurance contracts, and then examine potential borrowers directly. Absent a government guarantee, there is a strong element of "reputation" in these institutions, as those investing in the intermediary typically do not know the quality of the loans or investments.

Non-financial intermediaries issue or hold non-marketable securities in support of their main activities rather than as an activity in itself. Examples include firms that issue trade or consumer credit to facilitate the firms' operations; in time these credit operations may grow to become financial intermediaries almost independent of the firms that first created them. In these latter cases, there are a large number of small pools that create market-like allocations, but they are based upon firms' decision rules. So there is a substantial element of hierarchy or control in the decision making, and no assurance that similar projects are treated the same across the economy. (This is why economists have seen them as less desirable than complete markets).

When firms within groups of firms provide credit to others within the group, the lenders depend upon a strong sense of mutual trust, based upon close mutual knowledge and the understanding that any member of the group could harm others by a failure. This situation tends to require strong personal ties and norms against shirking, as well as strict observation of others to detect shirking or potential failures. Group members thus lose some individual freedom, as their fate is in part in the hands of the other group members. In groups with a bank, the non-financial firms may delegate much of the task of monitoring members' performance to the bank.

Financial systems differ not only in the relative importance of direct channels vis-à-vis indirect channels but also in the importance of the two major types of claims, debt and equity. If we combine these two elements, "channel" and "claim," we arrive at a 2X2 matrix such as Figure 1 below, based on a related chart of Hennart's (1994).

Modern financial systems in market economies exhibit all four components; the systems differ in the relative importance of each component. (We also have ignored for simplicity government ownership of corporate debt and equity.) Thus we get such classifications as bank (continental Europe and Japan) versus market (US and UK) - oriented financial systems (Rybczynski, 1984) or what Walter (1992) calls outsider (US and UK), insider (France and Germany) and ultra-insider (Japan and probably Italy) financial systems. Admittedly, recent research has called these distinctions into question.

Mayer (1993), Corbett and Jenkinson (1996), and Scholtens (1997) have challenged the meaningfulness of this categorization, at least regarding putative effects on the financing of industry. Allen (1993) accepts the categorization but critiques the association (e.g., (Ellsworth 1985; Porter 1992)) of bank-oriented systems with more rapid economic growth than that evident in market-oriented systems. Still, the different systems may have implications for dimensions other than financing patterns or economic growth.

Figure 1: The Components of a Financial System

		Channel	
		Market	**Intermediary**
Claim	**Debt**	Bonds	Bank debt or trade credit
	Equity	Public stock market	Private, bank, investment company, or group equity ownership

2.1 Debt and Equity

Traditionally, economics has identified capital flows with debt and has neglected the role of equity. However, Allen (1993) has a particularly insightful discussion of the relative importance of debt and equity in financial systems. He argues that traditional, well-understood industries in which monitoring of management is relatively straightforward will use debt rather than equity. Allen argues that new or rapidly changing industries where there little agreement among observers on how to run companies will tend to use equity. Similarly, small firms at start-up generally use personal equity because the uncertainty around the quality of the firms' management and prospects deters lenders. Later, public equity markets provide an incentive for many analysts to follow a company and come to a view on the optimal corporate strategy for the company. Equity markets then push management towards the consensus strategy through the market for corporate control (mergers and acquisitions). However, the small firms begun by personal equity are not able to participate in these equity markets.

In Allen's view, the relative importance of debt versus equity depends on the sectoral composition of the corporate non-financial sector, both in terms of well-understood industries and new industries, and in terms of the size and stability of firms. The composition of the non-financial sector in turn depends on the development of the economy and changes over time as firms and industries develop.

2.2 Markets and Intermediaries

Next we turn to the issue of markets versus intermediaries. As a number of the authors we have cited point out, highly developed securities (debt or equity) markets are slow to develop and represent a later stage of the evolution of financial systems. Securities markets require an infrastructure that assures disclosure of sophisticated accounting information, including internal financial systems, internal accountants, and a climate of compliance with financial rules. This requires an infrastructure of arms-length observers such as accounting firms, securities regulators, financial economists working for securities firms, and financial journalists. (It may be that this represents a phase of large, old, well-understood firms, and the infrastructure will shrink if smaller, newer, less well-understood firms come to dominate the economy). McKinnon (1993) has described how difficult it has been for developing countries to develop securities markets because of the weakness of this infrastructure.

The papers in Cameron (1972; 1967), however, show that it was also difficult for commercial and investment banking to develop and become stable in Europe in the 19th century. Banks in this period often appeared to be careful and responsible, but still made lending decisions that later turned out to be imprudent. Many banks in 19th century European emerging markets eventually collapsed, harming their depositors, owners and managers in the process. Well-operating securities markets also require a capable and determined government to bring about effective regulatory institutions. The government had to maintain these institutions over a considerable number of years to bring financial institutions to understand how to operate effectively under these regulatory institutions. It is very unlikely that the countries of Eastern Europe will be able to establish the necessary infrastructure within the next decade, even assuming that such markets were appropriate.

The MMM Ponzi scheme in Russia shows how far Russians are from a sophisticated understanding of financial markets. A series of similar Ponzi schemes occurred in Bulgaria in 1994-1995, with people admitting that they knew they were investing in a pyramid scheme, but still "hoping" that they might profit from it. This was after the collapse of a similar Romanian scheme in early 1994. Even after these Bulgarian schemes collapsed, many people have continued to defend them and still hope to get their money back (Bulgarian Business News, 1995, 1996, various issues). Also in Bulgaria, there are very popular unregulated non-banks that take high-interest term deposits and employ credit officers who appear to be disproportionately large, strong, aggressive young men. People guess that these non-bank financial intermediaries may collapse or "disappear" at some point. (A number of them did collapse in Spring 1996).

2.2.1 Financial System Debt

Diamond's (1984) seminal article is a particularly effective analysis of the factors influencing the relative importance in an economy of bank and insider debt versus bond debt. Diamond argues that firms will borrow from intermediaries rather than markets when uncertainty about the borrower's prospects is high. This uncertainty may derive from the fact that the borrower is new (i.e., has no reputation) or from general economic uncertainty. The intermediary will learn more about the borrower and the business than any outsider can. In the case of bank debt, banks monitor each company and one monitor is enough (Sheard 1994). The Japanese "main bank" system appears to fit this model (Aoki and Kim 1995; Aoki, Patrick, and Sheard 1994). With bond debt, two or so rating agencies provide the monitoring.

Thus bank and insider debt will predominate among new borrowers and in economies undergoing turbulence, as in Eastern Europe. Bank debt will be prominent when bankers build up substantial expertise in "sizing up" new loan prospects. This can occur in a variety of ways.

Historically, one route to bankerly expertise was through the banker's personal knowledge of a community. A banker, being a leading citizen of the business community, came to know the different business-people and to learn (through gossip, casual conversation, and direct inspection) about their business. Combining good judgment with this information gave a banker the ability to lend. Bankers in earlier eras often began their careers in business and embarked on banking as they saw a need for credit in their own business and in the community. Frequently businessmen clubbed together to create banks to serve their needs. A similar story applies to banks operating in particular industry sectors, as was common in 19th Century Europe (e.g., Spain, Austria, Serbia, Bulgaria) and Japan, as well as the U.S. Some U.S. banks betray their industry origins in their names: Chemical Bank, Farmers and Merchants Bank, Boatmens Bank. By the time a bank had achieved some size, it had developed a great deal of expertise across varied industries and so could evaluate a wide variety of new ventures effectively.

Over time, firms develop reputations and some economies embark on stable growth paths. A natural consequence is disintermediation; firms graduating from receiving bank loans and semi-equity insider loans to issuing bond debt. Technical progress in finance has also given rise to securitization - the creation of marketable debt from non-marketable debt (e.g., securities based on pools of credit card loans).

2.2.2 Trade Credit

There is little theoretical literature on debt intermediation through non-financial corporations—a pattern observed in Japan and the early U.S. Emery (1984) provides a general argument for trade credit in the face of financial market imperfections. Leff (1976) has a valuable paper on corporate groups (whether they contain a bank or not) as representing an internal financial market when governments engage in financial repression. Hodder and Tschoegl (1985) take this argument and point out that the Japanese financial system used more trade credit than did other major developed country systems.

Future research should be able to extend this argument and show how the current emphasis on arms-length banking and on bond markets misses these insider or group credit relations.

Trade credit has been important in the transition economies, but has also been misunderstood by some as being the failure of debtors to pay their bills (the interfirm debt "problem"). Koford and Miller (1995) find that trade credit in Bulgaria is very common and that firms do not give substantial trade credit lightly. However, in the early part of the transition, numerous firms did fail to pay their bills, leading to bad debts being carried by many firms.

2.2.3 Private and Public Equity

Ragazzi (1981) discusses the reasons for issuing stock in public offerings versus private placement. In closely-held companies, majority owners may achieve rents from control at the expense of minority shareholders. Although this provides an insight on the problems of going public, it does not address the cases where (as in Eastern Europe and the 19th century U.S.) virtually all the shareholders are insiders. Ekelund and Tollison (1980) argue that stock markets developed from the need of partners in private companies (or their heirs) to cash-out their capital. Cartel owner-managers in the early companies found transferable property rights in rents a way of reducing problems of succession. These rents to entrepreneurship imply that entrepreneurs would prefer private equity. The benefits to stockholders of diversification and of liquidity favor public equity. The tradeoff between these two factors suggests that public shareholding will develop as owner-founders retire or die.

In economies with a starting date, such as Germany and Japan after World War II, Japan after the Meiji restoration, newly settled regions in the 19th century U.S., or currently the former East Bloc countries, this implies that the supply of public equity will grow as the starting date recedes. Before owner-entrepreneurs or their descendants start to cash-out their shares, the major issuers of public equity will probably be large, privatized companies in well-understood industries. Utilities (including railroads) with high dividend yield shares that are very much like perpetual debt are likely to be the main companies with access to the public equity market. This also suggests that efforts by emerging economies to emulate established stock markets may be premature.

The Japanese post-World War II experience and the development of the main bank system has given rise to a large literature on banks owning the shares of the companies to which they lend. Much of the literature on the Japanese case has focused on the implications of bank ownership (Aoki, Patrick, and Sheard 1994; Hoshi, Kashyap, and Loveman 1994; Morck and Nakamura 1999; Sheard 1989; Weinstein and Yafeh 1994). Firms holding each others' shares also receive some attention, both as a way for firms to use the equity market while retaining control in friendly hands and for possible corporate collusion (Flath 1993; Hodder and Tschoegl 1985; Miyajima 1994; Wallich and Wallich 1976; Weinstein and Yafeh 1994). But the literature has ignored company ownership of banks. We believe that our concept of insider groups helps explain this phenomenon. Thus, the image of banks controlling the groups would be inaccurate. The banks are as much controlled by the borrowers as controlling them. The banks control particular firms, especially those in difficulty, but answer to the large, successful firms.

2.2.4 Groups

The economic group consisting of a closely-knit group of business owners who also own a bank is similar to the original development in Japan of the zaibatsu (and the postwar keiretsu). Japanese city banking after the Second World War emphasized short-term lending (except for the long term credit banks), at "arms length" for some years, but by the 1950s, closely knit groups including banks and firms had reestablished themselves (Hoshi 1995; Miyajima 1995; Teranishi 1995).

The literature on German banks is less extensive but growing (Cable 1985; Edwards and Fischer 1994; Fohlin 1995). In Germany, banking-industrial groups that were quite similar to the Japanese model dominated lending from the middle of the 19th century (Chandler 1990; Fohlin 1994; Fohlin 1995). (Such groups are also dominant in Swedish industry and, no doubt, other countries with which we are less familiar). Still, theorists have either neglected or decried the German-style universal bank as monopolistic.

Similar economic groups existed in the early U.S., particularly in New England before the Civil War (Lamoreaux 1991; Lamoreaux 1994). Most U.S. bank lending outside of groups up through the First World War was very short-term. Long-term investment capital came from such organizations as the House of Morgan, which provided essentially equity finance and also involved a close-knit group of major business leaders (Chandler 1990; DeLong 1991; Lamoreaux 1991; Lamoreaux 1994).

All of these models share certain characteristics. First, lending is personalized. The bank can lend to business owners because the directors know the reputation and prospects of the members of the circle. Formally, all of the business owners monitor each other and will punish any deviation by withdrawing business connections. Firms without a very long and solid history cannot expect to obtain arms-length credit for investments. So firms that need money for investments will go to investors or firms that know the firm and its management well, and the debt the firms issue will be high yield (i.e., analogs to junk bonds, which are like equity in their riskiness but with the legal rights of debt).

Traditionally economists have regarded personalized lending practices, for example, in villages in India, as a primitive form that is quickly outgrown with development. We note that recent work by Townsend (1995) gives a far more nuanced theorist's view of the village lending economy. Rotating credit associations such as the Grameen Bank in Bangladesh work on similar principles. They too employ a mutual monitoring of debtors. However these micro-lending institutions are not the focus of our paper.

Second, in the cases of Japan, Germany and the United States, at least before WW I, several factors meant that the group members, not the government, bore the costs of mistakes. One factor was the smallness of individual groups relative to the situation later or to the size of the economy. The failure of any one group then had little in the way of systemic consequences and so did not call for government remediation. A second factor was the absence of state protection of deposits, and particularly the absence of deposit insurance. Deposit insurance automatically involves the state in the failure of any institution. The third factor was a generally *laissez faire* state that did not try to channel funds to particular activities and sectors.

In time, all three factors waned. As groups and banks became bigger, the failure of any one came to have important external effects. As banks became bigger and came to hold more of society's savings, the need for depositor safety grew. Governments came to take responsibility for the safety of deposits, especially in the case of mass bank failures which tended to be the consequence of government macroeconomic policy. Deposit insurance, however, is a relatively new technology. The more usual technologics were some combination of regulation of banks and banking that ensured that even the least well-run bank would survive and that discouraged entry and encouraged banks to be large. Lastly, governments came to assume responsibility for economic performance and economic development.

2.3 Deregulation

When dealing with financial systems, one cannot ignore regulation. Walter (1992) notes that the development of the US and UK (outsider) market-oriented systems owes much to the limited role of the state. Even more critical is the role of specific regulations, particularly on the permitted operations of banks and on financial innovation. Kanda (1993) has an insightful article on the role of regulation (in code law-based legal systems and especially in Japan) in stifling innovation in financial markets and slowing the evolution of the financial system towards a greater use of markets. Coleman (1994) has an interesting article on the political power of financial intermediaries in countries. He finds that in the Continental countries that he studies, financial intermediaries are well-organized in associations that play a critical role in designing legislation governing financial intermediaries in markets. In the Anglo-Saxon countries financial intermediaries are more disorganized and can at best only slow change in the regulations that apply to themselves. The result is that in the Continental markets, the intermediaries are in a position to slow the development of arms-length markets that would compete with the activities of the intermediaries themselves. Lastly, we can also note the warning raised by the long life of regulatory measures taken in the 1930s (Cassesse, 1984). Legislation, once in place, becomes a force for conservatism and against the evolution of the financial system in its totality. Typically it requires a new crisis to unfreeze the status quo.

Still, the history of financial markets is in large part a history of financial crises. These have occurred in both bank-centered systems (see Cameron 1972; Cameron and al. 1967) and Tamaki (1995) for numerous historical examples), and in market systems. Common reasons given are insider dealing or reliance upon government guarantees against losses. However, these crises have occurred under so many different systems that they may be a fundamental fact of banking—essentially, there are so many potential sources of risk that banks fail to guard against them all. Then an "unexpected" calamity occurs, causing banks to fail. We suggest that it may be very difficult for bankers to avoid all major risks. The literature on bank failure (Caprio Jr. and Klingebiel 1996; Caprio Jr. and Vittas 1995) suggests that the most important cause is macroeconomic shocks. Admittedly, a few countries' banking systems have been quite stable—Swiss and German banks come to mind. But such examples are rare, and Switzerland has a long history of macroeconomic stability to draw upon.

If history is a useful guide, the inexperienced bankers of Eastern Europe are very likely to make a series of disastrous errors, causing their own bankruptcy and even causing financial crises. No regulatory policy can avoid these problems, however, without also stifling the ability to lend. The fact is that in the late 1980s and early 1990s, the banking systems of Australia, Canada, Denmark, Finland, France, Japan, Norway, Sweden, the UK, and the United States all saw system-wide problems related to real estate lending and subsequent deflation of real estate values (Ball 1994; Bartholomew 1994; Caprio Jr. and Klingebiel 1996; Caprio Jr. and Vittas 1995; Kindleberger 1995; Mishkin 1996). These crises culminated in some countries in bankruptcies amongst the largest banks. This suggests that even the regulatory authorities in well-developed financial systems cannot forestall all problems.

Overall, we return to our distinction between market-based and bank-based systems. The different financial systems are the result of different historical evolutions and different political values. Insider (bank-based or cross-holding) financial systems based on personal knowledge seem to be more appropriate for emerging economies than outsider (market-based) systems. However, this is not a permanent phenomenon; over several decades of evolution and growth, financial markets will tend to grow absolutely and in relative importance.

Because the economy will evolve, it is important for policymakers to structure a financial system that can evolve readily to remain congruent with the needs of the economy it serves. Again, one may recall that some experts claim that the Japanese and German banking systems have been too rigidly tied to an insider model, and have had difficulty adjusting to a more market-based system in recent years (Kanda 1993). A key challenge for the transition economies is to build the evolutionary path into the present structure of the systems they create.

3. Policy Application to Eastern Europe

The newly ex-communist countries of Eastern Europe lack the financial and accounting infrastructure of developed market economies. Banks previously made loans on the basis of state plans; the profitability or solvency of the borrower was irrelevant. Consequently, neither banks nor firms have any expertise in proving creditworthiness or solvency. Accounting practices concentrated on the detailed assurance that monetary amounts expended were the same as what was planned, but not on the "broader" accounting functions of capital value or realization of gains or losses. Thus, neither firms nor banks can apply their past skills or current knowledge to the efficiency and profitability issues that are critical to Western accounting systems.

In a recent study of Bulgarian firms, Koford and Miller (1995) found that both private and state firms very often have difficulty in obtaining sufficient working capital. Koford and Miller's results are consistent (with the exception of a survey of firms in St. Petersburg), with a series of surveys of firms in Eastern Europe carried out by the World Bank (de Melo and Ofen 1994; Webster and Swanson 1993). Analysis of the widely-discussed problem of interfirm debt in Eastern Europe suggests that the problem very often is not unprofitable firms, but rather a general lack of working capital, causing a debtor with cash constraints to fail to pay. With a chain of payment failures, one cash constraint can cause many constraints and failures to pay.

Nevertheless, Dobrinsky (1994), like the 1992 World Bank report on Bulgaria, follows the traditional approach, decrying the absence of credit and complaining that banks fail to make arms-length loans, and then noting that bankers lack experience and knowledge for making loans. Miller (1993) finds that the Bulgarian central bank, in cooperation with the U.S. Treasury Department, is aiming at creating an arms-length banking system comparable to that of the U.K. or U.S., though with German-type expertise.

3.1 Encouraging, Not Decrying, Group-Based Lending

The Bulgarian central bank defines a major problem it must face as the tendency for banks to develop close ties with borrowers and to form "groups." (Koford and Miller's discussions with firms and bankers indicate that much lending occurs within these groups.) Russia provides similar stories (Prokop 1995). The similarity with the Japanese experience suggests that firms in a different time and place are finding a similar solution to the similar problem of a credit shortage, despite misguided opposition. While these "groups" vary, the critical common element is a number of business owners who know each other well, have mutual business dealings, and (largely) trust each other, plus in the center of the group a bank. However, the bank does not control the group; rather, the group controls the bank.

Group lending does not eliminate all risks or problems. In the past two years, a number of Bulgarian banks have collapsed, usually bringing down several related firms.

The collapses seem to have been due to incautious lending and over-expansion (Bulgarian Business News, various issues).

The business leaders have generally owned rather extensive groups that collapsed along with the banks, bringing down friends and relatives as well. (One prominent bank collapse involved a Plovdiv bank with strong Turkish ethnic connections). The bulk of the businesses owned by the related "group" appear to have been sound, but the over-expansion of the bank's lending caused an overall collapse. The collapse implies a lesson for other bankers.

Not all failures represent entrepreneurs' business errors. The recent collapse of First Private Bank, the largest privately owned bank in Bulgaria, may point to other problems in transition economies. Although the central bank and some others claim that First Private Bank was overextended and had made bad loans to friends of the owners, the owners claim that the bank was sound, and that its collapse was political, caused by a faction of the ruling Socialist Party. If bankers expect political interference, they may see no reason to emphasize safe banking; if their party or faction wins, the government will bail them out of high-risk and even unwise loans but if their party loses, even wise loans will not save the bank.

These facts suggest that, for the immediate future, bankers in Eastern Europe should be allowed to associate with "groups," with bank solvency the responsibility of the group as a whole. The insolvency of a bank should lead to investigation and pursuit of the principals on the Board of Directors; that will give group members a stake in caution. Historically, the expectation of outsiders that group members were legally and morally responsible for any problems in a bank considerably reduced the chance of a run or collapse at unlucky banks in the early U.S. (Lamoreaux, 1994).

3.2 Public Justice as a Cure for Private Justice and Extortion

News reports and the results of surveys (of non-criminal businesses) suggest that most groups in Russia may have semi-criminal overtones. However, it would be useful in future examinations of business dealings to distinguish between aggressive (private or non-legal) enforcement of contracts and use of violence to extort protection money.

The problem in many emerging economies that it is difficult to collect commercial debts by public legal methods is likely to lead to private justice methods. Numerous groups have rather tough "enforcers" (known as "wrestlers" in one Bulgarian group). Stories involving people known to one of us include physical punishment for failure to pay debts. Certainly among some Bulgarian business-people, failure to pay one's debts is not a mark of shame—rather, the reverse! (This may be a legacy of years of Marxist ideology that emphasized rapaciousness as the essence of capitalism. It is in strong contrast with the New England businessmen studied by Lamoreaux (1994), but close to the early U.S. financial markets of the Gilded Age).

However, the highly varied stories of group activities do not indicate either a pattern of stern devotion to traditional business or a pattern of mafia-like semi-criminal activities. Rather, in Bulgaria, business heads seem to be involved in a tough quest for profit, with many joint activities involving credit and loans and joint ventures. Sizing up partners before making credit available is critical, and surely helped reinforce the "family and friends" element of business arrangements.

This distinction between enforcing contracts by private means and extortion suggests that public policy in Eastern Europe toward aggressive "groups" involved in lending should focus on stopping and punishing potential "shake-down" activities. In contrast, when groups attempt to collect debts on commercial loans in an aggressive manner, government policy might best be aimed at improving the legal enforceability of commercial contracts. In particular, in the U.S. and Britain, there is a crime, commercial fraud, which applies when people are able to pay their debts but claim that they cannot do so. Enforcement of criminal penalties against those defaulting on debts would reduce firms' incentive to enforce contracts through violent methods. (For criminal penalties to be effective, prosecutors cannot make essentially political decisions on who to prosecute—as many businessmen claim occurs in Bulgaria and in Russia.)

3.3 Encouraging Short-Term Debt and Long-Term Equity

Banks in Eastern Europe should not be expected or pushed to make arms-length investment loans; investments must come from wealthy individuals or firms willing to take equity risks. Rather, banks should specialize in short-term commercial loans (as is currently common); government support for registration and attachment of collateral can help develop arms-length bank lending and give firms the opportunity to establish good credit records. IRIS, in cooperation with USAID, is making a major effort to assure more complete collateral records.

Finally, banks should be encouraged to make loans based on accurate financial accounting information, but only when this becomes available, a process that will take a number of years. That will encourage both banks and firms looking for credit to develop more accurate financial data in order to obtain loans. Foreign banks with established ways of evaluating financial data, and international accounting firms, can play a substantial role in this process.

3.4 Letting Banks be Banks

Firms should not need to go to the banks to finance investment or growth. Banks should not be either venture capital firms or long-term lenders. Bankers are providers of short-term liquidity (Rajan 1996). The use of banks in both roles in Bulgaria and other transition economies reflects both history and the current lack of alternatives.

Under the planned economy, banks were simply arteries and accounting organs that moved funds on the basis of decisions made elsewhere and then kept track of the sums. Absent market interest rates the tenor (duration) of the allocation was irrelevant. Because banks were the only channel for funds, the tendency is to continue to treat them as the only channel. However, in a market economy, banks should have a more limited function.

3.5 Reducing Reliance on Collateral

The Bulgarian banking system's reliance on collateral seemed excessive. Requiring collateral aims to ensure that borrowers borrow only when they expect to be able to repay the loan, and that bankers are made whole if the loan turns bad. In practice, these hoped-for results did not occur. Bankers seem to have abdicated their responsibility to screen borrowers. Instead they have been willing to lend to bad risks while relying on collateral to save them from their mistakes. Bankers must be in the business of determining who are good borrowers, and making judgments about the quality of firms and of managers.

In developed economies, banks do not act as venture capitalists. The problem in Bulgaria and the other transition economies is that the proportion of new ventures among all firms is greater than in more mature economies, and the supply of venture capital is less. In most capitalist economies there are numerous wealthy individuals and families prepared to place money (and influence) in promising ventures. It appears that informal routes to obtaining private investments are very weak in Bulgaria, leading firms to try to obtain more bank financing than would be normal in a market economy.

Also, in mature market economies, much, perhaps most, long term capital comes from non-bank channels. Debt comes from commercial credit companies, specialized long-term banks, and bond markets. Equity comes from equity markets.

Firms' efforts to find long-term capital — their need to do so — cause substantial problems in banking. The problems are of two types: banks generally should provide only some long-term debt, and banks should not provide debt when the firm needs equity.

First, banks are specialists in liquidity, both for borrowers and for depositors. When banks fund long-term debt with demand and other deposits, as typically they are asked to do in transition economies, they expose themselves to interest rate risk from the maturity mismatch. Banks generally do not issue long-dated deposits. These are non-negotiable and so illiquid and therefore not very popular. Ideally, banks should issue bonds, but this requires functioning bond markets.

Second, firms need to be able to issue equity rather than to substitute debt for unavailable equity. Otherwise the firms become undercapitalized, or equivalently, too leveraged. Bulgaria needs to develop the stock market and perhaps create an informal, over-the-counter market for shares in closely-held firms.

4. Conclusion

Over a period of decades, Eastern European countries will develop the background to move to a more market-oriented financial system,. But policymakers should be aware of the pitfalls in attempting to do this prematurely. There is a kind of natural evolution of credit and equity markets, that develops the infrastructure, the information, and the reputation needed for these markets. Without these, forced creation of financial markets is likely to be a costly mistake. At the same time, the governments must ensure that the creation of a bank and group oriented financial system does not become an impediment to the evolution toward a greater role for markets.

References

1.Allen F. (1993), Strategic Management and Financial Markets, *Strategic Management Journal* 14, p. 11-22.

2.Amsden A. (1989), *Asia's Next Giant: South Korea and Late Industrialization*. New York: Oxford University.

3.Aoki M. and Kim H.K., eds. (1995), *Corporate Governance in Transitional Economies: Insider Control and the Role of Banks*, EDI Development Studies. Washington: World Bank.

4.Aoki M., Patrick H., and Sheard P. (1994). The main bank system, an introductory overview, in *The Japanese Main Bank System: Its Relevancy for Developing and Transforming Economies*, edited by Aoki M. and Patrick H. New York: Oxford University Press.

5.Ball M. (1994). The 1980s property boom. *Environment and Planning A* 26, p. 671-695.

6.Bartholomew P. (1994). Comparing Depository Institution Difficulties in Canada, the United States, and the Nordic Countries. *Journal of Housing Research* 5 (2), p. 303-309.

7.Cable J. (1985). Capital Market Information and Industrial Performance: The Role of West German Banks. *Economic Journal* 95 (377), p. 118-132.

8.Cameron R., ed. (1972). *Banking and Economic Development: Some Lessons of History*. New York: Oxford University.

9.Cameron R., Crisp O., Patrick H., and Tilly R., eds. (1967). *Banking in the Early Stages of Industrialization*. New York: Oxford University.

10.Caprio Jr., G. and Klingebiel D. (1996*). Bank Insolvency: Bad Luck, Bad Policy, or Bad Banking?,* Paper read at Annual Bank Conference on Development Economics, at Washington, DC.

11.Caprio Jr. G., and Vittas D. (1995*). Financial History: Lessons of the Past for Reformers of the Present,* World Bank.

12.Cassesse S. (1984). The Long Life of the Financial Institutions Set up in the Thirties. *Journal of European Economic History* 13 (2), p. 272-294.

13.Chandler A. (1990). *Scale and Scope: The Dynamics of Industrial Capitalism.* Cambridge, MA: Harvard University.

14.Coleman W. (1994). Banking, interest intermediation and political power. *European Journal of Political Research* 26, p. 31-58.

15.Commander S. and Coricelli F. (1995). *Unemployment, Restructuring and Labor Markets in Eastern Europe and Russia.* Washington, DC: World Bank.

16.Corbett J. and Jenkinson T. (1996). The Financing of Industry. *Journal of The Japanese and International Economies* 10, p. 71-96.

17.de Gregorio J. and Guidotti P. (1995). Financial Development and Economic Growth. *World Development* 23 (3), p. 433-448.

18.de Melo M. and Ofen G. (1994). *Private Service Firms in a Transitional Economy: Findings of a Survey in St. Petersburg.* Washington, D.C.: World Bank.

19.DeLong B. (1991). Did Morgan's Men Add Value?, in *Inside the Business Enterprise: Historical Perspectives on the Use of Information*, edited by Temin P. Chicago: University of Chicago.

20.Diamond D. (1984). Financial intermediation and delegated monitoring. *Review of Economic Studies* 51, p. 393-414.

21.Dobrinsky R. (1994). Reform of the Financial System in Bulgaria. In *The Development and Reform of Financial Systems in Central and Eastern Europe*, edited by Bonin J.P. and Szekely I.P., Aldershot: Edward Elgar.

22.Edwards J. and Fischer K. (1994). *Banks, Finance and Investment in Germany.* Cambridge: Cambridge Univ.

23.Ekelund R. Jr., and Tollison R. (1980). The Mercantilist Origins of the Corporation. *Bell Journal of Economics* 11 (2), p. 715-720.

24.Ellsworth R. (1985). Capital markets and competitive decline. *Harvard Business Review* 63, p. 171-183.

25.Emery G. (1984). A Pure Financial Explanation for Trade Credit. *Journal of Financial and Quantitative Analysis* 19, p. 271-285.

26.Flath D. (1993). Shareholding in the Keiretsu, Japan's Financial Groups. *Review of Economics and Statistics,* 75, p. 249-257.

27.Fohlin C. (1994). *Relationship Banking and Firm Liquidity Constraints: Evidence from the Heyday of the German Universal Banks,* Caltech.

28.Fohlin C. (1995*). Relationship Banking and Corporate Governance in the Kaiserreich,* Caltech.

29.Hayek F. (1948). *Individualism and economic order.* Chicago: Univ. of Chicago.

30.Hennart J.F. (1994). International Financial Capital Transfers: A Transactions Cost Framework. *Business History* 36, p. 51-70.

31.Hodder J. and Tschoegl A. (1985). Some Aspects of Japanese Corporate Finance. *Journal of Financial and Quantitative Analysis* 20, p. 173-191.

32.Hoshi T. (1995). Cleaning up the Balance Sheets: Japanese Experience in the Postwar Reconstruction Period. In *Corporate Governance in Transitional Economies: Insider Control and the Role of Banks*, edited by Aoki M. and Kim H-K. Washington, DC: World Bank.

33.Hoshi T., Kashyap A., and Loveman G. (1994). Financial System Reform in Poland: Lessons from Japan's Main Bank System. In *The Japanese main bank system: Its relevance for developing and transforming economies*, edited by Aoki M. and Patrick H. New York: Oxford University.
34.Kanda H. (1993). The Regulatory Environment for Japanese Capital Markets. In *Japanese Capital Markets*, edited by Takagi S. Cambridge, MA: Basil Blackwell.
35.Kindleberger Ch. (1995). Asset Inflation and Monetary Policy. *Banca Nazionale del Lavoro Ouarterly Review* 48 (182), p. 17-38.
36.King R. and Levine R. (1993). Finance and Growth: Schumpeter Might Be Right. *Quarterly Journal of Economics* 108 (3), p. 717-737.
37.Koford K. and Miller J. (1995). Contracts in Bulgaria: How Firms Cope when Property Rights are Incomplete, *IRIS working paper*.
38.Lamoreaux N. (1991). Information Problems and Banks' Specialization in Short-Term Commercial Lending: New England in the Nineteenth Century. In *Inside the Business Enterprise: Historical Perspectives on the Use of Information*, edited by Temin P. Chicago: University of Chicago.
39.Lamoreaux N. (1994). *Insider Lending: Banks. Personal Connections and Economic Development in Industrial New England*. New York: Cambridge University.
40.Leff N. (1976). Capital Markets in the Less Developed Countries: The Group Principle. In *Money and Finance in Economic Growth and Development*, edited by McKinnon R. New York: Marcel Dekker.
41.Mayer C. (1993). Financial systems in Eastern Europe: lessons from the West. In *The New Europe: Evolving Economic and Financial Systems in East and West*, edited by Fair D. and Raymond R. Amsterdam: Kluwer Academic.
42.McKinnon R. (1993). *The Order of Economic Liberalization*. Baltimore: Johns Hopkins University.
43.Miller J. (1993). *The Bulgarian Banking System*. Sofia: Bulgarian National Bank.
44.Mishkin F. (1996). *Understanding Financial Crises: A Developing Country Perspective*. Paper read at Annual Bank Conference on Development Economics, at Washington, D.C.
45.Miyajima H. (1994). The Transformation of Zaibatsu to Postwar Corporate Groups: From Hierarchically Integrated Groups to Horizontally Integrated Groups. *Journal of the Japanese and International Economies* 8, p. 239-328.
46.Miyajima H. (1995). The Privatization of Ex-Zaibatsu Holding Stocks and the Emergence of Bank-Centered Corporate Groups in Japan. In *Corporate Governance in Transitional Economies: Insider Control and the Role of Banks*, edited by Aoki M. and Kim H.K. Washington: World Bank.
47.Morck R. and Nakamura M. (1999). Banks and Corporate Control in Japan. *Journal of Finance* 54 (1), p. 319-339.
48.Porter M. (1992). Capital disadvantage: America's failing capital investment system. *Harvard Business Review* 70 (5), p. 65-82.
49.Prokop J. (1995). Industrial Conglomerates, Risk Spreading and the Transition in Russia. *Communist Economies and Economic Transformation* 7 (1), p. 35-50.

50.Ragazzi G. (1981). On the Relation between Ownership Dispersion and the Firm's Market Value. *Journal of Banking and Finance* 5, p. 261-276.
51.Rajan R. (1996). Why Banks Have a Future: Toward A New Theory of Commercial Banking. *Journal of Applied Corporate Finance* 9, p. 114-122.
52.Rybczynski T. (1984). Industrial Finance System in Europe, U.S. and Japan. *Journal of Economic Behavior and Organization* 5, p. 275-286.
53.Scholtens L. (1997). Bank- and Market-oriented Financial Systems: Fact or Fiction? *Banca Nazionale Del Lavoro Quarterly Review* (202), p. 301-323.
54.Sheard P. (1989). The main bank system and corporate monitoring and control in Japan. *Journal of Economic Behavior and Organization* 11, p. 399-422.
55.Sheard P. (1994). Reciprocal Delegated Monitoring in the Japanese Main Bank System. *Journal of the Japanese and International Economies* 8, p. 1-21.
56.Sowell T. (1980). *Knowledge and Decisions*. New York: Basic Books.
57.Tamaki, N. (1995) *Japanese Banking: A History, 1859-1959*. Cambridge: Cambridge University.
58.Teranishi J. (1995). Savings Mobilization and Investment Financing during Japan's Postwar Economic Recovery. In *Corporate Governance in Transitional Economies: Insider Control and the Role of Banks*, edited by Aoki M. and Kim H.K. Washington: World Bank.
59.Townsend R. (1995). Consumption Insurance: An Evaluation of Risk-Bearing Systems in Low-Income Economies. *Journal of Economic Perspectives* 9, p. 83-102.
60.Wallich H. and Wallich M. (1976). Banking and Finance. In *Asia's New Giant: How the Japanese Economy Works*, edited by Patrick H. and Rosovsky H. Washington: The Brookings Institution.
61.Walter I. (1992). The Battle of the Systems: Control of Enterprises and the Global Economy. *Journal of International Securities Markets* 6, p. 309-317.
62.Webster L., and Swanson D. (1993). The Emergence of Private Sector Manufacturing in the Former Czech and Slovak Federal Republic: A Survey of Firms. Washington, D.C.: World Bank.
63.Weinstein D., and Yafeh Y. (1994). Japan's Corporate Groups: Collusive or Competitive? An Empirical Investigation of Keiretsu Behavior. *Journal of Industrial Economics* 43 (4), p. 359-76.

Chapter 7

LABOR MARKETS AND MIGRATION: A POLISH PERSPECTIVE[1]

Krystyna Iglicka-Okolsla
School of Management, Warsaw University

1. INTRODUCTION

This paper focuses on the immigration into Poland, from both the East and the West, in the context of social and economic transformation. It emphasizes also the impact of this mobility on the labor markets. We stress that along with the transformation new and completely unexpected population phenomena occurred in Poland. These phenomena have influenced labor markets from the point of view of supply and demand for labor. Official statistical data and survey results that were used in this study show that Poland – Central European latecomer to the global stage - may serve as a model in the analysis of changes on labor markets from the perspective of immigrants' impact and role in this process.

Different literature in economic theory noted the segmentation of the labor market into primary and secondary sectors (Gordon, 1972, Edwards, 1975, Piore 1979, Portes, 1981). As far as the foreign labor force is concerned, primary labor market generally tends to occur through the legal channels, thus the legal status of immigrants is regulated and it is mainly on the basis of work-permit visa or the permanent residence. Ethnicity does not play an important role here since workers are hired mainly according to ability. Immigrants tend to have mobility chances comparable to those of native workers. They may start at the bottom of the job ladder but work conditions and remuneration are equal with the domestic labor. Finally, the function of primary sector is usually to supplement the domestic labor force rather than to discipline it (Portes, 1981).

[1] Shorter and modified version of this chapter was published in Iglicka, 2000.

Primary sector in the receiving countries is strongly correlated with the phenomenon of the brain drain in the sending countries. Thus, for example, the third and sixth preference categories of the amended 1954 U.S Immigration Act are reserved for professionals, technical, and skilled workers in short supply in the country[2].

In the contrary, secondary labor markets recruits jobs which do not need prior training, have little or no mobile opportunities and are at the bottom of the wage scale. Therefore immigration flows into this market possess opposite characteristics of that absorbed by the primary sector. First of all legal status of immigrants on this market varies from illegal to temporary stay. It is rarely a permanent residence. Ethnicity plays an important role here since workers are hired according mainly to the ethnicity. Immigrants are hired for short-term jobs (sometimes seasonal only) what does not create opportunities for upward mobility. Since the main role of immigrants is to discipline the domestic labor force the main function of the secondary sector is to lower the prevailing wages (Portes, 1981).

> "Within receiving societies, once immigrants have been recruited into particular occupations in significant numbers, these jobs become culturally labeled as 'immigrants jobs'. The stigma comes from the presence of immigrants, not from the characteristics of the job. In most European countries, for example, jobs in automobile manufacturing came to be considered 'immigrants jobs', whereas in the United States they are considered 'native jobs'"
> ***(Massey and al, 1999, p. 453).***

In the following sections the changes in population mobility in Poland after the collapse of the communist system and its impact on labor markets are discussed. We distinguish two flows of migration into Poland (divided into different categories of migrants): from the East and from the West and their inputs on the primary and secondary labor markets. Following Portes (1981, p. 291), we assume that the formation of a foreign labor force or immigrant enclave on the labor market is not a product of deliberate economic policies by the state or labor needs of the capitalist class, but depends on the initiative and resources of the immigrants themselves.

2. Foreign Labor Force in Poland – Basic Pool

Immigration is defined by the law as the stock of foreign citizens who, after being granted a permanent residence permit, were registered at any specific address as permanent residents of Poland and, until a given moment did not leave for any other country nor acquired Polish citizenship. Barring a few exceptions, immigration as recorded by official Polish sources displayed an astonishingly stable pattern in the post-war period – since the beginning of 1960s annual inflows ranged from 1,500 to 3,000 (Okolski, 1998). The sudden increase in the number of immigrants occurred after the collapse of the system only (see figure 1).

---

[2] See Portes (1981), p. 283.

Figure 1:
Flow of Immigrants in Poland (1950-1997)

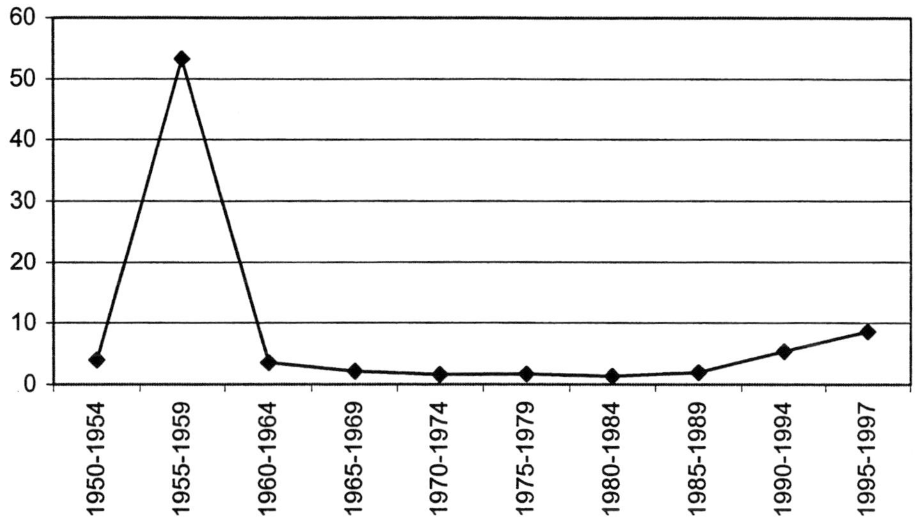

Sources: Central Statistical Office - Various issues

The fall of the communist system and the slow and sometimes painful birth of the new one have generated phenomena, which were completely unexpected both by people and governments in Western, Central and Eastern European countries (Iglicka and Sword, 1999). Seen from the point of view of the situation of the labor markets, the most important characteristics were:

1. An influx of persons from neighboring countries, particularly the former Soviet Union, arriving as a part of shuttle movements;
2. An influx of foreigners who require visas to enter Poland;
3. 'Permanent' immigration (both from the East and from the West).

Apart from the category 1 the other categories are divided in the official statistical registers of foreigners as:

- Persons granted a permanent residence permit (PRP): these are persons who have been granted permission to reside and settle in Poland;
- Persons legally employed by a Polish employer: these are persons who received permission to reside in Poland (resident visa 06) before they crossed the border into Poland. This visa is granted abroad by the Polish Consulate when documents are presented which confirm that the Polish employer has permission from the director of a given *voivodship's* [3] labor office to employ the foreigner;

[3] Voivodeship is the biggest administrative unit in Poland (a province).

- Persons granted permission to reside in Poland for a determined time period: these are persons who can present justifiable reasons for residing in Poland. Such reasons are: a) employment permitted by the authorities; b) economic activities; c) studies; d) marriage to a Polish citizen or to a foreigner who has permanent residence status;
- Persons who have come from abroad to reside permanently: these are persons who have 'registered' for permanent residence after they have arrived in Poland (according to unpublished estimates of the Central Statistical Office approximately half of those registering for permanent residence in Poland have Polish citizenship) (Glabicka and Sakson, 1996).

According to Okolski (1998) a rough (minimum) estimate of the pool of foreign population legally staying in Poland in 1997 oscillated around 70,000 persons. However, an influx of persons from the former Soviet Union, arriving as a part of shuttle movements (a flow that is almost completely impossible to be measured and to be categorized in official registers) has played a very important role in the changes on labor markets in Poland after 1989. Therefore we start the analysis of migration from the East with the description of this phenomenon.

3. Migration from the East

The new spatial mobility of people of the former Soviet bloc countries was perceived at the beginning of transition mainly as a threat. Then it turned out to have many positive effects (Iglicka and Sword, 1999). As Morokvasic and de Tinguy have pointed out at the beginning of 1990s;

> "The most characteristic of the post 1989 migrations, and the least known in the West, are the circulatory migrations or commuting of tourists; these involve various types of income-generating activities, mostly trading. They existed on a limited scale before the rise of the iron curtain. These 'tourists' stay for periods ranging from several hours to several months. Given their visibility on street corners and markets, these movements nourish fears of invasion among Central Europeans"
> ***(Morokvasic and de Tinguy, 1993, p. 253-4).***

As far as numbers of visitors from the former Soviet Union are concerned in 1989 fewer than 3 million of them entered Poland. Their number more than doubled the next year and continued to grow up to more than 14 million in the peak year 1997. In January 1998 Polish authorities complying with commitments arising from the forthcoming EU enlargement changed the Aliens Law[4] and regulations on documents for entry to Poland.

[4] Alien Law is a comprehensive document that regulates: 1) entry, exit, transit and residence of foreign nationals; 2) activities of the state and competence of various government agencies with relation to migration; 3) rights of foreigners in accordance to the international standards; 4) repatriation of ethnic Poles (Stachanczyk, 1998; Jagielski, 1997).

This immediately affected movements from Belarus and Russia as Ukraine and Lithuania had signed new agreements on visa-free movement with Poland. With new, more strict entry regulations[5] and the Russian crisis in 1998 the numbers dropped; to date (mid-1999) this trend has not reversed (see figure 2) (Stola, forthcoming).

Figure 2:
Border crossings on the eastern border, 1990-1998

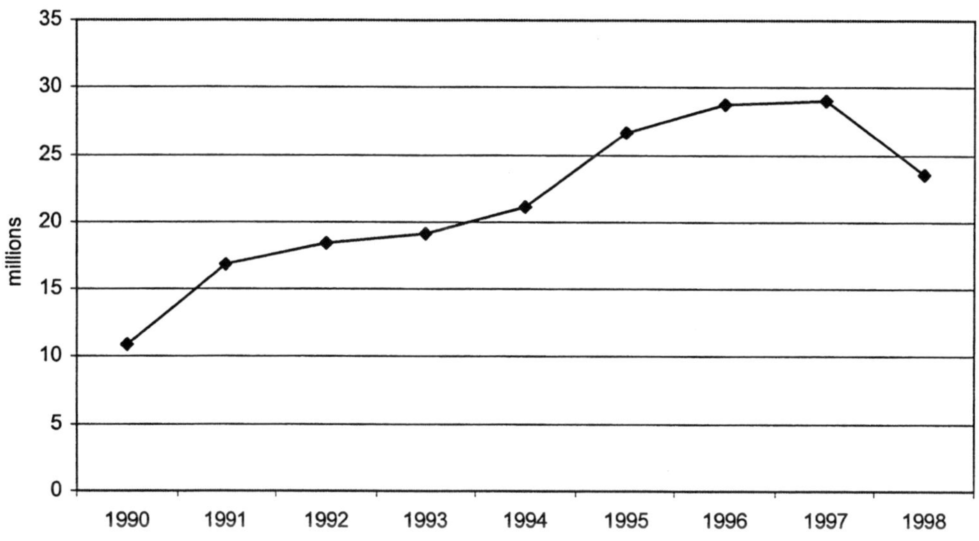

Sources: Border Guard Statistics - Various issues

Citizens of the former Soviet Union do not come to Poland to enjoy recently obtain freedom of movement. Most movements is a side effect of a sick post Soviet economy and take a form of 'shuttle' mobility which last from 3 to 7 days and is mainly for the purpose of trade (Iglicka, 1999). The remainder comes to work since besides an easy access to Polish territory, migrants have also a relatively easy access to Poland's informal labor market (Stola, forthcoming). An estimate made on the basis of survey conducted in Ukraine and Poland in 1995 suggest that there may be more than 500,000 Ukrainians who during travelling to Poland work illegally. A great majority of them are petty-traders who as a side effect of their trade activities engage in a various, usually very short work contracts. The estimate for 1995 shows that migrants with valid work permits constituted only 0.2 % of that figure (Okolski, 1998). According to the Polish Ministry of Labor and

[5] Citizens from the former USSR do not need visa in order to visit Poland. They still benefit from the old Polish-Soviet agreement signed in 1979. According to this agreement the only requirement to enter Poland is a voucher and an invitation from a Polish citizen. Till 1998 these were possible to buy for few dollars at kiosks on eastern border. The more strict policy means that Border Guard started to control whether the required documents are not false and whether the tourists hold a required, minimal quota of money.

Social Policy's estimates there are about 100,000 – 150,000 foreigners working illegally each year in Poland (Informal Labor Market, 1995). Majority of them comes from the 'East'. Although, according to that estimate, a substantial proportion of those people are seasonal workers, it probably omits foreigners who were employed for a very short period of time, e.g. for two weeks or shorter (Okolski, 1998).

Interview 1:
Pavlo: "There are now a lot of rich people in Poland. They want new houses. Our young men are working there. Form a team and go. When work in Poland, we stay at our boss's place – in a garret of his stable. Our entire furniture consists of two mattresses on a floor. We wash and eat in the yard"
(Khomra, 1994, p. 98).

The massive flux of arrivals from the former Soviet Union had many positive sides such as the development of some sectors of the Polish economy, competition on labor markets, etc. For several years, the citizens of the former Soviet Union visiting Poland to shop fostered local economic growth. Foreign demand for textile and leather products was one of the main factors, for instance, behind the boom in the growth of small, private textile and shoe businesses (Okolski, 1996). Foreigners (especially those from the East) spent also a lot of money in Poland (see table 1).

Table 1: The Value of Expenditures made by Foreigners from Neighboring States in Poland, 1994-1996.

Country	1994 (in mln PLN*)	1995 (in mln PLN*)	1996 (in mln PLN*)
Belarus	456.9	778.1	1184.7
Czech Republic	421.2	512.5	870.7
Germany	3628.2	4470.1	4965.6
Lithuania	116.4	130.7	118.8
Russia	109.2	84.0	138.9
Slovakia	133.7	160.3	251.3
Ukraine	317.8	578.2	1248.9

Note: 1 US$ = 2.9 - 3.4 PLN.
Sources: Ruch graniczny i wydatki cudzoziemcow w Polsce, 1994-1996. GUS (Central Statistical Office), Warsaw, (1997), p.23.

A very good example of the 'international petty-trade' arising in Poland since the beginning of 1990s is the example of the Warsaw Bazaar (Sword, 1999). With growing participation of foreigners from the East (not only citizens of the former Soviet Union but Asians as well – almost 60 per cent of customers at the fair are foreigners), the bazaar turned into a huge, predominantly textile-oriented market place. In 1995 the estimated turnover was more than US$ 500 million and this made the bazaar one of the biggest Polish enterprises in term of turnover (see table 2).

Table 2: Purchases made by Foreigners at the Polish Bazaars

Bazaar	Foreign Customers (% of Turnover)	Of which wholesale (%)	Amount in million PLN based on 1996 turnover (*)
Kostrzyn	93	0	112 (9)
Cedynia	93	0	150 (8)
Slubice	92	0	175 (7)
Cieszyn	91	0	46 (14)
Swinoujscie	88	0	62 (12)
Legnica	87	0.1	348 (4)
Bialystok	83	22	432 (3)
Gubin	82	0	90 (10)
Zgorzelec	80	0	72 (11)
Przemysl	67	10	60 (13)
Warsaw	58	32	870 (1)
Tuszyn	31	29	589 (2)
Rzgow	24	14	204 (6)
Gluchow	19	19	238 (5)
Krakow	1	0	13 (15)

Note: (*) 1 US$ = 3.4 PNZ.
Sources: Sword (1999), page 153

The Warsaw Bazaar gives employment to over 6,500 people. Caution estimates show that at least 3,000 are foreigners (Kozlowski, 1999). But altogether the Warsaw Bazaar activities (including factories supplying the fair) give employment to as many as 60,000 people (Okolski, 1996: 16). The other important fact is that the Warsaw Bazaar and other bazaars created for needs of traders from the East is considered to be a schooling and a first leg on the ladder for would-be entrepreneurs from the former USSR who will go on and create more orthodox and established businesses (Sword, 1999).

When new, more strict policy regulations towards the flux from the East were introduced in January 1998 sales at big bazaars in eastern and central Poland declined dramatically. This immediately caused a heavy lobbying of Polish traders and manufacturers who made Polish government reconsider certain regulations (Stola, forthcoming). As a result the costs of tourists' vouchers and a required at the entrance to Poland minimal quota of money were lowered (Iglicka, 2001a). After a decade of penetration of Polish trade and labor markets by petty-traders and seasonal workers one can observe that some of them, and especially those with already established network in Poland, having realized restrictions in West European policy towards mobility from the

'East', consider possibility of long-term or permanent emigration to Poland [6] (Iglicka, 2001a). It means that the foreign labor force will get regulated legal status and therefore will probably be visible more frequently on the primary labor market.

Interview 2:
Anna: "I started to go to Poland, to the town of Chelm, which is close to the border. There my trade business perked up and I left my job. Although the profits from my trips were not large, they were much greater than my salary as an art critic. Once I met a person who was an owner of a small private shop producing practical small-sized and not expensive kitchen units. These units were easily assembled and rather compact. Thus I started to bring them. In Kiev it was not a problem to sell these units through advertising them in local newspaper. The profits started rising. This allowed me to rent a car to take more units. During my regular cross-border travels I developed good contacts with customs officers and local people. One of them, who used to help to load the furniture, in time became my partner. He bought a truck and started to take furniture directly from producers to Kiev. Now he can take fifteen suites altogether and recently we have started transporting upholstered furniture. In one of the Kiev cinema-theatres which, are nowadays closed I agreed with the managers to exhibit the furniture in the lobby. Thus I have a permanent job now. When the furniture arrives I sell it. Now I can avoid these exhausting journeys. I order furniture by phone and my companion brings them. I have only to give him the money."
(Khomra, 1994, p. 165-166).

There are some ways of channeling the phenomenon of conversion the shuttle mobility into immigration. The most visible in official statistics are applications for a permanent residence permit, applications for a visa with work permit and a marriage to a Polish citizen.

Since 1990 there has been an increasing influx of foreigners arriving in Poland to work in accordance with the regulations set out in the Act of Employment and Counteracting Unemployment of December 14, 1994. Since the beginning of transition *Voivodship* Labor Offices have issued yearly 10,000 to 15,000 work permits for foreigners working for Polish employers (Glabicka and Sakson, 1996). During the period of 1990 to 1998 a total of 80,127 work permits were issued, 63% of which was comprised of individual permits and 27% of which were issued for export services and accepted contracts. Statistical data on work permits issued by *voivodships* indicate an accumulation of foreign manpower in large, urban agglomerations and in the following *voivodships*: Warsaw, Gdansk, Katowice, Szczecin and Cracow.

Labor migration to Poland is a recent phenomenon that gathered momentum only in the 1990s. Official statistical data indicate that the access to economic sectors in Poland for foreigners is segmented according to ethnicity. As far as the movement from the East is concerned Eastern Europeans prevail as unskilled manual workers, skilled manual workers and artists. Thus even those with work permits occupy so far mainly the secondary sector of labor market (see table 3). Nationals of Asian countries hold

[6] As a result of the understanding reached by the European Union member countries in September 1995, all of the countries of the former Soviet Union (on the contrary to the other non-Soviet former countries of the Communist bloc) were put on the 'visa-rule list'.

executive positions in sectors in which they invest, for example restaurants, trading companies, and so on. Asian nationals are most often employed however in food industry (60 % Vietnamese, for example, work in this sector) and by trade companies (Rudolph and Hillman, 1998:62). The trends visible in table 3 are maintained till to date (mid 1999).

Table 3: Work Permits for Foreigners from the Eastern Europe According to Type of Work (1994 and First Half of 1995) (%).

Region	Year	All management function	Owners	Experts specialist and consultant	Administrative personnel	Medical professions	Teachers trainers	Artists	Skilled manual workers	Unskilled manual workers	Other
Eastern European Countries	1994	25.0	33.0	50.5	51.7	89.5	43.2	98.1	95.8	99.8	82.4
	1995	18.5	36.0	40.1	45.0	42.4	56.5	98.5	73.3	62.5	88.0
Total	1994	1651	633	792	224	68	532	666	573	1816	177
	1995	1053	320	351	31	66	285	272	30	24	84

Sources: Sprawozdanie z badania sondazowego zezwolenia na prace udzielane cudzoziemcom przez wojewodzkie urzedy pracy w okresie 1994 i 1 Styczen – 30 Czerwiec 1995, Warsaw, Ministry of Labor Press, (1995).

Official statistical data indicates an increasing tendency of people from the former USSR applying for work permits and permanent residence permit (PRP). As far as visas with work permit granted from the beginning of 1990s till 1996 Ukrainians were on the first place, since 1996 until today (mid 1999) they are on the second place. If we look at the nationality of foreigners granted the permanent residence permit (PRP) we see that the most numerous nationality is undoubtedly Ukrainian (see table 4 and 5).

Table 4: Visas with Work Permit Granted in 1994-1998 by Most Numerous Nationalities (%).

Country	1994	1995	1996	1997	1998
Ukraine	13.0	14.0	15.8	15.2	13.1
Vietnam	11.0	13.0	14.6	17.8	15.1
Russia	8.5	7.5	7.6	6.5	5.6
USA	7.0	7.0	6.0	5.3	4.1
China	7.8	7.0	7.8	6.5	6.7
Great Britain	7.0	7.0	6.0	5.0	5.0
Belarus	5.0	3.5	3.0	3.3	4.0
Germany	4.6	5.0	6.0	6.0	5.5
Total (absolute numbers)	8690	9057	7019	8978	10505

Sources: Poland – Statistical Data on Migration 1994-1998, Office for Migration and Refugees, Warsaw, (1999).

Table 5: Foreigners Granted the Permanent Residence Permit (PRP) in Poland According to the Most Numerous Nationalities, 1993-1998 (%).

Country	1993	1994	1995	1996	1997	1998
Ukraine	15	21	19	22	23	24
Russia	11	12	11	10	8	7
Belarus	7	6	7	7	8	7
Germany	5	5	6	5	4	4
Vietnam	4	4	7	9	8	10
Kazakhstan	1	2	8	8	15	10
Lithuania	3	3	2	3	2	2
Armenia	1	2	2	2	2	5
Total (absolute numbers)	1964	2457	3051	2844	3973	1567

Sources: Poland – Statistical Data on Migration 1994-1998, Office for Migration and Refugees, Warsaw, (1999).

The result of the study on spatial distribution of the foreign born population of Ukrainians holding PRP in 1991 show that they were situated in big cities, in ethnically Ukrainian territories and territories where Ukrainians and Lemkos were resettled in 1947[7]. Thus some links between old diaspora of Ukrainians living in Poland for centuries

[7] In 1947 Polish security forces unable to destroy Ukrainian national guerilla movement (UPA) operating since 1943 in southeastern Poland dislocated approximately 150,000 Ukrainians and Lemkos from this region Poland (an area which was ethnically Ukrainian) to the northern and western territories (formerly part of Germany). This operation was named Akcja Wisla (Vistula Action).

and new arrivals are visible. Furthermore, a map of territorial distribution of Orthodox and Greek Catholic church covers spatial distribution of 'new' Ukrainians. It proves that network between 'old' and 'new' group plays an important role in the spatial formation of the latter (Jerczynski, 1999).

The other interesting phenomenon that links immigration with the presence of foreigners on labor markets is a phenomenon of mixed marriages. Sudden growing trends in number of people (especially women) from the former USSR may suggest that this is the beginning of the process only and that there may be some pressure from this channel on labor markets in the nearest future (see table 6).

Table 6: Mixed Marriages; 1990-1996 (Selected Years).

Foreign wife	1990	1995	1996	Foreign husband	1990	1995	1996
Ukraine	-	331	340	Ukraine	0	89	108
Russia	-	119	151	Russia	-	-	-
Belarus	-	95	104	Belarus	-	-	-
Lithuania	-	41	40	Lithuania			
Armenia	-	27	28	Armenia	0	44	64
Latvia	-	6	10	Latvia	-	-	-
Kazakhstan	-	13	11	Kazakhstan	-	-	-
USSR	255	-	-	USSR	210	0	0
Germany	370	61	63	Germany	1494	748	698
Vietnam	-	15	42	Vietnam	0	44	64
USA	88	46	33	USA	263	185	138
United Kingdom	14	-	-	United Kingdom	44	-	-
Canada	-	17	15	Canada	0	46	43
Others	184	149	140	Others(*)	1318	1164	1062
Total	911	920	977	Total	3329	2320	2177

Notes: (*):Mainly Western European countries
Sources: Roczniki Statystyczne (Statistical Yearbooks), Central Statistical Office, GUS, Warsaw, various years.

As it was already mentioned from the beginning of 1960s until the beginning of 1990s the immigration flows to Poland were statistically not significant. However, one of the existing and quite visible inflows was movement of students from Vietnam – who arrived in Poland under a government's sponsored program of 'socialist co-operation' or academic exchange. After graduation majority of them returned to home country where having a European diploma they placed high positions in social hierarchy.

After 1989 irrespective of being still communist country Vietnam started to pursuit more liberal migration policy that caused inflows to Poland, not only students (from privileged families), but people who were looking for place to work and to live.

Since the end of 1993, the number of Vietnamese citizens applying for work–permit visas has seen a sharp increase, and has resulted in rise in the number of Vietnamese legally coming to Poland. Until 1996 Vietnamese were the second largest group (after Ukrainians) as far as the number of visas with work permit granted (see table 4). Since 1997 they are on the first place. Moreover, the growing presence of Vietnamese was also due to an illegal flow. Some of these illegals attempted to legalize their stay through an application for permanent residence permit or through marriage with Polish residence. At the end of 1995, the Vietnamese were the third largest group of immigrants receiving residence permits (see table 5). In 1996 they were the second, and this tendency was maintained till today (mid 1999). According to estimates there are around 30,000 Vietnamese living in Poland (Halik, 2000).

Vietnamese carry on a lively economic activity and not only in the field of small trade and gastronomy. The Association of Vietnamese Businessmen in Warsaw has been legally registered. Vietnamese trade firms and enterprises are present in more than half of the *voivodships* of the country.

Contrary to what was expected at the beginning of 1990s it seems that there are more positive than negative aspects of the influx from the East. Foreigners applying for a visa with work permit and a permanent residence permit in Poland and, as we know people from the East prevail here are quite highly educated. Each year the majority had either a secondary education (41%) or university education (31.7%). The percentage of persons with only a primary education or with a (non-secondary) vocational education oscillated around 11 per cent only (Glabicka and Sakson; 1996).

4. Migration from the West

The transformation of the political and economic structure at the end of the eighties disturbed the stabilized migration trends. Although Poland is still a country whose net migration outflow is higher than its influx, new qualitative changes which, have begun to accompany immigration to Poland lead some policy makers and scientists to state that Poland is slowly becoming a destination and transit country (Korcelli, 1991; Salt, 1996; Kozlowski, 1999).

During the past ten years the movement from the East to Poland has been carefully studied in many research projects (Morokvasic and de Tinguy, 1993; Iglicka and Sword, 1999; Wallace and Stola, forthcoming) whereas the mobility on the West-East axis is almost totally neglected by researchers. Additionally to that statistical data on the phenomenon of return migration and mobility from the West are incomplete. Therefore this section will be based almost totally on the findings from the only survey conducted by German researchers from the *Wissenschaftszentrums Berlin fur Sozialforschung* in 1995 on managerial migration from the West into Poland[8]. The basic finding that occur in

[8] Project was conducted in co-operation with the Center for Migration Research, Warsaw University. During this study semi-structured interviews were conducted with high-level

this study is that contrary to the movement from the East mobility from the West pertains only to the primary labor markets and moreover it is a highly institutionalized phenomenon. The transfer of skills and knowledge from the West accompanies transformation of the economies in the East. This process takes a shape of human mobility on the West-East axis. The mobility from the West is one of the factors behind the phenomenon of the 'reverse brain-drain' visible since 1994 in migratory trends in Poland (see figure 3). This is because the percentage of immigrants with the high standard of education is much higher than the percentage of emigrants and also because more immigrants than emigrants occupy managerial or professional posts at the time of registration (Okolski, 1995; Iglicka, 2001b).

Figure 3: Emigrants and Immigrants by education, 1996

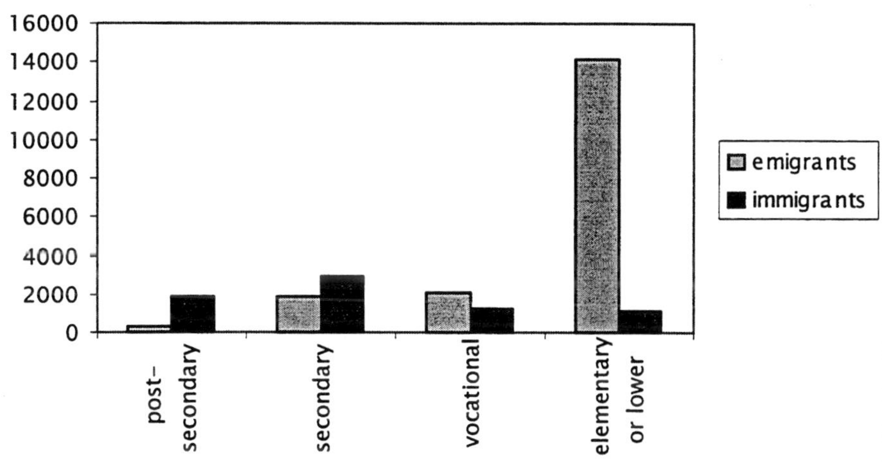

Sources: Okolski, 1998

Table 7 shows that Western Europeans and Americans held majority of managerial functions and were employed more frequently as experts, specialists and consultants. They find their place in the primary labor market in Poland through three channels - institutions: political organizations, multinational companies and joint ventures and, through the network of freelance professionals (Rudolph and Hillman, 1998).

managers in some 50 multinational companies/joint ventures, as well as interviews with experts, managers and professionals.

Table 7 Work Permits for Foreigners from the Western Europe and the US According to Type of Work (1994 and First Half of 1995) (%).

Region	Year	All management function	Owners	Experts specialist and consultant	Administrative personnel	Medical professions	Teachers trainers	Artists	Skilled manual workers	Unskilled manual workers	Other
Western European Countries and USA	1994	75.0	67.0	49.5	48.3	10.5	56.8	1.5	4.2	0.2	16.6
	1995	81.5	64.0	59.9	55.0	57.6	43.5	2.5	26.7	37.5	12.0
Total	1994	1651	633	792	224	68	532	666	573	1816	177
	1995	1053	320	351	31	66	285	272	30	24	84

Sources: Sprawozdanie z badania sondazowego zezwolenia na prace udzielane cudzoziemcom przez wojewodzkie urzedy pracy w okresie 1994 i 1 Styczen – 30 Czerwiec 1995, Warsaw, Ministry of Labor Press, (1995).

Among international and national organizations hiring foreign experts one should mention Poland and Hungary Action for Reconstructing the Economy (PHARE), and the *Centrum für Internationale Migration und Entwicklung* (CIM) (the German public recruitment agency for highly skilled manpower).

PHARE has been oriented on fields such as: food, humanitarian and medical aid, 'know-how' about state and management restructuring, education and technical assistance for privatization process, economic and regional restructuring, development of human resources, infrastructure development, provision of financial support for large infrastructure programs and towards adaptive measures in view of integration into the EU. During the first half of 1990s Poland received a quarter of the total investment made under the PHARE program (Rudolph and Hillman, 1998). Within the framework of this program a substantial but impossible to estimate a number of Western experts occurred in Poland (Salt, 1989).

> "The experts and consultants hiring by CIM are given local work permits but the German government provides the funds for topping up their salaries. Poland is the major recipient of CIM activities; in 1994, 25 of 70 experts on CIM's staff in this region were employed in Poland. These experts are earmarked for specific organizations with crucial functions for the promotion of the privatization process, such as the Polish bank for development, the bank for export promotion and the agency for regional development (which supports in particular small and medium sized enterprises)"
> ***(Rudolph and Hillman, 1998, p. 68).***

As far as the second channel of West-East migration is concerned i.e. multinational companies and joint ventures they are of particular significance in shaping the flow of highly skilled professionals in Poland. *"Very few of the multinational companies act without expatriates and sometimes the trend to substitute them is only declared"*

(Rudolph and Hillman, 1998). However, at the beginning of the transformation what also means at the beginning of the existence of such companies in Poland there were not enough Poles who could be able to work on the lower levels of the management positions or in the sectors of marketing, and public relations. Such sectors did not exist in the socialist economy and domestic highly skilled labor force was not skilled enough for this. Therefore the strategy of multinationals was to train Polish personnel in order to substitute the foreign managers and experts as quickly as possible. In the mentioned here study the average stay of foreign managers and experts was about two or three years.

It is also interesting to know who were these foreign experts. First of all they were expatriates. Secondly they were also people who have the same position as the expatriates but did not benefit from the "expat-package" (such package includes many incentives among them e.g. free flights home, subsidies for an apartment rent, etc.). This category is called "hybrid" and has usually a weaker bargaining power on the market at the time of recruitment because, for example, they are already in the country. Thirdly they were also Polish return migrants, usually children of the emigrants of the Solidarity and the martial law period (first half of 1980s) (Rudolph and Hillman, 1998). As far as the basic socio-demographic characteristics of this group are concerned they were in majority men, relatively young (most often between 30 and 39 years of age), and highly educated. *"They come from different background, but all of them are engaged in white-collar professions"* (Rudolph and Hillman, 1998, page 73).

As far as the third channel of mobility on the West-East axis is concerned i.e. freelance foreign experts consultants and teachers in this group prevail significantly. The demand for native English speakers at the beginning of transition was very high, not only because the English language is a language of international communication but also because until 1989 it was the Russian language that was though as a first foreign language in Poland. Therefore there was a huge demand for English language teachers who could quickly fit-in into the changes in the educational system. As a result, ten years after the collapse of the system the English language is introduced as a first foreign language in the kindergartens (also it is not obligatory at that level), and in the majority of grammar and high schools all over the country.

> "Polish Ministry of Labor statistics show that in 1994, 44 per cent of the total work permits issued to UK nationals were for training and teaching purposes, in the first half of 1995 the corresponding figure was still 31 per cent. There is an empirical evidence however, that these flows of 'native speakers' are driven not only by the demand in Poland, but also due to the effects of the current recession in Britain"
> ***(Rudolph and Hillman, 1998, p. 76).***

In this place it is important to mention yet another phenomenon concerning migration on the West-East axis and its impact on the labor markets however, this phenomenon is not described and analyzed in the literature very well. Moreover this kind of mobility has an impact not only on Polish but German labor markets as well but it seems important to me to mention it here. I have in mind the phenomenon of return migration from Germany to southwestern territories of Poland (Silesia) of people with dual citizenship. These are people who had emigrated to Germany in the 1970s and 1980s as so called *Spataussiedler* [9] (late emigrants). By comparison to other Polish emigrant groups in Germany this group comprised in majority young, dynamic and highly educated people. It included engineers, doctors, scientists, managers, teachers, as well as artists, musicians and so on (Heffner, 1999). They (in majority) did not resign from their Polish citizenship while, living for years in Germany, they had being granted German citizenship.

Some of these emigrants decide to return to Poland now. The number of such returns equals 1,500 –2,000 annually (Heffner, 1999). But it is still not a definite return. German passport gives these people today an opportunity to work in Germany (seasonally, for a half of a year or so) and benefit from the German social welfare system while investing earnings in Poland. They set up businesses here what means that in the nearest future they will spend probably the most of the year in Poland. 'They are trying to make the most of the professional skills and contacts gained in the German economic system' (Heffner, 1999, page 193). The representative of German Minority Society in Opole Silesia, senator Gerhard Bartodziej said:

> "This is the beginning of the process only. But returns to Upper Silesia will happen in the tens of thousands soon. Those people who left the region during the last few years, those who did not get rid off all they had, those who have dual citizenship and homes here will come back to Upper Silesia soon"
> ***(Heffner, 1999, p. 204).***

So far these who return move into the larger urban centers, mostly to Opole, a capitol of Opole Silesia region, return migration to the rural areas takes place on a relatively low level. The disappearing differences between living and working conditions between Poland and Germany, the process that has already begun, may incline in the future to permanent return of the bigger numbers of those who did not root in Germany. The estimated potential of such returnees oscillates around 200,000. So far however, short and long-term commuting to Germany in order to work have become a significant and stimulating factor in the development of the regional economy (Heffner, 1999).

[9] The term *Spataussiedler* refers to a person displaced in the 1970s or 1980s. The German distinguished between earlier and later evacuees since the cultural, social and motivational differences and also the causes of their emigration to Germany were clearly different from those which characterized the earlier 'Aussiedler' group. It is stressed in the literature now that the economic factor played a very important role in the emigration from Poland of this group (Heffner, 1999).

5. CONCLUSION

The geography of migratory flows into Poland during the transition period reflects recent changes in the global division of labor. Highly skilled flows from the "West" and a small part of the flow from the "East" find an employment on the primary labor market. Immigrants have a regulated legal status and are used to supplement domestic labor force here.

Decisive majority of the flows from the "East" finds an employment (legal or illegal) on the secondary labor market. Flows into the primary labor market are highly institutionalized whereas flows from the "East" reflect rather the dynamic process of migration that transforms temporary entries into settlement. I assume however, that in the future it is just immigrants from the "East" who would play an important role on both primary and secondary labor markets in Poland. Since the migratory potential lies on the "East" the process of globalization of migration will inevitable increase the flows from the "East" into Central European countries.

> "When immigration stream begins, it displays a strong tendency to continue because of the growth and elaboration of migrant networks (social capital theory). The concentration of immigrants in certain destination areas creates a 'family and friends' effect that channels later streams of immigrants to the same places and facilitates their arrival and integration. If enough migrants arrive under favorable conditions, an enclave economy may form, which further arguments the specialized demand for immigrant workers."
> ***(Massey, 1999, p. 306)***

The future of the migration flows depends on the stability of the central and eastern European economies, social and political changes in the countries of the former Soviet Union but above all it depends on the Polish (European Union) migration policy. Brussels and Berlin have already made it clear that strengthening control on Poland's eastern border – the future border of the Union – should be a priority task in Polish preparations for the accession (Stola, forthcoming). On the other hand one should not forget that the process of globalization of market economy brings dualization of central European labor markets thereby increasing the mobility of people and circulation of capital and goods. A case of German, French, Dutch, and other western economies of the 1970s happens now in Central and Eastern European region. Although the western European labor market is becoming increasingly constrained by restrictive immigration policy one should not forget that central European labor markets would need foreign labor. Positive aspects of the presence of immigrants in Poland are the fundamental socio-demographic traits of these societies. The young age of migrants as well as their being in the possession of a trade skills or occupation mean that there is a great potential, which should be taken advantage of by the local labor markets.

New and exotic for this part of Europe Diaspora of foreigners as Vietnamese or Chinese are rapidly formatting. In the future they might create "global tribes", with their own ethnic and cultural identity which will not disappear despite the spatial distance from their homelands. These tribes are groups, which are based on classical cosmopolitanism. Their arrival in various spots on the globe has resulted in the advancement of new technologies, industry and culture. Their departure has always resulted in the withering of these spheres. Their arrival has been the harbinger of technological, economic and intellectual advancement and has contributed to the development of the global market place.

REFERENCES

1. Edwards R.C. (1975), The Social Relations of Production in the Firm and Labor Market Structure, in R.C. Edwards, M. Reich and D.M. Gordon (eds), *Labor Market Segmentation*, Lexington: D.C. Heath.
2. Glabicka K. and Sakson B. (1996), Imigracja do Polski w swietle danych statystycznych [Immigration into Poland – in the lights of statistical data], Warsaw: *ISS Working Papers*.
3. Gordon D.M. (1972), *Theories of Poverty and Underemployment: Orthodox, Radical and Dual Labor Market Perspectives*, Lexington: D.C. Heath.
4. Halik T. (2000), The Vietnamese in Poland. Images/Scenes from the Past, Present and Future, in: F.E.I. Hamilton and Iglicka K. (eds), *From Homogeneity to Multiculturalism. Minorities Old and New in Poland*, London: SSEES, University College of London Press.
5. Heffner K. (1999), The Return of Emigrants from Germany to Upper Silesia: Reality and Prospects, in K. Iglicka and K. Sword (eds*) The Challenge of East-West Migration for Poland*, London: Macmillan.
6. Iglicka K., and Sword K. (eds), (1999), *The Challenge of East-West Migration for Poland*, London, New York: Macmillan, St. Martin's.
7. Iglicka K. (1999), The Economics of the Petty-Trade on the Eastern Polish Border, in K. Iglicka and Sword K. (eds), (1999) *The Challenge of East-West Migration for Poland*, London, New York: Macmillan, St. Martin's
8. Iglicka K. (2000), Ethnic Division on Emerging Foreign Labour Markets in Poland, *Europe-Asia Studies*, vol. 52, no.7, p. 1237-55.
9. Iglicka K. (2001a), Shuttling from the former Soviet Union to Poland, *Journal of Ethnic and Migration Studies,* vol. 27, no. 1, p. 1-21.
10. Iglicka K. (2001b), Migration From and Into Poland in the Light of East-West European Migration, *International Migration*, no1.
11. Informal Labor Market (1995), Warsaw: Ministry of Labor Press.
12. Jagielski J. (1997), *Status prawny cudzoziemca w Polsce* (Legal status of foreigners in Poland), Warsaw.
13. Jerczynski M. (1999), Patterns of Spatial Mobility of Citizens of the Former Soviet Union, in Iglicka K. and Sword K. (eds*) The Challenge of East-West Migration for Poland*, London: Macmillan.
14. Khomra A. (1994), Torgova migratsiya ukrainskovo naselennyja v Polshu (Petty-trade migration of Ukrainian population to Poland), *Kiev: NISS report (typescript).*

15. Korcelli P. (1991), International Migrations in Europe: Polish Perspectives for the 1990s, *International Migration Review*, 24(2).
16. Kozlowski T.K, (1999), Migration Flows in the 1990s: Challenges for Entry, Asylum and integration Policy in Poland, in: Iglicka K. and Sword K. (eds), *The Challenge of East-West Migration for Poland*, London, Macmillan.
17. Massey D., J. Arrango, G. Hugo, A. Koucouci, A. Pelligrino and J. Edward Taylor (1993), Theories of International Migration: Review and Appraisal, *Population and Development Review,* 19(3), p. 431-465.
18. Massey D.S. (1999), International Migration at the Dawn of the Twenty-first Century: The Role of the State, *Population and Development Review*, 25(2), p. 303-322.
19. Morokvasic M. and de Tinguy A. (1993), Between East and West: A New Migratory Space, in: Rudolph H. and Morokvasic M. (Eds), *Bridging States and Markets: International Migration in the early 1990s*. Berlin: Sigma.
20. Okolski M. (1995), *Trends in International Migrations. Poland: the 1995 SOPEMI Report*, Paris: OECD.
21. Okolski M. (1996), *Trends in International Migrations. Poland: the 1996 SOPEMI Report*, Paris: OECD.
22. Okolski M. (1998), *Recent trends in international migration – Poland: the 1998 SOPEMI Report*, Paris: OECD.
23. Piore M.J. (1979), *Birds of Passage: Migrant Labor and Industrial Societies*. Cambridge: Cambridge University Press.
24. Poland – *Statistical data on migration 1994-1998* (1999), Office for Migration and Refugees, Warsaw.
25. Portes A. (1981), Modes of Structural Incorporation and Present Theories of Labor Immigration, in: Kritz M.M., Keely C.B. and Tomasi S.M. (eds), *Global Trends in Migration*, New York: Center for Migration Studies.
26. Roczniki Statystyczne, various years, *(Statistical yearbook),* GUS (Central Statistical Office).
27. Ruch graniczny i wydatki cudzoziemcow w Polsce, 1994-1996, (1997), GUS (Central Statistical Office), Warsaw.
28. Rudolph H., and Hillman F. (1998), The Invisible Hand Needs Visible Heads: Managers, Experts and Professionals from Western Countries in Poland, in Koser K. and Lutz H. (eds), *Social Constructions and Social Realities*, London: Macmillan.
29. Salt J. (1989), A Comparative Overview of International Trends and Types, 1950-80, *International Migration Review*, 15(3):431-56.
30. Salt J. (1996), *Current trends in international migration in Europe*. Council of Europe (paper presented at the 6th Conference of European Ministers responsible for migration affairs).
31. Sprawozdanie z badania sondazowego zezwolenia na prace udzielane cudzoziemcom przez wojewodzkie urzedy pracy w okresie 1994 – 1995 (30 czerwiec), (1995), (A Report on the basis of work permits for foreigners granted by

Voivodships' Labour Offices in 1994-1995 (30 June), Warsaw: Ministry of Labor Press.

32. Stachanczyk P. (1998), *Cudzoziemcy. Praktyczny przewodnik do ustawy o cudzoziemcach*, (Foreigners. A practical guide for an Alien Law), Warsaw.
33. Stola D. (forthcoming), Migrations in Central Europe: Poland, in: C. Wallace and D, Stola (eds), *Central Europe. The New Migration Space*, London, Macmillan.
34. Sword K. (1999), Cross-Border 'Suitcase Trade' and the role of Foreigners in Polish Informal Markets, In: Iglicka K. and Sword K. (eds), *The Challenge of East-West Migration for Poland.* London: Macmillan.
35. Wallace C. and D. Stola (eds), (forthcoming), *Central Europe. The New Migration Space*, London, Macmillan.

Chapter 8

INTERNATIONAL BUSINESS STRATEGIES TOWARDS ECONOMIES IN TRANSITION: THE CASE OF JAPANESE MULTINATIONALS IN CHINA AND EASTERN EUROPE

J. Jaussaud
IAE Tours
J. Schnaper
IAE Poitiers

1. INTRODUCTION

Eastern Europe and China have been opening up their economies quasi simultaneously as part of a transition process towards more liberal inspired economies. However, all Central and Eastern European countries (CEEC) have clearly rejected communism, whereas China practices a policy of economic liberalization and opening up, while preserving at the same time references to socialism and to some extent centralized planning. The transition process attracts the Western, Japanese and even Korean companies which see new opportunities in terms of markets as well as in terms of reduction of production costs by means of delocalization. In this chapter however, we concentrate only on the attitude towards transition processes of Japanese multinational enterprises (MNE). We expose how multinational firms try to keep control over business operations when they set up subsidiaries in countries in the midst of economic transition. On the basis of a sample of 394 subsidiaries of Japanese multinationals in China (218) and in Central and Eastern Europe[1] (176), we concentrate on two main instruments of control which are the control of capital and expatriation policies.

---

[1] CEEC countries include in this chapter: Bulgaria, Croatia, Czech Republic, Hungary, Poland, Romania, Russia,. Slovak, Slovenija and Ukraine.

Figure 1 displays the growing interest of Japanese multinational companies to establish themselves in countries in economic transition. At the beginning of the transition process, both China and Central and Eastern European countries received every year a growing number of foreign subsidiaries. Then the Japanese plants in CEEC stabilize, whereas in China they increase sharply. Indeed, China opened more clearly after 1992 probably as a result of the speeches of *Deng Xiao Ping* in the south of the country.

Figure 1: Tendencies in the Creation of Subsidiaries in China and Central and Eastern European Countries by Japanese Multinational Firms (Number of Units)

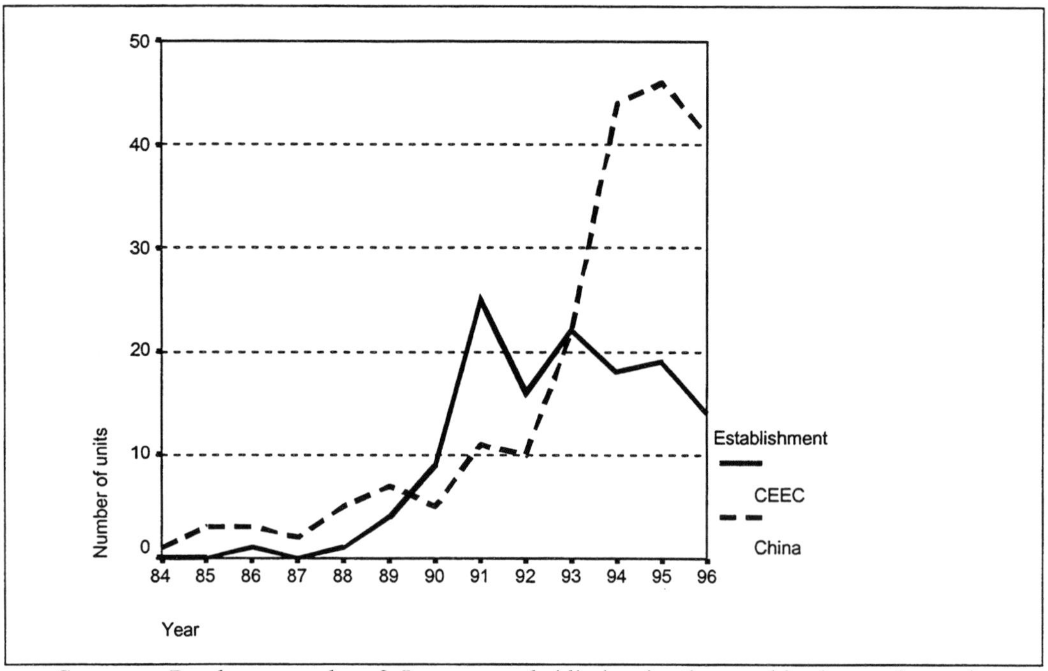

Sources: Random sample of Japanese subsidiaries in the world, drawn from the subsidiaries companies listed by Tôyô Keizai (1999)

The question of the control of subsidiaries abroad, in particular when they are equity joint ventures, has been widely studied during the last two decades, (Harrigan, 1985; Kogut, 1988; Geringer and Hebert, 1989; Kumar and Seth, 1998). Scholars have underlined the diversity of instruments of control and insisted upon the interest of combining judiciously different instruments of control according to the context of implantation. The distribution of capital of a joint venture between partners and the expatriation policy of top executives constitute two essential instruments of control, to which we recently devoted two publications (Jaussaud, Schaaper and Zhang, 2000 a and b).

In the first of these texts, we showed that when the subsidiary company is a joint venture (JV), the behaviors as regards the share of capital, deduced by Beamish (1992) and other authors he quotes, evolved deeply during the last years. Even in developing countries, the multinationals now often create majority JV's, undoubtedly because of a relaxing of the position of the authorities of these countries with regard to foreign investments.

In the second publication, we mainly tested the expatriation model of Perlmutter (1969, 1974), according to which firms send on average more expatriates to subsidiaries settled in developing countries than to subsidiaries settled in industrialized countries. Perlmutter states that multinationals mostly adopt ethnocentric behavior towards developing countries. Ethnocentric behavior means that values, practices and know-how of the home country are higher and must be transferred to the subsidiaries abroad. Thus the number of expatriates coming from the head office and detached to the subsidiaries will be high and only a reduced number of management positions will be offered to local managers. On the other hand, multinationals mostly adopt polycentric behavior towards industrialized countries. Polycentric behavior means that the values and practices of a host country are difficult to understand. Thus within such a framework a manager sent from the home office of the firm would have difficulty to act efficiently. In this case it is better to entrust responsibilities to local managers. Then, according to the degree of maturity of the multinational itself, expatriation policies may be of the geocentric or the regiocentric type, in the perspective of globalization or regional integration.

Following our empirical findings, this model can only be validated when reasoning within a certain type of subsidiaries, mainly when comparing minority joint ventures settled in developing countries to minority joint ventures settled in industrialized countries, as well as when comparing majority joint ventures settled in developing countries to majority joint ventures settled in industrialized countries. However, the model of Perlmutter has not been validated in the case of wholly foreign owned enterprises (WFOE), to which multinationals send globally more expatriates than to joint ventures, independently of the level of development of the host country. It appears that multinationals create massively full owned subsidiaries in industrialized countries while the creation of joint ventures remains the dominant rule in developing countries. Two contradictory effects play, less expatriates are sent towards industrialized countries and more expatriates towards full owned enterprises. Thus the Perlmutter's model of expatriation cannot be validated globally when mixing the cases of joint ventures and fully owned enterprises. We also validated in this contribution specific expatriation policies, as analyzed by Edstrom and Galbraith (1977). We found that towards the United States, Japanese multinationals send much more expatriated managers than to any other country in the world. The two authors explain such behavior for reasons of enrichment of experience for the expatriated managers and for reasons of the organizational development of the firm.

In this chapter, we wish to reconsider these two variables of control, distribution of capital and expatriation policy, in the case of establishment in the countries in economic transition. On the basis of a sample of 394 subsidiaries of Japanese multinationals in China (218) and in Central and Eastern Europe (176), we compare the structuring of the subsidiaries in these countries, and the policies of expatriation. However we shall first start with a short presentation of the activities and size of the subsidiaries in these countries.

2. Size and Activities of Subsidiary Companies Created in China and CEEC

We work on the basis of a random sample drawn from the *Kaigai Shishutsu Kigyô Sôran '99* directory (Tôyô Keizai, 1999), which lists subsidiary companies of Japanese mother firms settled in the whole world. This directory, published each year, is founded on a vast survey held completed by Japanese multinationals (5762 head offices for the 1999 edition with a response rate of 60%, permitting to identify 19036 subsidiary companies in the world). The widespread professional use of the Tôyô Keizai directories in Japan suggests that companies answer carefully. We compare, on the basis of our random sample, subsidiary companies created by Japanese multinationals in China and in the CEEC group. First we look at their sizes, then at their nature of activity: simple commercialization subsidiary or integrated subsidiary (production and commercialization).

2.1 Sizes of the Subsidiary Companies in China and in the CEEC

Total added value is by far the best indicator of the size of a company. However, lacking the necessary data, we shall retain three other main indicators of size here which are the registered capital, the turnover and the number of employees of the subsidiary. To make our statistical analysis more appropriate, we compare the figures on the basis of a rectified average eliminating extreme values.

Table 1: Comparison of the Sizes of the Subsidiaries in CEEs and China (Millions of US Dollars for the Variables "Capital" and "Turnover")

Comparison of the Sizes of Subsidiaries		**China**	**CEEC**
Capital	Trimmed mean (without 5% of extreme values)	4,3	2
	Median	3,4	0,2
Turnover	Trimmed mean (without 5% of extreme values)	6	19
	Median	2,9	6,3
Number of employees	Trimmed mean (without 5% of extreme values)	179	48
	Median	115	19

Sources: according to our sample extracted from the Tôyô Keizai (1999).

Graphical representation of the sample distribution of the capital and the turnover of the subsidiaries gives deeper insight into some of the characteristical differences in the economic transition process in China compared to that of the CEEC:

Figure 2: Comparison of the Sizes, Measured by the Registered Capital and the Turnover, of Subsidiaries in CEEC and in China (millions of US dollars)

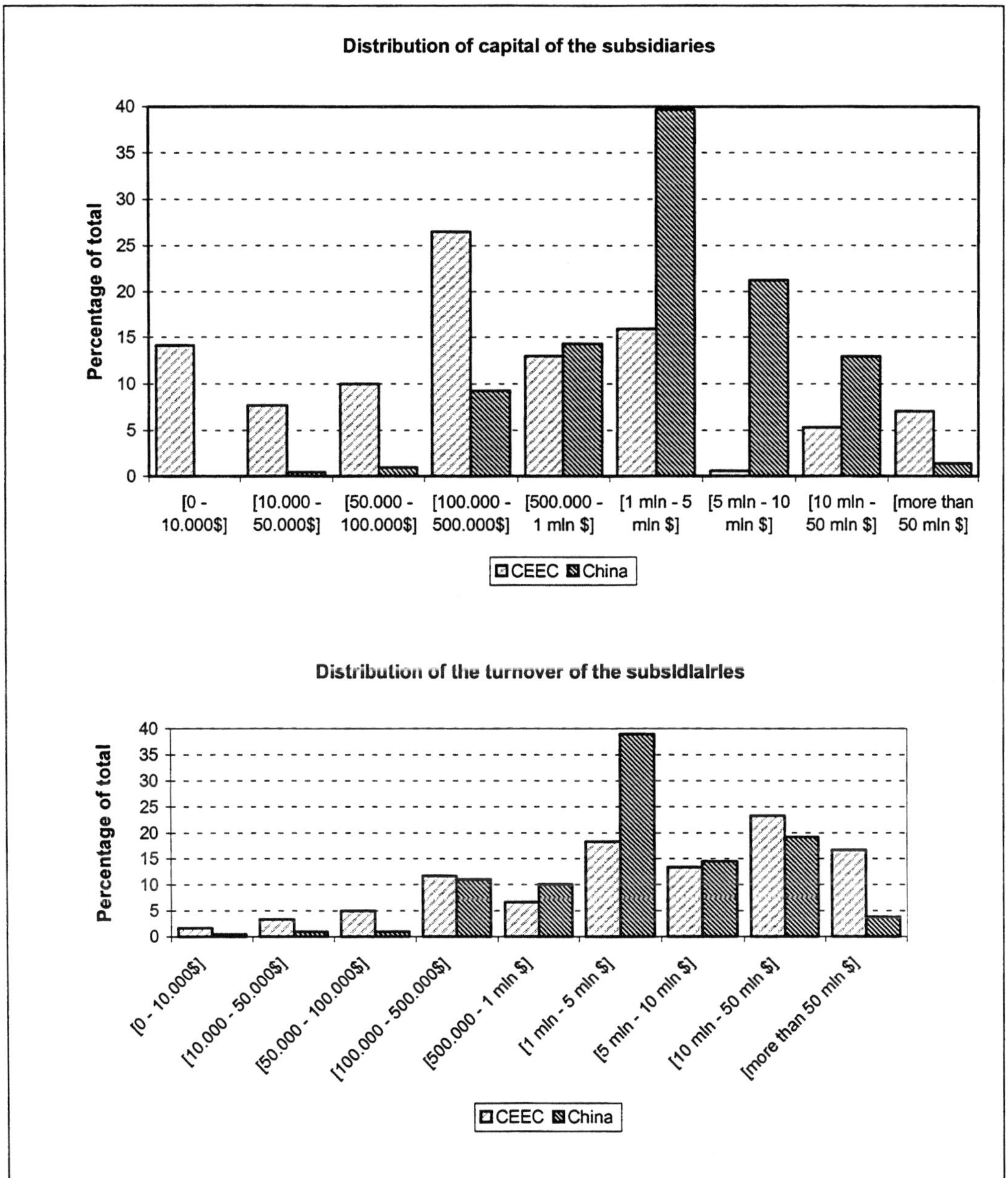

Sources: according to our sample extracted from the Tôyô Keizai (1999)

The average amount invested by the Japanese partners is higher in China than in the CEEC. However, as figure 2 shows, the diversity of the cases is much larger in Eastern Europe than in China. This is in the first place due to the fact that in China, when a foreign investment does not exceed a fixed threshold (30 million dollars in the coastal provinces, 10 million in the interior provinces - Chow, 1998; CCPIT, 1996), the authorization of setting up a JV is easier to obtain, because it is then granted by the local authorities and not by the national authorities. Furthermore, there are few small investments in China, maybe because most of subsidiaries there, as we shall see in the following paragraph, are carrying production activities. In Central and Eastern Europe, investments are done in countries at different stages of transition and whose market sizes vary considerably and therefore involve investment projects of different importance.

The same phenomenon can be observed in the diversity of turnovers realized by Japanese subsidiaries in the CEEC compared to China. However, it might appear surprising that the average capital invested in China is twice as high as the invested capital in Central and Eastern Europe, whereas the average turnover is three times weaker. In fact, as we shall see in the following paragraph, subsidiaries in China are much more often production plants whereas subsidiaries in the CEEC are more often simple commercialization offices.

2.2 Nature of the Activities of the Subsidiary Companies

Figure 3, shows that 80% of the subsidiaries in China concern production activities against only 25% in the CEEC globally. These production plants require to generate equal turnover, a larger starting capital than simple commercialization subsidiaries.

It is clear that Japanese firms settle JV's in China in order to delocalize their production, either to sell in the host country itself or to re-export back to Japan or to other countries. Because in China GDP per capita is amongst the lowest in the world (662$ in 1996; Bank of Japan, 1998), the wage costs are also very low leading to low production costs. In the countries of Eastern and Central Europe, the Japanese multinationals seem rather to establish subsidiary companies in order to commercialize. These strategical differences, as we shall see, will influence the way the joint ventures are structured as well as expatriation policies towards the foreign establishments.

Figure 3: Nature of the Activities of Subsidiary Companies Created in China and in CEEC by Japanese Multinationals

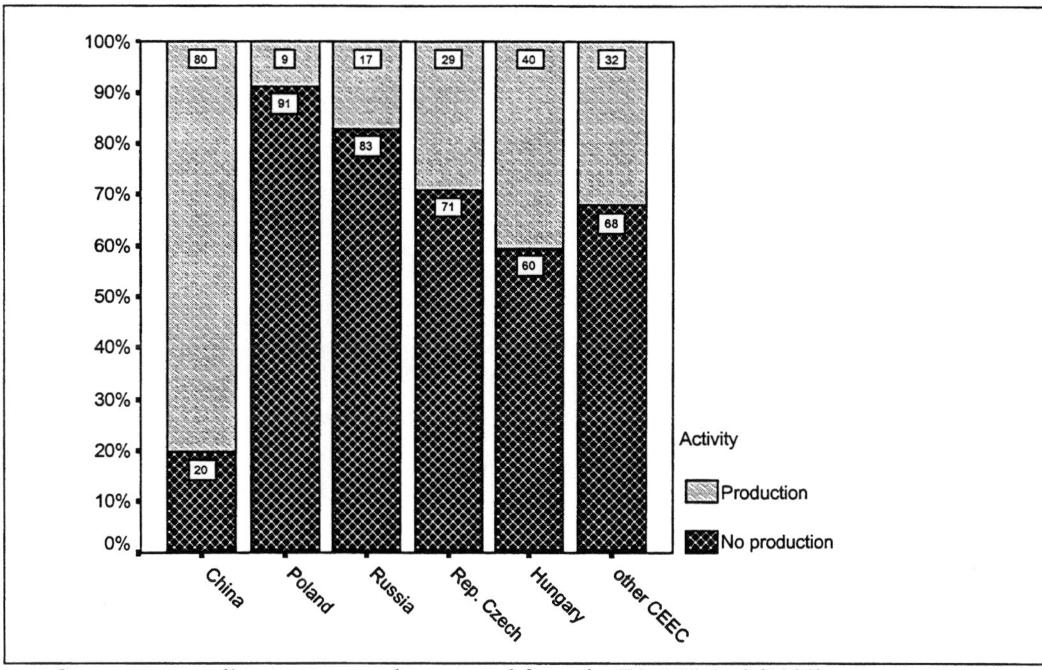

Sources: according to our sample extracted from the Tôyô Keizai (1999)

3. CONTROL OF THE CAPITAL AND STRUCTURING OF THE ESTABLISHMENTS

When a mother company establishes a subsidiary in a foreign country, it must first choose between settling as a full owned enterprise of which it holds 100% of the capital, or as an international joint venture, of which it shares the capital with a local partner. When it chooses to settle a joint venture, it must determine the level of participation which can be a minority, an equal (50/50) or a majority participation. Holding a majority share of the capital theoretically allows keeping the control of the strategical decisions, especially those relating to the appointment of the managers, and obtaining thus an effective control of management of the joint venture (Stopford and Wells, 1972). In practice however, a minority partner will not agree for a long time to contribute to the functioning of the joint venture if the decisions do not protect its interests and do not take into account its vision of problem solving. The capacity derived from a majority detention of capital must consequently be put into broader perspective, without however being concealed.

We first study what kind of control of capital Japanese multinationals prefer when they establish subsidiaries in China and in the CEEC. We shall then see that in Central and Eastern European Countries, Japanese subsidiaries are often controlled by means of another subsidiary company set up elsewhere in Europe.

3.1 Distribution of Capital

Table 2 and figure 4 specify the modes of establishment with regard to the distribution of capital of the Japanese subsidiaries in China and in the CEEC.

Table 2: Distribution of Capital of Japanese Subsidiary Companies Set Up in China and in the CEEC

		International Joint Venture				100% WFOE	Total
		Minority JV	50%-50% JV	Majority JV	Sub-total JV		
CEEC	Number	18	11	34	63	113	176
	Percentage of total	10,2%	6,3%	19,3%	35,8%	64,2%	100 %
China	Number	47	22	85	154	64	218
	Percentage of total	21,5%	10,1%	39,0%	70,6%	29,4%	100 %

Sources: according to our sample extracted from the Tôyô Keizai (1999)

Figure 4: Distribution of Capital of Japanese Subsidiary Companies Set Up in China and in the CEEC

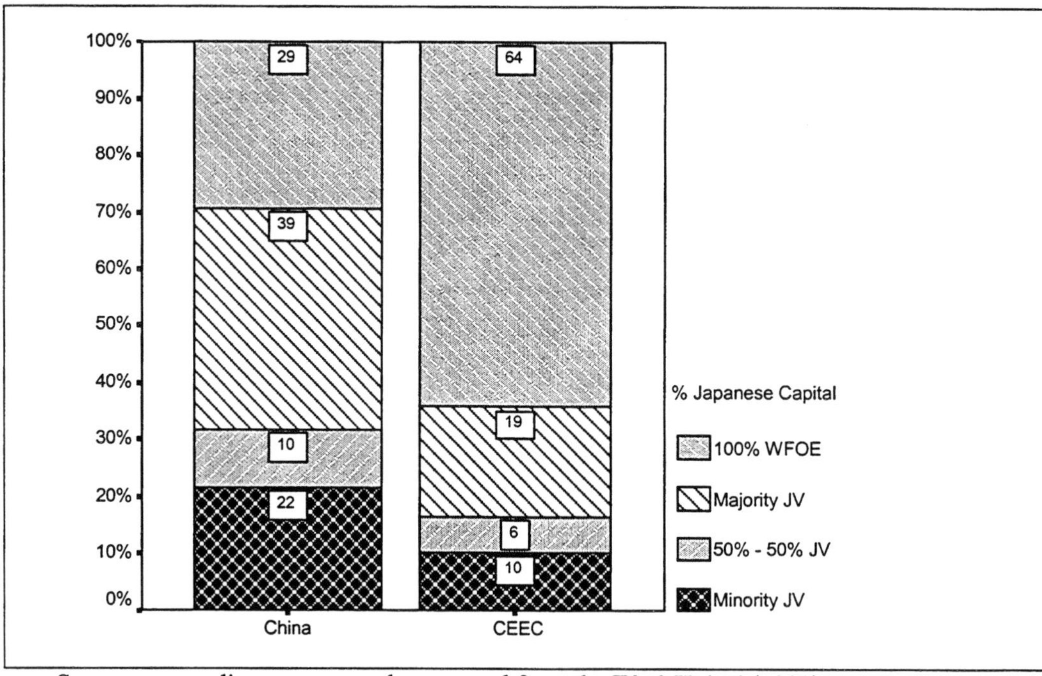

Sources: according to our sample extracted from the Tôyô Keizai (1999)

China is generally perceived as difficult to penetrate because of political and economic constraints imposed by authorities, because of imperfect distribution and transport systems and the language obstacle. Consequently, only 29% of the Japanese subsidiaries in China are fully foreign owned against 64% in the CEEC. In China,

Japanese companies prefer to associate with a local partner, although the law has allowed since 1986 (Xie, 1995) the creation of subsidiary companies with foreign capital only.

According to Chow (1998), if a Western partner in China wants to have significant control over a joint venture, it may be necessary for him to invest at least 70 or 80% of the capital. Otherwise, Chow suggests that the Chinese partner endeavor to acquire real influence on the management of the subsidiary company. Our data, as figure 5 shows, pinpoint the weakness of this idea. In China, as elsewhere, it is undoubtedly by means of combining various methods of control (distribution of managerial key positions, voting power in the board of directors of the subsidiary, etc.) that partners try, at the same time, to consolidate their positions and avoid situations of conflict (Geringer and Hebert, 1989; Kumar and Seth, 1998). This is also what Zhang (1998) found for the case of the Sino-French joint ventures settled in China.

Figure 5: Distribution of Capital of Japanese Joint Ventures Set Up in China (Number of Units)

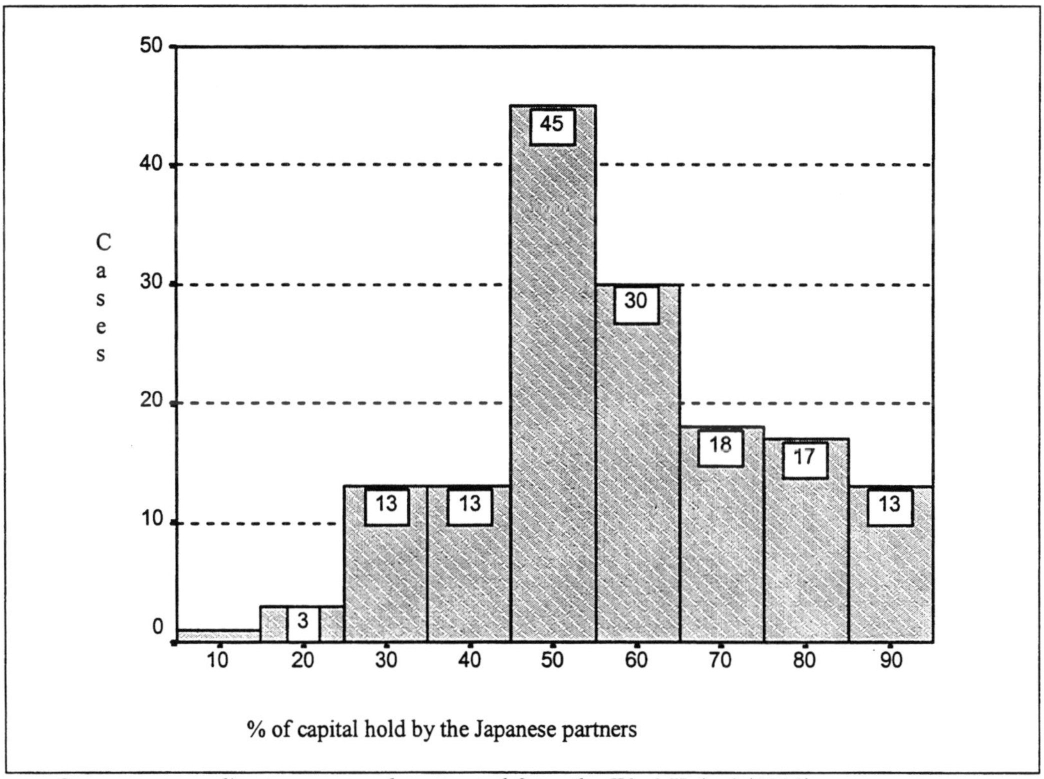

Sources: according to our sample extracted from the Tôyô Keizai (1999).

To study the distribution of capital for subsidiaries settled in the CEEC in more detail and in order to preserve representativeness, we retain only those countries for which the number of observations is higher than 30 (figure 6). Within these countries, Russia seems to constitute a specific case. The establishment in the form of international joint ventures with a Russian partner (63% of our observations) is preferred to wholly foreign owned enterprises (WFOEs), probably because the country is still perceived as being unstable and politically risky. The percentage of joint ventures compared to the WFOE's is even close to the percentage for China. Moreover, we remark a relatively high number (17%) of equal 50/50 joint ventures. However, a more thorough analysis over time shows a clear change in establishment strategy in Russia from 1993 onwards. Before 1993, we primarily observe minority and 50/50 joint ventures but no WFOE's at all. After 1994 we observe almost exclusively 100% WFOE's.

Figure 6: Distribution of Japanese Subsidiaries in Central and Eastern European Countries Following the Share of Capital Held

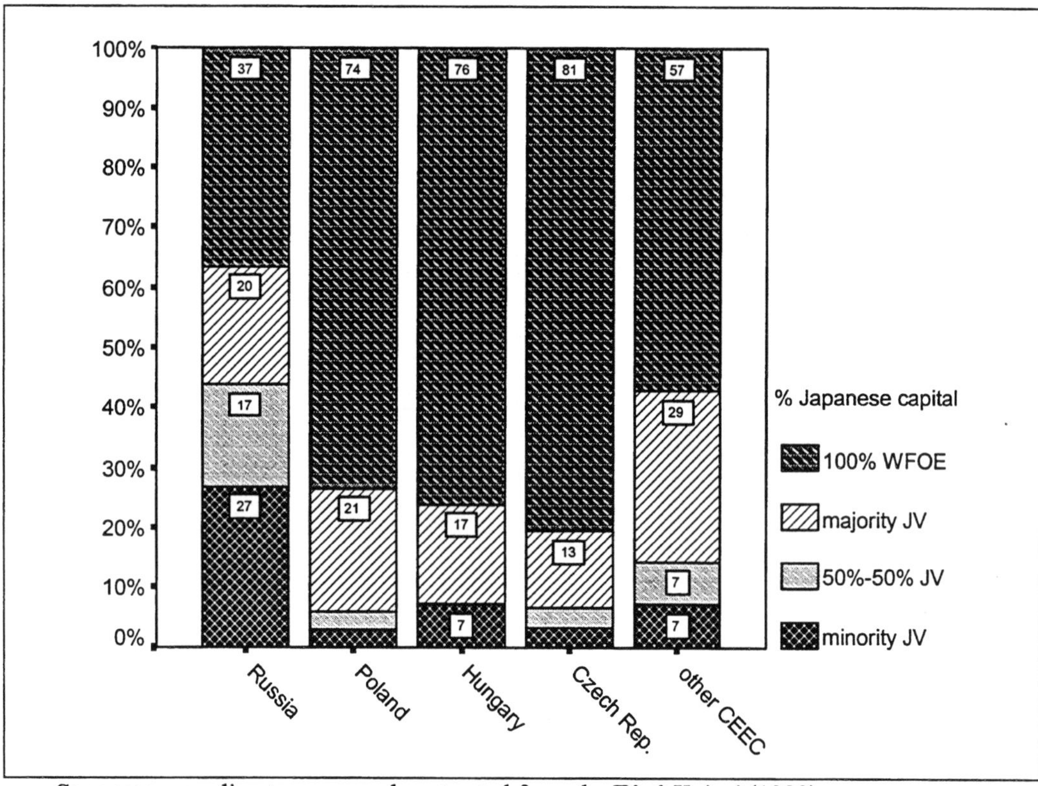

Sources: according to our sample extracted from the Tôyô Keizai (1999).

Poland, Hungary and the Czech Republic are considered political stable countries, preparing their future entry in the European Union, which impose few constraints on foreign investors. Hence, 75% to 80% of the Japanese subsidiaries in this group of countries are WFOE's. Also, minority participation is very rare in those countries. Did Japanese firms readjust their strategies of capital control in this group of countries as well as in China during the transition process, as they did in Russia? The two following graphs compare the creation of joint ventures to that of WFOE's in China and in the CEEC over the period 1984-1996 and 1985-1997 respectively.

Figure 7: Modes of Establishment in China and in the CEEC (WFOE vs. Joint Ventures) since 1984

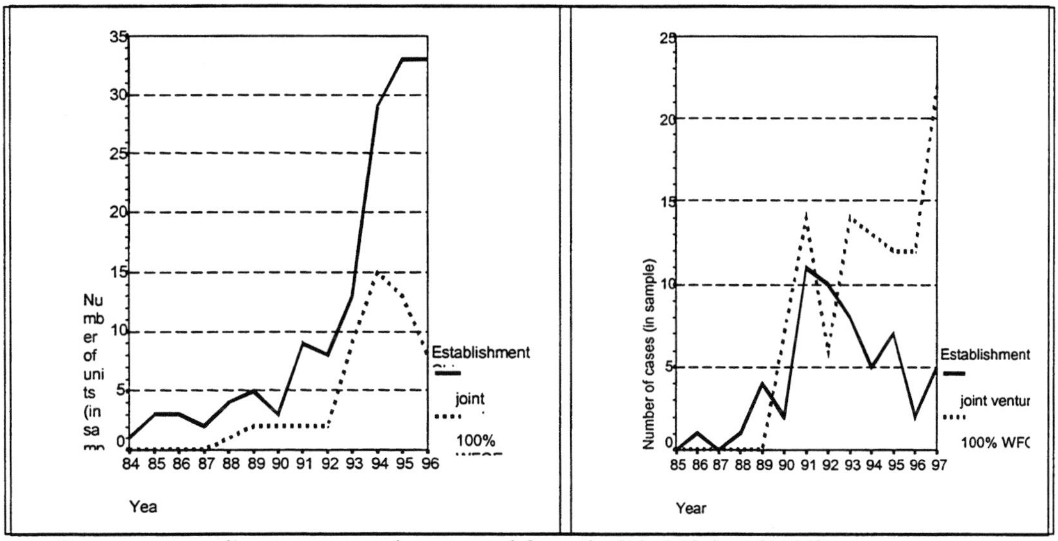

Sources: according to our sample extracted from the Tôyô Keizai (1999)

During the entire transition period, Japanese multinationals prefer the creation of joint ventures in China while in most of the Eastern and Central European countries since 1991, and since 1994 in Russia, they primarily set up fully owned subsidiary companies. China seems to be durably perceived as more difficult to access and a riskier market than the CEEC. The Central European and Eastern countries are increasingly considered as being part of the vast European market. Hence, Japanese firms delegate the control of their subsidiaries in the CEEC to other subsidiary companies they settled in the European Union, as we shall now see.

3.2 The Creation of Subsidiaries of European Subsidiaries in the CEEC

When we studied more thoroughly the rough data of our sample, we observed that subsidiary companies in the CEEC are frequently set up through the intermediary of another European subsidiary that the Japanese MNE already controls. This latter subsidiary enters into the capital of the new subsidiary in a country of the CEEC group. We shall designate this structure as "subsidiaries of subsidiary companies" that table 3 presents in more detail. In China, the subsidiary companies of our sample are all directly held by the Japanese head offices, whereas almost one of two in the CEEC are subsidiary companies of subsidiary companies, apart from Russia however.

Table 3: Establishment of Subsidiaries by Means of Subsidiary Companies of Subsidiary Companies (SOS) in China and in the CEEC

Host country	Number of SOS	Number of observations	Percentage
China	0	218	0%
Russia	4	41	9,8%
Hungary	20	42	47,6%
Poland	19	34	55,9%
Czech Republic	18	31	58,1%
other CEEC	11	28	39,3%

Sources: according to our sample extracted from the Tôyô Keizai (1999).

Japanese companies, in the CEEC, resort to a subsidiary of subsidiary structure to manage their WFOE's in 51% of the cases and in 35% of the cases of a majority joint venture. However, when the Japanese partners take part in equal or minority joint ventures, the management of the subsidiary company by interposed subsidiaries remains rare: only 2 cases out of 29 of our sample. The management of a subsidiary company by an another subsidiary company thus seems to depend on the level of participation in the capital. This phenomenon of creation of subsidiary companies managed by subsidiary companies is coherent with regional integration efforts which develop multinationals in order to benefit from the economies of scale between close markets (Ellis and Williams, 1995), which are here the markets of Europe (European Union and CEEC). The fact that it relates mainly to fully owned subsidiary companies seems also to be coherent with these efforts, because in order to be integrated into a regional scheme, it is useful that the unit be strongly controlled. Such a difference in methods of establishment in China and in the CEEC, as we shall see, will affect the practices of expatriation directed to these two zones.

4. Modes of Establishment and Expatriation Policies

It seems that the expatriation practices of managers by the multinational firm, as Perlmutter (1969, 1974), enriched by the suggestions by Edström and Galbraith (1977). Perlmutter, as we recalled in our introduction, has underlined the ethnocentric behavior of the multinationals in their expatriation practices towards their subsidiary companies established in developing countries, whereas they adopt polycentric, regiocentric or geocentric behavior elsewhere, according to context and the degree of maturity of the multinational company itself,. Edström and Galbraith (1977) interpreted for their part the paradox of a strong tendency of expatriation towards some specific industrialized countries, the United States in particular, for reasons of enrichment of experience of the managers concerned and for organizational development of the firm. Our recent contribution on this question (Jaussaud, Schaaper and Zhang, 2000 b) based on a sample of 868 Japanese subsidiary companies in the whole world, validates with some reserve, this enriched Perlmutter model. However, the whole of the CEEC and China belong to the group of slightly developed countries, it is theoretically difficult to interpret the expatriation policies according to Perlmutter's model. We can however ask, with regard to countries in transition, if expatriation practices by Japanese multinationals differ between China and CEEC? In this case, how do they differ?

4.1 Expatriation Policies towards Countries in Transition

Table 4 compares the mean number of expatriated managers sent towards Japanese subsidiary companies in China and in the CEEC.

Table 4: Mean number of Expatriated Managers towards Countries in Economic Transition (China, CEEC Globally)

	Number of observations	Mean number of expatriates	Standard deviation
CEEC	115	1,17	1,67
China	216	2,66	2,92

Sources: according to our sample extracted from the Tôyô Keizai (1999).

The global comparison of the mean number of expatriates towards China and the CEEC shows a significant difference (Student's t = 5,9, sign.= 0,000), which is worth further analysis. By detailing the practices in direction of countries of the CEEC for which the number of observations is higher than 30 (table 5 and figure 8), more subtle differences appear:

Table 5: Mean Number of Expatriated Managers in Direction to Countries in Economic Transition (China, Specific Countries of the CEEC Group)

Host country	Number of observations	Mean number of expatriates	Confidence intervals
China	216	2,66	[2,27 - 3,05]
Russia	26	1,92	[1,20 - 2,64]
Hungary	29	1,45	[0,83 - 2,06]
Poland	23	0,78	[0,46 - 1,10]
Czech Republic	21	0,48	[0,17 - 0,79]
Other CEEC	14	0,23	[0 - 0,50]

Sources:_according to our sample extracted from the Tôyô Keizai (1999).

Figure 8: Mean Number and their Confidence Intervals of Expatriated Managers Sent to Subsidiary Companies Established in China and CEEC (Differences are Significant when the Confidence Intervals do not Overlap)

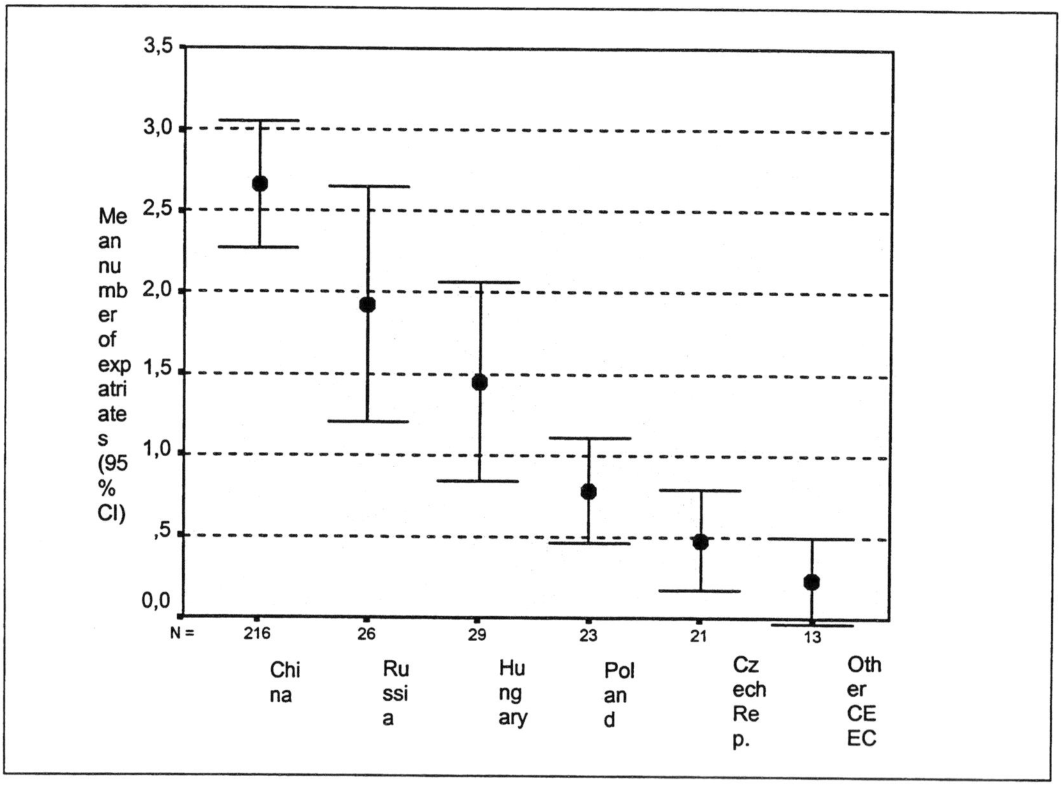

Russia once again occupies an intermediate place between China and the other CEEC. The difference in the number of managers expatriated to China and to Russia is not significant. On the other hand, the differences between the number of managers expatriated to China and to the other countries of the CEEC group are significant. As the level of economic development of the host country cannot explain these differences, three other variables are likely to bring an enlightenment on the differences in the expatriation policies: the level of participation in the capital, the nature of the activities of the subsidiary company and the management of the establishment by means of an intermediate subsidiary company.

4.2 The Effect of the Share of Capital on Expatriation Policies

Our own work (Jaussaud, Schaaper and Zhang, 2000 b) has shown the joint use of two main instruments of control which are the share of capital held and the expatriation policy. This result is coherent with the suggestions of Geringer and Hebert (1989) and Kumar and Seth (1998), according to which it is useful to combine judiciously various instruments of control. We remarked that Japanese firms send more expatriated managers towards majority joint ventures than towards minority ones, independently of the degree of development in the host country. Also, they send many more expatriate managers towards their WFOE's than towards joint ventures in which they take part. The two variables of control thus reinforce each other in the same direction. We subject these conclusions to a new empirical verification for the case of subsidiaries implanted in countries in economic transition.

Table 6: Mean Number of Expatriates in Relation to the Level Participation in the Capital in Countries in Transition (Significant Differences are Printed in Fat Characters)

	Minority JV's	50%-50% JV's	Majority JV's	Sub total of JV's	100% WFOE	Mean Difference	T-test
China	1,4	2,1	2,6	**2,1**	**3,9**	**- 1,8**	**-4,3**
Hungary	2,0	-	2,0	2,0	1,2	0,8	1,2
Poland	0	-	1,0	0,8	0,8	0	0
Russia	1,6	2,7	3,0	**2,4**	**1,2**	**1,2**	**2,0**
Czech Republic	1,0	0	0	0,3	0,5	-0,2	0,3
other CEEC	0	0	3,0	1,7	0,3	1,4	0,9

Sources: sample extracted from the Tôyô Keizai (1999).

Figure 9: Expatriation Practices and Participation in the Capital in the Countries of Transition

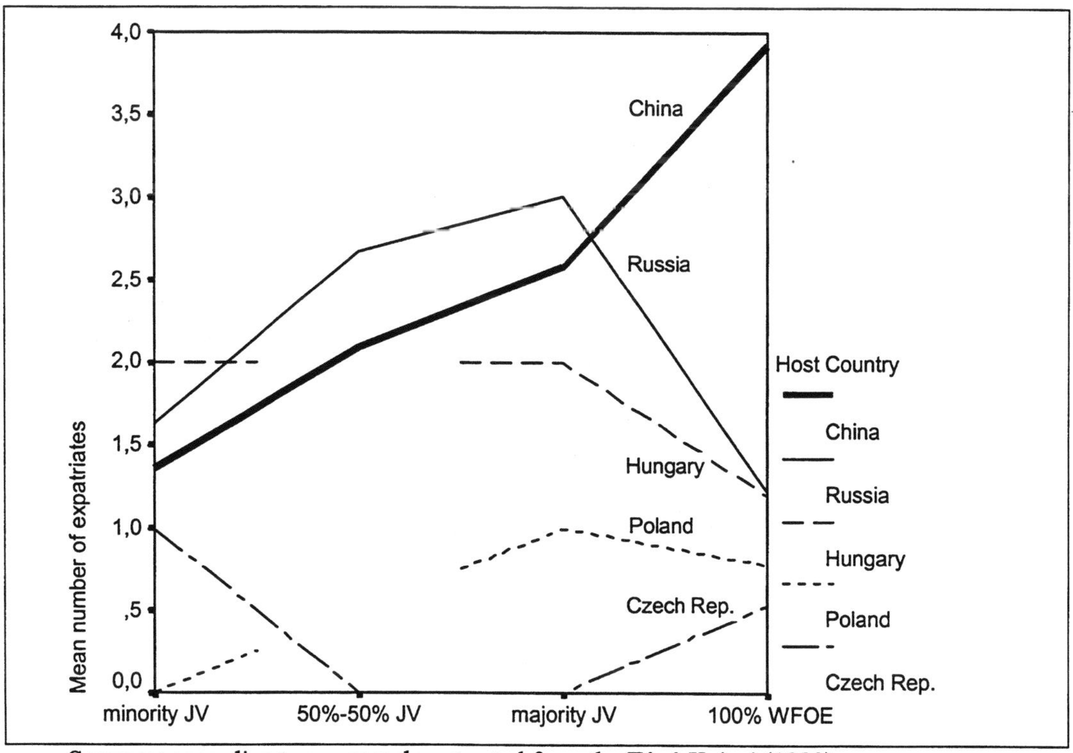

Sources: according to our sample extracted from the Tôyô Keizai (1999).

Our assumption is again corroborated for China: the higher the participation, the more the Japanese firms send managers to their Chinese subsidiary companies. For Russia, as figure 9 shows, our assumption seems only corroborated for the case of joint ventures without considering the case of WFOE's. On the other hand, we note a general tendency to send few expatriated managers to other countries of the CEEC group. In Hungary and Poland, one notes again, as in Russia, that an even fewer number of expatriated managers are sent to the WFOE's than to joint ventures. This paradoxical situation can be explained by considering another explanatory variable, which is the creation of an intermediate subsidiary company structure which enters into the capital of subsidiary companies in the CEEC. This implies that expatriated managers do not come directly from the head office but indirectly from the intermediate subsidiary companies, mostly settled in the European Union, which manages the subsidiary company implanted in the CEEC.

4.3 The Effect of Production Activity of the Subsidiary Company on Expatriation Policies

One may suppose that the nature of the multinational firm activity influences the number of expatriated managers. In our sample, we have classified subsidiary companies of Japanese multinationals in two main categories, those which have a production activity and those which carry only out commercialization operations. Production activities, because of their relative complexity, undoubtedly require more strict command which induces a delegation of more expatriated managers. Table 7 allows to study this assumption.

Table 7: The Effect of the Activity Practices of Expatriation in the Countries of Transition

Host Country	Production Activity				Mean Difference	T-test
	Yes	Number	No	Number		
China	2,8	175	2,3	43	0,5	1,05
Hungary	**2,2**	17	**1,1**	25	**1,1**	**2,17**
Poland	0,5	3	0,8	31	-0,3	0,63
Russia	3,0	7	1,7	34	1,3	1,65
Czech Republic	0,3	9	0,6	22	-0,2	0,99
other CEEC	**3,3**	9	**0,1**	19	**3,2**	**5,70**
CEEC globally	***2,0***	*45*	***1,0***	*131*	***1,0***	***3,22***

Notes: significant differences are printed in fat characters);
Sources: according to our sample extracted from the Tôyô Keizai (1999).

In China, the fact that there are production activities or not does not influence the expatriation policy: the Japanese partners seem to choose strong supervision of 2,66 expatriated managers on average in this country. For some specific countries of the CEEC (Poland, Russia and Czech Republic) the number of production subsidiaries in our sample is not high enough to draw significant statistical conclusions. However, when we consider the CEEC globally, the multinationals send on average one more expatriated manager when the subsidiary company has production activity. This general tendency can in particular be observed for Hungary, Russia and the other CEEC. Our assumption is thus invalidated in the case of China but is confirmed for most of the CEEC's.

4.4 The Effect of the Subsidiary of Subsidiary Company Structure on Expatriation Policies

Let us finally state the following assumption: the number of expatriated managers sent towards subsidiary companies managed by an intermediate subsidiary company is on average less important than towards subsidiary companies managed by the head office itself. Table 8 allows us to study the degree of validity of this assumption.

Table 8: The Effect of the Structure "Subsidiary of Subsidiary Company" on Expatriation Policy in the Countries in Transition

Host Country	Managed by the Mother Company		Managed by a Subsidiary of a Subsidiary		Mean Difference	T-test
	Mean number of expatriates	Number of observations	Mean number of expatriates	Number of observations		
China	2,7	218	-	0	-	-
Hungary	**2,2**	22	**0,5**	20	**1,7**	**4,0**
Poland	**1,2**	15	**0,3**	19	**0,9**	**3,5**
Russia	**2,1**	37	**0,3**	4	**1,8**	**4,4**
Czech Republic	**1,0**	13	**0,2**	18	**0,8**	**3,4**
other CEEC	1,2	17	0,3	11	0,9	1,04
CEEC globally	**2,4**	322	**0,3**	72	**2,1**	**12,2**

Notes: significant differences are printed in fat characters
Sources: according to our sample extracted from the Tôyô Keizai (1999).

It appears very clearly in table 8 that when the subsidiary company is managed by an intermediate subsidiary company, the head office sends practically few directly expatriated managers. When we consider both the existence of an intermediate subsidiary structure and the level of participation in the capital, including the 100% WFOE structure, we see that control of capital and expatriation policy do not always reinforce, as we assumed, but are sometimes exclusive in CEEC countries:

Table 9: Mean Number of Expatriated Managers according to the Existence of an Intermediate Subsidiary Structure crossed by the level of Participation

Subsidiary of subsidiary (CEEC only)	Level of participation			
	Minority	50%-50%	majority	100% WFOE
No	1,4	1,3	2,6	1,3
Yes	-	-	0,3	0,4

Sources: according to our sample extracted from the Tôyô Keizai (1999).

Tables 8 and 9 make it necessary to refine our hypothesis of double control exerted by multinationals with regard to their subsidiaries. In Jaussaud, Schaaper and Zhang (2000 b), we observed the presence of reinforcing control policy, combining a high number of expatriated managers with high levels of participation of capital in a subsidiary, in two groups of countries. The first group consists of the USA, the U.K and Germany which can be considered as the group corresponding to the Edström and Galbraith assumption. Managers are sent to these countries not only in order to control subsidiaries but also to enrich their personal and organizational development (Edström and Galbraith, 1977). The second group, in the case of Japanese multinationals, is made up of countries such as Indonesia, Thailand, Malaysia etc., but also includes China. It is broadly speaking the group of South East Asian countries where Japanese multinationals massively delocalized their production and thus want to keep strong control for highly strategic reasons.

Although the CEEC countries don't seem to belong to either group of countries, can we observe there reinforced double control? We can detect this kind of policy in the case of joint ventures managed by the mother company itself: the multinationals send on average twice as many expatriates (2.6) to majority joint ventures than to minority (1.4), or equal ones (1.3), corroborating our hypothesis of double reinforcing control. However, when the subsidiary is a 100% WFOE, multinationals send less expatriates than to majority joint ventures. One reason may be that in this case, subsidiaries are integrated in the European network of the Japanese multinational, its management being supervised by Japanese executives assigned in one of the countries of this area. This may be the case both for subsidiaries of subsidiaries, for which we have a very small number of expatriates (0.4 on average), but also for those directly held by the mother company in Japan subsidiaries (1.3 expatriates on average), which does not prevent the integration of their management in the European network of the multinational.

5. Conclusion

Concerning the study of the modes of establishment of multinationals outside their country of origin, the variables most often taken into account are the degree of development of the host country and the degree of maturity of the firm itself (Perlmutter, 1969 ; Perlmutter and Heenan, 1974 ; Beamish, 1992, etc.). As we compare in this contribution subsidiaries in China and in the CEEC, the variable "degree of development of the host country" is neutralized. However comparison of modes of establishment shows considerable contrasts, which suggests the complexity of the system of parameters determining the choices of structures and organization of the subsidiaries abroad.

We found several characteristical differences between establishments in China and in the CEEC. First, in China, the subsidiaries generally have a production activity whereas in the CEEC they are generally limited to commercialization activities. Secondly, in China, the majority of the subsidiary companies are joint ventures, whereas in the CEEC, 64% of them are wholly foreign owned subsidiary companies. Thirdly, the subsidiary companies in China are directly held by the Japanese head offices, whereas in the CEEC they are frequently managed by the intermediary of another subsidiary company established in the European Union, Austria or Germany generally. Fourthly, the policies of expatriation also differ whilst the number of expatriated managers is clearly higher towards China than towards the CEEC.

One can imagine, although more thorough qualitative research would be useful to confirm this intuition, that China is perceived by the Japanese multinationals as a highly strategic country of establishment within the framework of their world activities, but also difficult to access and at high risk. The CEEC, for their part, seem to be better integrated into the regional strategies of these multinationals in Europe.

BIBLIOGRAPHY

- Bank of Japan, (1998), Comparative Economic and Financial Statistics – Japan and Other Major Countries, Tokyo.
- Beamish P. (1985), "The Characteristics of Joint Ventures in Developed and Developing Countries", Columbia Journal of World Business, Fall.
- Beamish P. (1992), The Characteristics of Joint Ventures in the People's Republic of China, Journal of International Commercialization, October.
- Ccpit – China Council for the Promotion on International Trade, (1996), China Business Guide, Huaxia Publishing House, Beijing.
- Chow D.C.K. (1998), The limited partnership joint venture model in the peoples Republic of China, Law and Policy in International Business; Washington; Fall 1998
- Dzever S., and Jaussaud, J., Eds., (1998), China and India, Economic Performance and Business Strategies of firms in the Mid-1990s, Macmillan Press.
- Edström, A., Galbraith, J.R, (1977), Transfer of Managers as a Coordination and Control Strategy in Multinational Organizations, Administrative Science Quarterly, June, vol. 22.
- Ellis J., and Williams D. (1995), International Business Strategy, Pitman Publishing, London.
- Geringer J. M, and Hebert L., (1989), "Control and Performance of International Joint Ventures", Journal of International Business Studies, Summer.

- Hennart J.F. (1988), "A Transaction Costs Theory of Equity Joint Ventures", Strategic Management Journal, Vol. 9.
- Harrigan K. (1985), Strategies for Joint Ventures, Lexington Press.
- Jaussaud J., Schaaper J. and Zhang, Z-Y. (2000a), Sur le Contrôle des Entreprises Conjointes Internationales: répartition du capital et politiques d'expatriation, Actes de la IXème Conférence Internationale de Management Stratégique, Montpellier, 24-26 mai.
- Jaussaud J. Schaaper J. and Zhang Z-Y. (2000b), Gestion Internationale des Ressources Humaines: Pratiques d'Expatriation et Contrôle des Filiales au sein des Groupes Multinationaux, Revue Gestion des Ressources Humaines, n°38, novembre.
- Killing J. (1982), "How to Make a Global Joint Venture Work", Harvard Business Review, May-June.
- Kogut B. (1988), "Joint Ventures: Theoretical and Empirical Perspectives", Strategic Management Journal, Vol. 9.
- Kumar S. and Seth A. (1998), "The Design of Co-ordination and Control Mechanisms for Managing Joint Venture – Parent Relationships", Strategic Management Journal, Vol. 19.
- Perlmutter H. (1969), The Tortuous Evolution of the Multinational Corporation, Columbia Journal of World Business, January-February.
- Perlmutter H. and Heenan, D. (1974), How multinational should your top managers be, Harvard Business Review, November - December.
- Schaan J. L. (1973), Parent Control and Joint Venture Success: the Case of Mexico, PhD-Thesis, University of Western Ontario, Canada.
- Stopford J.M., and Wells L. (1972), Managing the Multinational Enterprise, Basic Books, New York.
- Tôyô Keizai (1999), Kaigai Shinshitsu Kigyô Sôran '99, (in English: "directory 1999 of Japanese investments abroad"), Tokyo. Publication in Japanese language.
- Xie, Z.H. (1995), Comprehensive Guide to Chinese Business Laws, Publishing House of Law, Beijing.
- Zhang Z.Y. (1998), Etude exploratoire sur l'organisation, le contrôle et la performance de l'entreprise conjointe franco-chinoise, PhD-thesis in Management Science, Institute of Business Administration, University of Poitiers.

Chapter 9

FDI AND THE ENVIRONMENT: IS CHINA A POLLUTER HEAVEN?

Sylvain H. Zeghni
University of Marne-la-Vallée
Nathalie H. Fabry
University of Marne-la-Vallée

1. INTRODUCTION

Since the economic reform and open door policy of 1978 (*kaifang zhenze*), China has been extraordinarily successful in attracting FDI[1]. By the end of 1998, China had approved over 324.700 FDI projects, with a contractual value of US$ 572.5 billion[2]. The accumulated actual inflows of FDI amounted to US$ 267.5 billion. Over the pas few years, China has been the second largest recipient of FDI in the world, and the largest among the developing countries. Over 170 countries and regions, and 300 of the world's largest MNEs have establishments in China. FDI has contributed to China's economic growth and development, and also facilitated the introduction of market-oriented reforms (Wu, 1999; Wei and al., 1999). In general, FDI has brought in financial resources, transferred technology and management know-how, stimulated institutional innovation in State-Owned Enterprises (SOEs), generated employment, upgraded work-force skills,

[1] In the late 1970's the Chinese government wanted to increase economic growth and catch-up with its neighbours. It has initiated a program of pragmatic and step by step reforms in 1978. According to Naughton (1993), when Deng Xiaoping visited Nissan Motors in Japan in 1978 he said"*today I have learnt what modernisation is like*" and his inscription in Nissan's visitor's book read: "*learn from the great, diligent valiant and intelligent Japanese people*". This story shows us the pragmatic spirit of the Chinese reforms.

[2] See the China Statistical Yearbook various year

promoted exports, and ultimately, contributed to the growth of output and incomes of the host country[3].

However, problems and impediments do exist with respect to FDI in China. First, FDI is concentrated in the manufacturing sector, generating some excess supply capacity in certain product markets (car industry), while-the level of FDI in infrastructure, energy and agriculture has been very low and the share of FDI in Hi-tech industries has also been modest. Second, FDI inflows are concentrated in the coastal areas[4] and accentuate regional unbalances between inland China and coastal areas (Broadman and Sun, 1997; Naughton, 1999; Wei and al., 1999).

The third great problem is linked to the environmental damage. For example, about 1490 foreign affiliates whose products are detrimental to the ozonosphere were established during the period 1985-1994 (Song, 1997). Due to the lack of systematic empirical evidence and a sound analytical framework, it is difficult to quantify either FDI's actual positive or negative effects on the Chinese environment. It is also difficult to determine whether foreign affiliates' environmental performance is better or worse than that of comparable local firms'.

As FDI stock reaches a significant level and the emphasis shifts from quantitative to qualitative FDI, one important issue is the impact of FDI on China's environment: has China emerged as a "polluter haven" for MNEs? Is China better off or worse off with respect to its environment by hosting huge amounts of FDI? What environmental standards should be applied for MNEs operating in China? What is the proper role of the Chinese government in maximizing the positive role of FDI and minimizing its negative impact?

The section 2 of this chapter analyses the polluter haven hypothesis (PHH). The section 3 presents an overview of policies and practices in environment protection. The study shows that FDI generates both positive and negative effects on China's environment, but identifying the scale of such environmental effect remains extremely difficult. As many FDI projects are located in the so-called pollution-intensive industries (PII), the risk of environmental damage has increased.

2. The Polluter Haven Hypothesis: An Overview

The international dimension of environmental problems is not an environmental pollution *per se* but rather a matter of competitiveness and attractiveness. Hence, if polluters do not have to pay for their actions (i.e. polluter pay principle), the host country may attract more inward-FDI in polluting activities. Foreign firms may benefit from additional cost advantages by producing under such a jurisdiction. Host country becomes a *Polluter Haven.* The polluter haven hypothesis (PHH) stipulates that some countries attract pollution-intensive investments through lax or non-enforced environmental

[3] These benefits from FDI in China have to greatly nuance see for example: Bjorkman and Lu 1999; Child and Stewart, 1999; Tsang, 1999a and b.

[4] There are only 10% of FDI flows to the inland China.

regulations. Consequently, pollution-intensive firms would shift operations to these countries to take advantage of lower production costs, the *"industrial flight hypothesis"*, leading to a *"race-to-the-bottom"* in environmental standards (ecological dumping). In the literature, a first set of studies on PHH analyzes the impact of environmental policies on competitiveness. A second set focuses on the relationship between firms' location strategies and lax environmental standards countries (Tsai and Child, 1997; Klassen and Whybark, 1999).

In the first part of the debate mentioned above the main question is "which strategies firms will adopt to face environmental pressures?" According to Faucheux and Nicolaï (1998) we can make a typology of firms' strategies regarding environmental innovation:

Table 1: Typology of Firms' Strategies for Environmental Innovation

The defensive strategy	In this case, environmental policies do nothing but increase production costs so firms do not declare their polluting activities and get round or thwart environmental regulations. They may also transfer their facilities or new plants abroad. This kind of strategy has been dominant and explicit in the whole pollution intensive industry until the mid-1980s.
The follower strategy	In this case, environmental compliance costs are non-productive. The firm does not take part either in the innovative process or in lobbying activities. It just adapts itself to new regulations.
The pro-active strategy	In this strategy, environmental policy can increase competitive advantage (Porter's win-win pollution-halos: foreign firms transfer cleaner technologies that they diffuse to the host country). A green label can provide a competitive advantage over dirtier competitors, providing better quality and more diversity in their product range (Hawkins and al., 1995; Howes and al., 1997)

The second part of the debate can be summarized by this question: "*How serious is the assumption saying that pollution-intensive industries will choose the relocation strategy?*" In other words, is ecological dumping a myth? Among many others examples we chose to mention the Bhopal accident (India, 2/12/84, 6500 death). Before setting up its highly toxic gas facility in India, Union Carbide tried to set up production facilities to Canada and several other industrialized countries. They all refused, even if they had the technological capacity to handle its risky production process. India, who was looking for new investments to foster its development, accepted, despite its lack of control over the technology (Nussbaumer & Worter, 1999).

We need analyses to provide conclusions that might be useful for policy making. We can summarize the more important economic literature in table 2.

The econometric analyses of the PHH concentrate on the relation between trade and the environment, introducing an environmental variable in models of international trade. One good example of this methodology is Tobey (1990). He measures the impact of environmental policies on the structure of international trade of polluting goods by predicting their impact on the net exports of five polluting industries (mining, paper, chemicals, steel, non-ferrous metals). In an Heckscher-Ohlin-Vanek model, he introduces a qualitative variable to represent the stringency of environmental pollution (varying from 1 to 7): some countries can be abundantly endowed with lax environmental standards. Compared to the previsions of the model, his results do not allow him to prove that the introduction of strong environmental constraints and controls changed the structure of international trade. But in industrialized countries environmental costs at the end of the 1970s and at the beginning of the 1980s were not important enough to affect significantly the patterns of trade between countries with high and low environmental standards. Moreover, in these analyses the environmental variable is too simplistic to get a good grasp on environmental stringency. The model will not capture trends in technological change because they are not necessarily related to factor endowment. In fact, one country can gain greater technology-intensive comparative advantage while having a mediocre scientific expansion. So, what happens if one industry gets cleaner through incremental innovations?

Table 2: The Economic Analyses of the Polluter Haven Hypothesis

	Modeling	**Statistical analysis**	**Case studies**
In favor of the Hypothesis	Becker & Henderson (1997) Castro Guerra & Santos (1998) Esty & Gerardin (1998)	Becker & Henderson (1997) Sun (1998) Sun (1999)	Jaffe & al. (1995) Mabey & McNally (1999)
Against the Hypothesis	Bui (1998) Jaffe & Palmer (1997) Markusen (1997) Rauscher (1995) Tobey (1990)	Kolstad & al. (1999)	Jenkins (1998a) Levinson (1996a) Mani & al. (1997) Ratnayake (1998)

The statistical analyses of the PHH are well represented by the Mani and Wheeler's approach (1997). Authors analyze the displacement of pollution-intensive industries (PII) using international information on industrial production, trade and environmental regulation for the period 1960 to 1995. They assess the environment Kuznets' curve (EKC) and analyze the evolution of the share of the five most PII (iron and steel, non-ferrous metals, industrial chemicals, pulp and paper, non-metallic mineral products) in the domestic industrial output of several regions. In Latin America and Asia they find a steady upward trend in pollution-intensive production share.

However, three main reasons explain why Polluter Havens have not had major significance: (1) a highly income-elastic demand for basic industrial products (Vernon's product life cycle); (2) with continued income growth, this elasticity has declined (EKC); (3) the persistence of energy subsidies in many developing countries. These subsidies are decreasing. But, we know that according to Vernon's product life cycle, it is normal that developing countries tend to be specialized in PII: such industries are old industries that are not as research-intensive as the one that constitute the main sources of growth for industrialized economies. However, even if such "involuntary Polluter Havens" existed, industrial flight would still be an issue at stake and Vernon wouldn't helped much in explaining firms' reaction facing increasing environmental standards in developing countries.

Moreover, according to Grossman and Kruger (1994) its applicability is limited to some local urban airborne pollutants for which it has been found that emissions declined after a level of income per capita around $8.000. As energy-intensive FDI are also pollution-intensive energy subsidies act as a strategic incentive to attract pollution-intensive FDI. Besides, subsidies are not the only factor influencing firms' location decisions, the proximity of sources of raw materials, of large markets, and strong environmental policies can also influence them.

Jenkins (1998a) analyses the patterns of industrial pollution at national and firm levels in Mexico and Malaysia. He compares the growth of industrial pollution over the past two decades and he surveys environmental management and performance at firm and plant levels. He concludes that there is a substantial increase in industrial pollution for both countries. International markets value positively environmental performance (firms producing for international markets have a better environmental performance than firms producing for local markets). However, Foreign ownership was not found generally to be a major factor in environmental performance. Domestic exporters tend to be positively influenced by national environmental regulation.

Therefore there are many ways for a company to be flexible as regards environmental-compliance. To understand firms' behavior one needs to understand the process of enforcement. For example, in the process of environmental enforcement, the behavior of a firm plays a much greater role than the pollution intensity of its production processes (Jenkins, 1998b).

In fact, most empirical studies (both econometric and survey) have failed to discern any relationship between low environmental standards and the amount of polluting investment inflows. A good example is the review by Levinson (1996b) and the study of four foreign investment patterns in Mexico, Venezuela, Morocco and Côte d'Ivoire by Eskeland and Harrison (1997). They also reject the hypothesis that the pattern of US FDI is biased towards industries with high pollution abatement costs. This could be for a number of reasons. For instance, environmental pollution will reduce productivity and increase health and related costs, thus raising domestic unit labor costs. However, *a priori*, a country with low environmental standards (pollution havens) may not automatically be seen as an attractive production base. Indeed, to the extent that some of the poorest and slowest growing countries are among the most polluted, rather than strategic or opportunistic gaming by the governments to attract FDI, it may be a sign of incompetent administrative and governmental management or a lack of qualified workers and reliable infrastructures[5]. A good case study of such policy mismanagement is the

[5] Since the 90's, FDI attraction is not exclusively based on factor cost, but rather on their quality. Foreign firms search a combination of cheap labour cost, technological capabilities, labour qualification, dynamic local demand, efficient market organisation, stable political, institutional and legal

ecological disaster in Bhopal by Union Carbide (Bailey, 1993). Further if multinational enterprises (MNEs) already have considerable sunk cost in their home base in environmentally friendly production techniques and technologies, the incentive to move to pollution havens is mitigated. This is referred to as the "*Bhopal effect*", which forced a rather lengthy litigation and costly compensation settlement by union Carbide, not to mention the substantial (though not necessarily unwarranted) negative reputation costs.

Moreover, the other mobile factor, skilled labor, may be not interested to enter and work in a highly polluted country. Given this complementarity between the two factors (skilled labor and capital) and the importance of each in output growth, MNEs (capital providers) will need to offer a premium for skilled labor to work in these countries. That will probably more than offset the direct cost savings (if any) from not having to adhere to strict environmental standards. Different environmental standards may not necessarily lead to destructive competition. Various jurisdictions could conceivably maintain differing environmental standards and tax burdens (i.e. lower quality environment corresponding to lower tax burdens or lower levels of public services and amenities). Skilled labor will then be free to weigh the various tax burden-benefits packages/tradeoffs and decide their preferred jurisdiction accordingly (i.e. they could vote with their feet). This result is derived from the famous Thiebout's model[6]. Finally, empirical studies seem to suggest the existence of an inverted "U-shaped" relation between per capita income of a country and the extent of environmental degradation (referred to as the EKC). This shape may be rationalized in a number of ways (see succinct review in Andreoni and Levinson, 1998). For instance, in the early stages of its industrialization and development drive, the quality of the environment deteriorates, the predominant goal being to increase income level. This is commonly referred to *the "growth now, clean up later*" philosophy. However, once the per capita income reaches a certain threshold, there will be increased awareness of and demand for enhanced overall quality of living, which includes better environmental conditions and recognition of the concept of sustainable development (i.e. pollution-free environment is a luxury good). Further, higher incomes have generally led to lower fertility rates and population growth, which also directly reduces environmental degradation. Andreoni and Levinson (1998) have argued that EKC may be simply rationalized by scale economies in pollution abatement technologies. This suggests that the environmental quality is hardly used as a strategic tool to increase the rate of growth and capital inflow by developing countries but, rather, is a natural process of development (i.e. it is an endogenous variable) due to expanding markets, changing tastes, and the like[7].

---

environment, and safe and reliable infrastructures (Van Den Bulcke and Zhang, 1998). Thus, unskilled human capital, unsafe infrastructures, weak capacity of absorption of the transferred technology, weak financial institutions, may discourage inward-FDI, in spite of polluting facilities (Fabry and Maximin, 2000).

[6]Of course, immobile factors (unskilled labor) will not have this luxury, and will therefore be worse off. This is a specific instance of the asymmetry of benefits and costs of globalization between mobile and immobile factors, discussed in Rodrik (1997).

[7]This does however not preclude explicit government action from reducing environmental degradation at every income level (i.e. shifting down of the EKC).

To conclude, the preceding discussion suggests that the national (competitiveness) or strategic argument is dubious, and thus, the likelihood of a race to the bottom among countries is low[8]. Moreover, as shown by Letchumanan and Kodama (2000, p. 59), *"positive measures enhancing FDI is not only crucial for technology upgrading, but at the same time brings about enhance environmental welfare through transfer of eco-friendly product and production processes".*

3. FDI AND ENVIRONMENT IN CHINA

This section focuses on the link between FDI and Environment in China. We present here an overview of policies and practices in environment protection. We examine first (3.1.) the environmental regulatory framework regarding MNEs. Then, we study the positive and negative impacts of MNEs on China's environment and policy debates arising therefrom (3.2).

3.1. Regulatory Framework for Environment Protection

- *China's Environmental Management System*

China's institutional setting for environmental protection has undergone several transformations over the last decades, reflecting different stages of restructuring, and an increasing emphasis by the Government on environmental issues. The first National Conference on Environmental Protection was held in 1973. The Steering Group on Environmental Protection of the State Council was established subsequently. The Steering Group was upgraded to an Environmental Protection Bureau under the Ministry of Urban and Rural Construction and Environmental Protection in 1982. In 1984, the Commission on Environment Protection of the State Council was founded to coordinate environmental affairs in the country. In 1987, the National Environment Protection Bureau (NEPB) was set up, with a mandate for overall environment management throughout the country. Now the Bureau has been renamed: The National Environmental Protection Administration (NEPA).

The legal framework has also evolved over the past three decades. "The Draft Rules (provisional) on the Protection and Improvement of the Environment" was issued in 1973. Six years later, the Steering Group on Environmental Protection of the State Council promulgated the "Key Points in the Environmental Protection Report". It stated that China could not afford to adopt the approach of "polluting first and controlling

[8]See Palmer and *al.* (1995) for a critic. Jaffe and *al.* (1995) have concluded that the relatively higher environmental regulation standards in the US have posed negligible threats to US industrial competitiveness and do not justify substantial cutbacks in domestic environmental regulation. Porter and Van der Linde (1995a,b) have gone so far as to suggest that relatively more stringent environmental regulations are cost less and in fact may be beneficial to firms operating in a regulated environment, as it will spur innovation.

later". Subsequently, China formulated "The Basic Law (provisional) on Environmental Protection". As experience accumulated through the implementation of the provisional Law, the formal "Environmental Protection Law of the People's Republic of China" came into effect in September 1989, which sets a firm basis for China's environmental protection system. Now, there are in effect some 30 national laws and regulations related to environmental protection. 364 environmental standards in China and local authorities have issued over 600 rules and regulations. All this forms a comprehensive, though complex, legal framework on environmental protection.

The current environmental management system contains four important components (see table 3).

Table 3: Components of the Chinese Environmental Management System

The environmental impacts report system	The Environmental Protection Law stipulates that every project should go through an environmental impact review process, if it is perceived to have possible negative effects on the environment. Project proposals should contain an analysis of environmental impact and the corresponding preventive measures, and be submitted to the environmental administrative authorities for screening. After the review of the proposal, the applicant will further engage a qualified firm to prepare an environmental impact report. It is only after the approval by NEPA or local EPB, that the project can be legally established.
The principle of the "three simultaneous steps".	According to Article 26 of this Environmental Protection Law, the system requires that a pollution- preventing facility must be designed, constructed and operated simultaneously with the design, construction and operation of the main production line of the project. To ensure the effective implementation of this system, the environmental authorities are mandated to check the project design in the review process and monitor the construction. Once the construction of the project is completed, inspection and approval by the environmental authorities are required before the project starts operation.
The registration and licensing system for the discharge of pollutants	According to Article 27 of the Environmental Protection Law, those institutions and enterprises that emit polluted substances must register and report in accordance with the stipulations of the environmental protection authorities. This is an important tool in controlling environmental pollution and monitoring environmental damage.
The system of effluent charges	Any firms that dispose of polluting materials above the prescribed standard will be charged an excess effluent fee. However, the charge paid for discharging pollutants does not legalize the pollution process itself. After paying the charges, the enterprises should also bear the costs of controlling and eliminating the pollution, pay fines and compensate for the resulting losses, and face other liabilities. For those enterprises that have already paid the effluent charge, but still failed to meet the effluent standards, the charge will increase by 5% annually, starting from the third year after the original charge is levied

In China, the mandate of the NEPA covers the overall supervision and management of environmental protection for the entire country. The Environmental Protection Bureau (EPB) at provincial, city and county levels are responsible for the supervision and management of environmental protection in the respective judicial areas. EPBs have also been established in various industrial authorities, such as the National Marine Administration, the Harbor Supervision Administration, the Fishing and Fishing Port Administration; as well as in the military forces, the public security, transportation, railway system and airlines administration. The administrations of land, mining, forestry, agriculture and waterpower also carry out supervision and management functions relating to environmental protection.

With the rapid economic development, some huge construction projects such as water power plants, iron and steel plants, coal and charcoal enterprises, petrochemical and chemical industry, nonferrous metallurgical industry and nuclear power plants, etc. inevitably have an impact of the environment. Therefore, there are some detailed clauses in various environmental laws and regulations on the implementation and enforcement of the requirements for environmental impact reporting.

In the past several years, the pollution control system in China has expanded from limited control over key polluting sources to a wide coverage of regional and industrial projects. China has established a nation-wide network for environmental monitoring, with over 4,000 environmental monitoring stations. These stations monitor acid rain, the atmosphere, earthquakes, and important river systems and marine pollution.

Owing to the strict management by the environmental protection administrations, most large-and medium-sized projects with a potential environmental impact have followed the environmental assessment system. The principle of the "three simultaneous steps" for project construction which come within the purview of the national and local EPBs was applied in about 87% of the projects in 1995, as compared with only 18% in 1976. The effluent charge for pollution reached US$ 325 million in 1995, rising from US$ 8.5 million in 1978. The money was transferred to the environment administration fund. Performance in the implementation of the environmental management system apparently varies among different regions and cities. The management is stricter in large cities and softer in small towns and rural areas where township enterprises are concentrated. Some coastal areas, such as some cities and towns in southern *Jiangsu Province*, have a better environmental management system. They formulate relevant regulations and plans based on a careful assessment of the impacts of local economic development on the environment, and implement them effectively.

Table 4: Responsibilities for Environmental Problems in China

Institutions	Responsibilities
NEPA	• Setting national environmental standards, in line with the existing economic and technological conditions in the country; • Establishing nation-wide environmental monitoring system, including the formulation of regulations thereon; coordinating with relevant ministries in re-enforcing environmental laws and regulations; and issuing bulletins on environmental status. • Setting and implementing the rules for environmental impact reports, assessing the impact of large construction projects on the environment, and evaluating the effectiveness of pollution prevention measures.
Local environmental protection authorities	• *Local standard setting*. Governments at provincial and city levels, under the direct leadership of the central government, can set up local standards for environment quality for those projects that are not covered by the national standards. Such standards should be reported to the NEPA. In cases where national standards already exist, local standards are expected to be stricter than the national ones. • *Environmental management.* EPBs are responsible, by virtue of their jurisdiction, for formulating plans for environmental protection, screening and approval of investment projects that have environmental implications, monitoring the implementation of laws and regulations, and carrying out field investigations on pollution cases. All local environmental protection authorities are supposed to issue environment status bulletins on a regular basis. • *Coordination*. The environmental protection authorities (above the county level) are responsible for the coordination with other relevant administrations in conducting investigation and assessment of the environmental status of the area concerned. They are also responsible for negotiating solutions; or presenting the case to higher authorities for coordination and settlement, when environmental pollution needs to be prevented and controlled at a cross-regional level.

Though the present system has played an important role in controlling industrial and municipal pollution, there still exist numerous problems and difficulties. For example, many administrative procedures of environmental protection have been followed mechanically. Some local governments have overemphasized the growth of the industrial output and the quantity of FDI inflows, due to the overriding concern for the economic development of the region. The local EPBs are usually under the supervision of the local governments and are not invested with sufficient authority to screen the environmental aspect of the projects. They are very cautious in checking the projects launched by local leaders or FDI projects. As a result, some projects that are not up to the environmental standards are carried out. Furthermore, some local EPBs do not have adequate enforcement capacity nor the qualified professionals needed. This has seriously impeded the execution of their functions and responsibilities rigorously and effectively. Some enterprises, particularly township enterprises and foreign investment enterprises, take advantage of the loopholes in the environmental regulatory framework to start some projects which are engaged in pollutant production, and are detrimental to the environment. The transfer of pollution-intensive industries to China has become a manifest phenomenon over the past years. The issue will be dealt within next point 3.2.

To sum up, with great efforts to control pollution and protect environment, China has succeeded in avoiding the rapid deterioration of its environment as its economy grew rapidly in the past two decades. For example, the discharged industrial wastewater remained at virtually the same level since the beginning of the 1980s (i.e. 23 billion tons in 1982 and 22.7 billion tons in 1997). Forest coverage ratio increased from 12.4 per cent in 1977 to 13.9 per cent in 1996. However, the density of suspended particles is higher than the international standard level in almost all cities in China. Acid rain has become even worse than before, with a rapid expansion in coverage. In 1996 rivers and lakes were polluted in various degrees, and underground water in almost half of the cities in China was contaminated. Industrial pollution caused by township enterprises has been rapidly increasing over the past 10 years and tends to expand further in the foreseeable future.

- *The Environmental Regulatory Framework Regarding Transnational Corporations*

In general, China does not have separate environmental standards for foreign investment, although some relevant clauses governing foreign investors' environmental behavior can be found in a number of national environmental, as well as FDI laws and regulations. Foreign investors must abide by Chinese environmental laws and regulations and meet the host country's environmental standards. Article 18 of the Constitution stipulates that foreign companies, economic organizations and joint ventures operating within the Chinese territory must abide by Chinese laws and regulations. Furthermore, in order to prevent PII from shifting into China, Article 30 of the Environment Protection Law stipulates that the importation of environmentally unqualified technology and equipment is forbidden.

There are, however, some specific policies and administrative procedures governing the screening and monitoring of FDI with respect to environmental protection. The "Provisions for Guiding Foreign Investment" clearly set out environment protection requirements for foreign investment projects. There are specific provisions encouraging investment in environmentally sound technologies, and new technologies for controlling environmental pollution, such as those for recycling or the comprehensive utilization of resources. In the meantime, the "Guidelines" limit foreign investment in exploring rare and precious mineral resources, and prohibit investment in those that threaten human health or destroy natural resources. According to the "Notice on Reinforcing Environmental Protection Management of Foreign Investment Projects" issued in 1992 foreign investors should respect the Chinese environment protection laws and regulations. They should prevent environmental pollution and ecological damage, and accept monitoring and supervision by environmental protection authorities. The "Notice" also set out procedures for screening the environmental implications of FDI projects and monitoring their implementation of environment protection measures. Item 5 of "Implementing Regulations on Joint Venture" also stipulates that projects with negative environmental impacts should not be approved. In accordance with the "Regulations of Ocean Oil Exploring by Foreign Firms", foreign investors are required to abide by the relevant environmental laws and regulations in their oil exploration activities, and to protect the environment of the atmosphere, oceans, rivers, lakes and lands. In principle, the procedures for regulating the environmental aspects of FDI are similar to those for domestic firms. The reporting system of environmental impacts, the principle of the "three simultaneous steps", the registration and licensing systems for the discharge of pollutants and the system of effluent charge elaborated earlier are equally applicable to FDI projects. Furthermore, according to Article 4 of "Project Construction and Operation in Part III of the Application Form (Sample) for Establishing Foreign Invested Enterprises in China", foreign invested enterprises (in the manufacturing and mining industries) should present the indices of Three Wastes (air, land and water pollution) treatment and security.

3.2. Environmental Issues Related to FDI in China

The overall environmental impact of FDI in China is a mix of positive and negative effects. Due to the lack of systematic empirical evidence and a sound analytical framework, it is difficult to quantify either its actual positive or negative effects on the environment. It is also to determine whether foreign affiliates' environmental performance is better or worse than that of comparable local firms'. With that caveat, this section presents preliminary analysis and findings of some existing studies, as well as a number of highly publicized positive and negative cases.

- *Environmental Problems Related to FDI*

Some foreign investors transfer production facilities and technical processes that are forbidden in other countries into China through direct investments. There are cases where foreign investors bought second-hand production equipment that do not meet environmental standards elsewhere and used them in China. This has been a notable phenomenon as about 75 per cent of the foreign direct investment is "investment in kind", i.e., in the form of production equipment (Zhan, 1994).

The transfer of production lines that have negative effects on the ozonosphere is a case in interesting point. Although there has been strict control over such production lines, some 1490 foreign-investment firms were established between 1985-1994, most, of which produce foaming and rinse products. The majority of them (about 60 per cent) came from, or via, Hong Kong, as some of the firms are subsidiaries of companies headquartered in some developed countries. Others were mainly from the Republic of Korea, Japan, the United States and a couple of European countries (Song, 1997). This has caused grave concern to the Government as well as the public. Subsequently, administrative decrees relating to the screening and monitoring of environmental aspects of FDI came into being with a view to strengthening the relevant mechanisms. One general perception is that more environmentally sound technologies have been used in the projects financed by firms from developed countries. Therefore, the environmental performance of these projects is better than those financed by firms from developing Asia. Nevertheless, even in the projects executed by firms from industrialized countries, the environmental performance of some MNEs is not as good as would be expected. A recent survey of a limited number of samples of European affiliates in China shows that their environmental performance was uneven in various aspects (Di, 1997).

Some foreign investors have set up enterprises to decompose, renovate and process waste metals, electronic appliances, tires, and harmful chemical pollutants. Most of them have a serious impact on the environment. Some of these investors even import foreign garbage into China, ostensibly for the purpose of recycling. Taiwan used to be an important location for recycling hazardous materials from the United States. In 1993, its Environment Authorities banned trading in waste metal materials. A number of Taiwanese investors relocated their production facilities to the eastern coastal areas, such as *Shenzhen, Zhuhai* and *Changzhou*. They continue importing tons of waste materials such as used cells, vehicle plates, computers, adapters and other electrical and electronic components for recycling in China. The impact on the surrounding environment is enormous.

Some foreign firms do not pay enough attention to pollution prevention, nor do they adopt adequate and effective measures to treat pollution. Some of them even try to elude the environmental monitoring mechanism. Most of the incidents happened in the projects financed by medium and small-scale foreign firms. There are, however, incidents involving large MNEs, many of them highly publicized environmental incidents (Box 1), some of them have had serious consequences. In 1996, Fumao Phosphor-Chemical Industrial Ltd. Co., a joint venture set up by a Chinese fertilizer manufacturer, and a Taiwanese chemical company in *Guizhou* province, discharged their sewage into the *Yanchang River*. It caused very heavy environmental pollution, and over 400 persons were poisoned by phosphorus. The company had ignored the environmental law for a long time. It even refused inspection by local EPB. When its vitriol factory started to operate in September 1995, its accessory environment protection facilities had not even been installed. Furthermore, it switched to the use of an inexpensive raw material of high dense phosphorus content. The facilities could only reduce acidity, but not eliminate phosphorus. The water of high-density phosphorus was directly discharged and resulted in severe pollution. An investigation revealed that the phosphorus content of the sewage discharged from the factory was up to 703.45mg/litre, 250 times higher than the national standard. The *Yanchang River* polluted by the sewage had phosphorus 20 times higher than the national standard. The EPB of the province fined the factory and directed it to take effective measures to eliminate the pollution (Ru, 1996).

Workplace safety is another serious problem. Some MNEs that conduct operations with a high safety-risk do not address health and safety issues effectively in accordance with relevant laws, regulations and policies on labor protection. Efficiency in export processing is the motivation behind investing in China. They employ cheap labor from the inland rural areas. The footwear industry of *Fujian province*, for example, has a significant share in both China's domestic market and its exports (bearing in mind that China has been the world's single largest footwear exporter). There are numerous foreign affiliates, some of which use a large amount of solvents. There is lack of effective disposal measures for discharged *triphenylmethylene*. Some employees in these factories were poisoned or died of exposure to noxious substances without protection.

In general, China's environmental standards are much lower than those of developed countries. This provides opportunities for some MNEs to take advantage of the lax environment standard and transfer their out-of-date technologies and pollution-intensive products to China. For example, the standard for effluent in some developed countries is based on the total quantity of discharge, while in China it is based on the density of the effluent. Some firms can dilute their effluent before discharging it (Zhan, 1999).

The screening and monitoring mechanism in China is also much more flexible than those of developed countries and even those of the more developed developing countries. Furthermore, the significant decentralization of the FDI approval authority from the central government to provincial, and from provincial, to city levels has, to a certain extent, further weakened the screening and monitoring mechanism on environmental protection. Indeed, no one argues publicly that lower environmental standards should be applied to foreign firms, nor can that environmental problems caused by the foreign investors be ignored.

However, there is some local government officials who try to accommodate, even to lure foreign investors whose projects have serious implications for the environment. Some local governments over-emphasize their local economic growth, and do not insist on following the principles of environmental protection. This has been the cause of many environmental problems. According to a survey made by the relevant administrations, only 97 out of 382 economic development areas in 16 provinces have conducted regional environment assessments. Some local officials even ignored the environmental protection laws and regulations, and decided to build polluting projects in water-source areas or in natural conservation zones.

- *FDI and Pollution-Intensive Industries*

Over the past two decades, industries such as chemical, petrochemical, leather, printing and dyeing, electroplating, pesticide, paper, mining and metallurgy, rubber, plastic, construction material and pharmaceutical production have been among the "bright spots" for foreign investment in China. They are often referred to as PII, as they usually rank high in emissions intensities of pollutants. Pollutants are waste residuals-harmful by-products of industrial processes that are not profitable to recycle or resell at current prices. Sometimes, they are also intensive in the use of other inputs, particularly bulk raw materials, energy and land (Mani and Wheeler, 1997). Those industries have been perceived as one of the major sources of environmental pollution in China.

A study based on the industry survey of 1995 shows that about 30 per cent of the FDI in China were in pollution-intensive industries, out of which 13 per cent were in highly-pollution-intensive industries (see Table 5).

Table 5: FDI in Pollution-Intensive Industries in China, 1995

	Number of firms	Industrial output (in yuan)	Employees
FDI PII[1]	14.189	379,3 billion	2,19 million
FDI PII share of national total	2,8%	6,9%	2,6%
FDI PII share of total FDI	28,6%	35,4%	33,1%
FDI in HPII[2]	6.493	186,7 billion	0.91 million
FDI in HPII share of national total	1,27%	3,4%	1,1%
FDI in HPII share of total FDI	13,1%	17,4%	13,8%

Notes: (1) FDI in PII includes FDI in HPII; (2) PII and HPII refer to pollution-intensive industries and highly pollution-intensive industries
Source: Xia (1996), based on China Third National Industrial Survey, 1995

It should be noted that the magnitude of FDI shown in Table 5 only reflects the FDI inflows before 1995. A large number of FDI projects came into operation between 1996-1998. FDI share of pollution-intensive industries in the country's total should be much higher today. Furthermore, measured by foreign affiliates' share of the assets or sales in a particular industry, the degree of FDI involvement in those pollution-intensive industries is generally higher than the average level of involvement by FDI in all industries. In 1995, FDI involvement (measured by share of assets) in those industries was 20.3 per cent higher than the average level of FDI in China (16.9 per cent) (Wang, 1997).

Among other determinants, an increasing tightening of regulations in major home countries, a lower level of environmental standards and weak monitoring mechanisms in China are the main reasons for inducing FDI into those industries. In fact, the relocation of pollution-intensive industries is not a unique phenomenon in China. As one study of cross-country analysis (Mani and Wheeler, 1997) shows that pollution-intensive output as a percentage of total manufacturing has fallen consistently in the OECD and risen steadily in the developing world. Moreover, the periods of rapid increase in pollution-intensive products net exports from developing countries coincided with periods of cost of pollution abatement's rapid increase in the OECD economies. There can be greater environmental implications by FDI from more developed developing Asia than from developed countries. The share of developing Asia in total FDI in PII is consistent with its overall share of FDI stock in China. This is possibly due to the rapid change in location advantage for PII and the tightening of environmental regulations in the home economies.

Indeed, some studies suggest that such transitions actually occurred in Asia. One analysis (Mani and Wheeler, 1997) shows that the growth experience of PII in Asia reflects a cascading pattern. It begins in Japan in the early 1970's, and continues for two decades in the NIE's and later on to ASEAN, and now China, Vietnam and the South. It can be assumed that such cascading pattern coincides with the "flying geese formation" in Asia (Zhan, 1999). A rather prevailing view holds that large amounts of FDI flows into PII can have serious negative implications for China's environment. This has caused deep concern in China.

However, there can be a different argument in this respect. One should differentiate the relocation of production into those PII from the transfer of pollution itself (Zhan, 1999). First, massive FDI into those PII may not be mainly due to environmental considerations. Other determinants, such as labor costs and skills as well as infrastructure, are usually more important. Second, not all-foreign affiliates in those industries produce severe environmental damage. Some foreign affiliates utilize environmentally sound technology and produce no pollution at all. This has been particularly the case in the pharmaceutical industry, where MNEs facilitated the transformation of that industry into a much more environmentally friendly one. Third, it is true that the expansion of production capacity in PII has increased the burden of environmental protection. But, such expansion could make it easier to achieve economies of scale and employ advanced environmentally sound technology. Furthermore, in the absence of FDI, it may take China a long time to develop such a production capacity with much inferior technology, causing more serious environmental damage. Consequently, the cost of development would have been much higher than it is today. One should also note that over 60 per cent of the FDI are in the form of joint ventures. The decision on the level of technologies utilized in the production facilities may not always be in the hands of foreign partners, particularly in ventures where Chinese partners have ownership control. In conclusion, one should not only focus on industry location, but rather on the environmental performance of foreign ventures relative to domestic firms. The important quest is not "where firm locates", but "how it performs once it produces locally.

- *Positive Environmental Contributions by MNEs*

MNEs, particularly the world major's, have contributed to China's environmental protection in one way or another. Apart from the advantages of technology and management, MNEs are usually large compared to domestic firms. Being large means that a company has greater resources for investment in research and development, as well as environmental management systems. Some MNEs have been actively involved in environmental services such as waste management and cleaning projects; others use environmentally friendly technologies in their production. They also generate demonstrative impacts on domestic companies in implementing ISO 14000 standards on Environmental Management Systems.

Some MNEs are active in building infrastructures of environmental protection in China and cooperate with the Chinese Government in dealing with environmental problems. They transfer environmentally sound technologies through FDI. Examples are abundant (see table 6):

Table 6: Example of Firm Action in Favor of the Environment

Firms	Action
Linde Co.	It has established 6 sewage disposal facilities and two urban sewage disposal facilities in China. Other companies, such as **WABAG, Hochtief, Sulzer, Geiger, Brochier Westfalia Separator**, also produce sewage disposal equipment or parts and components in China
Preussag-Noell Co.	It is very active in supplying sulfur-detaching facilities to China and participating in building demonstration garbage disposal facilities in two areas of Beijing.
Siemens, Deutsche Babcock	It took part in upgrading a project of Yangshupu Electricity Factory in Shanghai. **Uhde, Lurgi, ABB, Steag and Lentjes** also participated in constructing and upgrading the electricity generation plants and supplied the technology for efficiently utilizing energy and filtering equipment
Canadian Ruiwei Environmental Protection Co	It has technological advantage in generating electricity by garbage incineration. It invested US$150 million in a power generation plant in Guangdong, which has a capacity of 500 tons of garbage disposal daily. The plant uses 5 CAO garbage incinerators with a capacity of 12Mw.

Sources: based on Di (1997), Hansen (1999b), Xian and Zhang (2000)

In its industrial guidelines for foreign investors, China encourages FDI in the production of pesticides that are highly effective, of low toxicity and hazard-free, as well as fertilizers of high concentration. Many MNEs, particularly large ones, have introduced new types of fertilizers, which contributed to the improvement of the product structure of fertilizers in China. For example, Aigefu's affiliate in *Tianjin* produces insecticide-deltamethrin, which has improved the product line in the market. A joint venture between DuPont and Shanghai Pesticide Factory produces a new patent herbicide, which is highly popular for its high-effectiveness and low toxicity.

Some MNEs have taken the lead in adopting international environmental standards. For example, Shanghai Gao Qiao BASF Dispersions Ltd. Co. is the first chemical firm to obtain ISO14000 certificate on international environment standards in China (Xia, 1996). BASF also set up R&D fund for research projects in the fields of organic pigment, dyestuff chemistry, and polymer chemistry, in new material and natural effective components, as well as new design of chemical engineering and factory construction. Shanghai Squipp Co., a Sino-American joint venture is the first pharmaceutical manufacturer in China to obtain ISO14000 certificate on international environment standards. Since 1996, 36 companies in China obtained ISO 14000 certificate, of which 25 were foreign affiliates (Xian and al., 2000). Since 1994, China embarked on environmental labeling certification, 40 out of the 86 firms that obtained such certificates were foreign affiliates. This has certainly exerted pressure on the domestic firms to apply high environment standards in their production. As illustrated above, through the establishment of joint ventures in China, MNEs can upgrade the overall level of technology in local industries and help domestic enterprises manufacture products of low-pollution and low-energy consumption. For example, Liebherr Co. has been over the years cooperating with the Chinese manufacturer Haier to produce fluorine-free refrigerators. In the pharmaceutical industry, a large number of major domestic producers have formed joint ventures with foreign MNEs, and pollution by this industry is now greatly reduced, even disappeared owing to advanced technology and a sound environmental management system. In many cases, MNEs transfer managerial skills, including those related to environmental management to their local partners.

Many MNEs have established advanced pollution disposal facilities. A survey conducted by EPB in *Shenzhen* in 1986 covered 75 per cent of the industrial companies operating in the city. The survey showed that most foreign investors follow environmental regulations. In general, their negative impact upon the local environment is less than that of domestic firms. The results of the survey also showed that most foreign affiliates enjoy higher efficiency. Their resource consumption was lower than that of domestic firms. What is most impressive is that foreign investors invested much more than domestic firms in facilities in environmental protection. Their environment protection facilities were either imported or made in the host country. In regard to the efflux of the three wastes, the coefficient of product value of waste water discharged from foreign-investment firms is only around 57.5% that of the local firms, but the pollutant density of waste water of foreign investment firms is higher than that of local firms. In term of effluent waste gas, the ratio of product value of waste gas discharged by foreign investment firms is only 21.7% that of local firms. It is not only due to the environmentally sound technologies used by the foreign investment firms, but also to their low level energy consumption and their energy consumption composition (Liu, 1990).

The above comparison was made only between the foreign investment firms and local firms in the same industries, and only between firms in *Shenzhen*. Further research work on a larger scope and in greater depth is required in order to understand better the cross-border environmental behavior of MNEs. Some large MNEs with good track records are environmentally sensitive in their investment decisions. They conduct careful investigations on environmental conditions of the sites before building their production facilities, so as to avoid future disputes on environmental impact. Environmental conditions, therefore, become one of the location determinants in investment decisions for some of those MNEs investing in PII (Xian and al., 2000).

It is hard to reach any general conclusions on whether MNEs helped local industries to improve environment management through their forward or backward linkages. This remains a subject for further investigations in the case studies. Nevertheless, MNEs exert demonstrative influence to the local industries in utilizing low-energy-consuming, low-polluting technologies, and by adopting environmental management techniques systems in their ventures in China.

- *Policy Debates and Public Concerns Regarding MNE Related Environmental Issues*

There are different views on the question of which environmental standards should be applied to MNEs operating in China (see table 7):

Table 7: Views of Different Chinese Actor about Environmental Standards for MNEs

Actors	View
Some environmentalists	They hold that in principle MNEs should be encouraged to apply the standards of their home countries. Nevertheless, they are, for the time being, allowed to adopt standards lower than those of their home countries, but they must be higher than the current standards in China.
Some Government officials, notably those dealing with economic affairs (e.g., MOFTEC and SETC)	They believe that China should adhere to the principle of national treatment. The same environmental standards, i.e., host country standards, should be applied to all firms operating in China, be they state-owned, township or foreign owned.
Officials from NEPB	They have suggested that, in principle, host country standards should be used. But, for those projects with high levels of pollution and high-environmental risks, particularly in the absence of an ideal solution to their environmental damage, high standards should be established. Regarding those special cases in which China has not yet set relevant standards, home country standards should be required (Xia, 1996).

From a local perspective there is no obvious disagreement on the environmental impact of FDI among areas in China. The degree of importance attached to it by local governments, and their environmental performances, however, vary from one area to another. In the coastal areas the desire for environment protection is stronger because of a higher economic development level and a pervasive environmental pressure resulting from rapid economic growth. Therefore, it is easier for these areas to achieve consensus on environmental protection, and the implementation of environmental policies is rigorous and effective. In the areas of lower level of development, local governments have greater interest in hosting FDI than environmental protection. Economic development is often considered as important and environmental protection is given a low priority. Environmental measures are frequently remedial rather than preventive. This is based on the argument that the region will become less polluted as rising incomes make a cleaner environment more desirable and affordable. Economic development will eventually take care of pollution.

Public attitudes towards environmental protection in China are paradoxical. Although every one believes in protecting human living conditions and improving the quality of the environment, a strong voice often comes out to debase environmental protection when there is conflict between economic growth and environment protection in China. According to a survey of residents around Beijing (EPCSC, 1996), housing and security were considered the issues of deepest concern among all social and economic issues listed. Health care and education ranked second and then the environment, traffic and employment. The results show that environmental problems are not considered as the most important, although they are very severe in the municipalities like *Beijing*.

This explains why favorable policies are accorded to FDI by local governments in order to improve their local investment climate for foreign investors. In the meantime, the authorities of local environmental protection administrations are often eroded, giving way to economic considerations. Many people argue that strict environmental regulation will make investment less attractive and frighten foreign investors away from China. Only those people who were direct victims of environmental damage voice strong opinions on the control of the environmental performance of foreign affiliates.

4. Conclusions and Implications for Further Research

In addition to their positive impact on China's economy, MNEs, notably large ones, have also made remarkable contributions to China's environmental protection both through direct investment in environmental protection and by improving products and production processes in a number of industries. They also pave the way for domestic firms in adopting higher environmental standards. As was shown earlier, large numbers of FDI projects are located in those so-called pollution-intensive industries. Among other determinants, increased tightening of regulations in major home countries, and lower-level environmental standards and a weak monitoring mechanisms in China are the main factors in inducing FDI into those industries. This has certainly increased the risk of environmental damage and the burden of environmental protection in the host country. Highly publicized environmental incidents are numerous. However, differentiation needs to be made between *the relocation of production* into those PII and *the transfer of pollution*. Foreign affiliates in those industries have varying environmental performance, depending on the size of the firms, type of ventures, source of investment, type of industry, motivation of investment and business performance. The study shows that FDI generates both positive and negative effects on China's environment. To identify the scale of such effects, however, is extremely difficult. Moreover, the degree of government intervention in environmental regulation remains highly controversial. Although data restrictions have prevented us from providing a comprehensive assessment of the FDI impact on China's environment, our study points some interesting findings and implications for future research and policy analysis. Further examination, especially at firm level, is highly desirable, with a view to providing a solid basis for the Government to formulate effective policy measures. Case studies need to focus on the investigation of the cross-border environmental management systems within the MNEs' integrated production networks, and on the identification of the actual level of technologies employed, be it at home country level, host country level or the level in between.

Based on this contextual study, large, notably world leading, MNEs tend to consider their environmental performance as part of their image-building endeavors. Furthermore, their production is usually standardized globally, and it is more financially viable for them to invest in environmental protection. Therefore, they are more sensitive to environmental protection in the host countries. Small firms, especially those involved in short-term investment and footloose ones are sometimes reluctant to invest in environmental protection.

There seems to be greater environmental implications by FDI from more developed developing Asia than from developed countries. This is possibly due to the rapid change in location advantage for pollution-intensive industries and the tightening of environmental regulations in the home economies. It can be assumed that the cascading pattern of pollution-intensive industry in Asia coincides with the "flying geese formation" in Asia (Hansen, 1999b; Zhan, 1999).

The overview of FDI patterns in terms of source, types, sector, and regional distribution has indicated the possible magnitude of implications of FDI for China's environment. All these factors need to be brought into perspective in assessing the environmental impact of FDI. Government intervention in environmental performance of the MNEs, even if appropriate, remains a challenge. To what extent a trade-off can be made between economic development and environmental quality needs to be addressed further. Effective ways and means have to be identified with a view to attracting environmentally friendly investment and encouraging the transfer of cost-effective pollution-control technologies. Screening and monitoring mechanisms clearly need to be strengthened in order to maximize the economic benefits and minimize the negative environmental effects of MNEs' operations (Hansen, 1999a).

REFERENCES

- Andreoni J. and Levison A. (1998) "The simple analytic of the environmental Kuznets curve", *NBER Working Paper 6379*, Cambridge MA
- Bailey N. (1993). Foreign direct investment and environmental protection and the third world. In D. Zaelke, Orbuch P. and Housman R. (eds.), *Trade and the environment*, Washington D. C.: *Island Press*,
- Becker R. and Henderson V. (1997). "Effect on air quality regulation on decision of firms in polluting industries", Working Paper n°6160, NBER
- Bjorkman, I. and LU, Y. 1999. A corporate perspective of the management of human resource in China. *Journal of World Business*, 34(1): 16-25.
- Broadman H. & Sun X. (1997). The Distribution of Foreign Direct Investment in China. Policy Research Working Paper, n°1720, The Wold Bank, Washington DC.
- Bui T. M. (1998). "Gain from trade and strategic interaction: equilibrium acid rain abatement in the Eastern United States and Canada", *American Economic Review*, vol. 89, n°4, p.984-1002
- Castro Guerra A. and V. Santos (1998). Environmental Regulations and Foreign Direct Investment Flows Within European Union, pp. 36-48. In S. FAUCHEUX and I. Nicolaï, (eds.) *Sustainability and Firms*, London: *Edward Elgar*.
- Child J. and Stewart S. 1999. Regional differences in China and their implication for Sino-foreign JV. *Journal of General Management*, vol. 23 (2). Winter.
- Di C. (1997), "Survey on the environmental situation of European affiliates in China", *Foreign Direct Investment in China*, February.

- Eskeland G. and Harrison A. (1997). "Moving to greener pastures? Multinationals and the pollution-haven hypothesis", *Policy Research Working paper* n° 1744, World Bank
- Esty D. and Gerardin D (1988). "Environmental protection and international competitiveness: a conceptual framework", *Journal of World Trade*, vol. 32, p. 5-46
- Environment Protection Committee of State Council (EPCSC) ed., (1996), A complete compendium of the policies and regulations Concerning Chinas's environment and national resources Protection, Beijing: CITIC Publishing Co.
- Fabry N. and Maximin B. (2000). FDI, industrial Labor transformation and growth: the case of Korea, Malaisia and Thailand, Working Paper n° 1999-5, University of Marne-la-Vallée. Forthcoming in Jaussaud J., Callagan O. and Bassino J., editors *Changing Economic Environment in Asia – Implications for the Firm's Strategies in the Region*, London: Mc Millan.
- Faucheux S. and Nicolaï I. (1998). "Les firmes face au développement soutenable : changement technologique et gouvernance au sein de la dynamique industrielle",*Revue d'Economie Industrielle*, n°83, p. 127-146
- Grossman G. and Krueger A. (1993). Environmental impacts of a North American Free Trade Agreement. In Garber P. (ed.), *The Mexico-US Free Trade Agreement*, Cambridge MA: *MIT Press*
- Grossman G. and A. Krueger (1994). "Economic Growth and the Environment", *NBER Working Paper*, N° 4634, Cambridge MA.
- Hansen M. W. (1999a). "Environmental management in transnational corporation", Working paper, Department of Intercultural Communication and Management, Copenhagen Business School, June
- Hansen M. W. (1999b). "Environmental management in transnational corporation in Asia: Does foreign ownership matter?", Working paper, Department of Intercultural Communication and Management, Copenhagen Business School, November
- Hawkins R., Mansell R. and Skea J., (1995). Standards, Innovation and competitiveness: The politics and Economics of Standards in Natural and Technical Environment. Aldershot: *Edward Elgar*
- Howes R, Skea J. and Whelan B., (1997). Clean and competitive? Motivating environmental performance in industry. London: *Earthscan*
- Jaffe A. Peterson S., Portney P. and Stevens R. (1995). "Environmental regulations and the competitiveness of US Manufacturing: what does the evidence tell us?", *Journal of Economic Literature*, vol. 33, p. 132-163
- Jaffe A. B. and Palmer K. (1997). "Environmental Regulation and Innovation: A Panel Data Study", *The Review of Economics and Statistics*, vol. 79, n°4, p. 610-620
- Jenkins R.O. (1998a). "Pollution, Trade and Investment: Case Studies of Mexico and Malaysia", Report to the ESRC Global Environmental Change Program, SPRU.
- Jenkins R.O. (1998b). "Environmental Regulation and International Competitiveness: A Review of Literature and Some European Evidence", in *UNU/INTECH Disc. Papers*, No. 9801, January

- Klassens R. D., and Whybark D. C. (1999). "The impact of environmental technologies on manufacturing performance", *Academy of Management Journal,* vol. 42, n°6, p. 599-615
- Kolstad C. D., and Kelly D. L. (1999). "Bayesian learning, growth and pollution", *Journal of Economic Dynamic and Control*, vol. 23, n°4, p. 491-517
- Letchumanan R. and Kodama F. (2000), "Reconciling the conflict between 'the pollution-haven' hypothesis and an emerging trajectory of international technology transfer", *Research Policy*, n°29, p. 59-79
- Levinson, A. (1996a). "Environmental Regulations and Manufacturers' Location Choices: Evidence from the census of Manufactures", *Journal of Public Economics*, vol. 62, n°1-2, p. 15-29
- Levinson A. (1996b). Environmental regulation and industry location: international and domestic evidence. In Bhagwati J. and Rudec R. (eds.), *Fair trade and harmonization : prerequisites for free trade?*, volume 1 Economic Analysis, Cambridge MA: *MIT Press*
- Liu, S. (1990). *Environment Impact of Foreign and Joint-ventures in Chin*a, China's Environment Science Publisher, Beijing.
- Mabey N. and R. Mcnally (1999). Foreign Direct Investment and the Environment: From Pollution Havens to Sustainable Development, WWF-UK Report, October
- Mani M., Pargal S. and Huq M. (1997). "Is there an environmental race to the bottom? Evidence on the role of environmental regulation in plant location decision in India", *Working Paper* n°15, Research Project on Social and Economic Consequences of Growth-Oriented Policies, Policy research Department, World Bank
- Mani M. and Wheeler D., (1997), "In search of pollution havens? Dirty industry in the world economy, 1960-1995", mimeo
- Markussen J. (1997). "Costly Pollution Abatement, Competitiveness and Plant Location Decisions" R*esource and Energy Economics*, v19, n4, p. 299-320
- National Environment Protection Administration ed. (1997), Collection of the laws and rules of environmental protection (1982-1997), Beijing: *Chemical Industry Publishing*
- Naughton, B. 1993. Deng Xiaoping: The Economist, *China Quarterly* v0, n135, pp. 491-514
- Naughton, B. 1999. Causes et conséquences des disparités dans la croissance économique des provinces chinoises. *Revue d'Economie du Développement*, 1999-4: 33-70
- Nussbaumer J. and Worter M. (1999). "Industrial accidents: risk of industrial development – an empirical study". Available from Martin.Worter@uibk.ac.at
- Palmer K., Oates W. and Portney P. (1995). "Tightening environmental standards: the benefit-cost or the no-cost paradigm", *Journal of Economic Perspectives*, vol. 9, p. 119-132

- Porter M. and Van der Linde C. (1995a). "Toward a new conception of the environment-competitiveness relationship", *Journal of Economic Perspectives, vol. 9,* p. 99-118
- Porter M. and C. Van der Linde (1995b), "Green and Competitive: Ending the Stalemate", in *Harvard Business Review*, Sept.-Oct., p. 120-134.
- Ratnayake T. (1998). "Do Stringent Environmental Regulations Reduce International Competitiveness? Evidence from an Inter-Industry Analysis", *International Journal of the Economics of Business,* v5, n°1, p. 77-96
- Rauscher M. (1995). "Environmental Regulation and the Location of Polluting Industries", *International Tax and Public Finance*, v2, p. 229-44
- Rodrick D. (1997). Has globalization gone too far? *Institute for International Economics,* Washington D. C.
- Ru E., (1996) "400 People Poisoned by Pollution of Fumao Accident", *China Environment Daily,* April 18, 1996.
- Song W. and al.(1997), "Inducing foreign investors to protect ozonosphere", *Foreign direct investment in China, february*
- Sun J. (1998). "Changes in energy consumption and energy intensity: a complete decomposition model", *Energy Economics*, vol. 20, n°1, p. 85-100
- Sun J. (1999). "Decomposition in aggregate CO2 emission in the OECD: 1960-1995", *Energy Journal*, vol. 20, n°3, p. 147-155
- Tobey J.A. (1990). "The Effects of Domestic Environmental Policies on Patterns of World Trade: An Empirical Test", in *Kyklos*, Vol. 43, Fasc. 2 p. 191-209.
- Tsai S.H.T. and Child J. (1997). "Strategic responses of multinational corporations to environmental demands", Journal of General Management, vol. 23, n°1, p. 1-21
- Tsang E. 1999a. Internationalization as a learning process: Singapore MNCs in China, *Academy of Management Executive*, Vol. 13(1): 91-101
- Tsang E. 1999b. Can Guanxi be a source of sustained competitive advantage for doing business in China? *Academy of Management Executive*, Vol. 12(2): 64-73
- Van Den Bulcke H. and Zhang H. (1998). Foreign Equity Joint Ventures in China: Interactions between Government Policies and Multinational Investment Strategies. In Tharakan P.K. and Van den Bulcke D. (editors), *International Trade, FDI and the Economic Environment*, London: McMillan.
- Wang L. ed. (1997), Report on foreign direct investment in China, Beijing: Economics and Management Publishing Co.
- Wei Y., Liu X., Parker D., & Vaidya K., (1999). The regional distribution of foreign direct investment in China, *Regional Studies*, vol. 33.9.
- Wu, Y. 1999. *Foreign Direct Investment and Economic Growth in China*, Cheltenham: Edward Elgar.
- Xia G. (1996) Investigation and thinking of environment pollution caused by foreign firms", *China Environment Daily*, December 31, 1996.
- Xian G. and Zhang C. (2000), "Environmental management in transnational corporations in China", Working paper Department of intercultural communication and management, Copenhagen Business School, January 2000.

- Zhan J. X. (1994). "The role of FDI in market-oriented reforms and economic development: the case of China", *Transnational Corporations*, Vol. 2(3), 1994, United Nations, pp. 121-148.
- Zhan J. X. (1999). "Relocating pollution-intensive industries through FDI: costs and benefits analysis from a host country perspective" (mimeo).

Chapter 10

THE FOREIGN-INVESTED SECTOR AND THE REFORMS IN VIETNAM

C. Pottier
University of Paris 10 Nanterre

1. INTRODUCTION

The current economic difficulties of Vietnam shed a particularly sharp light on the general issue of the relationship between the transition process and the economic opening, which has been spectacular in Vietnam. As measured by the ratio (imports + exports)/GNP, the trade openness rate in 1997 was 78%, not far from that of Thailand (79.7%) (ADB, 1998). Moreover, one fundamental feature of Vietnam's development strategy is its reliance on inward foreign direct investment (FDI) mainly in the productive sectors. Between 1988 and 1997, Vietnam's economy growth was led by FDI and sustained by macro-economic policies aiming at stabilizing fundamentals. The East Asian crisis (1997) was an important shock that provoked the blockage of this opening process. Lacking an open financial system, Vietnam was not directly affected but suffered the consequences of the crisis in terms of trade and inward FDI. Investments have diminished rapidly since 1997 and consequently contributed to a net slowdown in growth. However, the flows of FDI had already reduced before the crisis because of persistent restrictions on the activities of foreign enterprises, and more generally, because the transition process towards a market economy was too slow. Two issues, therefore, emerged simultaneously: the adequacy of the opening process chosen by Vietnam (as revealed by the crisis), and the transition process itself.

The aim of the present chapter is firstly to illustrate the significant role of FDI in the Vietnamese economy. Section 2 deals with the importance of FDI, its geographical origin and its destination by sector. Above all, it shows the FDI's place in industrial production, in international trade, in the balance of payments and in investment in general. This analysis leads to an examination of the political options emerging in response to the strong slowdown in these investments (section 3). Since the Vietnamese Communist Party already opted for a convergence towards market economy, this choice will not be looked at here. The discussion will be restricted to an examination of two questions. The first concerns the coherence and the rhythm of the transition process: is it compatible with economic opening? The second concerns the way in which opening takes place: how can Vietnam insert itself into the international division of labor resulting from the multinational corporations' networks?

2. The Significant Role of Foreign Direct Investment in the Vietnamese Economy

The accumulation of FDI during the 1990s led to the formation of a foreign-invested sector, which takes an important place in the Vietnamese economy. Furthermore, the flows of inward FDI play a major role in the country's economic fundamentals.

2.1. Intensity and Nature of Foreign Direct Investment

The political changes of 1986 launched the slogan for renovation *("doi moi")*, and the law on FDI was adopted in 1987. The flow of inward FDI was particularly large, representing an average of 9% of GDP during the period 1993-1997, with a peak of 11.3% in 1995 (IMF, 1999). From 1988 to 1996, inward FDI, relative to GDP, was in fact nearly twice as high as that in China (Haughton, 1998). In 1997, the stock of FDI in Vietnam, as a proportion of GDP, was 55.8%, the highest in Asia after Singapore (UNCTAD, 1999).

An analysis of the origin of FDI shows that five countries have invested strongly in Vietnam (Table 1). These are Japan and the four Asian NICs, which are responsible for two-thirds of the cumulated investment commitments in Vietnam by April 2000. Up to the 1997 crisis, they were indeed the source of a growing share of the investment flows (Nguyen Trong Xuan, 1997).

Table 1: Origin of Foreign Direct Investment in Vietnam
(cumulative commitments as of April 2000)

	$ billion	%
1 Singapore	7.33	20.0
2 Taiwan	4.79	13.1
3 Hong Kong	4.66	12.7
4 Japan	3.80	10.4
5 South Korea	3.49	9.5
6 United States	2.02	5.5
7 France	1.79	4.9
8 British Virgin Islands	1.70	4.6
9 Malaysia	1.57	4.3
10 Russia	1.45	4.0

Sources: MPI (Ministry of Planning and Investment), in Vietnam Economic Times, May 2000.

However, one should emphasize the great uncertainty as to the nationality of the investors, which should not be confused with the country's origin of an investment. This is most notably the case for investments from Singapore, which houses the regional headquarters of multinationals and, also, has an excellent banking network that may provide the source of the investment. Thus, for example, the investments of Coca Cola and Heineken in Vietnam originated in Singapore. At the end of 1996, the Indonesian firm Ciputra committed itself to a very large investment in Vietnam of $3.3 billion (DREE, 1998). This investment in fact came from Singapore and represented 45% of the cumulated investment from this country. At the same time, direct investment from the Chinese diaspora, part of which lives in Vietnam, does not show up directly in Table 1, but represents a large part of the investments from all the Asian countries, notably Hong Kong, Taiwan and Singapore.

An analysis of FDI by sector shows the predominance of industry, which forms one third of investments made during the period. The share held by this sector grew fairly regularly from the beginning of the 1990s (IMF, 1999). However, adding in FDI in the hotel, tourism and real estate sectors represent 41.6% of all FDI (Table 2).

Table 2. FDI by sector in Vietnam (cumulative commitments as of April 2000)

	$ million	%
Industry	12,160	33.1
Hotels and tourism	8,090	22.0
Real estate	7,210	19.6
Transport and communications	3,200	8.7
Oil and gas	3,060	8.3
Agriculture, forestry, fisheries	1,410	3.9
Finance and banking	233	0.6
Other services	846	2.3
Others	490	1.3
Total	36,700	100.0

Sources: MPI, in Vietnam Economic Times, May 2000.

In conclusion, till 1997, inward FDI in Vietnam had three main characteristics: it became more and more important, it originated predominantly and increasingly from other East Asian countries and it was directed more and more towards industry. But this evolution came to an abrupt end in 1997, the year in which commitments to investment were reduced by 48%. They went down by a further 14% in 1998, then by 61% in 1999. This was followed by a reduction in disbursements, after a delay of one year following commitments (Table 3).

Table 3. Evolution of FDI in Vietnam ($ billion)

	1991	1992	1993	1994	1995	1996	1997	1998	1999
Commitments	1.3	2.0	2.7	4.1	6.6	8.6	4.5	3.9	1.5
Disbursements	0.2	0.4	1.1	1.9	2.7	2.6	3.3	2.0	1.5

Sources: MPI, in Vietnam Business, Aug. 1-15, 1999 and Vietnam Investment Review, Jan. 17-23, 2000

2.2. Importance of the Foreign-Invested Sector in the Vietnamese Economy

In July 1999, the foreign-invested sector, i.e. the subsidiaries of overseas firms and the joint ventures of whom they were majority capital owners, employed 281,000 people[1]. This represented 15% of employment in manufacturing industry in 1995 (UNCTAD, 1999). If FDI's impact on global employment is relatively weak (given that two-thirds of the working population are still employed in agriculture), it is however crucial for the development (Hoang Van Huan et alii, 1997). FDI in Vietnam permitted the introduction of new technologies and facilitated the acquisition of skills by local workers. Above all, it represented about one third of total investment between 1991 and 1997, far more than in the other East Asian countries (UNCTAD, 1999). The foreign-invested sector is the source of a growing share of exports: 21% in 1998. It plays a crucial role in industrial production, with a 35% share during the first six months of 1999[2]. Furthermore, this role is becoming more and more important since growth in industrial production is faster in the foreign-invested sector (20% in 1999) than in the local industry (4.5% in the public sector, 8.8% in the private sector) (DREE, 2000). It should be noted that, in 1998 and 1999, despite the strong slowdown in FDI and in the growth of GNP, industrial production in the foreign-invested sector continued to grow rapidly (Table 6.)

2.3. FDI in Relation to General Economic Indicators

The sustained growth in Vietnam up to 1997 was attributed to both inward FDI and a macroeconomic policy based on fundamentals' stabilization. The contraction of FDI upset this virtuous circle by provoking a serious problem of investment financing. Until 1997, the IMF was satisfied with the Vietnamese government way to manage the macro-economic fundamentals from the beginning of the 1990s. The budgetary deficit reduction was the most striking result, which was achieved principally by the suppression of grants to State-owned enterprises from 1990 and 1991, years in which the number of civil servants and their pay were reduced (Riedel and Comer, 1997). The aim was to limit the deficit to under 5% of GDP and to reserve it to finance investments. It stood at 3.5% in 1997 and 4% in 1998 (Table 4). Above all, this deficit was no longer financed by money creation but by saving mobilization and external aid (Vu Van Truong, 1998). The

[1] *Vietnam Economic News*, no. 27, 1999.

[2] *Le Courrier du Vietnam*, 21 August 1999.

improvement in saving mobilization was the result of Government loans and raising interest rates, notably on current account and three-month deposits.

The rise in interest rates was one element of a restrictive monetary policy that helped to limit and control inflation. The price stabilization was also obtained by a strong increase in supply, whether of internal production, of imports or of smuggling (Le Van Cuong et alii, 1998). Thus, following the period of hyperinflation, which corresponded to the price liberalization, the inflation rate was brought back to 17.5% in 1992. It was only 4.5% in 1996 and 3.6% in 1997. In 1998 it rose to 9.2% because of the devaluation of the national currency (*dong*) following the Asian crisis. But it was practically zero in 1999 (Table 4).

Table 4. Evolution of the Main Economic Indicators, Vietnam

	1991	1992	1993	1994	1995	1996	1997	1998	1999
Budget deficit (% GDP)	1.5	1.7	4.8	1.5	1.3	---	3.5	4	---
Inflation rate (%)	67.0	17.5	5.1	14.5	12.7	4.5	3.6	9.2	0.1
Trade deficit ($ billion)	0.2	0	1.2	1.8	3.2	3.2	1.3	1.0	0.1
Growth in GDP (%)	6.1	8.1	7.5	8.5	9.5	9.3	8.8	5.8	4.8

Sources: IMF (1999); World Bank (1997); Ministry of Commerce; Vu Van Truong (1998); DREE (2000)

The increase in national currency investments (relative to dollar investments), due to the rise in interest rates, and the increase in currency reserves provoked by FDI, produced a relatively stable exchange rate from 1991 to March 1997, when a gradual depreciation of the dong began.

Finally, the deficits in the trade balance and current account balance have been clearly reduced over recent years, From 1992 to 1997 trade flows were multiplied nearly by five. This development was accompanied by a growth in the trade deficit that reached $3.2 billion in 1995 and 1996. The deficit was then brought back to $1.3 billion in 1997, $1 billion in 1998 and only $100 million in 1999 (Table 4). At the same time, the current account deficit, which stood at 13.1% of GDP in 1995, was reduced to 4.2% in 1998.

These sharp reductions of the trade deficit and of inflation resulted in a contraction of the economic activity. The annual growth rate of GDP, which was at least 8.5% from 1994 to 1997, fell to 5.8% in 1998 and 4.8% in 1999. Several factors affected purchasing power. Among these were lay-offs in State-owned enterprises, reduced wages in the private sector (Nguyen Dinh Tai, 1999) and also the various monetary readjustments, carried out in 1997 and 1998, meaning a devaluation of the dong by 20% relative to the dollar. Before the 1999 stabilization, these readjustments led to a large increase in prices (Table 4). As to the elimination of the trade deficit, this was obtained by import stagnation during 1997 and 1998, while exports continued to grow, even though very weakly in 1998 (Table 5). This import stagnation was due to a slowdown in growth, to the depreciation of the dong and to measures temporarily restricting imports, taken by the government in 1998.

Table 5. Evolution of External Trade, Vietnam ($ billion)

	1993	1994	1995	1996	1997	1998	1999
Imports	4.2	5.9	8.4	10.5	10.4	10.3	11.6
Exports	3.0	4.1	5.2	7.3	9.1	9.3	11.5
Deficit	1.2	1.8	3.2	3.2	1.3	1.0	0.1

Sources: IMF (1999); DREE (2000).

As the Asian countries constitute the origin of 70% of inward FDI in Vietnam (cumulated sums as of June 1999) and the destination of 55% of exports from this country (in 1997), the East Asian crisis largely contributed to this activity contraction (Pham Ngoc Long, 1998). The reduction in demand and the currency depreciation in the Asian countries created a slowdown in Vietnamese exports, and also in the sub-contracting activities in manufactured products destined for Japan and South Korea. However, the impact of the crisis on exports from Vietnam was limited since the opportunity cost was estimated by the authorities at $400 million for 1997 and $800 million for 1998 (DREE, 1999), or 4.4% and 8.6% respectively of total exports. The negative effect of the crisis on economic activity was, however, not limited to a slowdown in export growth. It also showed up in a strong reduction in inward FDI.

Beyond the crisis itself, the impact of inward FDI on long-term growth should be analyzed. There are two main issues here: first, the contribution that FDI makes to growth and second the dependence of Vietnamese economy on FDI for financing its investments. In spite of the spectacular reduction in FDI, the foreign-invested sector showed a clear increase in industrial production from 1997 to 1999. Therefore, FDI plays a role of crisis softening in a context of strong slowdown in production by local enterprises, notably in the public industrial sector (Table 6).

Table 6. Evolution of Industrial Production in Vietnam (Annual Growth Rate)

	1997	1998	1999
Public sector	11.0	7.9	4.5
Private sector	9.5	6.7	8.8
Foreign-invested sector	20.6	23.3	20.0
Total	13.2	12.1	10.4

Sources: Vietnam Investment Review, 5-11 July 1999; DREE (2000).

On the other hand, Vietnam's dependence on FDI for investment financing is a real concern. In the five-year plan for 1996-2000, the program of public investment for this period stood at $42 billion. Half of it should have been financed externally, with two-thirds coming from FDI and one third from official development assistance (Le Van Sang and Dinh Quy Do, 1998). Certainly the predominance of inward FDI is good for growth, but it has its reverse effect: the reduction of inward FDI in 1998 not only suffocated the economy, but also made it much more difficult to achieve the balance of payments equilibrium.

Table 7. Balance of Payments of Vietnam ($ Million)

	1997	1998[1]
Trade balance	- 1315	- 981
Current account balance (1)	**- 1664**	**-1067**
Capital repayments (2) :	**- 1418**	**- 2773**
Long term loans	- 632	- 690
FDI loans	- 174	- 372
Short term loans	- 612	-644
Need for external finance (1+2)	**- 3082**	**- 2773**
External finance :	**+ 3082**	**+ 2773**
FDI	+ 2074	+ 800
Official development assistance	+ 550	+ 796
Commercial loans	+ 457	+ 326
Reserve-related liabilities[2]	- 319	- 15
Arrears	+ 323	+ 126
Debt relief	0	+ 413[3]
Errors or omissions	+ 1	+ 327

Notes: 1. Estimate; 2. Net credit from the IMF and short term borrowing between monetary authorities; 3. Debt rescheduling by the London Club in 1998
Sources: author's presentation of IMF (1999) data

Between 1997 and 1998, the need for external finance, corresponding to the sum of the current deficit and the capital repayments, went down from $3.1 billion to $ 2.8 billion. But in the same period, the FDI disbursements collapsed, going from $2.1 billion to $800 million, so that they covered only 29% of the need for external finance in 1998, compared with 67% in 1997 (Table 7). In addition, it should be noted that in recent years FDI has increasingly taken the form of intra-company loans, forming 70% of it in 1997. This means that the burden of repaying these loans will increase in coming years.

Resorting to other methods of finance is not easy, as the level of external debt is already very high, despite the debt relief obtained by Vietnam: 50% of its official debt, by the Paris Club at the end of 1993, 45% of its private debt by the London Club at the end of 1997. The Vietnamese government does not make public the total sum of the country's debt, which is estimated very differently by various international organizations. The Asian Development Bank values it at $14.5 billion for 1997 (ADB, 1998), which means a rate of 115% of GDP for 1996, far higher than that of other countries in the region (60% for Indonesia, 50% for Thailand, 47% for the Philippines, 42% for Malaysia). Medium and long term debt in convertible currencies, according to the IMF, stands at $9.6 billion in 1997, of which $5.3 billion is for public and publicly guaranteed debt (IMF, 1999). The cost of servicing this debt, standing at 13.4% of exports in 1998

(ADB, 1999), is therefore already considerable, and may become even more important as the slowdown in growth persists. An excessive increase in debt would weaken the value of the national currency.

Moreover, the pace of reforms increasingly conditions international aid. The pace demanded by international organizations and foreign States is faster than that the Vietnamese government wishes to or can achieve. With the Asian crisis, the IMF hardened its position, as it did in the other countries in the region. Thus, from 1997, it suspended its payments to Vietnam under the title of *"Enhanced Structural Adjustment Facility"*. Other organizations have frozen part of their aid (World Bank) or have threatened to do so (Asian Development Bank). However, in December 1999, the annual conference of Vietnam donors granted it development aid of $2.1 billion for the year 2000 ($2.2 billion in 1999) and additional aid of $700 million, on condition of an acceleration of reforms.

3. Political Options in the Context of FDI Reduction

The strong reduction in FDI undermines one of the bases of Vietnam's economic policy, while provoking a crisis in the financing of investment. Thus the government is obliged to make its economic choices clear, whether it intends compensating for the lowering of FDI or encouraging its renewal. For this, two issues appear essential. The first is global as it concerns the pace and nature of structural reforms: how to make the productive and financial system more efficient from the perspective of transition towards the market economy? The second question might be the key for development in the current context of globalization: how can Vietnam achieve what the other countries of South East Asia have already done, i.e. becoming part of the international division of labor set up by the multinational corporations?

3.1. The Pace and Nature of Structural Reforms

The withdrawal of FDI has made apparent not only Vietnam's dependence on these investments, but also the weakness of domestic saving, or at least, it's insufficient mobilization. For this to improve, Vietnamese economy needs to be supported by reliable and efficient monetary and financial institutions. Besides, State-owned enterprises should be more profitable. This raises the issues of the reform of the monetary and banking systems, of the privatization of State-owned enterprises, of the creation of a financial market, and more generally of the convergence towards a market ruled economy. On all these points, Vietnam, like China, has adopted an approach called "*gradualist*"[3]. Beyond

[3] One can however challenge the use of the term "*gradualist*" to characterise the whole transition in Vietnam towards a market economy. Thus Marie Lavigne underlines the fact that this country "*has passed far more rapidly than any other ex-socialist country to an agriculture based on small private property (in fact) and market forces*" (Lavigne, 1999, p. 99).

merely being an "approach", the slow progress of these transformations can be explained, more prosaically, by the protection of particular interests. This is shown fairly clearly in the process of "*equitisation*" of enterprises, prior to privatization. But more globally, the government is confronted with the problem of economic and social equilibrium. A too rapid privatization would mean an increase in unemployment, a contraction in demand, and finally the development of poverty.

- ***The Mobilization of Saving***

According to official figures, the domestic savings ratio remains low compared to those of other Asian countries: 21.5% in 1997, in proportion of GDP, against 32.9% in Thailand and 43.8% in Malaysia (ADB, 1998). However, as Lavigne (1999) emphasizes, this ratio is very difficult to measure in Vietnam and it is probably under-estimated, given the importance of the informal credit sector in the countryside. The problem would therefore not be the amount of savings but their mobilization. From 1989, by fixing real positive rates of interest and by stabilizing the exchange rate, the Vietnamese government has achieved a noticeable increase in the amount of bank deposits. The domestic savings ratio seems to have increased regularly. According to the Asian Development Bank, it went from 14.8% in 1993 to 24.6% in 1998 (Table 8).

Table 8. Domestic Investment and Savings Ratios in Vietnam (% of GDP)

	1993	1994	1995	1996	1997	1998
Gross domestic investment ratio	20.5	24.1	27.6	28.1	28.3	28.7
Gross savings ratio	14.8	17.6	19.1	17.8	21.5	24.6
Difference	5.7	6.5	8.5	10.3	6.8	4.1

Sources: ADB (1999).

However, till 1996, the rate of domestic investment grew faster than that of savings, to the extent that the difference between the two ratios grew to about 10% in 1996. On the other hand, in 1997 and 1998, the rate of domestic investment grew very little, thus reducing the difference to 4% in 1998 (Table 8).

- ***The Reform of the Banking System***

Better mobilization of savings presupposes the reform of the banking sector or, in any case, cleaning it up. From 1988, the government transformed the banking system by diversifying it. Currently, it is dominated by four State-owned commercial banks, which are the source of 80% of credit. But it also includes 51 joint-stock banks (whose shareholders include State-owned banks, State-owned enterprises and private institutions), 23 branches of foreign banks and 4 banks in joint venture with foreign capital. According to an IMF study (IMF, 1999), profitability is low in the four State-owned commercial banks (two of them have made no profits in the past four years). They are heavily in debt. The Central Bank however did re-capitalize them in October 1998. The sum of their non-performing loans is very large, as, according to audits using international standards, at the end of 1997 it represented between 30% and 35% of their total loans. As to the joint-stock banks, they are in the most vulnerable situation, as many of them are in deficit. At the beginning of 1999, the government elaborated a plan to reorganize the whole banking system.

The poor state of the banks is partly explained by the speculative operations that took place, especially in real estate[4]. It is also the result of the weakness of prudential regulation and supervision mechanisms. But most of the difficulties of the banking sector are due to the poor performances of the State-owned enterprises that absorb over half of all credit. The central issue that has to be dealt with is thus that of the reform of State-owned enterprises.

- ***The Reform of State-owned Enterprises***

In 1998, State and local public enterprises still held a central place in the Vietnamese economy, representing about 30% of GDP, 20% of investment and 15% of non-agricultural employment. They even held a predominant position in the industrial sector, with 55% of production. At the end of the 1980s and at the beginning of the 1990s, they were affected by three important decisions taken under the country's new political orientation: to make their management autonomous, to eliminate subsidies and to liberalize prices. These measures led to an improvement in performance (Le Van Cuong et alii, 1998). In addition, mergers and closures led to a strong reduction in the number of State-owned enterprises, which went from 12,000 in 1989 to 5,800 in 1998, with a high degree of concentration, since the largest 200 represented 60% of public capital and 40% of the total debt of these enterprises. With the aim of improving their performance, the government consolidated State-owned enterprises into kinds of conglomerates. Thus 23 "general corporations" were formed between 1995 and 1997. The idea was to create giant corporations able to compete on an international scale, in the image of the Korean

[4] FDI in real estate, hotels and tourism represented 20.4% of total FDI in 1997 (IMF, 1999), this proportion going down to 14.1% in 1998. Vietnam therefore seems to have known, to a much smaller extent, the process of over-investment in real estate that was one of the causes of the crisis in the South East Asian countries in 1997.

chaebols. It does not seem that the aim of improved performance was attained, on the contrary[5].

The profitability of State-owned enterprises remains too weak. According to the Vietnamese Ministry of Finance, only 40% of them make any profit, 44% are sometimes in deficit and 16% are chronically in deficit (IMF, 1999). The Vietnamese government accepted a World Bank program, financed by Japan, aimed at auditing the 100 largest State-owned enterprises by 2002. The Asian Development Bank launched a program, in 1999, to improve the management of all these enterprises.

State-owned enterprises keep on mobilizing a large share of national resources, not in the form of subsidies, which have been eliminated, but as bank credits. Certainly, they absorb a decreasing share of them: little more than 50% in 1998 (ADB, 1999) compared with 90% in 1988. But they also benefit from loan conditions that are preferential in comparison to those for the private sector: interest rates 20% to 30% lower and a State guarantee (including for foreign loans). This explains their high level of debt. According to the Vietnamese Ministry of Finance, the ratio debt/assets reached 59% for the State-owned enterprises at the end of 1997 (IMF, 1999) and went even higher in 1998 when they benefited from a 22% increase in credit (compared with 11% for the private sector).

In addition, these enterprises will be increasingly concerned by the progressive liberalization of Vietnam's external trade, beginning with that resulting from the free-trade agreement, (AFTA), with which Vietnam is linked since its adhesion to ASEAN in 1995. A large number of State-owned enterprises are engaged in import-substituting industries, currently protected by high import duties. The Vietnamese government obtained a deferment till 2006 for the elimination of most tariff barriers. But it seems to be thoroughly committed to respecting its engagements, according great importance to the process of regional integration. Its orientation towards free trade in fact goes even wider, as witnessed by its application for membership of the WTO in 1995 and its commercial agreement with the United States in 1999.

The insufficient profitability of State-owned enterprises raises the issue of their reform. The Vietnamese authorities do not officially speak of privatization, but, in 1992, launched a process of "equitisation". This means first transforming State-owned enterprises into joint-stock companies, and then selling shares. The process was re-launched in 1996 and in 1998, the year in which selling shares to foreigners was allowed. But the implementation of the reform has been very slow since, in December 1999, only 237 enterprises had been "equitised"[6], a large majority of them being local enterprises. This delay can be attributed to different factors, whose respective importance is difficult to evaluate. There are firstly technical difficulties linked to issuing shares and setting their value (Nguyen Dinh Tai, 1996). This value should actually be negative for the enterprises whose debts are greater than their assets. Then political and social resistance also seems to be important. The disappearance of public enterprises would mean, for local authorities, the loss of considerable tax revenues. At the central level, it seems that some ministries also put up barriers to the operation. This blockage comes in part from

[5] *Vietnam Economic News*, No. 35, 1999.

[6] *Vietnam Investment Review*, 20-*26* December 1999.

the State bureaucracy. However, it is difficult to say whether this is due to questions of power or to the perception of the obvious social damage that a rapid "equitisation" would lead to. Officially, the unemployment rate was 10% in June 1999. The French Embassy in Vietnam estimated it at 20% (DREE, 1999). The context of the present economic crisis, that means lay-offs in State-owned enterprises, can only encourage the government to be cautious. In this respect, it is contradictory for institutions such as the IMF and the World Bank to demand the rapid dismantling of State-owned enterprises while at the same time setting themselves up as champions in the fight against poverty.

To sum up our analysis, a major difficulty confronting these reforms is that their timing always seems wrong: large inflows of FDI prevented considering them to be a matter of priority, and now the contraction in these investments makes them urgent but more difficult to achieve. At the Vietnam donor's conference in December 1999, a three-year reform program was worked out between the IMF, the World Bank, the UNDP and the Vietnamese government. But the latter, in its concern for preserving social stability, refused to commit itself on the deadlines for achieving this plan[7].

- ***Towards the Creation of a Financial Market***

As the process of "equitisation" is very slow, few shares have been issued and it has not been possible to create a financial market. However, this is the government's goal. In 1997, it set up a *State Securities Commission*, with the aim of setting up two stock markets in 1998: one at Hanoi and the other at Ho Chi Minh City. In 2000, these had still not been opened. As well as the lack of share issues, there are also serious technical problems, notably the adoption by firms of a coherent and transparent accounting framework. Actually, when the financial markets come into existence, their initial operations will not concern shares but bonds: firstly those currently issued by the Treasury and the Central Bank, and then those issued by enterprises (Lavigne, 1999). The creation of financial markets is coherent with the liberalization of the economy. It will also eventually help to attract new foreign capital. However, the Mexican and Asian crises have underlined the dangers of opening the economy too rapidly. On one hand, the banking system must be reformed, with strict prudential rules, and on the other, the existence of these rules is no protection against the volatility of speculative capital.

3.2. The Insertion of Vietnam into the Multinational Production System

The implementation of structural reforms would create an environment favorable to FDI. However the government had to take immediate measures supposed to stop the decline in FDI. The law on foreign investment, adopted in 1987 and modified in 1996, was therefore completed by important measures taken in January 1998[8] and March 1999[9].

---

[7] Ibid.

[8] Decree No. 10-CP, cf. *Vietnam Investment Review*, 9-15 February 1998.

[9] Decree No. 53-CP, came into force 1st. July 1999, cf. *Vietnam Investment Review*, 29 March – 4 April 1999.

These measures represented a response to the wishes of foreign investors who had expressed their disillusionment even before the crisis. The weight and complexity of the bureaucratic procedures that necessitates dealing with many levels of administration and local organizations, encouraging red tape and corruption, has proved more durable than expected (Mason, 1998). This is why the 1998 decree set up the "one-door principle" for the formalities to be fulfilled by foreign enterprises.

Beyond this principle, the 1998 and 1999 measures facilitated the setting up of foreign enterprises and allowed them to transform the existing joint ventures into 100% subsidiaries. Above all, since 1999, most of their costs are fixed in dong and no longer in dollars. To begin with, this concerns wages of local workers. At the same time, electricity, telephone and water bills are now paid in dong, as also the registration fees for the establishment of plants and representative offices. Thus enterprises will be able to benefit from the progressive depreciation of the local currency. In addition, the dual pricing system, which discriminates between local and foreign firms, will progressively be dismantled. From 1999, a single price for water and telephone installation was instituted. The excess cost paid by foreign firms for electricity and telephone communications will be progressively eliminated. However the dissatisfaction of foreign investors remains, notably over limiting access to hard currencies and the sometimes officious and arbitrary nature of customs duties. Another serious problem is the ban on enterprises recruiting their personnel directly. They have to do it via the intermediary of the labor service of the local Popular Committee or use a specialized agency. In the face of the foreign firms' protests, this system was somewhat eased in 1999. From then on, they could recruit directly if the labor service did not fulfil their demands within a month.

However, from the perspective of development, the liberal strategy of attracting FDI does not seem sufficient if it is not accompanied by an industrial strategy. From this point of view, Vietnam is struggling to become a productive base for multinational firms, like other East Asian countries (Nguyen Van Tam, 1996). This raises the questions of regional integration of production and Vietnam's degree of competitiveness, which in turn involves the issues of exchange rate, cost of labor and skill levels.

- ***Regional Integration of Production***

In December 1997, the Vietnamese Communist Party reaffirmed its plan to make Vietnam a productive base for exports. It therefore put forward three objectives: setting up effective special economic zones, developing the labor-intensive industries for which Vietnam has a comparative advantage, and publishing a timetable for reducing customs duties.

The decrees of 1998 and 1999 extended the tax advantages that benefited foreign exporting enterprises. In addition, from 1991, export-processing zones were created. These are free zones where imports do not incur customs duties and where land lease rate is reduced (Do Van Dong and de Lestrange, 1996). Of six zones set up, two are located near Ho Chi Minh City. In these two zones, Tân Thuân and Linh Trung, the number of foreign establishments fell in 1998: only five in all, against forty per year in preceding years. However, the enterprises that were already set up increased their capital and developed their exports by 50%. By 1999, 95 foreign enterprises are active in the two zones, employing 30,000 persons. There is a net predominance of Taiwanese and Japanese enterprises, both in terms of number and of capital invested[10]. By sector, the textile, clothing and leather industries are the most important.

However, exports from the six export-processing zones only represent a small part of foreign firms' exports. These zones in fact form part of a group of 63 industrial zones in which over half of foreign capital is invested. To understand how Vietnam is inserted into multinational firms' production networks, one should examine the activities which enable these firms to set up a division of labor between production units by making them specialized in one type of production or in one group of products (Pottier, 1998). Since neither the service industries nor industries using local raw materials (energy and food industries) lend themselves easily to this division of labor, one can restrict the discussion to manufacturing. This reveals that, in the period 1988-1997, the rank order of the main investing countries for FDI in the manufacturing sector differs markedly from that for all FDI (Table 9).

Table 9. Origin of FDI Commitments in the Two Main Investment Sectors in Vietnam (1988-1997)

	Total FDI $ billion	FDI in manufacturing industry $ billion	%	FDI in real estate, hotels and tourism $ billion	%
Singapore	5.5	2.0	37	1.9	35
Taiwan	4.1	1.1	26	1.9	47
Hong Kong	3.7	0.7	18	2.2	59
Japan	3.5	1.2	33	0.9	27
South Korea	3.1	2.2	69	0.8	25

Sources: MPI, DREE (1998)

South Korea, which concentrates 69% of its FDI in manufacturing industry, is the leading investor country in this sector, though it is only the fifth for all FDI. Conversely, Hong Kong's FDI is relatively weak in manufacturing industry, below even those of the United States and Malaysia, which do not appear in Table 9. This table shows that a high proportion of FDI from Hong Kong (59%), and also Taiwan (47%), is directed towards real estate, hotels and tourism. One can see here a specific feature of FDI, linking the Chinese diaspora of Hong Kong, Taiwan, Singapore and other countries, to the large population of Chinese origin living in Vietnam. Thus the FDI from Hong Kong and Taiwan is concentrated in Ho Chi Minh City, where about one million Vietnamese of Chinese origin live (the "Viet Hoa").

The feature of investment in manufacturing industry is very different. It consists of setting up plants in protected sectors in order to profit from the development of the

[10] *Vietnam Investment Review*, 11-17 January 1999.

internal market, or, on the contrary, of establishing a production base for export, notably towards the country of origin. This explains the implantation of the Korean chaebols, the Taiwanese and Japanese firms.

The crisis and the depreciation of regional currencies further increased cost constraints. The advantage gained by devaluation for the export of finished goods is limited if there is a considerable import of intermediate goods. For reasons of cost, delay and delivery, and more generally of productive efficiency, the multinationals need to rely on a network of local producers. This is something that is not yet well developed in Vietnam. For example, Japanese assembly plants for motorbikes and cars import numerous parts and components from Japan and from ASEAN countries. Facing the contraction of domestic demand, these firms are trying to develop their exports but are, then, even more constrained by costs.

- ***The Issue of the Exchange Rate***

Even before the crisis, the dong was considered over-valued by about 10%. With the crisis and the currency depreciations in the region, this over-evaluation became unsustainable. The Vietnamese government reacted in 1997 by progressively lowering the central rate of the dong and by widening its trading band to 10%. Then, in 1998, it limited the band to 7% but devalued by 10%. All these measures led to a depreciation of 20%, relative to the dollar, in two years. However, the dong remained over-valued because it retained its floor value. In February 1999 the Vietnamese authorities therefore adopted a new system, which is a sort of crawling peg, by which the central rate is equal to the average rate for the interbank market, established the day before, with a 0.2% band. This means that the exchange rate is now fixed by the market, but with a delay. This system allows for a progressive currency depreciation[11], while avoiding the possible effects of a brutal devaluation, namely, a financial shock for banks and enterprises, whose debt denominated in foreign currencies is considerable, and an economic and social shock from a sudden rise in inflation and from a reduction in purchasing power. One condition for making this new policy of dong depreciation effective was that the salaries and operating costs of foreign firms should be paid for in national currency, something that was agreed the following month, in March 1999.

The very weak growth in exports from Vietnam in 1998 (+2%, compared with +25% in 1997 and +41% in 1996) (IMF, 1999), was seen as an indicator of the over-valuation of the dong. However, the contraction in demand in Asia played an essential role, since, in 1998, exports from Vietnam to Japan and ASEAN countries went down by 30% and those destined for South Korea by 40% (ADB, 1999). Actually exports have again shown a clear increase in 1999, including of manufactured products destined for Asia (DREE, 2000). Furthermore, exports from foreign enterprises have grown strongly in 1998, when they reached nearly $2 billion, against $1.5 billion in 1997, or an increase of 33%[12]. This seems to be due to the progressive increase in the production capacity of foreign plants, which is partly independent of the dong value. The three main export items from foreign

[11] In fact, it remained stable in 1999.

[12] *Vietnam Economic News*, No. 37, 1999.

firms are electronic products, shoes and clothing. The company Fujitsu Computer Vietnam, which set up in the province of Dong Nai, employing 1,500 people, is the largest foreign exporter from Vietnam. This firm produces electronic circuit boards for computers made in Japan. In March 1998, its managing director, Mr. Kawashima, declared that, due to regional currency depreciations, it was more advantageous from now on for the parent company in Japan to import its components from Thailand or the Philippines than from its Vietnamese subsidiary. It therefore saw its exports attaining only $320 million to $330 million, while the initial objective had been $400 million[13]. Its forecasts were however belied by the facts, since the firm's exports rose to $490 million in 1998[14]. The over-valuation of the dong is therefore not as high as it is held to be, and the solution adopted by the Vietnamese government, allowing for a progressive depreciation, seems adequate.

- ***The Competitiveness of Labor***

Before the Asian crisis and the subsequent currency depreciations, the cost of labor was much lower in Vietnam than in most of the other countries of the region. Table 10 shows that, in January 1998, while the currencies of Thailand and the Philippines had already reached their lowest level and the 10% devaluation of the dong had not yet been carried out, the cost of labor in Vietnam remained competitive compared to other countries.

Table 10. Cost of Labor in Vietnam, the Philippines and Thailand, January 1998

	Vietnam	Philippines	Thailand
Workers' monthly salaries ($)	57	71.5	75.5
Managers' monthly salaries ($)	169	199	305
Annual bonus	1 month	1 month	2 months
Welfare contributions	50%	25%	14.3%

Sources: Fujitsu Computer Vietnam, in Vietnam Investment Review, 16-22 February 1998

But if wages were clearly lower in Vietnam, welfare contributions were far higher (Table 10), to the extent that, for a worker, the cost of labor was about the same as that in the Philippines and Thailand. Therefore, the supplementary depreciation of the dong was welcomed. For managers, the cost of wages plus welfare contributions was of a similar level in Vietnam and in the Philippines but was far higher in Thailand.

As stated above, the foreign enterprises established in Vietnam come up against another difficulty that is the impossibility of directly recruiting their personnel. On the other hand, official inquiries carried out in these firms show that they often do not respect work regulations. Thus by 1996, 30% to 40% of them had not established employment contracts and 45% had not contributed to social insurance schemes for their employees.

---

13 *Vietnam Economic News*, March 1998.

14 *Vietnam Economic News*, no. 37, 1999.

Besides, many of these employees were made to work for between 12 and 14 hours per day (Do Minh Nghia and Vu Ngoc Lan, 1996). In addition, union representation only existed in 30% of foreign enterprises. In 1998, in the two export-processing zones near Ho Chi Minh City, 10% of employees of foreign enterprises had no employment contracts[15].

The labor competitiveness is the result of a combination between cost (wages + welfare) and skill levels. Levels of adult literacy and education are relatively high in Vietnam, thanks to the socialist orientation. Thus, though the country was ranked 147th in the world, in 1995, for real GDP per inhabitant, it was 122nd for the human development indicator established by the UNDP[16]. However, education is not sufficiently directed towards vocational training. For the education year 1996-1997, 500,000 students were registered at university, but there were only 172,000 students in training schools and 70,000 apprentices[17]. University graduates hired by foreign firms should receive one or two years' training[18]. State-run vocational training is in crisis. Due to lack of funding, many schools have closed, their number going down from 366 in 1997 to 129 in 1998[19]. The Minister of Labor declared in 1999 that, from now on, the State-run training schools would only guarantee 15% to 20% of vocational training, the remainder being the business of private and local schools. But the private sector also experienced severe financial difficulties. The government counts on foreign investment and official development assistance to improve vocational training[20].

4. Conclusion

It is doubtful that in coming years growth will be rapid in Vietnam if the reduction in flows of FDI continues. FDI has played an important role in growth and its reduction has provoked a crisis in financing investment. Vietnamese firms would therefore have to take over this role. The reforms carried out at the end of the 1980s and beginning of the 1990s permitted a net increase in the efficiency of State-owned enterprises, but this remains insufficient. The indebtedness of these enterprises handicaps the banking system and hinders the distribution of credit to private enterprises. New reforms are therefore necessary. They will take time. In the short run, the government tries to re-launch FDI. It is responding partially to the expectations of foreign investors by measures that increase the Vietnamese attractiveness. But, firstly, other countries in the region are outbidding each other to attract FDI, and, secondly, implementing these measures has to confront the nature of Vietnam's socio-political structures. Thanks to the low cost of its labor force and the recent flexibility of its exchange rate, Vietnam can however hope to form a

[15] Report by the Ministry of Labor, War Injured and Social Affairs, in *Le Courrier du Vietnam*, 25 May 1999.
[16] UNDP, *World Report on Human Development*, 1998.
[17] *Business Vietnam*, No. 7, 1999.
[18] *Vietnam Economic Times*, July 1999.
[19] *Business Vietnam*, No. 7, 1999.
[20] *Vietnam Investment Review*, 25-31 October 1999.

productive base for the multinationals, as the other countries in the region have become. In order to do this, it must rapidly improve its infrastructure and its network of suppliers and sub-contractors. Furthermore, it is imperative that it allocates substantial resources to the development of vocational training so that it can fit foreign investors' needs.

References

- ADB (Asian Development Bank) (1998), *Key Indicators of Developing Asian and Pacific Countries*, Oxford University Press.
- ADB (1999), *Asian Development Outlook* 1999, Oxford University Press.
- Do Minh Nghia and Vu Ngoc Lan (1996), "La situation réelle du travail dans les entreprises à capitaux étrangers", *Tap Chi Cong San*, no. 10, in CID Vietnam, bulletin signalétique, no. 2, 1996.
- Do Van Dong and De Lestrange A. (1996), "Le développement au Vietnam des Zones de Production pour l'Exportation", *Ouverture Economique*, no. 2, Centre Franco-Vietnamien de Formation à la Gestion, Hanoi.
- Dree (Direction des Relations Economiques Extérieures, French Ministry of Finance) (1998), *Les investissements directs étrangers au Vietnam*, T. Blin, Poste d'Expansion Economique de Hanoi.
- Dree (1999), *Economie du Vietnam*. Poste d'Expansion Economique de Hanoi
- Dree (2000), *Situation économique du Vietnam et investissements étrangers en 1999*. Poste d'Expansion Economique de Hanoi.
- Haughton J. (1998), "Walking the walk", *The Vietnam Business Journal*, April.
- Hoang Van Huan, Nguyen Anh Tuan and Phan Huu Thang (1997), *Foreign Direct Investment in Vietnam*, Hanoi, The Gioi Publishers.
- IMF (International Monetary Fund) (1999), *Vietnam: Selected Issues and Statistical Appendix*, Staff Country Reports, No. 99/55 and 99/56, July, Washington, D.C.
- Lavigne M. (1999), *Economie du Vietnam*, Paris, L'Harmattan.
- Le Van Cuong, Tran Hai Hac and Tran Thi Anh Dao (1998), "L'économie vietnamienne de 1976 à 1994" in Le Van Cuong and Mazier J. (dir.) *L'économie vietnamienne en transition*, Paris, L'Harmattan.
- Le Van Sang and Dinh Quy Do (1998). "The Investment Policies of Vietnam in the Period of Accelerating Industrialisation" in Vo Dai Luoc (ed.) *Vietnam's Policies on Trade and Investment and the Development of Some Key Industries*, Hanoi, Social Sciences Publishing House.
- Mason M. (1998). "Foreign Direct Investment in Vietnam; Government Policies and Corporate Strategies", *Exim Review*, February.
- Nguyen Dinh Tai (1996), "The equitisation of the state enterprises", *Vietnam's Socio-Economic Development*, no. 8, Winter.
- Nguyen Dinh Tai (1999), "Social Impacts of the Asian Financial Crisis to Vietnam", *Vietnam's Socio-Economic Development*, no. 18, Summer.

- Nguyen Trong Xuan (1997), "The attraction of foreign direct investment: a comparison between Vietnam and other ASEAN countries", *Vietnam's Socio-Economic Development*, No. 11, Autumn.
- Nguyen Van Tam (1996), "Policy of trade and tariffs and strategy of industrialisation and modernisation" in Vo Dai Luoc (ed.) *Vietnam's Industrialisation, Modernisation and Resources*, Hanoi, Social Sciences Publishing House.
- Pham Ngoc Long (1998), "Impact of the Asian monetary crisis on the Vietnamese economy", *Vietnam's Socio-Economic Development*, No. 13, Spring.
- Pottier C. (1998), "Le système productif Japon-Asie: quelle division internationale du travail?", *La Revue de l'IRES*, No. 27, Spring-Summer.
- Riedel J. and Comer B. (1997), "Transition to a Market Economy in Viet Nam", in Woo W.T. et alii (eds.) *Economies in Transition: Comparing Asia and Eastern Europe*, Cambridge, The MIT Press.
- UNCTAD (United Nations Conference on Trade and Development) (1998, 1999) *World Investment Report*, New York and Geneva, United Nations.
- Vu Van Truong (1998), "La politique budgétaire du Vietnam dans la période de transition (1990-1995)", in Le Van Cuong and Mazier J. (dir.) *L'économie de Vietnam en transition*, Paris, L'Harmattan.
- World Bank (1997), *Vietnam: Deepening Reform for Growth, an Economic Report*, Report No. 17031-VN, October, Washington, D.C.

INDEX

A

B

C

D

E

F

G

H

I

J

K

L